HESBURGH

A BIOGRAPHY

HESBURGH

A BIOGRAPHY

MICHAEL O'BRIEN

THE CATHOLIC UNIVERSITY OF AMERICA PRESS

WASHINGTON, D.C.

Copyright © 1998
The Catholic University of America Press
All rights reserved
Printed in the United States of America

The paper used in this publication meets the minimum requirements
of American National Standards for Information Science—
Permanence of Paper for Printed Library materials, ANSI Z39.48-1984.

∞

Library of Congress Cataloging-in-Publication Data
O'Brien, Michael, 1943–
    Hesburgh : a biography / Michael O'Brien.
        p.   cm.
    Includes bibliographical references (p.) and index.
    1. Hesburgh, Theodore Martin, 1917– .   2. University of
Notre Dame—Presidents—Biography.   1. Title.
    LD4112.7.H47O37   1998
    378.772'89'092—dc21
    [B]   98-17978
    ISBN 0-8132-0921-8 (alk. paper)

For Sally O'Brien

CONTENTS

ILLUSTRATIONS

The University of Notre Dame Photographic and Television Production Center provided the illustrations used throughout the book and on the book jacket. Their assistance, and that of Jaime Owen Cripe in particular, is greatly appreciated.

ACKNOWLEDGMENTS

Once again, I have incurred many debts in preparing a book and am delighted to express my deep gratitude. Thanks to Richard Conklin and Lyn Magliola for graciously helping me through the clippings in the Office of Public Relations and Information at the University of Notre Dame. I owe a primary debt for the valuable assistance of librarians and archivists, including Charlotte Ames, Wendy Clauson Schlereth, and especially William Kevin Cawley, all at the Theodore M. Hesburgh Library of the University of Notre Dame; Tony Zito at The Catholic University of America; Jacqueline Dougherty at the Province Archives Center at the University of Notre Dame; and Mark Alnott at the Onondaga County Public Library, Syracuse, New York. All of them expertly guided me to materials and answered numerous questions.

Several persons graciously gave me (or loaned me) valuable papers at their disposal. Among them were Edward Fischer, Rev. Dennis Geaney, James Grant, Florence Lynch, Sr. Joellen McDonnell, John O'Connor, Edmund A. Stephan, Thomas Stritch, and Jean Wilkowski.

This is not an authorized study. I did not ask permission of Fr. Theodore Hesburgh or officials at the University of Notre Dame to write my book, preferring instead to write independently. Nonetheless, I appreciate the consideration of Fr. Hesburgh and the kindness and hospitality of numerous people at Notre Dame.

Several people criticized manuscript versions of the book, catching errors, helping me overcome problems of writing and interpretation, and offering their encouragement. For their efforts I deeply appreciate Rev. David Burrell, Walter Langford, and Sally O'Brien. My colleagues Daniel Putman and Ken Anderson offered valuable suggestions for improving specific aspects of the biography.

As in my previous books, I have placed a heavy burden on the staff at the University of Wisconsin–Fox Valley who have, nonetheless, responded with good humor and patience. For the third time, Kathy Hosmer typed many drafts and Patricia Warmbrunn efficiently processed hundreds of interlibrary loan requests. Former Dean Robert Young kindly supported my project from the start and offered his advice and assistance.

In the early stages of my study I received important and timely grants from the University of Wisconsin–Fox Valley and the University of Wisconsin–Fox Valley Foundation, Inc. In addition, the University of Wisconsin awarded me a sabbatical during the critical, last stage of my writing.

My voluntary research assistant, Marguerite Hagen, located and photocopied many important articles and newspaper clippings. I have been especially fortunate to have an excellent voluntary typist, Reighe Nagel, who for over three years expertly and quickly typed many drafts of the manuscript.

My wife Sally was a valuable critic and patiently endured her husband's fourth book with encouragement and love. Also thanks to Tim, Sean, Jeremy, and Carey for all the love and enjoyment they bring me.

INTRODUCTION

Throughout the spring of 1987, Fr. Theodore Hesburgh granted scores of newspaper, magazine, television, and radio interviews, and he received tributes, special presentations, requests for autographs, and emotional farewells. After thirty-five years as President of the University of Notre Dame, he was about to retire. The most versatile and most highly respected priest in the United States, he was known for his rare energy and his ability to carry out a staggering variety of assignments with distinction, both at home and abroad, for the church and the state. He was "Mr. American Catholic" to Monsignor John Tracy Ellis, dean of U.S. Catholic historians. "With all due respect to our archbishops and bishops, there isn't one who can touch him," said Ellis. "He's miles and miles ahead."[1]

Almost all the testimonials listed his astonishing accomplishments. During his career at Notre Dame the enrollment doubled, the endowment grew from $9 million to $350 million, and the number of buildings on campus increased from 48 to 88. By 1987 his signature was on the degrees of four out of five living Notre Dame graduates. The tributes also mentioned that he was in the Guinness Book of Records as the person who had received the most honorary degrees in history (112 and counting).

Recalling one category of his public service, testimonials described the fourteen Presidential appointments he had received, which included chairmanship of the U.S. Civil Rights Commission. Because of his low threshold for boredom, his idealism, and his extreme intellectual curiosity, his job as President of Notre Dame wasn't fascinating enough to sustain his interest and energy. "His challenges are so enormous," said his friend Edmund Stephan, "that I don't think Notre Dame . . . itself could contain them." His vita filled eleven typed pages, and included the thirty-six boards and commissions on which he was currently serving. "Few people are willing to accept the weight of concern for all the world's problems," a newspaper wrote a few years earlier, but Fr. Hesburgh "picks up that weight, throws it over his shoulder and carries it with him around the globe."[2]

Not everyone was pleased with the results of his long career. Notre Dame continued to have problems attracting minority students. Year after year the minority enrollment barely climbed. Only 3.3 percent of the students were black in 1986. Faculty and students had earlier complained that he occasionally lapsed into a somewhat haughty paternalism. Others thought his personal crusades away from Notre Dame removed him too much from the day-to-day functioning of the university. Some wondered if Notre Dame had really embraced the values of Christ or the acquisitive, individualistic goals of the larger, secular society. "Perhaps the most pointed of these criticisms," said a writer for the *National Catholic Reporter*, "is that Notre Dame has become something of a cult of self-adoration fanned by alumni more enraptured by the lure of success than the lessons of the Gospels."[3]

For the most part, though, he was thrown far more bouquets than bricks. On May 1, students bid him farewell with a special Mass and a picnic on the South Quad. Normally reserved and dressed in his Roman collar and black suit, he stunned thousands of students by arriving at the picnic on a Honda scooter, clad in Blues Brothers sunglasses, leather gloves, a black windbreaker, and red crash helmet. Students presented him and Fr. Edmund Joyce (executive vice president who was also stepping down after thirty-five years) with oil portraits and a farewell card signed by the student body.[4]

He worried about his valedictory speech. What should he say about himself? After thirty-five years, "How do you go out?" he wondered. On May 9, 1987, his address was beamed via closed-circuit television to 126 Notre Dame alumni gatherings, mostly at hotels, in every state, plus Canada, Mexico, and Puerto Rico. The one-hour telecast featured a sixteen-minute film retrospective of his life narrated by Walter Cronkite. "To have been president of such a company of valiant searching souls,"

Fr. Ted told the gathering, "to have walked at the head of this 35-year-long procession, to have shared with you the peace, the mystery, the optimism, the joie de vivre, the ongoing challenge, the ever-youthful, ebullient vitality, and, most of all, the deep and abiding caring that characterizes this special place and all of its people, young and old, this is a blessing I hope to carry with me into eternity when that time comes."[5]

On May 17, Harvard's reticent president, Derek Bok, ventured to Notre Dame to deliver a rare extramural commencement address in tribute to his friend. At the commencement ceremony, graduating students cheered and applauded as Fr. Ted, a few days short of his seventieth birthday, accepted Notre Dame's Laetare Medal, one of American Catholicism's highest awards for distinguished performance. He tried to inspire them about some of his favorite causes. "I associate myself with each of you," he told the graduates. "We don't know where we're going and what we'll be doing, but I can guarantee you there are a lot of battles yet to be won for justice. There are a lot of mountains yet to be climbed to overcome human ignorance and human prejudice."[6]

When a reporter for the *Boston Globe* questioned some graduates about what they would most remember about their retiring president, they most often mentioned values. "He pretty much gives you a sense of values from day one," said Al Ridalla, an engineering major from Latrobe, Pa. "You read about what he does on campus, off campus, in the nation and around the world, and if you didn't have that sense of values when you came here, you leave here with them." "I think as a leader, as a role model, he hasn't only participated, he has shown us we need to go out and take what we have learned here and serve the country," said Nellie Hautzinger of Omaha, a science major.

"So now the Hesburgh era is ended," editorialized *The New York Times* after the commencement ceremony, "and the Hesburgh legend begins."[7]

1 ⌁ EARLY LIFE,
1917–1945

THEODORE MARTIN HESBURGH was born on May 25, 1917 (four days before John F. Kennedy), in Syracuse, New York, the second of five children of Theodore Bernard and Anne Marie Hesburgh. A mixture of German and French, the Hesburghs had come to America from the Grand Duchy of Luxembourg in 1848. Ted's great-grandfather and his wife had two sons and a daughter. One of the sons, Theodore Bernard Hesburgh, Ted's grandfather, was a remarkable man. College educated, he learned Yiddish, Russian, German, French, Italian, and Spanish, as well as English, and during their infrequent meetings he fascinated his grandson Ted by his wizardry in expressing the same thoughts in different languages.

A schoolteacher most of his life, Grandfather Hesburgh also wrote columns for the *New York World* under the pen name Knickerbocker. His columns explored politics, religion, economics, and labor relations. One particularly outspoken and ironic article, written in 1886, opposed Archbishop Michael Corrigan, New York's Catholic leader, for suspending Father Edward McGlynn from his priestly duties after McGlynn had endorsed Henry George's controversial Single-Tax Program. "Surely the present corrupt and destructive political methods of government would in time be swept into oblivion," wrote Grandfather Hesburgh, "were clergymen of decided honorable intentions to assume a strong and wholesome activity in the conduct of public affairs."

In 1891 an extraordinary personal tragedy severely distracted Grandfather Hesburgh. Within about a two-week period his wife and two of his three children died. In his autobiography, *God, Country, Notre Dame* (1990), Fr. Ted Hesburgh observed of his grandfather: "Undoubtedly these tragedies caused something within him to snap." Severely depressed, he abandoned his Catholic faith, quit his job, and hauled his remaining three-year-old son, Ted's father, off to live with relatives on an Iowa farm. For a time, while living in Iowa, Theodore apparently taught all eight grades (including his son's) in a small rural schoolhouse. Several years later he essentially abandoned his son and allowed an aunt from New York to take the boy back East to live with her.[1]

The son, Theodore Bernard, may have been scarred by his difficult early life, but he persevered. He lived with the aunt in New York and set pins at a bowling alley while he finished high school. He then started to work for the Pittsburgh Plate Glass Company, and after a few years of climbing the ladder he was sent to upstate New York as a salesman to develop a new territory. Apparently at parties in New York City and picnics on the Hudson, Theodore Bernard met and courted Anne Marie Murphy and on February 2, 1913, the couple married at St. Augustine's Church in the Bronx, and then moved to Syracuse.[2]

Ted's maternal ancestors came from Ireland. Grandfather Martin Murphy arrived in the U.S. with his parents when he was only seven weeks old. A plumber, he lived in the Bronx with his invalid wife; Anne was their only child. Schooled in New York by German nuns, after high school Anne worked as a secretary at the telephone company. Although possessing an excellent soprano singing voice, she gave up a promising singing career to marry.[3]

Ted's father was steady, organized, and kind. Intellectually a self-made man, he read extensively, devoured cross-word puzzles, and cultivated an excellent vocabulary. An avid sports fan, he especially enjoyed baseball, studying the batting average of each of his favorite players. (His oldest son would never share his father's ardent interest in sports.) A hard working, respected businessman, he returned to his office for a few hours on Sunday after church to sort his mail and prepare for the next week. He was an excellent salesman. One day he tried to make a difficult sale to a resistant owner of a hardware store. The owner was about to throw him out the door when Mr. Hesburgh noticed a picture of Theodore Roosevelt on the wall. "This is a great man," he shrewdly said to the store owner. "What do you know about Colonel Roosevelt?"

the store owner demanded. Mr. Hesburgh mentioned the charge up San Juan Hill. By the time Ted's father had left the store, he had made his biggest sale of the week.

Yet Ted's father seemed emotionally bruised by his difficult early life. At home he was usually quiet, serious, and reserved. "He felt deeply," his daughter Betty speculated, "but he never quite let you know." John O'Connor, a friend of Ted's and a neighbor, recalled vividly Mr. Hesburgh sitting in a chair, his head barely visible, immersed in his newspaper, usually reading about sports. "He was a very laconic guy, almost dour," said O'Connor; "not at all like Ted."

Because of Theodore Bernard's extreme reserve, and because he was on the road most of the week, Ted never grew emotionally close to him. His dad, Ted reflected, "just wasn't a demonstrative, touchy-feely kind of person. Nor was he given to much gaiety." James, Ted's younger brother, enjoyed an excellent relationship with his father. "Jimmy developed a closeness to my dad that I never had," Ted admitted. (Mr. Hesburgh died of liver cancer in 1960.)[4]

Anne was different. Bubbly, gregarious, and happy, her personality complemented her husband's. She was 5'1" and grew increasingly heavy; Theodore was 6'2" and slim. "Mom and Dad looked like Mutt and Jeff," said Betty. Anne had dark hair and dark eyes, and Ted was the only one in the family who inherited her dark Irish looks. Ted also expressed more affection for her. "My mother . . . was easily the romantic one of the pair," he said. "An aura of joy and merriment seemed to surround her all the time." The children's love of music came from her. She often played the piano, and on Saturday evenings the children gathered around her and harmonized. Ted later speculated on the influence of his ethnic heritage: "My German side gave me a sense of order and discipline; my Irish side gave me the ability to understand people [and to] get along with them."[5]

Theodore and Anne Hesburgh raised three daughters and two sons. Mary, the firstborn, was nineteen months older than Ted. After Ted came Elizabeth (1920), Anne (1925) and James (1933). Because they were nearest in age, Ted and Mary became particularly close. Bright, artistic, and funny, Mary became a teacher, but died tragically of cancer in her early forties, leaving a husband and four children.

The Hesburgh family lived briefly in two different apartments in Syracuse and then in 1925, when Ted was eight, they moved into a new, two-story, three-bedroom, colonial home at 609 Charmouth Drive, in the Strathmore section of the city. In this mostly Protestant, German and Irish neighborhood, the Hesburghs lived a comfortable middle class life. "We never wanted for anything," said Betty.[6]

Although neither Theodore nor Anne had gone to college, they strongly encouraged their children's education. All but one of the children completed college. They earned a total of four bachelor's degrees, four master's degrees, and one doctorate. The Hesburghs were a close family. In their unique Franklin auto, with its unusual air-cooled engine, the family went on picnics, and vacationed for two weeks at a cottage on Lake Ontario in upper New York State. Because the children deeply respected their parents, they carefully avoided doing anything to upset or disappoint them. Nor did the children challenge their parents' authority. "In those days you never questioned your family's authority on anything," said Betty. "Their word was law."[7]

In most respects Ted led a normal childhood. For twelve years— first grade through high school—he attended Most Holy Rosary School, about a mile walk from his home through Onondaga Park. The school was located on a hill on Bellevue Avenue in an area dubbed Bellevue Heights. Like many Catholic communities, the parish built a school before it built the church, and parishioners worshipped in the school's auditorium. Most Holy Rosary had been founded in 1913. The heavy debts incurred by Syracuse churches in the expansive 1920s posed serious problems when the Depression hit, catching parishes like Most Holy Rosary in the midst of ambitious plans. In July 1932, with a total debt of more than $500,000, Most Holy Rosary was near bankruptcy and was saved from disaster partly by support from the Diocese of Syracuse.

In order to fulfill his dream of building a new church, the founding pastor, Fr. George Mahon, constantly implored parishioners for more donations. From the pulpit he urged that the collection basket be silenced, meaning that he preferred the "silence" of greenbacks in the baskets to the "noise" of coins. Still, the church was not completed for many years.

With the Boy Scouts Ted went to summer camp and earned numerous badges. He dabbled in sports. He was a lineman on a neighborhood football team, the Robineau Terriers. "I wasn't very good," he later said. He also played softball in the summer. "I wasn't any good at that [either]." "I would say he was just plain not an athlete," said John O'Connor. He supported the school's athletic teams, said another friend, Frank Corso, "but he had small interest in participating himself in sporting events."[8]

He loved building model airplanes, and at age ten convinced his father to allow him a taste of the real thing. He and a friend went to the local airport and flew with a barnstorming, daredevil pilot in a creaky biplane with a wooden prop and an open cockpit. "The view was stunning," he recalled in his autobiography, "farms, woods, cars, people, downtown Syracuse, the neighborhoods, and, of course, Lake Onondaga." The ride lasted only fifteen minutes, but he was hooked for life.[9]

One of the greatest thrills of his childhood occurred in June 1927, when he was ten. While attending a cousin's ordination to the priesthood in St. Patrick's Cathedral in New York, as luck would have it the ceremony occurred the same day Charles Lindbergh made his triumphant return to New York after his flight to Paris. Up to his knees in tickertape, he watched Lindbergh come up the street in a motorcade with New York's mayor, Jimmy Walker.[10]

At age twelve Ted was nearly killed in an accident. While he sat next to an ice skating rink, spiked-shoed horses pulling a sleigh ran over him. Fortunately he lay down flat and emerged unscathed. "I could have really been squashed," he said. "Everyone marveled that he survived," added Betty. When someone pointed out he could have been killed, Betty remembered him responding, "Oh, no, God has other plans for me."

"It was a wonderful place for young people to live," he later remembered. "We had great winter sports, tobogganing, skiing, skating in Onondaga Park. The winters were rough but you loved them because you had so much going on. In summertime, it was gorgeous. I just have nothing but good memories."[11]

Except for the few Catholic families, Strathmore was mostly a WASP community. There were a few blacks in Syracuse, but Ted didn't encounter any in his neighborhood, in school, in the YMCA, in Boy Scouts, or at summer camp. Nor did the subject of blacks and race relations ever come up. "Race just never entered the picture," said Betty.

However, he did learn an unforgettable lesson about prejudice. As he was growing up, he thought vaguely that Jews were "somewhat different," and he considered being somewhat different a "bad thing." Years later he recalled his youthful thoughts on Jews: "They're not like us. . . . Why can't everybody be like us?"

One afternoon he arrived home from grade school and encountered a neighbor lady weeping in the arms of his mother. He retreated to the kitchen to get a sandwich, but later asked his mother what the fuss was about. His mother explained that the lady had moved into the neighborhood a few years earlier and was now leaving because no one would talk to her. "Why not?" Ted asked. "She's Jewish," Anne replied. "So what?" Ted persisted. Anne sat her son down and explained further. "We are living in a segregated neighborhood. It's almost completely Protestant, and there are no other Jews in it, and very few Catholics. The only reason some of them tolerate the few Catholics who live here is because we have a little money. Otherwise, we would not be welcome here, either." Why was his mother different? Ted inquired. Why did she befriend the Jewish woman? Anne replied that, where she grew up in the Bronx, the Irish and Jews were interspersed, got along, and supported each other. "There's no way on earth I could be prejudiced against Jews," she said. The incident had a profound impact on Ted: "That was my first contact with [prejudice] . . . and it shocked me."[12]

The values stressed in the Hesburgh household were honesty, hard work, and patriotism. But fidelity to the Catholic faith was paramount. The Hesburghs were devout Catholics and abided by strict moral standards. All the children attended Catholic schools, never missed Mass on Sunday (and some went almost every day), never ate meat on Friday, didn't cheat, steal, or lie. "And," Ted recalled, "we never, never talked about sex—in any way, shape, or form." Ted's father belonged to the Knights of Columbus, prayed the rosary in his auto, and made an annual retreat. When the family went on a trip, they always prayed the rosary together.

Many devout Catholic parents hoped that when their first son arrived they might be lucky and he would become a priest. Theodore and Anne Hesburgh may have entertained such a thought, but they never pressured their first-born son. "It wasn't drummed into him," recalled Betty. Religious faith was natural in the Hesburgh household. "It wasn't forced on us," Betty added.

Most Holy Rosary parish, though, stimulated many of its parishioners to enter the religious life. By the thirtieth anniversary of the parish, thirty-six graduates of the school had become priests and twenty-eight more were vowed religious. As far back as Ted could recall, he wanted to be a priest. There was never any special moment when he felt called to the vocation. "I *always* wanted to be a priest," he said; "I never went through a fireman stage." He was an altar boy, and while school was in session, students attended Mass and communion every day. He started going to daily Mass in first grade. He expected more challenge and satisfaction as a priest than in any other vocation. The thought of standing between God and man, with the "traffic going both ways," was romantic and adventurous. "I visualized that I would be endowed at ordination with a great power to do great good for everyone I would ever meet."[13]

When Ted was in seventh or eighth grade, four missionaries came to Most Holy Rosary and fanned the flame. Members of the Congregation of Holy Cross, which had been founded in France in 1837, they preached "fire and brimstone sermons about sinners dying in whorehouses and spending eternity in hell." The altar boys were considered too young to listen to such horror stories, so one of the priests would talk to the youngsters in the sacristy. When Fr. Thomas Duffy asked Ted what he wanted to be when he grew up, Ted replied with strong conviction, "I'm going to be a priest, Father. Like you." Ted liked the friendly Holy Cross priests, particularly Fr. Duffy. Equally impressed with Ted, Fr. Duffy scribbled down his name and attributes ("fine boy, bright"). Before long Fr. Duffy was urging Ted's mother and father to enroll him in the Holy Cross high school seminary at the University of Notre Dame. Anne Hesburgh approved of her son's desire to be a priest but was leery of allowing him to enter the seminary after eighth grade, fearing he was too young. "If he doesn't come and he goes to high school here [in Syracuse], he may lose his vocation," Fr. Duffy retorted. But Anne insisted. "It can't be much of a vocation if he's going to lose it by living in a Christian family," she responded. So Ted continued on to high school at Most Holy Rosary.

In describing his own Catholic childhood, the writer Garry Wills vividly recalled habits which Ted Hesburgh also experienced:

prayers offered, heads ducked in unison, crossings, chants, christenings, grace at meals; beads, altar, incense, candles; nuns in the classroom alternately too sweet and too severe, priests garbed black on the street and brilliant at the altar; churches lit and darkened, clothed and stripped, to the rhythm of liturgical recurrences; the crib in winter, purple Februaries, and lilies in the spring; confession as intimidation and comfort (comfort, if nothing else, that the intimidation was survived), communion as revery and discomfort; faith as a creed, and the creed as catechism, Latin responses, salvation by rote, all things going to a rhythm, memorized, old things always returning, eternal in that sense, no matter how transitory.

From the time of their arrival in America, Catholics were often viewed with suspicion. Catholics were clannish, attended their own parochial schools, accepted rigid ecclesiastical discipline, produced large families, were led by unmarried clergy, held peculiar religious practices, and granted allegiance to a foreign authority. For the first sixty years of the twentieth century it wasn't clear that a Catholic could be elected president.

Catholics separated themselves and developed their own culture, their own viewpoint. Catholics were told to stay out of non-Catholic churches. "Attendance there would be sinful," observed Wills, "a way of countenancing error." The pronouncements of the Catholic hierarchy in Syracuse highlighted the religious strictures imposed on Catholics in the diocese while Ted was growing up. In their private, nonworking life, Catholics in Syracuse were strongly urged to associate only with other Catholics, primarily because Catholics believed that their church was the "one true Church." Daniel J. Curley, the Bishop of Syracuse while Ted was in grade school, said, "We are bound to regard all other conceptions of God as false, an insult to his divine majesty." One should be charitable toward non-Catholics, but "we must unequivocally condemn the errors themselves and neither by word or conduct manifest any approval or compromise with their doctrine or form of worship." Catholic doctrines were "the keystone of the arch of all sound morality" and as such a bulwark against what Bishop Curley termed the "materialistic, unholy, Godless world."

In a 1930 pastoral Curley stated that the contemporary Church confronted "pagan practices" and "pagan morality" worse than that faced by the earliest Christians. One danger was "a putrid stream of the most despicable, the most iniquitous and the most dangerous variety of literature and of prints and pictures that were debauching the minds and morals of the young." Another was the "neo-paganism of birth control," based upon "lewdness and self-indulgence of the most degrading kind," and bringing about "a lustful perversion of the marital relationship" and "prostitution of motherhood." Another danger was communism, whose "agents spread sedition and unrest," "created conflict between capital and labor," and undermined national institutions, assisted by "callous employers" who forced people to live in misery while they built "swollen fortunes."

To avoid the scourge of immoral films, Catholics must follow the Legion of Decency. Pledge forms were distributed and as a matter of conscience Catholics were told to promise to abstain from attending indecent and immoral moving pictures.

Since modern Christians lived in a pagan environment, it was necessary to create an alternative environment—one that honored Catholic and American values. Speaking to Catholic students attending Syracuse University, Bishop Curley observed: "You cannot live among the icebergs without feeling the cold." Stay close to the Church, and stay close to each other in order to be safe from dangers.

Catholics could avoid "grave peril," said Bishop Curley, if they respected and followed God's law, prayed, and received the sacraments. Those who would be "numbered among the elect" must not "walk in the path of self-indulgence, of luxury and sin" but "in the mortification of the senses and evil inclinations."

David O'Brien, historian of the Diocese of Syracuse, observed, "Loyalty to the Church, submission to its requirements of faith and morality, and an attitude of humility and deference before priests, who embodied God's presence in the world, were the way to earn salvation. The sin of sins was pride, placing one's own thoughts, judgments or needs before those of God's Church." Bishop Curley told a congregation that it was "foolish pride" that explained the defection of "foolish Catholics who banish from their minds the light they have received." Concluded O'Brien: "The Church, then, was a source of truth and grace and at the same time a set of associations, family, friends, [and] companions."

At Most Holy Rosary School, officials also enforced strict rules. While Ted was in high school, Fr. Howard McDowell succeeded Fr. Mahon as pastor of Most Holy Rosary. Devout and strict, Fr. McDowell followed every rule of the Church right to the letter of the law. "He was not a warm man," recalled Mary Waters, an acquaintance of Ted. "He really was misplaced. In dealing with youth, his idea of a dance was boys dancing with boys and girls dancing with girls. He was very strict."[14]

All the students wore uniforms—the girls wore uniform dresses, the boys, white shirts and dress blue trousers. Nuns monitored the dress of the girls and discouraged any display of sexuality. The pastor, said John O'Connor, "tried to present a world that was not like the real world. Sexuality was not even a part of it." When sexuality was mentioned by school and church officials, it was considered reprehensible. "I think the emphasis then on the Sixth Commandment, or sex, was probably overdone," Fr. Ted reflected. Individual rather than social morality was emphasized.

Since social functions at school were frowned upon, boys and girls interacted at picnics, swimming outings, and birthday parties in homes. "It was a group activity most of the time," Ted recalled; "we had a lot of fun." Girls enjoyed Ted's company. He was strikingly handsome. Several friends thought he looked like a cross between actors Tyrone Power and Fredric March. In his junior and senior years Ted primarily associated with Mary Eleanor Kelley, a vivacious, attractive classmate who lived in an expensive home. "He cared a lot for Mary Eleanor," recalled John O'Connor. "She thought the world of Ted Hesburgh," said Donald Roth, a friend of Ted.

Many years later CBS television reporter Dan Rather interviewed Fr. Ted and tried to catch him off guard. "Before you became a priest," Rather asked, "did you ever raise hell? . . . I mean did you ever chase the girls or drink too much on occasion?" Looking slightly amused, Ted replied, "Well, we all chased the girls when we were young . . . but I think we did it in a more modest way than is done now."[15]

For a while in high school Ted and friends owned a run-down Model T Ford. Occasionally they got the car running and drove to the other side of town to visit friends. (They couldn't go any farther because the auto was likely to break down.) An avid fisherman and hunter, Ted and other boys fished for bass on a lake near the foothills of the Adirondacks and hunted pheasants near Rochester, New York. "We were very much into . . . hunting and fishing," said O'Connor. At a cabin for a weekend Ted and seven other high school friends hunted and fished, drank beer and smoked cigars, and raised a bit of Cain. "Typically, we would play poker all night long," O'Connor remembered, "and feel that we were quite macho." Ted worked at a variety of jobs—mowing lawns, hauling coal ashes, delivering newspapers. Because breaking news stories were known mainly from special editions of the local newspaper, Ted occasionally ran down the street with a stack of newspapers, yelling "Extra, Extra!" In his senior year of high school he got grease under his fingernails working forty hours a week as a gas station attendant.[16]

Besides his early ambition to be a priest, three features distinguished Ted from his young peers: his sense of propriety, his voracious reading, and his scholastic ability. "He never seemed to get in trouble or controversy with either the teachers or other students," said Frank Corso. "School-boy pranks [were] not part of young Ted's make-up." O'Connor agreed: "He always had a real good sense of propriety. . . . He always knew the limits."

O'Connor and Ted attended a film that portrayed a physician becoming romantically involved with a nurse, resulting in an illegitimate child. The couple were victims of circumstances and couldn't help themselves, the film's message seemed to convey. Afterwards, though, Ted disagreed with the film's message. "We always have free will and can control our affairs," Ted told his friend. On this occasion and others, O'Connor was impressed with Ted's maturity.[17]

"I've always been curious," Ted said. In the seventh grade he won first prize in a New York state geography contest, and the award stimulated his interest in "what was over the next hill." When he was a youngster, reading satisfied his voracious curiosity and also extended his imagination to exciting places far beyond Syracuse. He belonged to the high school's Literary Guild, where he and other students took turns presenting oral book reviews. At a meeting in March 1934, he reported on *Father McShane of Maryknoll* (1932). The book related the story of Fr. Daniel McShane of Columbus, Indiana, who served as a Maryknoll missionary in South China from 1919 to 1927. Exceptionally devoted and courageous, Fr. McShane died of smallpox contracted while taking care of an abandoned Chinese baby. "We need men who are pure of heart, who are truly humble, whose motives are single, whose courage is marked, who are fearless in the charity of Christ," the author said while eulogizing the book's hero; "and it is no exaggeration to say, . . . that these admirable qualities were found in [McShane's] character."

Ted's taste in reading ran to adventure, romance, and travel, and to stories about thoughtful, courageous Christians. Among his favorite books were stories of the early martyrs in the catacombs (*Fabiola*); Russian aristocrats under Soviet rule (*Silver Trumpets Calling*); the reflections of a devout Catholic during a pilgrimage to the Holy Land (*Crusade of the Anemone*); and a travel tour of modern Italy (*A Foot in Italy*). He loved the books by Edison Marshall, the short-story writer, novelist, and explorer. Marshall wrote tales of adventure, peril, and the excitement of cold, snow, and ice. Virtue was always rewarded and death was the penalty for transgressing. "Ted used to consume those," said O'-Connor. "Ted liked the macho appearance that was portrayed in many of those adventure novels." He especially liked the extraordinarily vivid *Trader Horn* (1927), Marshall's story of a young trader in Africa among cannibals, elephant hunters, and gorillas.[18]

In 1934, his senior year in high school, Ted helped edit the school newspaper, *The Rosarian*. In one remarkable article he brashly challenged his fellow students to elevate the quality of their reading. Dispense with the simplistic "dime novel," he urged, the kind where the western hero slaughters "the big bad bandit, marries the foreman's daughter and lives bloodily ever after." The "veracity" of such novels was "dubious," he argued. Forget the cowboys and bandits. "[You] will not miss them."

Instead, he urged they read "GOOD" books, ones that were "true to life" and "interesting," and would "satiate your most sanguinary tastes." They should read books "that will elevate your ideas, enlarge your vocabulary, and widen your perspective." Some classmates, he speculated, would retort that "only a pansy reads those books," but he reminded skeptics that Abraham Lincoln walked all day to procure a book. "And have you ever heard Abe Lincoln referred to as a 'Lily of the Valley?'"

Ted recommended nine books for his classmates to read—all adventure, travel, or religious books. He commented extensively on his current favorite, Fr. Bernard Rosecrans Hubbard's *Mush, You Malamutes* (1933). Fr. Hubbard, nicknamed the "Glacier Priest," told marvelous adventure tales. While describing the animals, flowers, and trees of Alaska, he took his readers mushing and camping, climbing unclimbed mountains, crossing uncrossed glaciers. Yet he was always the missionary priest as well, never missing Mass even though he may have driven his dogs 85 miles in 67 hours, and he always found time to say his breviary. It was a "great story," Ted told readers of *The Rosarian;* "[Hubbard] is a fine man and a fine writer. . . . With him you will fight grizzly bears, fall into crevasses, starve, and yet come out unscathed—more fun than a barrel of monkeys." Why waste time and energy with "improbabilities," Ted concluded his challenge to classmates, "when India, China, Alaska, Africa, Mexico, Spain, France—all the world of adventure, history, romance, and culture beckons?"[19]

Except for an occasional substitute, the teachers at Most Holy Rosary were all nuns of the Immaculate Heart of Mary. The nuns instilled a high level of piety and discipline. Most of them had master's degrees and were excellent teachers. In high school Ted took a core curriculum: four years of Latin, four of English, three of French and history, and one year each of algebra, geometry and chemistry. He also studied civics, art, drama, plus, of course, four years of religion. The only class he disliked was Latin, partly because an ineffective substitute teacher taught the course in his first year.

Two high school teachers stood out in his mind. Sister Veronica, who taught third-year English, brought literature to life by inspiring her students to read literary classics and by encouraging extensive writing, which she assiduously corrected. Sister Justina taught geometry, a subject Ted expected to be exceptionally difficult and boring. But on the first day of class she surprised the students with a challenge: whatever else they might learn from Euclidean geometry, it would never teach them to trisect an angle. That hooked Ted and his classmates, who took it as a personal challenge. Every time Sister Justina presented a new theorem, "we tried it out feeling sure that we would surprise her . . . and be successful at using the theorem to mathematically trisect an angle." Of course they failed, but the nun had cleverly aroused their interest in the use of Euclidean propositions. "In trying to prove her wrong and failing," Ted said, "we succeeded in something more important. We came to learn a lot of math."[20]

In April 1934, during three performances in the school's auditorium, two hundred students took part in a dramatic production of Christ's passion, titled the "Mysteries of the Mass." Ted played the lead part, Christ, an exceptionally difficult role requiring him to memorize a large portion of the New Testament. A local Catholic newspaper described the play as a "magnificent religious spectacle. . . . So dramatic was the performance that it thrilled the hushed throng for nearly three hours." The newspaper singled out three young actors for praise. "Particularly commendable was the portrayal of Our Lord by Theodore Hesburgh." "You would think he was Christ!" recalled a classmate. "He *was* the play. After the play, everybody thought for sure he would [enter the priesthood]."[21]

Only once did Ted get in trouble at school. On the first day of pheasant-hunting season in his senior year, he skipped school to hunt. His parents were called in to talk to the principal. "Only vulgar people go hunting," the principal declared. (Probably under his breath, Ted said, "Yea. Like Teddy Roosevelt.")[22]

At the end of his senior year Ted ranked about third in his class. During an honor's assembly before graduation he won the award for excellence in English and earned honorable mention for the award in religion. At commencement, on June 24, 1934, a Sunday afternoon, school officials selected Ted to deliver the Address of Welcome. He thanked the teaching nuns for being "wonderful dispensers of His holy word. You have taught us all that we know and what you have taught us we know to be the truth. You have prepared us for life's conquest even as the knights of old were prepared to fare forth against the infidel. You have bestowed upon us for our protection, the ample armor of knowledge and right thinking."

After expressing his appreciation to the parents of the graduates, Ted concluded pompously: "The door of the past is swiftly closing and naught but cherished memories remain of the happy days spent here at Rosary. Father Time has turned another page in the book of life, and we stand upon the threshold of the coming years while the bright future beckons. May it be a happy one—as happy as the years gone by."[23]

While Ted was in high school, his parents put no pressure on him to enter the priesthood. "Not even vaguely," said Betty. Nonetheless, his classmates knew he intended to be a priest. "There was little doubt in anyone's mind on the course that Ted's life career would follow," said Corso. The class prophecy for the 1934 graduating class predicted the occupations of graduates a decade later. Some were expected to be journalists, librarians, actresses, and college professors. The prophecy for Ted Hesburgh: "Pastor of St. Peter's in Split Rock."

Although he attended dances and dated girls, he never wavered in his desire to be a priest. "There were many nights when I'd roll in at 2 A.M. after having a good time and I'd just sit on my bed and say to myself, 'This isn't enough for me. There's something more that I need out of life.'" He interpreted his feelings to mean that God was telling him his priestly vocation was more important than his social life.

A priest who regularly heard his confession and knew he intended to enter the priesthood advised him to lead a normal high school social life, to date and have fun, but firmly added: "Just don't do anything you'll be ashamed of when you become a priest." Ted tried to abide by the admonition. The prospect of remaining celibate didn't seem to bother him. If he was to belong to "everybody," he reasoned, it would be hard to belong to "somebody."[24]

He frequently corresponded with Fr. Duffy, to whom he gave most of the credit for his entry into the Holy Cross order; but he also had reasons other than Fr. Duffy's influence for selecting the Congregation (in Latin, *Congregatio a Sancta Croce* or C.S.C.). During the Depression, Most Holy Rosary parish continued to suffer financial problems, and the burden of worry under which he saw the pastor and his assistants struggling caused Ted to rule out becoming a diocesan priest. "All

Theodore Hesburgh as a young man with his family.

we heard about was money," he later said. "I decided to join a religious order and take a vow of poverty, thus making sure the rest of my life would be free from the tribulations of money raising." The Holy Cross order also attracted because it had foreign missions. "That seemed a very exciting life," he later said. Besides being an adventure, missionary work was the ultimate in hardship and self-sacrifice.

Ted's parents were thrilled that he sustained his vocation throughout high school. He refused a college scholarship at Niagara University in New York and made plans to enter the seminary at the University of Notre Dame, near South Bend, Indiana. The night before he was to leave for the seminary he claimed he kissed goodby to thirty-six girls from his high school class.[25]

In mid-September 1934, Ted's father, mother, and sister Mary drove him from Syracuse to the University of Notre Dame. A world apart from what he had known, the campus "was shaded by giant oaks, quiet, lovely, and awe-inspiring in a medieval sort of way." After he checked into Holy Cross Seminary, he said his emotional farewell to his family. When they left, the seventeen-year-old suffered his first wave of "unequivocal homesickness," which remained for about a month, then slowly faded as he became absorbed in his classes and his life as a seminarian. As he contemplated the long periods of study and training, "I thought it would never end while [I was] going through it."[26]

The first year Ted was a postulant, one who intended to join the Holy Cross order. Except for chemistry and life sciences, which he took on the Notre Dame campus, his classes were conducted at the seminary. The seminarians were at Notre Dame but lived by different rules. They could not correspond with girls and could not date or attend social functions on campus. Homesickness and loneliness occasionally resurfaced. Other students cheerfully went home for Christmas vacation, while Ted and his fellow seminarians were left behind, lonely and cold.

To many Notre Dame students, a seminarian was a black-clad figure who on cold winter days emerged from the northwest, shoulder hunched against the cold, attended classes and then disappeared. "Where [the seminarian] comes from and where he returns to is a mystery to many," observed a Notre Dame student magazine. Moreover, at Notre Dame, Ted's social and cultural horizons remained narrow. There wasn't a single black student or faculty member at the university. In his courses he learned practically nothing about Asia, Latin America, or poverty.

After his first year Ted was sent to Rolling Prairie, Indiana, along with twenty-nine other novice seminarians and twenty brother postulants. Rolling Prairie was a small hamlet, thirty miles west of Notre Dame. It was also the name of the dilapidated, 720-acre farm that the Holy Cross order had recently purchased. Arriving on August 6, 1935, he went on an eight-day retreat, after which he received his religious habit. He was about to discover that there was more to becoming a priest than spiritual and intellectual development. Having heard about the rigors of life at Rolling Prairie, he nervously anticipated his upcoming thirteen-month ordeal. Would he make it? Would he persevere? "Would I get through that tough year and finally take my temporary vows for three years and make them perpetual after that?"[27]

During the winter at Rolling Prairie, Ted and his fellow seminarians followed an exceptionally rigorous and rigid schedule:

5:00	Rising
5:20	Meditation
5:50	Meditation Recollections
6:05	Mass
6:50	End of Thanksgiving. Make beds
7:00	Breakfast, followed by housework
7:55	End of work
8:10	Little Hours
8:35	Conference
9:20	Clean rooms. Study
10:00	Setting up exercises outdoors or in Recreation Room according to weather, followed by inspection
10:15	Study
11:00	Spiritual Reading
11:25	Study or Private Spiritual Reading
11:45	Particular Examen
12:00	Dinner
1:25	Visit. Vespers and Compline
2:00	Work until 3:00
3:20	Class or Study (See Schedule of Classes)
4:45	Meditation in Chapel
5:10	Meditation Recollections
5:20	Matins and Lauds
5:56	Scapular Prayers in Chapel
6:00	Supper
7:30	Hymn to Our Lady . . . followed by Spiritual Reading. Beads and Night Prayer in Chapel.
8:55	Bell for retiring
9:00	Lights out

Living conditions at Rolling Prairie were fine; each seminarian had a private room. But Ted had love-hate memories of his experience there. Life resembled Marine boot camp, and although he accepted the regimentation as a necessary initiation and learned lessons, his most vivid memories were of exceptional hardship and toil. The purpose was to instill physical, mental, and spiritual discipline and to weed out the men. They cleaned their rooms and prepared meals; waited on tables and washed dishes.

The hardest task, though, was coping with work assignments planned and supervised by Brother Seraphim. Born in Germany, Brother Seraphim Herrmann, 36, had served two years in the German Army during World War I before coming to the United States to become a Holy Cross brother. Hardworking and ingenious, he acted like a crusty, hard-nosed, Marine drill instructor. Ted and his fellow seminarians picked up huge piles of rocks, built a barn, tended cows, and harvested corn, wheat, and rye. Under Brother Seraphim's watchful eye they moved an old silo ("cement block by cement block") a mile and built the silo anew. Brother Seraphim then ordered them to paint it. "The next thing I knew," recalled Ted, "I was sitting on a kind of swing, a board suspended by a rope on either end, and I was hanging there on the outside of the silo about fifty feet off the ground."

After collecting honey from bee hives, Ted was covered with bees and had to dive into a nearby lake to get rid of them. He cut down large beech trees and sawed the wood for the wood-burning furnace. While wielding a huge, two-handled crosscut saw, he cut himself badly. "I have a scar just above my right knee, a reminder of when I got too close to the saw."[28]

Fiendishly inventive with his assignments, Brother Seraphim once made his crew pick the lice off sheep. "The sheep stank," said Ted, "and pretty soon we did, too. On top of that, we also became infested with their lice, and had to bathe that night in Lysol." By the end of the fall, the young seminarians thought they had endured every dirty job imaginable, but they had underestimated Brother Seraphim. In November he ordered them to butcher the pigs. Ted learned the task so well and remembered the process so vividly that he took two pages in his autobiography to explain the gory details.

They sang the office every day, like monks in a monastery, and for twenty-two hours a day they maintained silence. (At meals they communicated with sign language.) Ted also took classes, prayed, meditated, and listened to spiritual lectures and readings under the direction of Fr. Kerndt Healy, 43, the Master of Novices and the spiritual director at Rolling Prairie. Some of the readings were outdated, boring tomes, but the seminarians took them seriously and without question. Both "the Church and community life were very structured and disciplined," Fr. Ted reflected. "It certainly never occurred to any of us to challenge anything."

Despite the rigors and the work, Ted still found plenty of time to read, devouring over a hundred books mostly on spiritual subjects. He felt a sense of accomplishment at the end of his stay at Rolling Prairie.

At 145 pounds, he was in the best physical shape of his life and didn't have an ounce of fat on him. Twenty of the twenty-nine seminarians had dropped out by the end of the thirteen months. "One day [a person] wouldn't show up for a meal. Then you'd know [he] was gone." Two more dropped out the next year. Why did Ted stay? "I just knew I wanted to be a priest. I figured that if every priest I knew in the order went through that I guess I could go through it." Although he learned what farmers were up against, "I also learned I didn't want to be a farmer." With hindsight, he said, "It was a great year in many ways. I'm glad I had it."[29]

On August 16, 1936, he took his temporary vows of poverty, chastity, and obedience. In September he began his second year of college at Notre Dame. Living and studying at Moreau Seminary was almost cozy and homelike compared to Rolling Prairie. Nonetheless, there was still the drudgery of work assignments: waiting on tables and washing "thousands and thousands" of dishes at Moreau. He disliked the excessive time taken up by the work assignments, time that could have been spent on study. But, he reflected in his autobiography, "I never gave voice to those thoughts, you can be sure, because I had taken a vow of obedience, and mine was not to question my superiors."

The common goal was perfection, and the vows of poverty, chastity, and obedience were to make pursuit of the objective easier. Ted knew that he could never fully attain the goal, but at Moreau he had all the spiritual weapons possible. An article on the seminarian's life at Moreau noted, "There is Mass and Communion and meditation every morning; there is the recitation of the Little Office of the Blessed Virgin during the day, as well as spiritual reading and rosary; there are the countless reminders of his obligation such as the prayers before and after meals, the silence, the regimented schedule, and the bells which signal the end of one activity and the beginning of another."

The discipline, carefully organized schedule, and the quiet rooms allowed for more effective study than in the campus dormitories. In his two years of college courses, chemistry and math were sheer drudgery for him, but he found most of his other classes stimulating. He particularly enjoyed languages, literature, philosophy, and writing. A Protestant English professor left an indelible impression. "I learned more about a Christian view of sex in literature from him than [from] any Catholic professor I had [at Notre Dame]." The insights stuck with him many years later whenever he read a novel or watched a drama. Another English professor criticized his writing. "If you don't learn to simplify your style with simple words," the professor wrote on Ted's final exam, "you will wind up being a pompous ass." Ted noted that the professor's style was simple and clear.[30]

Ted earned the affection and respect of his fellow seminarians. "If people were talking about something that was fairly serious, when [Ted] came to talk, there [would] be more attention [paid] to him," recalled Fr. Chester Soleta, a fellow seminarian. "He was a very pleasant, very humorous man," added Soleta, "a man who laughed a lot, who liked simple jokes. . . . We would laugh a lot about silly things."

Once Ted began taking college courses he quickly caught the attention of his teachers, who decided to send him to Rome for further study at Gregorian University. In July 1937, as he was about to begin his junior year, his superiors informed him of the decision. How long would he be in Rome? he asked. Eight years, he was told. The prospect was daunting. "When you're twenty, eight years is a long, long time." The news gave him "considerable pause" and his excitement about going to Rome temporarily faded.

Gregorian University, the famous Jesuit-run theological and philosophical center, was to the Catholic Church what West Point was to the U.S. Army. Priests and seminarians from throughout the world were sent there to study. "It was the custom of the Holy Cross community," observed Professor Thomas Stritch of Notre Dame, a student of Hesburgh's life, "to send their best and brightest there." Despite his apprehension, Ted understood his selection was an honor. "Within the Congregation of Holy Cross," he later said, "those who went to the Gregorian most often ended up running things in one way or another." In late September 1937, he boarded the *Champlain* and steamed to Europe in time for classes, which began in early November.

In Rome, he lived with thirteen others in the three-story Holy Cross house on the Via dei Cappuccini, a fifteen-minute walk to Gregorian University. It was clear that his primary responsibility was to study, learn, and grow spiritually. Of his spartan room he observed, "In January I was so cold . . . my fingers were always too numb for me to do any typing. The marble floors were so cold that we used little wooden platforms under our desks to put our feet on. I don't remember ever being warm during those Roman winters."[31]

Work or no work, holiday or no holiday, he was up at 5 A.M. Like most of his life in the seminary so far, his routine was challenging and rigid: "Up at five, meditation and morning prayer, Mass, breakfast (bread, cheese, coffee), classes, noon chapel, lunch, classes, an afternoon walk, study, chapel, a light supper, half-hour recreation (Ping-Pong or bridge) in the front room, and then (at about nine) to bed or to study in your room for as late as you liked, just so long as you were up and at 'em at 5 A.M."

At Gregorian University he studied logic, metaphysics, cosmology, and epistemology. Although unhappy with the rigid, unimaginative, old-fashioned teaching, he appreciated receiving a thorough grounding in classical scholastic philosophy and theology. The only exams were at the end of nine months of study, when each student had to sweat through a frightening oral exam administered by a Jesuit.[32]

In the atmosphere of Rome, Ted's whole world suddenly became international. He developed a deep understanding of the universality of the Church, because he rubbed elbows in class with seminarians and professors from Germany, Italy, England, Scotland, Armenia, South America, almost every race and nationality on earth, with each group dressed in different colored cassocks. "It was visually a melange," observed Fr. Roy Rihn, a classmate, "as well as linguistically, culturally, ethnically." The years in Rome, said Stritch, left him with a "cosmopolitan polish and introduced him to the urbanites of the capital of the Catholic World."

Ted communicated in five different languages. To begin with, the Holy Cross residence in Rome was run by the French wing of the order. Fr. George Sauvage, the director, was meticulous, intelligent, and strict. At dinner the seminarians couldn't talk with each other, but only with Fr. Sauvage, who would ask them questions about religion or current events. All conversation was in the house language. Ted conversed in French, read lessons in French, and even prayed in French. Having studied French in high school, he was able to become fluent, though his accent remained American. At Gregorian University all of his classes were taught in Latin. He answered questions in Latin and took notes in Latin. He even studied Hebrew in Latin. On the streets of Rome, he conversed in Italian. "I also studied Italian intensely, buttonholing any unsuspecting Italian student at the university who did not speak English. I made it a point never to speak English if I could avoid it." One of his friends was Mexican so they always conversed in Spanish. Finally, through self-study, he learned German.

It became his habit to spend the fifteen minutes before lunch each day learning thirty new words—ten each in Italian, French, and German. Every year, therefore, he learned 3650 new words in each language—and he remembered the words. "I grew to love languages," he said, "and I have no doubt that the fluency I acquired in Rome helped me enormously in all the work I was to do the rest of my life."

In class the students listened to the lecture by the Jesuit instructor, who expected the students to learn by rote. "You were told what the conclusion was, and then you set out to prove it," reflected Rihn of his dogmatic theology course. "It was propagandizing rather than teaching." There were no papers assigned, no discussions, and usually no questions. "He just rattled on for 50 minutes," observed another classmate, Fr. William Schreiner.

Ted struck fellow seminarians as bright and intelligent. Rihn observed: "Here was an intelligent young man who was alive to what was going on in the world." Schreiner agreed. "What impressed me was his intelligence. He was . . . a deep thinker."

Intensely ambitious and hard working, Ted completed an astonishing self-directed study program during two summer months at a Tyrolean guest house near the Austrian border. In the bucolic setting, he performed all the exercises in a German textbook, conjugated all the irregular German verbs, practiced speaking German with area residents, and read the New Testament in German. Further, he read a textbook on philosophy (in French), a seven-hundred-page novel, a history of Italian art, and a six-hundred-page book on metaphysics (all in Italian).

How did he do it? He thought there were several factors. "One, I had acquired discipline over the years of my Catholic education, and Rolling Prairie taught me in particular just how much can be accomplished if one focuses on the task at hand without interruptions and without distractions. The free time between morning and evening prayers . . . had given me that opportunity to focus and to concentrate."[33]

In August 1940, Ted published his first article. It appeared in Notre Dame's *Ave Maria* magazine and chronicled with unbridled enthusiasm the election of Cardinal Eugenio Pacelli as the new pope. Early on the election day in March 1939, Ted had watched for the white puff of smoke signaling that the cardinals had decided on a new pope. The same evening, among a "huge black, seething mass of humanity," he reported that Cardinal Caccia Dominioni came to the rail of the balcony of St. Peter's and spoke slowly and deliberately through amplifiers. "It was a thrilling message," Ted said, "strangely reminiscent of the words of the angels on the first Christmas Eve: *Annuntio vobis gaudium magnum, habemus papam* . . . 'I announce to you a great joy, we have a pope . . . the most reverend and most eminent Eugenio.' The crowd needed no more. From end to end the thronged Piazza echoed with cheers of acclamation, joy and exultation." Cardinal Dominioni finished his announcement: "Cardinal Pacelli, Supreme Pontiff of the Holy Roman Catholic Church, who has chosen for himself the name of his predecessor." Cardinal Pacelli had become Pius XII.

When Pius XII appeared on the balcony to intone his first blessing, reporter Hesburgh felt as one with the excited crowd: "On all sides, people knelt and blessed themselves as his voice, strong and firm, pierced the dusk and gripped us with an indescribable feeling of trust and confidence. We felt ourselves repeating, as if to reaffirm the reality, *Habemus Papam!*"

After the pope left the balcony, Ted and the crowd turned to go home. "All about the city, jubilant church bells were ringing, adding to the already exuberant spirit of the hour. . . . We hurried past historic monuments, careless, and for the moment almost heedless of their age-old significance. Tonight we had been living history—the glorious history of a force that outlasts even these ancient piles of Imperial days."[34]

Less savory people also made appearances in Rome. On one occasion Adolph Hitler toured historical sites in the city in an open car and passed by the Holy Cross residence. A classmate, standing by the window, yelled, "Come over here and look out. Hitler is passing." Ted shrugged him off indignantly as a matter of principle: "I wouldn't walk ten feet to see that bum."

In May 1940, at the end of his third year in Rome, war tensions permanently interrupted his education at the Gregorian. France was being overrun by Nazi Germany, and Mussolini was about to enter the conflict. Because of the impending danger, the American consul in Rome ordered all U.S. citizens to leave the country. They were to board the *USS Manhattan*, leaving from Genoa on June 1st. "The announcement that we were going home threw us all into a frenzy," Ted said. The school term was shortened by a month, and in less than a week he completed his final exams, packed his belongings, and hustled to Genoa.

"It was a very, very sad moment when we pulled out [of Genoa]," said Emmett O'Neill, a fellow seminarian at the Gregorian and Ted's traveling companion aboard ship. "All the people on the pier were cry-ing." (Many were Jews who worried they would be unable to leave be-cause of the war.) Loaded with thirty-six-hundred people, far above nor-mal capacity, the *USS Manhattan* took nine days to reach New York. O'Neill enjoyed his personable, easygoing companion, but was most impressed with Ted's perceptive mind. They met daily and discussed theology and Catholic Action, the new reform movement within the Church. Ted helped O'Neill understand the movement. "You were car-ried away by his knowledge, by his awareness of things," recalled O'Neill. "You couldn't help but feel that this man [was] destined to be a leader." On June 10, 1940, the ship arrived in New York, and Ted's sister Mary met him at the pier. They took the train to Syracuse, where Ted had two weeks for reunions and vacation.

On June 15, while on vacation, Ted wrote his provincial superior at Notre Dame, Fr. Thomas Steiner, and reflected on the war and on the virtues of his own country:

We never appreciated so much the freedom of America until we saw the results of the lack of liberty in Europe. It really is sickening to see the lives of so many people ruined, their hopes frustrated, their families disrupted, merely because a dictator thinks he owns them body and soul. We can't pray too much for war torn Europe, and heart broken Europeans. One aspiration I bring from Rome is to do whatever I can to keep America true to her ideals.

One reason Ted's superiors liked him and saw great potential in him was his graciousness. While writing Fr. Steiner in June 1940, Ted asked his provincial superior to "please relay my best regards to Fr. Healy, and be assured of my prayers for yourself and the Community. I must also thank you for the fine opportunity you have given me, of studying three years at Rome. I have tried to be loyal in doing my best, and with the grace of God, will continue at Washington."[35]

For the next five years during World War II, Ted studied in Wash-ington, D.C., spending three years at Holy Cross College completing his theology studies (1940–43); then, after his ordination, two years at Catholic University working on his doctorate in sacred theology (1943–45). Dennis Geaney, a classmate at Holy Cross College, observed Ted doing much more than just his course work. "He seemed to be on top of every Catholic Church development in the greater Washington metropolitan area, without losing his identity with his local communi-ty," said Geaney.

One subject that captured Ted's attention was race. No blacks had attended the University of Notre Dame in the 1930s largely because the prevailing attitude at the university was that white Southern students would object, and possibly leave, if blacks were admitted. The first black Ted met was in Rome, not in the U.S.

But in 1940, at an informal seminar at Catholic University, Ted studied institutional racism and impressed his peers with his perceptive research and understanding. The seminar had been organized by a priest, a refugee from Mussolini's Italy, who lived in a parish in a black section of Washington. He invited six seminarians and several faculty members from Catholic University to the Sunday morning sessions, and at the first meeting he asked for a volunteer to make a presentation on the dimensions of institutional racism in the country. Ted, who had said little, volunteered. At the next meeting Ted delivered an incisive paper, analyzing the problem from every perspective. Dennis Geaney, a seminar participant, was impressed. "I thought the guy was a genius," reflected Geaney. "I knew from that day that [he] was a man of destiny."

Later, when Ted worked as a chaplain at the National Training School for Boys, a federal reform school, blacks occupied two cottages, and he counseled those who were Catholic. He also mingled with blacks in a Boys Club and helped start a Newman Club at all-black Howard University.[36]

On June 24, 1943, Ted was ordained in Notre Dame's Sacred Heart Church. Wearing white vestments, he and fifteen others prostrated themselves in the sanctuary. As he put his fingers and thumbs on the chalice and host, he heard the "wonderful" words: "Receive the power of offering the Mass for the living and the dead. Receive you the Holy Spirit, whose sins you shall forgive will be forgiven."

Speaking at a First Mass a few years after his own ordination, he said, "You could search far and wide in this world without finding a vision quite so noble or quite so ennobling as that of Christ's priesthood. And the reason is that his vision is the very vision of Christ himself. The priest is a priest because he is consecrated and committed to be what Christ *is*, to do what Christ *did*. The priest, more than anything else, is another Christ."

The priest was a Christlike go-between who sacrificed and taught at the altar, forgave sins in the confessional, consoled and guided, and who was "to give and give and give" with all the priestly powers he had received from Christ, "until the shadows lengthen, and his own day is done and the time comes to go home to the Great High Priest with his hands full of the souls he has saved in Christ's name along the high ways and by ways of this world."

Returning to Washington after his ordination and his First Mass in Syracuse, Fr. Ted (as he now preferred to be called) was eager to perform priestly duties. With much to be done, he was quickly swamped with assignments, yet diligently performed them all. He served as an assistant at several parishes, gave a three-day retreat for high school students, worked as a chaplain for juvenile delinquents at the National Training School for Boys, and as auxiliary chaplain at military installations.[37]

He heard hundreds of confessions at St. Patrick's Church. He felt a surge of power, "the power of God through my hands and through my voice, saying, 'and I forgive you your sins in the name of the Father, and of the Son, and of the Holy Spirit.'" He was convinced that people who had been spiritually dead emerged from the confessional box "full of eternal life, full of grace, full of a new power to be more Christian."

While he was working in parishes in Washington, kind mentors provided sterling models of compassion. For two weeks at St. Martin's parish he assisted with Fr. Bill, an exceptionally charitable pastor. Fr. Bill advised him not to worry about being conned or deceived by someone asking for money or a sandwich. If a panhandler asked for something, Fr. Bill tried to provide it, reasoning that it was better to give to someone who didn't need it than to withhold from someone who did. "Better to be conned ninety-nine times," Fr. Bill advised, "than to miss the one who really needs help."

Similarly, when Fr. Ted served at St. Patrick's parish, a fellow priest told him, "Ted, don't be too professional." By way of example he cited priests who thought it was "professional" to process efficiently requests for spiritual advice. The faster the priest got rid of the person the better the job done, some priests believed. But those priests were wrong to associate professionalism with speed and efficiency. "A good priest," he told Fr. Ted, "will spend time with the person at the door. He won't be satisfied until he knows why that person rang the bell."[38]

Fr. Ted helped run a huge USO club, located in the large Knights of Columbus Hall at Tenth and K streets. Because the club was in a red-light district, he tried to keep the service personnel off the streets. To lure them away from brothels, he helped bring in excellent military bands that entertained as many as fifteen hundred jitterbugging men and women. "It was a sight to see," he said.

Fr. Ted also did considerable writing for the USO in Washington. To fill a vacuum in the spiritual literature sent to servicemen, he and another Holy Cross priest, Fr. Charles Sheedy, wrote a pocket-sized booklet, *For God and Country*. (Sheedy did most of the writing.) Fr. Ted estimated that the USO distributed nearly three million copies of the booklet.[39]

While working at the USO, Fr. Ted became acquainted with many servicewomen. "A lot of them had spiritual problems that they talked to me about [and] came to confession to me." Disturbed that servicewomen were often stereotyped as "prostitutes in the service," he composed a moral and spiritual guide for them. The booklet, *Letters to Service Women* (1943), offered simple advice on how to cope with life in the service. Written informally as though he were writing to his three sisters—each letter began "Dear Mary, Bets, and Anne"—the booklet reflected his early views on God, values, sexuality, and women.

He dedicated the booklet to Mary Immaculate, the Mother of God, with a prayer that she might inspire and help women in the service "to give our darkened world a shining example of Christian womanhood." Women in service had many good opportunities, he contended, but dangers lurked. A woman should enhance the good opportunities—occasions to do God's work—while overcoming or avoiding the dangers.

Women could find and fulfill God's will in every task. Simple tasks, like typing a letter or answering a phone, "are worth eternity if done *for* Him and *with* Him." Living with other women also provided opportunities. "Try taking a kindly personal interest in all of them," Ted advised; practice the "virtue of consideration." Be cheerful and cordial and above all kind. "Kindness is the only way you will get inside those who desperately need help and are too proud to admit it."

Just as there were opportunities to exploit, there were dangers to avoid. Women must respect themselves and then men would respect them. A woman's body "is the Temple of God." Therefore, women must avoid "hot spots," like cocktail lounges, with their alcohol and disreputable men. Some men could not be trusted. "Keep them at arm's length. Don't go out with them. Never be alone with them." Be careful using alcohol because it "will sell you short every time. Some ways of talking and walking and carrying on generally cheapen you."

The corrosive influences of modern society made it difficult to avoid the dangers: "It is not going to be easy to attain this ideal of Christian womanhood in a world that ridicules modesty, sneers at purity, and thinks of women in terms of pin-ups." Nonetheless, the consequences of giving in to temptations were morally catastrophic. "A girl cannot philander around during her term of service and then expect to settle down and raise a good family after the war. It can't be done." The loose girl doesn't make a good mother. "Besides, men don't marry the free and easy type."

"The ideal Christian woman," he said, "should cultivate her unique attributes." If women were pure, pious and dedicated to the values of the home and the family, they would not only inspire men but improve the quality of civilization. Women "very definitely have their own place in the world, but it is not man's place."

"Women have always had the noble work of giving tone and refinement to the world they live in. The presence of a good woman is always an elevating influence on a man or a group of men. Even a tramp does not swear in the presence of his Mother."

One could judge the level of a civilization by the quality of its women. "When Roman and Greek women became dissolute—the mere tools of men's pleasure—the bottom fell out of marriage and the family and the whole Graeco-Roman world collapsed. Christianity restored this collapsing world by restoring woman to her rightful place as the inspirer of man, the queen of the home.

"Since then, whenever women have stepped off their pedestal and sought false freedom and liberty, they have ended in the lowest kind of slavery—without love, without true friends, with nothing but bitter emptiness to their lives."

Fr. Ted estimated that three million copies of the booklet for servicewomen were distributed. Both booklets generated a large amount of mail, leading him to speculate that "hundreds of thousands of lives were affected."[40]

After his ordination, Fr. Ted had itched to get out of Washington and into military service, specifically to become a Navy chaplain aboard an aircraft carrier in the Pacific. But his provincial superior at Notre Dame insisted he complete his Ph.D. "Get your doctorate now, or you will never get it," he was admonished. In the fall of 1943, therefore, he entered the Ph.D. program at Catholic University.

The Catholic University of America was founded in 1887 as a pontifical university governed by bishops of the United States. Soon after its founding, many religious orders (including the Congregation of Holy

Cross) built houses of study nearby. The university's School of Sacred Theology offered a more rigorous and broader education than any offered at ecclesiastical seminaries around the country and hoped to train "teachers and leaders" in the religious field.

Normally the doctoral program took three years to complete, but with the Navy chaplaincy as his goal, he decided to hustle and complete the program in only two. He took courses in Scripture, the sacraments, and fundamental, dogmatic, and moral theology. Because of his language proficiency and his training at the Gregorian, he had a considerable advantage over his classmates. He dove into his studies, reading books in French, Latin, Italian, and German. At one point in his second year he was taking six graduate courses, writing long papers for each, and simultaneously racing to complete a doctoral thesis of over five hundred pages. He claimed that for five months, October 1, 1944 to March 1, 1945, the date his thesis was due, he worked from 7 A.M. to midnight every day except Christmas.[41]

Several new developments within the Catholic Church stimulated his thinking and influenced the subject of his doctoral dissertation. A new understanding of the Catholic Church as the Mystical Body of Christ stressed the responsibility of the members of the body to one another. A second development, Catholic Action, encouraged lay people to become active modern apostles in society, thereby advancing the Kingdom of God on earth. Laymen should assist Christ with the same energy and spirit that the original twelve apostles had. A Belgian parish priest, Joseph Cardijn, developed the inquiry technique to implement Catholic Action. Catholics should systematically observe and discuss their environment, judge the situation in the light of the gospel, and then act. The thrust was on action, not study or education. At Notre Dame the Young Christian Students, a Catholic Action group, used the Cardijn method with surprising success. By circulating a student petition, YCS helped convince the administration that racial integration would be accepted, and Notre Dame began to admit black students.

The official Church version assumed that all Catholic Action would proceed under the guidance of the hierarchy, specifically the bishop. This interpretation saw the layman's role principally as a soldier whose chief virtue was his obedience to the hierarchy. But each country gave to Catholic Action its own specific form, and in the United States leaders of the movement sought to keep it as far removed as possible from the Church's hierarchy and official bureaucracy, which coincided with Fr. Ted's view.

At Holy Cross College he belonged to a study group focused on Catholic Action. "I was interested in Catholic Action," he recalled, particularly "a new concept at the time called the Mystical Body." He had come to believe that everyone had a function in the Church; yet the Church appeared at the time to be totally hierarchical. Rarely were lay people pictured as doing anything responsible in the Church. He was particularly disturbed with the prevailing definition that Catholic Action was the participation of the laity in the apostolate of the hierarchy, as mandated by the hierarchy. The problem with the concept, he believed, was that it was not the apostolate of the hierarchy as much as it was the apostolate of Christ.[42]

In his doctoral dissertation he proposed to show that a person received the power to participate in the liturgy from baptism and the power to participate in the apostolate from confirmation. Everybody participates in the priesthood of Christ, the laity as well as the priest. "That was always a big secret in those days," he later said. He proposed, therefore, to put Catholic Action in a sacramental context.

Members of his dissertation committee, though, objected to his proposal. "It came to them as kind of a practical pragmatic, not-too-important subject," he said. His advisor, Fr. Eugene Burke, instructor of Dogmatic Theology, urged him not to pursue the thesis because of the objections by the theology faculty. But Fr. Ted persisted and with Burke's cooperation shrewdly devised a "fancy" title for the dissertation: "The Relation of the Sacramental Characters of Baptism and Confirmation to the Lay Apostolate." With the cosmetic change, Fr. Ted observed, "we got it through."[43]

As finally drafted, his doctoral dissertation strongly endorsed Catholic Action and contended that the lay apostolate was the Church's answer to the increasing secularism of the time. In the past thousand years society had dramatically changed from an ecclesiastical to a lay civilization. Clerics had withdrawn from direct and practical guidance of human affairs. In the course of secularization, "God was gradually exiled from His world"—from politics, education, business, literature, recreation, and the home.

The solution to the evil of secularism, he argued, was the complete antithesis of the evil. Secularism separated the human from the divine; the lay apostolate could rejoin them. The Christian layman was the perfect bridge. He was in the temporal order because he was a layman, and in the spiritual order because he was a Christian. He could restore the harmony of the two orders in his person.

EARLY LIFE

The layman received the supernatural preparation for the apostolate through the characters of baptism and confirmation. The indelible character of baptism permanently incorporated the layman "into the Body of Christ and placed [him] under the life-giving influence of Christ's Headship." Confirmation completed the process: "The confirmed Christian is given a more perfect configuration to Christ the Priest, and a consequent full participation in his priestly work."

Although his thesis committee originally had judged his dissertation proposal as merely practical, it was actually slightly radical but not unique for its time. He had argued against those who were hierarchically minded and who wanted to make sure the laity was controlled. He came down firmly on the side of the laity in the debate. His thesis implied that the mark of the authentic layman was a spirit of discovery and autonomy and that the apostolic ministry was not merely an extension of the clerical or hierarchical Church.

On May 23, 1945, after easily defending his dissertation, he was awarded the Doctorate in Sacred Theology. He had to submit two hundred printed copies of his dissertation to Catholic University using the "glorified title." Then he had another thousand copies printed by the Ave Maria Press with the simpler title, *Theology of Catholic Action*, and they sold briskly, earning him enough money to pay for the copies he had presented to Catholic University.[44]

From 1934 when he entered the seminary to 1945 when he received his doctorate, Fr. Ted had been immersed in philosophy and theology. Underpinning all his studies was the philosophical system known as Thomism or scholasticism. Especially up to Vatican II, scholasticism infused much of Fr. Ted's thinking and left an indelible mark on his subsequent writings and speeches.

The great achievement of St. Thomas Aquinas (1225–74) was that he brought together, in a formidable synthesis, the insights of classical philosophy and Christian theology. In effect, he "Christianized" the philosophy of Aristotle. Aristotle had taught that truth and happiness were *human* achievements; he left no room for divine intervention. But in the totally Christian environment of the Middle Ages this was inadequate. Aquinas linked philosophy and theology, teaching that they complemented each other in man's quest for truth. Human happiness is only partial and incomplete without God; human truth is never the whole truth.

Among the key features of Aquinas's philosophy that influenced Fr.

Ted was the conception of what God is. Aquinas taught that, as First Mover, God is unchangeable and eternal. As First Cause, God is all-powerful to create and is pure actuality, in contrast with the imperfect potentially in all matter. As the ultimate truth and goodness, God is perfection itself, the orderer or designer of the universe, the supreme intelligence directing things. Aquinas took Aristotle's philosophical concept of cause and turned it into an argument for the Catholic theological position.

According to Aquinas the intellect is man's highest faculty and, based on truth supplemented by divine revelation, was designed to direct our will toward the greatest goods. In his analysis of Aquinas, the scholar Samuel Stumpf observed: "When the intellect directs the will, . . . it helps the will choose the good. The intellect knows, however, that there is a hierarchy of goods, that some goods are limited and must not be mistaken for man's most appropriate and ultimate good. Riches, pleasure, power, and knowledge are all goods and are legitimate objects of the appetites, but they cannot produce man's deepest happiness because they do not possess the character of the universal good that man's soul seeks. The perfect happiness is found not in created things but in God, who is the supreme good."

In his encyclical *Aeterni Patris* (1879), Pope Leo XIII decreed that the philosophical system of Aquinas was to be the official philosophy of the Catholic Church and must be taught in all Catholic colleges and universities, a practice followed through the 1950s. Thomism was not to be just another intellectual position, competing by its intrinsic merits. "Rather," observed Philip Gleason, church historian and professor at the University of Notre Dame, "with *Aeterni Patris* it was designated the *official* philosophy of the Church, and the immense authority of the papacy was mobilized to establish it as the only system orthodox believers could employ in elaborating the cognitive dimensions of the faith."

The Church's position claimed to "prove" that faith was perfectly compatible with reason, and, Gleason noted, "The breathtaking assertion was made that the power of human reason alone was sufficient to establish with certainty that God exists." Thomism was all accessible to human reason and most of it, said a college theology textbook, was "scientifically proven."

Before Vatican II the acceptance of Thomistic philosophy contributed substantially to the intense personal sanctity and piety in the

Church, and to the intense sanctity and piety of Theodore Hesburgh. As Gleason observed: "Knowing what they believed, having confidence in the truth of those beliefs, and seeing an intimate connection between their faith and the Church with her treasury of grace, Catholics could throw themselves with loving abandon into the search for personal holiness through assistance at Mass, reception of the sacraments, attendance at devotional exercises, spiritual reading, and of course private prayer."

The certitude brought about by the revival of scholasticism induced in Catholics a smugness, an intellectual complacency, an assumption that they already knew the answers to the important questions. An historian of the Catholic seminary system in the United States observed of the attempt to revive scholasticism, "It was not Thomism, as such, which created the intellectual desert which was the American seminary system, but the manner in which Thomism was masticated, pre-digested, and force-fed." Continuing, he said:

All across the country seminarians were indoctrinated in the science of matter and form, substance and accident, essence and existence. They were asked to memorize, in Latin, answers to questions and problems that had not been posed for hundreds of years. A combative atmosphere prevailed. Adversaries were seldom considered in their context; instead straw men were set up for swift knocking down. Students developed the weakest of all attitudes toward adversaries, that of contempt.

Many years after completing his doctorate, Fr. Ted criticized the deadening and regressive aspects of his theology training. "I was mainly asked to memorize during those . . . years, and much that I memorized is no longer good theology after Vatican Council II. I was not encouraged to read original documents, especially of our adversaries, but rather given capsule and misleading statements of their position which were easily demolished by similar brief statements of orthodoxy."[45]

Overall, though, Fr. Ted saw "great value" in his liberal education and enjoyed scholasticism. To some it would appear impractical, majoring in philosophy as an undergraduate and then taking six years of theology. "You might say that [it] prepares you for just about nothing" except to be a priest, he admitted. His theology training didn't even teach him how to baptize a child or how to marry people. His program had been entirely academic and philosophical. But because he had intensely studied, read, and learned, he greatly improved the quality of his mind and actually prepared himself effectively for wider experiences.[46]

2 ⟿ FROM TEACHER
TO PRESIDENT, 1945–1958

A
S FR. TED WAS ABOUT to receive his doctorate, he lobbied Fr. Thomas Steiner, his provincial superior at Notre Dame, about his next assignment. He still wanted to be a Navy chaplain. When he had broached the subject in the fall of 1944, Steiner had urged him to complete his dissertation. "By working very hard since then," Fr. Ted wrote Steiner on May 6, 1945, "through vacations and free days, and with the help of friends' prayers, I have completed all the work for the degree a year ahead of the rest of the class."

"I would still like very much to do a priest's work with the boys who still have a man-sized job on their hands in the Pacific," he told Steiner. The chaplain's position would provide experience working with young people and would prepare him to understand the postwar problems of veterans. "If a priest has shared . . . first hand the basis of a lot of problems, he would be on the ground floor and would have a perfect right to speak and write the Catholic answers," Fr. Ted explained. Nonetheless, he intended to be obedient and accept any assignment. "While taking the liberty to state my side," he concluded his letter, "I am glad that the decision is entirely in your hands and will do to the best of my ability, whatever you decide."

Fr. Steiner decided that the University of Notre Dame needed a bright, energetic, well-schooled theologian on its faculty more than the

Navy needed a chaplain, so he assigned Fr. Ted to teach at the university. In the summer of 1945, therefore, Fr. Ted returned to the University of Notre Dame, where he was to live and work for over half a century. No one could have foretold the impact he would have on Notre Dame or that his work there and outside the university would transform him into one of the nation's most highly respected leaders.

The University of Notre Dame dates to November 26, 1842, when Fr. Edward Sorin, 28, first viewed the 524 acres in northern Indiana on which the university was to be built. Within two years Sorin and his companions had built a Catholic men's college, a preparatory high school, a vocational school, and a religious novitiate. Sorin named his new home after his special spiritual patroness, Notre Dame du Lac (Our Lady of the Lake).

Notre Dame was located a mile from South Bend, Indiana, an old industrial town, ninety miles east of Chicago. It was not the oldest Catholic university in the United States. (Georgetown University had been established fifty-three years earlier.) Nor did Notre Dame have the largest enrollment in 1945 (Fordham University in New York enrolled more students). But Notre Dame was the best-known Catholic university, mainly because of its football team.[1]

In 1913 obscure little Notre Dame played powerful Army in Yankee Stadium and pulled off one of the biggest upsets in college football's history. Quarterback Gus Dorais and end Knute Rockne passed Notre Dame to a 35-to-13 victory. The stunning upset launched Notre Dame into the spotlight. "From nuns to working men, Catholics all over the country began praying on Saturday mornings for Notre Dame victories."

An excellent student and athlete, Rockne stayed on at the university after graduation, teaching and coaching, and in 1918 became head football coach and athletic director. "For the next thirteen seasons," said Thomas Schlereth in his history of Notre Dame, "[Rockne's] personal charm, salesmanship, shrewd scheduling, and immense knowledge of football technique propelled the University into the national limelight of spectator sports."

Rockne produced such outstanding teams that sportswriters used mythological images to describe their powers. The most famous example was Grantland Rice, the nation's premier sportswriter, who described Notre Dame's 13–7 victory over Army in 1924:

Outlined against the blue-gray October sky, the Four Horsemen rode again. In dramatic lore they are known as Famine, Pestilence, Destruction, and Death. These are only aliases. Their real names are Stuhldreher, Miller, Crowley, and Layden. They formed the crest of the cyclone before which another fighting Army football team was swept over the precipice of the Polo Grounds yesterday afternoon.

Rockne's teams won 105 games, lost only 12, and tied 5. Five of his teams went undefeated and two were national champions. Flamboyant, tough, and ambitious, Rockne became a legend in his own time. His tragic death at age forty-three in a 1931 airplane crash gilded his legend. His campus funeral, broadcast nationwide on radio, was treated practically as a national day of mourning.[2]

Those who touted football at Notre Dame argued that it enhanced university life by providing educational opportunities for the poor, unifying school spirit, molding character, and releasing excess energy. Because most of the national publicity was complimentary, Notre Dame became a cultural symbol with which thousands of Catholics could identify. Schlereth observed that "the 'Fighting Irish,' who were neither all Irish nor all Catholic, represented the effort of the predominantly immigrant and poor Catholic group in this country to get ahead." Catholics often felt like lesser people, but Notre Dame's football teams, said an alumnus, "were proof of the virility of the Catholic-American view, proof that the school's combination of belief, tradition and practice could produce all-American virtues: manliness, straightforwardness and a joyful belligerence." Football was a significant financial benefit to the university, as well, with annual profits reaching $529,420 in 1929. "This income," said Schlereth, "bolstered faculty salaries and built academic facilities and residence halls."

Yet football was a mixed blessing at Notre Dame. Because of its success on the gridiron, critics questioned the university's integrity and academic standards and tagged it a football factory. Most of the accusations were exaggerated. Some were not. Notre Dame's athletic department did not abide by the economic restrictions that governed the rest of the university's operations. "For example," observed Schlereth, "in 1929 football uniforms cost $15,400, nearly the same amount which was budgeted for library book acquisitions."[3]

Women on campus were about as rare an event as a football defeat. An alumnus of the class of 1936 recalled: "Some of us old-timers were reminiscing at what happened in our day when, on an infrequent Sunday, some innocent young lady (usually a student's sister) visited on campus. At the shout of '*girl*' every resident-hall window in the line of sight was crowded with faces pressed against the glass."

Notre Dame's Catholic character was a simple social fact. "Notre Dame had always been a Catholic university," observed Notre Dame historian Philip Gleason. "It was founded by a religious community, and Holy Cross priests played a highly visible role. Campus religious life was intense; daily communicants filled the hall chapels, the *Religious Bulletin* appeared several times a week, and there were frequent novenas and special devotions."[4]

The university's academic distinction lagged far behind the reputation of its football teams. Lack of intellectual distinction, though, was a national problem for Catholics. In his famous essay in 1955, "American Catholics and the Intellectual Life," Catholic historian John Tracy Ellis described the meager record of American Catholics in science, scholarship, and literature. Several reasons have been offered for the intellectual lag of Catholics in the United States: the pastoral emergency caused by the vast influx of Catholic immigrants; preoccupation with building churches, schools, and charitable institutions; anti-Catholic bias of many Americans; poor Catholic leadership in encouraging intellectual endeavors; emphasis on the supernatural life at the expense of human development; and the isolating and repressive aspects of the revival of scholasticism. Moreover, the position of the Catholic Church on scholarship was often one of censure, causing many Catholics to feel intimidated.

A Jesuit scholar thought that "the general Catholic community in America does not know what scholarship is." British political scientist Denis Brogan noted the irony that "in no Western society is the intellectual prestige of Catholicism lower than in the [United States] where, in such respects as wealth, numbers, and strength of organization, it is so powerful."

Catholics lived in a "ghetto," said critics, but not an economic or racial ghetto. "It was the ghetto mentality they referred to," observed Garry Wills, "an isolation from the intellectual currents of this country, from the 'right' schools and fashionable journals." In the 1950s Catholic liberals urged Catholics to abandon their separation, outgrow their siege mentality, and break out of the Catholic ghetto. "This message was often accompanied by praise for American pluralism," observed Philip

Gleason, "which was interpreted as requiring everyone to mix indiscriminately 'as Americans.'"

Notre Dame's most notable area of intellectual success was in science. In 1926 Fr. Julius Arthur Nieuwland, the university's foremost research scientist in the early twentieth century, disclosed his catalytic polymerization of acetylene, which resulted in the manufacture of synthetic rubber. Royalty income from the Nieuwland patents was used for part of the cost of building science facilities at the university. In addition, the university's renowned LOBUND Laboratories developed germ-free animals for medical research. Notre Dame also received good marks in English, history, chemistry, and math. On the whole, though, the university was not a distinguished academic institution.[5]

"A Catholic university is a contradiction in terms," George Bernard Shaw asserted. Many secular academicians agreed. Notre Dame and other Catholic universities were aliens in the intellectual world because they did not subscribe to its basic tenet: relentless pursuit of the truth, no matter how harsh or unpleasant the conclusion. "Catholic schools in general and Notre Dame in particular," said one commentator, "were committed to an almost contradictory endeavor: the production of dedicated believing Catholics. No matter if this created an atmosphere in which genuine scholarship and intellectual growth was reduced almost to zero. Faith, strengthened by the Catholic philosophy of St. Thomas Aquinas and other medieval schoolmen, was too precious to risk exposing it to the 'godless' rationalism of American secular thought."

It seemed that Catholic schools were too preoccupied with teaching religion to study seriously other fields. In the late 1940s Notre Dame had virtually no scholarship funds or endowment, no liberal arts building, no science building, an inadequate library, and a shortage of dormitories. Notably weak in the social sciences, Notre Dame didn't establish a Department of Psychology until the 1960s because some had thought the discipline "a Godless pseudo-scientific enterprise." Ironically, Notre Dame was also weak in theology. At Notre Dame, theology was not a subject for scholarship; any ordained faculty could teach it and the department was called the Department of Religion. The university selected visiting lecturers for orthodoxy rather than for probing intellect. Salaries were low and the lay faculty lived in genteel poverty. With most power vested in the president, the university was authoritarian in structure and neither lay nor religious faculty had influence on faculty appointments or promotions.[6]

When Fr. Ted returned to Notre Dame, he began teaching his first course, moral theology, in the Department of Religion. Initially one of the few with a doctorate in the department, he quickly judged most of his departmental colleagues to be inadequately trained and poor teachers. "Students had a choice, a painful choice," he later said, "because twelve hours of religion courses were required and one was as boring or as confusing as another." Notre Dame after World War II, he said, was a "sluggish, tradition-bound university."

The textbook he inherited for his course on moral theology was the worst he had ever seen, "full of casuistry" and riddled with pedantic instructions on how late a person could come to Mass and how early one could leave and still fulfill the Sunday Mass obligation. He thought the students needed ideals and goals. "I ignored the textbook and its minimalist moral approach as best I could, and instead stressed the Christian virtues."

While working as chaplain at the reform school in Washington, he had learned that the problem common among all the delinquent boys was the background of broken homes. His students at Notre Dame must learn excellent models of Christian marriage. To teach them about "good marriages," he developed a popular new course on marriage. "People loved his classes," said one former student.[7]

As he had done in Washington, Fr. Ted plunged into extra work. He spoke throughout the country on Catholic Action. In a roundabout way he became the military chaplain he had wanted to be. After World War II Notre Dame, like other universities, was inundated with veterans completing their education on the GI Bill of Rights. He helped found the Notre Dame Veterans Club on campus and became its chaplain, and the veterans became his favorite students. "They were no-nonsense Catholics," he later observed. "They believed [and] they practiced." Highly motivated, eager, serious, they knew what they wanted—a wife, children, and a decent job.

They also liked to party, and their drinking caused him problems. The Veterans Club's first outing was an afternoon picnic at the dunes on Lake Michigan to which they brought four kegs of beer. "The first two went down just fine," Fr. Ted wrote in his autobiography, "but somewhere into the third, most of our young veterans became downright drunk. Feeling responsible for their welfare and fearful of what might happen, I took the fourth keg of beer and broke it open on the sand. They were too drunk to notice, I think." When the group returned to

Notre Dame, he gathered the drunken veterans on the far edge of the campus. "I marched them up and down the roadway several times, shouting 'Forward march! Hut, hut, hut. To the rear, march! Hut, hut, hut.' When I judged them to be reasonably sober, I marched them briskly back to their dormitory."[8]

After four or five years of living and thinking for themselves, the ex-GI's took exception to the rigid paternalism at Notre Dame and helped create the awareness that changes had to be made. The university minutely regulated student life. (Some faculty members labeled the university the "Catholic West Point.") Visits to nearby South Bend were strictly monitored; students had to sign in and out of their dormitories; lights went out at midnight, and there were frequent bed checks. Students also had to attend Mass at least three times a week or they lost privileges.

Fr. Ted often heard gripes about the rules and, while opposing wholesale changes, he sympathized with many of the complaints. "He wanted no part of official discipline and officious policing," said Thomas Stritch. He noticed that someone would stand at the chapel door and check off the students who arrived for Mass. But many students went in one door, checked off, then sneaked out another. "I think that it was just a bad way for religion to operate," he recalled. "It was a typical French boarding-school–type thing."[9]

The regimentation at Notre Dame extended to student support of the football team. On October 25, 1950, the campus chaplain exhorted students in an article in the *Religious Bulletin* titled "MASS Formation for the Team Saturday." The chaplain noted the apparent correlation between two consecutive losses to Purdue and Indiana and a decline in Saturday communions from 2,010 to 1,487. "The best way to wreck a season is to prove you do not deserve a winning team," said the chaplain. He recalled nostalgically the good old days in 1933 when the student council organized a calling brigade, which visited every room on the campus at 6 A.M. on the Saturdays of games to make sure everyone got to communion and prayed for a victory. Those who resisted were unceremoniously dumped into the lake, bed and all. The chaplain urged students to "hit the rail" on the forthcoming Saturday to pray for Old Notre Dame.[10]

Fr. Ted focused most of his attention on the married veterans, a totally new phenomenon in campus life, the first large number of married students to attend Notre Dame. Former prisoner-of-war barracks at a military camp were hauled to Notre Dame and reconstructed on the edge of the campus, providing cheap housing for over a hundred families. "He had his hands full over there [in Vetville]," said John Schneider, a student at Notre Dame after the war. Supposedly tending only to the married veterans' spiritual needs, he ended up troubleshooting broader problems—rocky marriages, financial woes, children, inadequate housing, plus heavy class loads.

The Vetville community had exceptional spirit. A couple whose nine-month-old daughter died of spinal meningitis lacked the money to bury the child in Connecticut. "I went door-to-door with a milk bottle to take up a collection," said Fr. Ted. "By the time I had visited all 115 apartments, the milk bottle had enough money in it to get them to Connecticut and back."

He taught theology during the day and sometimes at night he babysat for a Vetville couple in exchange for sandwiches and beer. Working overtime trying to keep the married veterans happy, he counseled those with fragile marriages and badgered obstetricians for discounts for deliveries. He helped arrange dances on Saturday night, bringing in student musicians and charging twenty-five cents admission. To keep young wives from wrecking the family budget on new-style dresses, he offered prizes for the worst-dressed couples. He kept reminding couples that they probably would never be as poor as they were then, and probably never as happy.

As their advisor, Fr. Ted flourished. "He became confessor, baby-sitter, confidant, and friend to hundreds of these young people," observed Stritch, "and they in turn helped to form him into a warm, compassionate, tolerant, and sympathetic person." "You get the impression," wrote a reporter who interviewed him, "that of all Notre Dame, Father Hesburgh likes Vetville best." Of his work with the married veterans he would later say wistfully, "I loved that job. I'd have two or three baptisms every Sunday."[11]

From 1945 to 1948, while teaching theology and ministering to the needs of veterans, Fr. Ted was also the prefect of Badin Hall. There were many veterans in Badin, and he understood quickly that they were more worldly than the traditional young undergraduates. "Ted understood that right away," said John Schneider, who lived in Badin. He was not as strict as the other prefects. "He had a lesser rein on us in Badin," Schneider recalled. Students had an informal understanding with him. He had a refrigerator in his room in which he allowed students to store a small amount of beer. "This was when all alcoholic beverages were absolutely forbidden," said Schneider. "But he knew he wasn't going to tell us that we weren't going to have beer. We knew that if we didn't abuse it, it would be okay." On a sweltering evening Fr. Ted permitted them to drink one beer. "Not two," said Schneider.[12]

In September 1948, Fr. Ted became the rector of Farley Hall, where he supervised an explosive mixture of 330 seventeen-and- eighteen-year-old freshmen. He concentrated on memorizing the names of all his charges, dealt with them as individuals, and tried to be understanding. "He was a splendid rector," said John Powers, a freshman in the hall.[13]

Fr. Ted and his colleague Fr. Charles Sheedy, who also came to teach theology at Notre Dame, worked vigorously to improve their courses, and each produced a best-selling textbook. Late in the evening, starting at about midnight, when the young freshmen in Farley Hall had finally settled down, Fr. Ted banged away at his typewriter for two hours. His book, *God and the World of Man*, published by the University of Notre Dame Press in 1950, was expressly designed as a textbook for use in religion classes in college. The book described the content and structure of Catholic dogma; the Catholic position on faith; God and his attributes; the Holy Trinity; the creation of the world and of man; the elevation and fall of man; and the end of the world. He contended throughout that the truths of the Catholic religion were based on real evidence, but the evidence was not the kind a secular scholar would find convincing. Secular scholars ignored the book; Catholic reviewers, though, praised it. "Professors of religion will do well to examine this work," said the review in *The American Benedictine Review*. "It may be the text that so many have long been seeking." Others found it "invaluable," "interesting," "easy . . . to read." It sold briskly, earning royalties of $50,000 for the Congregation of Holy Cross.[14]

Fr. Ted was busy, but well organized, and, above all, contented. "It was a wonderful life, and I was loving it to the hilt." He could have continued "for the rest of my life doing what I was then doing—teaching, writing, and ministering." However, before his textbook was published, Fr. Ted had begun to rise, mostly against his will, in the administration of Notre Dame. His talents were being watched closely by his superiors, particularly by the progressive president of the university.[15]

Fr. John Cavanaugh served as President of Notre Dame from 1946 to 1952, during the university's postwar expansion. At age twenty-seven he had forsaken a promising business career with Studebaker Corporation in South Bend to enter the priesthood. A kindly man and a strong priest-executive, Cavanaugh held a doctorate from the Gregorian University and had wide-ranging intellectual interests. His most memorable speech, delivered after he left the presidency, charged that the intellectual prestige of American Catholics was shockingly low. "Even casual observation of the daily newspapers and the weekly news magazines leads a Catholic to ask, where are the Catholic Salks, Oppenheimers, Einsteins?"

The originator of modern Notre Dame, Cavanaugh revamped the university's administration and allowed undergraduate enrollment to jump from 3200 to more than 5000. In 1947 Cavanaugh established the Notre Dame Foundation, the first ongoing fund-raising program in the university's history. He recruited faculty from Europe, and these scholars helped enrich and professionalize the Notre Dame faculty. Because of Cavanaugh's presidency, said an observer, Notre Dame "was a university ready for take-off."[16]

Cavanaugh quickly recognized Fr. Ted as a potential successor. In 1947 in the kitchen of a small house in Evanston, Illinois, Cavanaugh whispered an aside to his host, Edmund Stephan, a young Chicago attorney and a Notre Dame graduate. "Keep your eye on that fellow," Cavanaugh said, pointing to Fr. Ted in the other room. "He's going to be president of the university one day." A few years later Cavanaugh said about him: "You'd have to be blind not to spot his talents."[17]

In September 1948, Fr. Ted met Cavanaugh in front of Sacred Heart Church, and they walked together to Corby Hall for prayers. "Ted, how would you like to go into administration?" Cavanaugh remarked. In his autobiography, Fr. Ted related his long, thoughtful response:

"Look, Father John, I didn't want to get a doctorate, but they said I should and I did, and now I'm glad I did. I didn't want to go into teaching because I wanted to do something more active, like being a Navy chaplain. Isn't it curious that by doing what I was told to do, rather than what I thought I wanted, I've managed to have a happy life. I'm enjoying teaching, I'm enjoying offering Mass for the students in the hall every morning, and I'm enjoying the counseling I do every evening. I like the student clubs I'm involved with. And I'm engrossed in writing this theology book, and looking forward to writing two more. I like what I'm doing. I don't want to sit behind a desk and write letters and do all those other things that administrators have to do. I'd much rather teach and stay active with the students. With all due respect, I must say, I really don't want to be an administrator."

Cavanaugh heard him out and then said with a sigh, "Well, it isn't all that bad, Ted."

"I'll take your word for it, but it's not for me," Fr. Ted replied. Cavanaugh disregarded Fr. Ted's objections. Shortly after their conversation, Cavanaugh appointed him to the administrative post as Chairman of the Religion Department.[18]

Then, after only one year as department chairman, Cavanaugh and Fr. Theodore Mehling, the provincial superior, arranged a huge administrative promotion for him. Unbeknown to Fr. Ted, Cavanaugh had reorganized and modernized the administrative structure of the university, creating four new vice presidents and an executive vice president. In June 1949, Fr. Ted received his "obedience assignment," the responsibility entrusted him as a priest of Holy Cross. At the meeting the four vice presidents were named, and when Ted's name was called, Fr. Mehling announced, "Ted Hesburgh, executive vice president." "I was stunned," Fr. Ted remembered. After the meeting, he asked Cavanaugh what the executive vice president did. "Oh," responded Cavanaugh, "that's the vice president who is in charge of the other vice presidents."[19]

Although very capable, Cavanaugh was so severely overburdened that he delegated a huge workload to Fr. Ted, putting him through a tough three-year training program. "I sometimes wondered about his seemingly unbounded faith in me," he later said of Cavanaugh. "And yet, somehow, I rose to the occasion; a job had to be done and one did it, and learned something on the way."

At first he felt overwhelmed with the complexity of his new position. In a report to Cavanaugh on July 28, 1949, he warned that his views "must be qualified by my inexperience in these matters, plus my ignorance of any previously decided policies." Nonetheless, he frankly and firmly stated his views on problems facing the university. Some of his colleagues wanted to defer difficult decisions, he informed Cavanaugh. But Fr. Ted disagreed. "Decisions may be delayed, but they must be faced eventually. Why not face some of them now?"[20]

Fr. Ted wrote administrative procedures and job descriptions for each of the new vice presidents, including his own. Cavanaugh also wanted him to write up articles of administration, lines of authority, organizational charts, and areas of responsibility. He quickly sensed some resentment, mostly because he was the youngest of the new vice presidents. "Who was I to be telling them what to do?" he thought. Yet he knew he had one major advantage: his subordinates had taken vows of obedience, too. When a priest colleague objected to his inexperience and intrusion, Fr. Ted said to him: "You're singing my song . . . but all I can tell you is that this wasn't my idea. I was instructed to do this by John Cavanaugh, who happens to be the president, and if you find it bothersome, I think you ought to take it up with him." The priest cooperated, but grudgingly at first.

Cavanaugh introduced Fr. Ted into the world of potential benefactors of the university. "A luncheon is to be held in the Dining Hall before each of the home games," Cavanaugh wrote him on September 20, 1949. "You are hereby invited to attend all of these luncheons. . . . Please try to acquaint yourself with all of the guests and do everything you can to make them feel welcome and at home here on the campus."[21]

Cavanaugh also assigned him to supervise the construction of five buildings. Initially he knew nothing about construction—nothing about contractors, materials, finance, or architecture. His education was "swift and awesome," he said. "I learned because I had to." He questioned how things had been done in the past, brought in an engineering consultant, and became an advocate of function before form. He also ended the practice of building on a cost-plus-basis, and instead reaped substantial savings by taking sealed bids on all construction contracts.

He constantly inspected new construction and had a keen eye for saving money. Faced with a heating expansion project costing $98,000, he began whittling down the cost. Engineers had planned to route the extension 980 feet at $100 per linear foot. Fr. Ted suggested a new route that cut the distance in half. Still not satisfied, he woke up one evening, phoned the engineer, and suggested an even shorter route. Then he whittled down the cost per linear foot. The final cost of only $14,000 meant a saving for the university of $84,000.[22]

He questioned the financial management and administration of LOBUND. After the public relations director at LOBUND listed unimpressive outreach programs, including speeches to a local women's club and a high school, Fr. Ted wrote Cavanaugh: "This seems to be the corn seed circuit—not public relations for a university institute."[23]

His most unpleasant task involved tangling with powerful Frank Leahy, the university's head football coach and athletic director. Leahy was one of the nation's most renowned, most respected, and most successful coaches. A Notre Dame graduate (1931) and Rockne protégé, Leahy had been hired by Notre Dame in 1941. His teams won 87 games, lost 11 and tied 9, a winning percentage second only to that of the legendary Rockne. Shy and introverted off the field, as a coach he was brilliant and imperious. Although he drove his players hard, they respected his authority. In the late 1940s Leahy's teams went undefeated four consecutive seasons until Notre Dame's thirty-nine game unbeaten streak ended in 1950.

Leahy was obsessed with winning, and his success renewed the charge that Notre Dame ran a football factory. (He occasionally brought shame to Notre Dame by his devious tactics, such as fake injuries.) "Winning was such a Leahy tradition," said Schlereth, "that University officials, including the president, constantly had to defend Leahy's success against the criticism of many contemporary coaches, teams, and writers." Displeased with some aspects of the athletic department, Cavanaugh wanted to reorganize it. The biggest problem was Leahy himself, who had become so powerful that he did whatever he pleased, running what amounted to an autonomous fiefdom. In order to rein in Leahy, Cavanaugh asked Fr. Ted to forgo his summer vacation in 1949 and directed him to write a new set of strict administrative rules for operation of the athletic department that would drastically restrict Leahy's power. Then Fr. Ted was to oversee the implementation of the new rules. Naturally, his training in philosophy and theology did not prepare him for the assignment. He knew virtually nothing about the athletic department and had to shore up all his courage to confront the "world famous" coach. "I dreaded the assignment," he recalled.[24]

Fr. Ted's new rules and directives curtailed the widespread distribution of complimentary tickets, granted the team doctor absolute authority in deciding if an injured athlete could play, and cut back the football team's traveling squad to thirty-eight players. He appointed Ed "Moose" Krause as the new athletic director and made sure that Krause reported directly to the executive vice president. "I expected Leahy to hit the ceiling," said Fr. Ted.

In the fall of 1949, a showdown occurred over the number of players on the traveling squad. The new rule required the coach to inform the executive vice president of the names of all the players selected to make the trip. Before the first game Fr. Ted learned by telephone that Leahy had forty-four players on his traveling squad, six more than allowed. He dispatched Herb Jones, the business manager of the athletic department, to secure Leahy's list.

"He says he's too busy to get you the list. He's getting ready for a big game," Jones reported.

"I'll give you a shorter message for him," Fr. Ted shot back. "Just tell him to give me the names of the six players who are going to reduce that number to thirty-eight, because if he does take all forty-four, the six extra players are going to be out of school for good because they will have missed classes without excused cuts. I'm approving only thirty-eight for excuses."

Thinking an explosion was about to occur, Fr. Ted stopped by Cavanaugh's office to secure his backing. Walking into his office, he said to the president, "We're at the crossroads, and if he doesn't comply, either he goes or I go." With a twinkle in his eye but with steely conviction Cavanaugh calmly replied, "Very simple. What you propose is the right thing to do. Either he complies, or he goes." Fortunately, Leahy buckled, came up with only thirty-eight names, and the crisis subsided. Fr. Ted breathed a sigh of relief. Subsequently, he and Leahy made peace with each other.[25]

After two years as executive vice president, Fr. Ted had a far better grasp of the strengths and weaknesses of Notre Dame. In the summer of 1951, during a conversation with Cavanaugh aboard a train, the president asked for his frank assessment of the problems facing Notre Dame. In a memo on August 3, 1951, Fr. Ted gave a litany of them, most involving poor administrative leadership.

"The first problem is that of Arts and Letters," Fr. Ted stated. "I do not think that anything definite or practical will be done about bettering this college until there has been a new top administration established. I know that this too involves certain personal problems that cannot be regarded lightly." (The "personal problems" amounted to one very personal problem: Fr. Francis P. Cavanaugh, the president's brother, was the ineffective Dean of Arts and Letters and needed to be replaced.) Fr. Ted wrote that he was "appalled at the poor organization and operation" of the College of Commerce and again recommended a change in the top administration. He continued his list of internal university problems—the College of Law, the library, faculty relations—pausing at one point to say, "This may begin to sound like the Anvil Chorus."[26] Another memo to Cavanaugh, in which he listed a host of financial woes affecting the university, concluded: "The only silver lining in the above dark cloud is the Lady on the Dome who has brought us [this] far without a budget. Maybe we should begin the budget meetings with a prayer to the Holy Spirit and end them with a Hail Mary."[27]

While Cavanaugh introduced his protégé into the world of administration, he also imparted sage advice about administrative leadership. The essence of administration is making decisions, Cavanaugh taught. Don't ask: "What is the easy thing to do?" Don't ask: "What will cost the least money?" Don't ask: "What will make me the most popular?" Simply ask: "What is the *right* decision." Despite the temporary uproar and disagreement, people will respect the administrator for following his conscience.

"So many things one learned from him," Fr. Ted later said. Observing Cavanaugh, Fr. Ted learned to simplify complicated problems by cutting through to the essential core; to be one's self even in the company of the powerful; to cherish intelligence; not to bear grudges; never to compromise one's convictions, whatever the cost.

Hire the best people you can find, delegate responsibility to them, and then share the credit, Cavanaugh advised. Don't expect a lot of praise for your own efforts. People are fickle and insensitive and the academic community is made up of people. Don't become pompous or think you are indispensable. "Remember," Cavanaugh taught, "the cemeteries of the world are full of indispensable people."

Cavanaugh personified integrity, Fr. Ted thought, and was probably the "biggest influence" on his life. "He knew so much more than I did. . . . In many ways he was like a father to me."[28]

In just a few years at Notre Dame, Fr. Ted had made a remarkable impression. "Hesburgh was like a breath of fresh air around here," said a colleague. "He was incredibly charming and energetic. He landed on both feet and started running." The 1951 edition of *The Dome*, the Notre Dame yearbook, described him as the "amiable Executive Vice President" who, "through his many contacts with the students and faculty, . . . has won the admiration and love of everyone connected with the University." From the beginning he also made a remarkable impression on the establishment. George N. Shuster, President of Hunter College in New York, first met him about 1950 when the newly established Ford Foundation was looking for innovative educational programs to support. Shuster served on a committee of advisors who listened to Fr. Ted speak at their first meeting. Shuster was impressed with Fr. Ted's charm, but "it wasn't just charm," said Shuster; "it was also his ability to think clearly and speak very much to the point. . . . I listened to the handsome, intelligent, forcefully speaking young priest from Notre Dame with almost unbounded admiration."[29]

Cavanaugh's six-year term as president ended in 1952. Since 1919 Notre Dame's president had also held the position of religious superior of the Holy Cross priests and brothers who worked and resided at the university. Canon law had restricted the president-superior to a term of six years.

On June 27, 1952, the university announced that thirty-five-year-old Fr. Theodore M. Hesburgh would be Cavanaugh's successor. Because he had been groomed and tested for three years, few were surprised by the announcement. After the annual retreat at which the appointment was announced, Fr. Ted and Cavanaugh were leaving the chapel when the retiring president reached in his pocket, pulled out his office key and handed it to Fr. Ted. "By the way," Cavanaugh added. "I promised to give a talk tonight to the Christian Family Movement over at Veterans Hall. Now that you're the president, you have to do it. Good luck. I'm off to New York."

Just like that, Fr. Ted was President of the University of Notre Dame. "No convocation, no installation, no speeches," he recalled. "Just go right to work. That's the way it was done in 1952."[30]

Almost immediately, Fr. Ted displayed a dynamic personality, a flair for publicity, and an aptitude for leadership. He talked openly of the difficult tasks ahead of him and impressed observers. He "radiates confidence," said a reporter for the *South Bend Tribune*. Although he spoke softly, "one senses a firm spirit behind the façade of gentleness. One can note the spirit of determination in his brown eyes, which can become almost piercingly black on occasion."

"Certainly, I pull the strings," he modestly told an interviewer after he assumed the presidency, "but it's the strings I pull who do the work." He expressed confidence in the "wonderful priests and laymen" who did the day-by-day jobs of running the university. Besides, Fr. Cavanaugh would be nearby for consultation. Another factor gave him confidence. "There must be a special providence that watches over Notre Dame," he said. "Good things happen to the university, and no one really knows the reason why. But it's been like that since Father Sorin founded Notre Dame."

What role should religion play at Notre Dame? he was asked. "We do not hold that piety is a substitute for competence, but it should not be divorced from competence," he said. "If a man is responsible to God he will be responsible to his neighbors, his family, and his country. Our emphasis on religion isn't something that is tacked on to the program, but a fiber running through our entire educational structure." Religion was important, he added, but it should not be taught in a "sentimental or superficial way."[31]

He acted decisively to rearrange personnel at the university, bringing in administrators who had his confidence. The best time to make changes in any organization was at the beginning of the new reign, he believed. "The hardest thing I had to do when I became President of Notre Dame," he later said, "was to shunt someone aside, or to talk someone into resigning, or, worst of all, to outright fire someone." But it had to be done, because some people were "not keeping up with the scholarship in their fields, or not working hard enough, or they were simply miscast in the first place."

He fired most of the rectors of the residence halls because he thought they were "old fogies who looked on the places as their fiefdoms." The process of weeding out ineffective deans and department heads had begun in the last six months of Cavanaugh's term. Cavanaugh had replaced Clarence Manion, the radical right-wing dean of the Law School, with Joseph O'Meara, an Ohio lawyer associated with the American Civil Liberties Union. "[O'Meara's] sweeping changes upset a good many people," Fr. Ted reflected, "but I backed him and took the heat."

On the advice of Fr. John Cavanaugh, Fr. Ted asked for the resignation of Cavanaugh's brother as Dean of Arts and Letters. He also fired LOBUND'S director. At one point in the reorganization he learned that the Dean of the College of Commerce had told his faculty, "Well, we've had two bad presidents in a row. We can't stand a third. But we probably won't have to worry about that, because we'll outlast Hesburgh." When Fr. Ted learned of the comment, he asked the dean if the remark was accurate. When the dean admitted making the statement, Fr. Ted told him, "Then I guess you know who's finished around here." He replaced the dean but gave him another position in the university at the same pay. In retrospect, Fr. Chester Soleta, an English professor, strongly endorsed Fr. Ted's dismissals, agreeing that the administrators were ineffective leaders. "All the people looked at [their positions] as a 9 to 5 job."[32]

With Cavanaugh's admonitions ringing in his ears, Fr. Ted tried to select the best people available to be his deans and vice presidents. "They all possessed talents that I lacked. They often disagreed with me and often they were right, so I changed my mind. It was not always easy working with them, but it would have been impossible without them."

Planning campus construction with Fr. Edmund P. Joyce, executive vice president.

He found his right-hand man in Fr. Edmund Joyce, whom he appointed as executive vice president. A magna cum laude Notre Dame graduate (1937) and a certified public accountant, Joyce would manage finances, buildings and grounds, university relations, and athletics. Fr. Charles Sheedy, the new Dean of Arts and Letters, provided a sense of purpose about being a college. "He exhausted people with his communal meetings and projects," observed Thomas Stritch. In 1952 and 1953, using a small grant from the Ford Foundation, Sheedy visited institutions generally considered America's best, quizzing deans and faculty members at Princeton, Harvard, Yale, Columbia, and Barnard College. Fr. John Cavanaugh served as Fr. Ted's special assistant and used his personal magnetism, business acumen, and wide network of friends to raise funds for the Notre Dame Foundation. From Fr. Cavanaugh he inherited his secretary, Helen Hosinski. "She ran the office and she ran much of my life with nary a misstep or mistake," he later said.[33]

He often told the story about one of his first press conferences in 1952 as the newly installed president. On the West Coast visiting Los Angeles, Seattle, and Vancouver, he intended to talk about his academic plans, but sportswriters attended every press conference wanting to know how Frank Leahy's football team would do. He grew irritated. "I asked if they wanted to talk about education." No, said the sportswriters. They wanted to talk about football. "Well, then this news conference is over," he responded. "I'm not the football coach." Sportswriters stopped attending his press conferences.[34]

By 1953 Fr. Ted had become concerned about Leahy's health. During a game against Georgia Tech, Leahy collapsed and had to be taken to a hospital. "Frank often worked himself into a frenzy of worry and concern over an upcoming game," Fr. Ted thought, "even when Notre Dame was heavily favored to win." Believing that Leahy's life was unbalanced and that the pressure to win at Notre Dame was too great, he urged Leahy to retire. Leahy said he would think it over. To push him toward retirement Fr. Ted shrewdly enlisted the assistance of two of Leahy's closest friends, who convinced him to step down. In January 1954, Leahy resigned, saying that he was acting on the advice of physicians. "I sweetened the pot," Fr. Ted recalled, "by telling Frank that, if his six boys qualified, we'd give them all full scholarships to Notre Dame." Subsequently, Notre Dame hired Terry Brennan as head coach.

"We don't apologize for our football," Fr. Ted said shortly after becoming president. "Notre Dame wants to be best in everything. We want the best professors and the best coaches." He believed that college football could develop character and responsibility in youngsters and wanted an excellent football team, but not at the expense of the university's academic accomplishments. Football had been overemphasized at Notre Dame, he believed, and needed to be brought into perspective. It was still only a game. He had once overheard a Notre Dame coach yell at his players, "What do you think this is, a game? Get in there and fight!" The remark puzzled him. "It struck me as crazy. Because it is a game."[35]

While football had publicized Notre Dame in the past, he said in December 1955, "the heartening thing is that the university is becoming known for other things." In his speeches he talked about "other things," not football. He told an alumni group that he would address "the less colorful" but "much more substantial" aspect of Notre Dame. In interviews with reporters he seldom mentioned football unless specifically asked. Reporters noticed. In a long article on Notre Dame in *The Chicago American*, the reporter observed: "If it seems strange that this story about Notre Dame does not mention football, the reason is that Father Hesburgh had many, many things to say that are more important than anything he might say about a game." Another reporter interviewed Fr. Ted for four hours before the subject of football was mentioned.[36]

As he settled into his new office, he began to think seriously about his goals. What did he want to accomplish? Young James Hesburgh, a sophomore at Notre Dame when his older brother became president, recalled, "When we would talk, he always had these visions of what Notre Dame should be and could be."

Fr. Ted wanted Notre Dame to be a great university and also to be a great Catholic university. The first was easier to accomplish than the second, he thought. There were many great universities, but not since the Middle Ages had there been a great Catholic university. "To be great," Fr. Ted wrote in his autobiography of his vision in 1952, "a university needs a great faculty, a great student body, and great facilities. In order to have those things, it needs a substantial endowment, which means you have to learn how to raise money—lots of it. And finally, a great university needs to be imbued with a great spirit, which is an inspirational and cohesive kind of ambience, and not be just a lot of separate parts that operate around a central heating plant. The spirit we had. The rest we didn't."

As Fr. Ted began trying to mold Notre Dame into a major Catholic university, he reflected on John Henry Newman's great classic of educational literature, *The Idea of a University*. Newman (1801–90) was the saintly British theologian, church leader, and the brilliant writer of eloquent books who converted to Catholicism and late in his life was named a cardinal. *The Idea of a University* suggested a vision for a Catholic university in which the liberal arts played a central role and teaching was important. Fr. Ted also liked Newman's description of intellectual virtues, including "the ability to tolerate fundamental diversity of beliefs and values without sacrificing conviction." Moreover, the one pervading thought that characterized Newman's writings on education was the belief that a university that teaches everything else but neglects theology, "the science of God," was not committed to being a true university. Newman stimulated Fr. Ted to build a great Theology Department. "I got some very good ideas [from Newman]," he later said, "especially on the primacy of theology in a Catholic university."

At first he dealt with Notre Dame's deficiencies on an ad hoc basis, but when he needed a comprehensive, modern, secular plan, he turned to the Ivy League model, specifically Princeton. "We wanted to be a Catholic Princeton," he later said. Why Princeton? Both Harvard and Yale had huge graduate schools, which Notre Dame did not. Princeton was close to Notre Dame's size, had a superb undergraduate program, and only about fifteen hundred graduate students. In addition, the Presbyterian-founded school had a similar religious and athletic tradition and an isolated physical setting. During his many visits to Princeton on educational and foundation projects, he had developed a natural affinity for the place. Therefore, in the 1950s, when he talked about Notre Dame, he used Princeton as a model. "What we need . . . is a real working library," he said in 1952, "one like they have at Princeton."[37]

For the time being he decided to retain most of the strict rules governing student activities, reasoning that the old tight system produced remarkably stable men. In April 1953, he argued that most colleges and universities were unwilling or unprepared to discipline students. "In forming its students morally as well as intellectually, Notre Dame has agreed to act 'in loco parentis,' in the place of the parent."

In order to devote as much time as possible to education in general and Notre Dame in particular, he cut back on his socializing and leisure activities. He departed from Fr. Cavanaugh's practice of attending parties and social events in South Bend. "I felt I could not afford the time, and if I accepted one invitation, I would have to accept the next."[38]

In 1956 *Time* labeled him a "Hustler for Quality" and noted that he sometimes worked until 2 in the morning. In speeches to alumni groups he hammered away relentlessly at the need to raise the academic quality of the university. He gave hundreds of speeches. Speaking on "The Notre Dame Story" to an alumni group in Texas on January 20, 1953, he explained that Notre Dame had three objectives: first, to make the student a good man; second, to make him professionally competent; third, to make him a person who was morally and socially responsible to the society in which he lived. Sometimes he spoke at half-a-dozen alumni functions across the country in a two-week period. After listening to his speech, an alumnus asked, "What about the ordinary boy? Why can't he find a place at Notre Dame?" Fr. Ted retorted: "What do you drive, a jalopy or a Cadillac?" The grad grinned and answered, "A Cadillac." "In his four years as president," said *Time*, "Fr. Hesburgh has made it abundantly clear that he intends to have his football-famed campus known at last as a university of Cadillac quality."[39]

In 1954 Fr. Ted had his first major controversy over academic freedom, with Notre Dame on one side and the Vatican on the other. Fought away from the glare of the media, the incident remained private until Fr. Ted described it in his autobiography in 1990. The focus of the dispute was John Courtney Murray, the prominent Jesuit theologian and expert on church-state relations, who had taken part in a symposium at Notre Dame. Afterwards the University of Notre Dame Press published the papers of the symposium participants in a book and sent out review copies. But powerful conservative theologians at the Vatican, led by Cardinal Alfredo Ottaviani, objected to some of Murray's beliefs. Through the Holy Cross Superior General in Rome, Father Christopher O'Toole, Ottaviani ordered Fr. Ted to withdraw the book from bookstores and suppress it.

Fr. Ted regarded the order as censorship. "[It] hit me like a challenge to action," he wrote in his autobiography. With the backing of his university council, Fr. Ted informed O'Toole that he would not suppress the book and if ordered to, he would resign as president.

Eventually a face-saving compromise was struck, one that conceded Fr. Ted almost everything he wanted, and the tension subsided. It was a "sorry episode," he reflected. "There was no way I was going to destroy the freedom and autonomy of the university and, indeed, the university itself, when so many people had devoted their lives to building it." Shortly after the incident Notre Dame boldly granted Murray an honorary doctorate at commencement.[40]

Ironically, while Fr. Ted defended academic freedom in the "Murray affair," he was simultaneously playing another role which probably curtailed academic freedom at Notre Dame. As president of the university, Fr. Ted had the responsibility for granting permission to petitioners who wanted to read books listed in the *Index (Index Librorum Prohibitorum)*. The Catholic Church's regulation of books had its roots in apostolic times, but the *Index* owed its existence to the Counter-Reformation in the middle of the sixteenth century, when the Church felt threatened by heresy from without and corruption from within. For the next four hundred years the Church issued numerous editions of the Index. The last edition, issued in 1948, banned 4,000 titles, including many classics of literature. Twelve groups of books explicitly prohibited included books "against" Catholic morals and Catholic faith, and books on "impure or obscene" matters. Publication of the *Index* ended in 1966.

Among the great thinkers of the Western world whose books appeared on the *Index* were Jeremy Bentham, John Stuart Mill, John Milton, Jean Jacques Rousseau, René Descartes, Immanuel Kant, John Locke, Jean Paul Sartre, Carl Jung, Karl Marx, and Sigmund Freud.

Fr. Ted supervised the *Index* on the Notre Dame campus from 1952 to 1965, reviewing hundreds of requests from faculty, staff, and students for permission to read banned books. Among those who had to petition him each year for permission were lay and religious faculty in philosophy, history, and theology; even department chairmen routinely requested special permission. On each occasion he granted permission, using almost exactly the same language each time. In January 1954, a student wrote asking permission to study Immanuel Kant's *Critique of Pure Reason*. Fr. Ted granted the permission to research the German philosopher's work, adding his standard rules:

> In accordance with the conditions under which my faculty is granted, I ask that the reading be limited to the works mentioned; that you adopt prudent and effective means of preventing spiritual and intellectual harm from coming to you through the reading of such prohibited books; that you understand the permission is good only for the time you are at the University doing work requiring the reading of such prohibited books.

Unlike Fr. Ted, Fr. John Cavanaugh was sometimes harsh and intimidating toward those who asked his permission to read books on the *Index*. In 1947 when a professor of modern languages asked to place two books in French on reserve in the library for two weeks, Cavanaugh replied sharply: "For undergraduate students, do you not think that readings other than those on the *Index* can be found for your purpose? . . . As a policy I think it wise to grant the permission to read books on the *Index* to undergraduates only in very rare instances. I know that you will see the wisdom of this policy and that you will try your best to help me put it into effect."

Although Fr. Ted always granted the special exemptions, the censorious role ran counter to his increasing public support for academic freedom. It seemed awkwardly restrictive when in 1959 an Associate Professor of Electrical Engineering wrote Fr. Ted saying, "The librarian informed me that I require your permission to use the following books, all by Jean Paul Sartre," and then listed ten books. Fr. Ted granted permission "for one year."

"Does the Church today wish to isolate itself from the current standards of literary greatness?" asked a critic of the *Index* in 1963. "Banning an author without furnishing cause smacks of thought-control today. . . . Mere mention of the *Index* reminds us of Torquemada's destroying 6,000 volumes at Salamanca on charges of sorcery; of Paul IV's banning 61 printing firms and all books by any printer who had published one heretical book."

By the early 1960s, some Notre Dame professors apparently were no longer taking the *Index* seriously; they assigned or studied whatever books they chose, and they went uncensured. Fr. Ted gave only perfunctory attention to his responsibility, treating it as a routine bureaucratic duty. Probably he didn't object openly to his role because he didn't want to arouse needless antagonism with the Church's hierarchy; besides, there was nothing he could do to overturn the four-hundred-year tradition. Many years later, after his retirement, when he was asked about the *Index*, he expressed his disgust. "I thought the sooner we got rid of it the better. Thank God we got rid of it sooner."[41]

Fr. Ted gave hundreds of speeches on a wide variety of subjects: on Christian families, juvenile delinquency, business, theology, education in South America, Atoms for Peace, astrophysics; on the wisdom of St. Thomas Aquinas, St. Thomas More, and John Cardinal Newman; on values in athletics, values in education, values in science; and, finally, on the traditions, spirit, challenges, and prospects of the University of Notre Dame.

At the beginning of each school year he spoke at an inaugural Mass, always trying to inspire the assembled faculty. "I happen to believe that a President who cannot inspire his faculty is not worth his salt," he said. In a speech to the faculty he joked that he had given so many speeches that he was in danger of becoming illiterate. "[The president's] opportunity to read and to write are in inverse ratio to his necessity of speaking frequently, often without advance warning, on a vast variety of subjects." Yet he felt obligated to speak. "It was a matter of speak or disgrace my position."

He tried to bring an element of spirituality to higher education and at the same time tried to bring an element of education to the spiritual. In September 1953, in an address to faculty members who had filed into Sacred Heart Church, he pointed to Christ's Incarnation as the most important fact in all human history. He declared, "There is no human event, no human progress in knowledge, science, or art that cannot be consecrated to a higher service, now that God has literally become man and dwelt amongst us." The university community must take part in the program of creative ideas, must become essentially an intellectual apostolate. "Our prime concern," he said, "must be to offer to the service of God and men a worthy gift. Certainly we should not offer as our part in this divine symphony of all creation, the sour notes of intellectual mediocrity or educational complacency."[42]

His commencement address at Dartmouth in the spring of 1958 illustrated his maturing thoughts, particularly about values. Using ornate but clear language, he pursued the theme that the unexamined life was not worth living. He challenged the graduates to do something useful with their lives and to assess the values they cherished. "Values, consciously examined and adhered to, are extremely important to the examined life that alone is really worth living."

He denigrated material values. What great human achievements have these values nurtured? "When accepted as ends in themselves, material values are the strongest possible deterrent to the achievement of the really significant human aspirations." He asked the graduates to reflect on the great spiritual values that have nurtured the giants of human history:

The pursuit and love of truth, that have inspired the great scholars, such as Socrates and Aquinas, who have illumined and guided man's faltering steps upwards through history; the passion for justice, which has given us our great advocates like Coke, legislators like Justinian, statesmen like Adenauer, and jurists like Marshall; the enduring love of beauty in all its forms, that gave birth to the artists who, like Beethoven, have filled the world with music, who have, with Cezanne, brightened our rooms with paintings, and who have lent dignity and grandeur to the simple and lovely aspects of life on earth—a woman's face, a sunset at sea, a child in the park; the intelligent use of human freedom, a value which has been the foundation of stable government, social institutions, and the great humane movements of our times.

Respect for the dignity of the individual, the capacity for sacrifice, and the reverence for things spiritual were other laudatory values to pursue.

Face great challenges, he urged, like overcoming the evils of communism, eliminating poverty in underdeveloped countries, and establishing racial justice in America. Another challenge was to use effectively the explosive scientific advances:

Inherent in this challenge is whether we will be able to master in a human and humane way, this Promethean power within our grasp, whether we will be able to use it for the good of mankind and not for his destruction, whether in the face of these new and dramatic scientific values, which are also good and extremely useful, we will be able to maintain the balance and the supremacy of those older and better treasures of mankind—the humanistic values that you have learned here at Dartmouth—the values that alone provide a human framework for science, a direction for its power, a meaning for its contribution, a family in which it can be an honored, but not a sole member. We fear the scientific and technological power of Russia, not because this power is essentially bad, but because without the supporting framework of a humanistic tradition and policy, it can become as dangerous as a bomb in the hands of an idiot.

Power, scientific or otherwise, is meaningful and fruitful in the world of man only when it reckons with . . . deeper spiritual values . . . and these values come from outside the realm of physical science.[43]

In 1957 Fr. Ted traveled nearly 150,000 miles. A reporter who interviewed him the following year observed: "Father Hesburgh stopped talking about education after three and a half hours to prepare for a trip that would take him to another part of the country where he was scheduled to talk about education." Some of his associates viewed his grueling schedule with alarm. "He works far harder than any human being has a right to," said Fr. Howard Kenna. "Father Hesburgh is fond of swimming," said another associate, "but it's all we can do to get him into Lake Michigan once every three years. He's very fond of bridge, but if we can coax him to the table for one night a year, we consider it a major triumph."[44]

Several times Fr. Ted spent a week at the Aspen Institute for Humanistic Studies in Colorado, taking part in stimulating seminars. When the seminars were not in session, he did relax. "We took [the seminars] seriously," recalled Fr. Chester Soleta, a fellow participant, but the two Holy Cross priests also had fun. "If we went to dinner, we enjoyed the dinner very much," said Soleta. "We went to the musical events and enjoyed them very much. We would take drives out into the mountains and enjoyed that very much. We didn't think we had to keep our noses to the grindstone all the time."

Fr. Ted was open to new suggestions. Commercial television programs rarely interested him, but he was concerned with the effect of television on education and served on several committees on educational television. Therefore, when John Schneider approached him with a proposal to build a television station on the campus, he immediately expressed interest because he thought it would assist journalism students. "He was absolutely open to everything," said Schneider. "He picked up on it right away."

Although busy and energetic, he was also amenable. Mike Ahren, a reporter for the campus radio station, interviewed him and observed: "We were all struck with how gracious he was. He was fairly well known then, a young man, gracious and warm even though he had heard all of the questions before."[45]

In the 1950s Notre Dame made substantial progress. Twelve new buildings sprang up during his six-year term. The university demanded higher Scholastic Aptitude Test scores from students, and reformed the curricula in arts and letters, law, commerce, and engineering. "We were trying to get a better integration of studies and greater impact," Fr. Ted explained in 1958. "We had the impression, generally, that students could be working a lot harder."[46]

He made three trips to Europe looking for ideas and faculty talent. In about 1954 he arrived at the University of Louvain in Belgium. A young Irish priest, Fr. Ernan McMullin, listened attentively to his presentation. "He spoke in French," said McMullin. "He was a very good linguist. . . . He was very eloquent and energetic, and full of vision and all kinds of plans." McMullin had several offers of academic positions, but he chose Notre Dame. "One of the main factors," he said, "was Hesburgh's presence. I was very impressed by him."

In 1954 the first comprehensive faculty manual was compiled, increasing the faculty's role in the governance of the university. Fr. Ted invited a galaxy of distinguished professors to be visiting lecturers—historian Arnold Toynbee, classicist Sir Richard Livingstone, and theologian Martin D'Arcy, S.J. A $2.6 million grant from the Ford Foundation was specifically earmarked for improving faculty salaries. Between 1952 and 1961, faculty salaries increased 90 percent, 120 Ph.D.'s were added to the staff, and the endowment tripled to $25 million.[47]

Although busy with his work at Notre Dame, he carried on his duties in fairly routine fashion, and the university was a placid, halcyon place. Outside the university, he began to get into "more exciting challenges." As his reputation spread beyond the Notre Dame campus, he was in demand as a speaker, committee member, and chairman. He joined the International Federation of Catholic Universities (and eventually became its president), the Association of American Colleges (and later became its president), and the American Council on Education. He also joined the Ford Foundation Committee for Liberal Arts Grants, the Carnegie Commission on the Future of Higher Education, and the Overall Panel of groups which wrote the Rockefeller Reports.

On the Carnegie Commission he served with prominent educators and public members. Every month for six years they met for three days, eventually producing over one hundred volumes of reports in one of the most comprehensive studies in the history of American higher education.[48]

On a Sunday afternoon in 1954, President Dwight Eisenhower's assistant, Sherman Adams, called from the White House and asked if Fr. Ted would accept an appointment to the National Science Board. Twenty-four persons, mostly prominent scientists, governed the National Science Foundation, which Congress had recently established to promote fundamental scientific research and education. Fr. Ted protested that he had been trained in philosophy and theology and knew nothing about science, but Adams retorted that Eisenhower wanted a moral perspective on the Board. "Well," said Fr. Ted, "if they can stand some philosophical and theological observations, I can certainly learn a great deal about science." And thus began his education in quantum mechanics, relativity theory, positivist psychology, cybernetics, atomic technology, and their effects on social and cultural life.

Fr. Ted plunged into the new fields, spending the next twelve years on the Board, as revolutionary changes in atomic energy, space, electronics, and biology took place. The position gave him the opportunity to develop friendships with many of the world's greatest scientists. The President of Cal Tech taught him about radio astronomy; Glenn Seaborg, Nobel Laureate in chemistry and Chairman of the Atomic Energy Commission, explained transuranium elements. "I had all the very best teachers," Fr. Ted said. He enriched his own life and could more effectively promote science at Notre Dame.

He had no illusions about becoming a scientist or engineer. "I started all this too late," he said. But he learned the language, the vision, and the adventure of science and technology, and came to respect scientific practitioners and their exacting standards. After 1954 he gave scores of speeches and wrote several articles on scientific topics, particularly on the theme of science, technology, and values.

And so it went. "When the scientists, diplomats, or businessmen got used to the Roman collar," wrote one observer, "they were impressed by Hesburgh's ability to learn quickly, to formulate issues clearly, and to be forthright without being offensive."

One thing led to another. "When you're young, and you do everything halfway decently," he said, "you get asked to do something else." He was always learning and always networking; one assignment led to another in a related field. From the National Science Board he went to the Midwestern Universities Research Association (working on a scheme in high energy physics), to the Nutrition Foundation Board, to the Policy Advisory Board of Argonne National Laboratory, and to the International Atomic Energy Agency.[49]

Representing the Holy See at the International Atomic Energy Agency meetings in Vienna.

In 1956 he visited every South American country except Paraguay and Panama, as President of Notre Dame and as Vice President of the Institute of International Education, an organization that sponsored the exchange of students and teachers. In every country he consulted with American ambassadors and cultural attachés, plus Latin American educational officials and university presidents. He also spoke to Notre Dame alumni clubs throughout Latin America.

By 1958 he had established himself as an expert in some areas of public service as well as higher education. Usually he was the only Catholic on the boards and commissions on which he served. At times he seemed to be just "the necessary Catholic." The tokenism puzzled him, but he made sure he attended meetings and had something intelligent to offer. He found out quickly that he could learn almost anything if he read. "I realize that I may be doing more than I should," he observed of his extensive work outside Notre Dame, but he was reluctant to abandon projects because he felt his new experiences and his association with important officials might benefit Notre Dame.[50]

He plunged into national debates, as well, like the uproar in education touched off in 1957 by Russia's Sputnik. He worried that the shrill reaction in America would stampede this country to throw the whole system out of balance in favor of science. Yes, youngsters were learning less science; but they were also learning fewer foreign languages, less history and less English literature. Science wasn't everything. Besides, Russia neglected other important aspects of life, the humanistic side of man, literature and the arts. "What good would it do us to send up 10,000 sputniks if we know nothing of the purpose of life and why we were placed on earth in the first place?" he asked. "We need excellence across the board in everything," he argued. "But our problem is more serious than the flimsy presentation in the papers today crying out for more scientists and technologists."[51]

Problems with Notre Dame's highly visible football team continued to plague him. Just before Christmas 1958, when Notre Dame announced that it was releasing Terry Brennan as football coach, an avalanche of criticism fell on Fr. Ted's head. The likable Brennan had started off well replacing Leahy. His 1954 team won 9, lost 1, and the following year Notre Dame was 8 and 2. But in 1956, when Notre Dame suffered the worst record in its history, losing 8 games and winning only 2, some alumni screamed for Brennan's dismissal. Brennan's 1957 and 1958 teams won a total of 13 games and lost 7, not a sterling enough record by the high standards expected at Notre Dame.

A storm followed Brennan's release. Editors, sportswriters, football coaches and even Brennan's players condemned Notre Dame's action. "A startling dismissal of [an] honest, personable, conscientious, and able young man," wrote the prominent syndicated columnist Red Smith, a Notre Dame alumnus. Many charged that Notre Dame had cut back the number of its football scholarships and raised academic requirements for its athletes, making it more difficult for Brennan to recruit effectively. Then, when he didn't win enough games, Notre Dame's administration callously fired him almost on the eve of Christmas. In an article, "Surrender at Notre Dame," *Sports Illustrated* noted that Fr. Hesburgh "has been striving mightily to raise academic standards, gain prestige and place football in its proper status in university affairs." But by firing Brennan, contended the magazine, the university had tragically surrendered its noble goals to football-crazy alumni and was in danger of becoming once again a "football factory." Bushels of mail accused Fr. Ted of pushing the Brennan family out into the cold. "Even New York taxicab drivers," said a Notre Dame devotee, "protested what Father Hesburgh [did]."

The criticism became so irritating that Fr. Ted sought to limit questions about the Brennan firing. He requested that reporter Norman Ross ask him only one question about the Brennan ouster. "Because it was a very big story," Ross later said, "I pressed my luck by asking him a second question, then a third. As I opened my mouth to venture a fourth, he fixed me with a look so cool and so penetrating that I quickly changed the subject."[52]

Two weeks after the appearance of the *Sports Illustrated* article, Fr. Ted responded in the same magazine, telling his side of the story. With controlled anger, he clearly defended the firing of Brennan and eloquently restated his academic and athletic philosophy. His primary goal was excellence, he contended. "Most of my waking hours are directed to the achievement of that excellence here in the academic order. As long as we, like most American universities, are engaged in intercollegiate athletics, we will strive for excellence of performance in this area too, but never at the expense of the primary order of academic excellence."

He had no intention of changing the strict rules and regulations governing athletics at Notre Dame. There would be no "softening of admission standards, no lowering of scholastic average for eligibility each year, no amending of scholarship requirements or numbers, in a word, no university athletic policy change at all."

He denied having given in to alumni pressure to fire Brennan. "I received a total of two negative communications from the alumni regarding football this past year." Most difficult decisions are not popular, he admitted, but sometimes they are necessary. "We could, for example, greatly improve the whole structure of American education tomorrow if we would make a few difficult and unpopular decisions. In any event, the important factor for an administrator is to be convinced that he is acting reasonably and rightly. With this conviction, I approved the recommendation of the faculty board, and frankly did so with mixed emotions—reluctance, if you will, because Terry Brennan is an attractive young man, a good friend of mine from his student days and my personal choice for head coach five years ago."

His final comment took a parting shot at the overemphasis placed by the sports world on the dismissal of a college football coach. "While I can appreciate the wide national interest in sports, I think it somewhat of an inversion of values that a university can appoint 20 distinguished professors, make broad and significant changes in academic personnel to achieve greater excellence, without attracting more than a slight ripple of attention. But let the same university make a well-considered change in athletic personnel for the same reason, and it sparks the ill-considered charge that it is no longer a first-rate academic institution and must henceforth be considered a football factory." There had, indeed, been a surrender at Notre Dame, he said, but it was a "surrender to excellence on all fronts, and in this we hope to rise above ourselves with the help of God."[53]

"I came off like Scrooge," Fr. Ted later admitted, but he insisted that the timing of the dismissal was at Brennan's request. Still, he gave two different versions of their mutual agreement. In *Sports Illustrated* in 1959 he had said: "We mutually decided to make it before Christmas rather than after the new year. This was decided mainly in the interest of the assistant coaches, considering the present availability of other coaching positions that might not be available later."

Thirty years later, in his autobiography, Fr. Ted had a different version: "I wanted to announce it early in December, but Terry told me his wife had already planned a Christmas party on something like the sixteenth or seventeenth of the month. She did not want the party to be ruined by the news, so I gave in on the date."[54]

For the most part, though, Fr. Ted's overall efforts won widespread praise. Fr. Charles Sheedy, who served for seventeen years as Dean of the College of Arts and Letters, witnessed Fr. Ted race through the early years of his presidency "as though shot from a cannon." Sheedy was not surprised, because he had observed his friend's energy and skill since World War II. "Moxie," said Sheedy of Fr. Ted. "Ha-ha, boy, he had the moxie."

"Father Hesburgh never spares himself," observed Fr. Cavanaugh. "He never has. . . . That's the way he is. Take the scientific positions he now holds. Like all priests, his training was in philosophy and theology. A decade ago his knowledge of science was little greater than that of the average, intelligent layman. He changed all that. He took a speed-reading course and ever since he's been reading at the rate of about four scientific books a week. Today, it's safe to say that he can hold his own in a discussion with the best nuclear physicists in the country."

Notre Dame's English Professor, Francis J. O'Malley, thought Fr. Ted's greatest contributions were intangible. "Much has been said of his accomplishments here—the buildings that have gone up since he took over and the amazing strides the school has made in scholastic attainment. The fact remains that his single greatest achievement here is the atmosphere he has created," said O'Malley. "It is an atmosphere of freedom and flexibility and good will, an atmosphere that has made of this university a human as well as an academic community. Father Hesburgh is able to generate this spirit because, in spite of all his experience and knowledge, he is still capable of wonder. He is still open to people, to existence, to ideas."[55]

In 1952, when Fr. Ted accepted the presidency, he was under the impression that, like Fr. Cavanaugh, he would serve his six-year term and then would pursue other assignments. His term ended in June 1958, and he expected to be transferred to another post. "I will go where they send me," he told a reporter.

But by 1958 his superiors considered him so dynamic, successful, and influential that they thought it was desirable—even necessary—for him to continue in the presidency. Since the six-year limit applied only to the post of religious superior, not to the university president, why not separate the posts? Consequently, in the spring of 1958, Fr. Mehling announced that a new religious superior would be appointed at Notre Dame, but that Father Hesburgh would continue as president for an indefinite period.

"I took those first six years like a 100-yard dash," Fr. Ted later said. "Then when I got to the tape, I had to keep going."[56]

3 ⟿ GROWTH AND CHANGE, 1959–1967

O N S E P T E M B E R 9, 1957, President Dwight Eisenhower signed the first civil rights act in eighty-two years. While following a tortuously slow and winding path through Congress, the act was substantially weakened. It survived conflicts between Northerners and Southerners, amendments and counteramendments, divisions within House and Senate, ambiguous Administration policy, and complex backstage maneuvers. Finally a persistent coalition of liberal Republicans and Northern Democrats salvaged a compromise. Most of the provisions, though, were weak and legalistic. Civil rights activists were disappointed. Senator Paul Douglas of Illinois said the law had as much substance as "soup made from the shadow of a crow which had starved to death." Indeed, the law did little to increase voting by blacks and did nothing to protect other civil rights. But one feature of the bill had potential. Title I of the new law established a Commission on Civil Rights to act as an independent, bipartisan, federal agency. The Commission was to investigate sworn allegations of denials of black voting rights; examine legal developments constituting a denial of equal protection of the laws; and appraise laws in the civil rights field. The Commission was a fact-finding and appraising agency with no enforcement powers, but it could issue subpoenas and call witnesses to testify under oath at hearings. The importance of the Commission seemed to lie in its future potential. The new panel was given a life of only two years, and its final report was to be made to the President by September 9, 1959.

Southern segregationists had objected strenuously to its creation. Senator Strom Thurmond of South Carolina carried on a record-breaking, one-man filibuster of 24 hours and 18 minutes. Later, Senator James Eastland of Mississippi tried to stall the creation of the Commission by repeatedly postponing committee hearings, delaying confirmation of Eisenhower's nominees for Commissioners.[1]

When the Commissioners were appointed, a wave of skepticism swept supporters of civil rights. If anything was dissonant in its composition, it was the new Civil Rights Commission. Eisenhower appointed three Democrats, two Republicans, and an independent; three were Southerners and three were Northerners. The selections seemed to guarantee a stalemate.

The six Commissioners were John Hannah, 55, President of Michigan State University, who was designated chairman; John Battle, 67, former governor of Virginia and a moderate segregationist; Robert Storey, 63, dean of the Southern Methodist University Law School in Texas; Doyle Carlton, 72, former governor of Florida; and Ernest Wilkins, 63, the only black on the Commission. The final appointment was Fr. Ted, who at age 40 was the panel's youngest member and the one designated as politically independent.

Some observers thought the new Commission would not move off dead center. White House assistant Fred Morrow lamented in his diary, "Things like this that vitally involve the Negro race are decided by men who have had little or no experience or contact with Negroes, and who must base their decisions almost entirely upon their own meager knowledge."

An editorial in the *Nation* observed skeptically that since the members were "deliberately chosen for their devotion to the cause of moderation, the Commission is not likely to break many lances crusading for civil rights." Reacting more favorably, *Time* contended that Ike had staffed the Commission with "earnest and judicially minded men."[2]

When interviewed about his new appointment, Fr. Ted strongly hinted that he, at least, would seek improvement in civil rights for blacks. Commissioners must bring patience, tolerance, consideration, vision, and courage to their task, he said. Still, he would approach his duties in the "moral knowledge that all men are created equal." Time would cure the problem, he remarked, but "we may have to nudge time a bit." He deplored the notion that human problems were timeless and could never be solved. "We are not just prisoners of time."[3]

On January 3, 1958, the six Commissioners were sworn in at the White House, and after the ceremony President Eisenhower privately visited with them. They were about to address the nation's most serious domestic problem, he told them. "To the extent that we can solve it, we will be worthy to hold up our heads in the company of the nations of the world." He added, "I don't know the answer. That's why you gentlemen have been commissioned. Now it is your problem. We'll do all we can to help."

After the ceremony, the Commissioners walked to their office across from the White House. The office was a shambles: one room with six chairs, a dusty desk piled high with unopened mail, and floor tiles commonly found in public toilets. An inauspicious start. In the initial meetings, the Commissioners found their basic thinking far apart. "It appeared that it was going to be very difficult, indeed, to make real progress," Hannah reflected.

The soft-spoken Hannah, a Republican, former Assistant Secretary of Defense in the Eisenhower Administration, was cool, tough, and competent, accomplishing things through quiet, effective pressure. He had firm convictions in favor of human rights but was not a zealot. Fr. Ted quickly built an alliance with Hannah. In fact, Fr. Ted made a point of reaching out to all the Commissioners.

Harris Wofford, Fr. Ted's legal counsel on the Commission, watched his boss closely in the early years of the Commission and was impressed by his ability to communicate with his colleagues. "I discovered a man of curiosity, compassion, conviction, and courage," said Wofford. "His approach was obviously to . . . reason with a person, not to manipulate or defeat him." He particularly set his sights on befriending Battle, the most outspokenly segregationist Commissioner. If they could work together and find common ground, Wofford observed of Fr. Ted's attitude, "the Commission might make a significant contribution."[4]

The Commission often met southern intransigence. Before the hearing scheduled for Montgomery, Alabama, in December 1958, the Commission sent agents to subpoena the voting records of various Alabama counties. To forestall the federal examination, Alabama Circuit Judge George Wallace impounded the registration files of two counties and warned, "If any agent of the Civil Rights Commission comes down here to get them, they will be locked up." Nonetheless, the Commissioners remained adamant and on December 8th opened its hearing in Montgomery.

At the panel's hearing in Montgomery the Commission experienced first-hand the indignity of segregation. Commissioner Wilkins and two black lawyers on the staff were turned down for room reservations, and the Commission ended up staying at an air force base. At the Alabama hearings black witnesses described their experiences in depressingly repetitive terms. Invariably they experienced great difficultly finding the place and the time to register to vote; waited endlessly in lines; filled out long, complicated forms. All blacks were required to copy a section of the Constitution. A single mistake in writing the Constitution or a form—a misspelling, a wrong date, or other minor error—would be seized upon as an excuse to deny them registration, all at the whim of the white registrar. But the black witnesses who testified were superb. Ten were college graduates and six held doctorates. Most owned property and paid taxes. Some were veterans and two had earned Bronze Stars. Nonetheless, they were prevented from voting. A college-educated woman, married to the chairman of the Biology Department at Tuskegee Institute, testified about her interest in voting: "It is the duty of citizens, and I have four children to whom I would like to be an example in performing that duty, and I want them to feel that they are growing up in a democracy where they will have the same rights and privileges as other American citizens." A Korean War veteran bitterly remarked, "I have dodged bombs and almost gotten killed, and then came back and being denied to vote—I don't like it."

The Commission listened to some of the "reddist-necked rednecks of the species," Fr. Ted recalled in his autobiography. "Many of them were high school dropouts, but in Montgomery they were telling black Ph.D.'s from Tuskegee Institute that they could not vote because they, the rednecks, were not yet 'ready' to let them vote."

As the Commissioners heard the same stories over and over, they grew more sympathetic to the blacks. After one black farmer told of being turned down time after time, Fr. Ted interrupted his testimony and asked, "Are you going to keep trying?" The farmer said, "Oh, yes, I'm determined to register." Departing from the Commission's usual impartiality, Fr. Ted responded, "God bless you."[5]

From Alabama the Commission moved on to public hearings in Texas, Georgia, Mississippi, and Louisiana, finding the same deplorable conditions. "Not a man of us failed to recognize that there were millions of people qualified to vote who probably would not be able to vote for the next President of the U.S., much less for their senators, congress-men, and state officials," Fr. Ted later observed. The Commissioners had listened to these people. "They weren't units to us. They were flesh and blood."

In July 1959, the Commission was in Shreveport, Louisiana, where a segregationist federal judge prevented them from holding a hearing on deprivations of voting rights in the state. The Commission was stymied and the deadline for their final report was approaching fast. They were staying at an air force base, again, because local hotels wouldn't accept them, and because of the heat, the terrible food, and the jet noise inter-rupting their sleep, they felt miserable and dejected.

"It seemed like a hell-hole to Father Hesburgh," recalled Wofford, "but he passed part of the late evening, as had become his custom, talk-ing with John Battle." He and Battle shared a taste for bourbon, and Fr. Ted brought a bottle along whenever the Commissioners met   or left a message for Battle that it was his turn. They talked about religion, fami-ly, and politics, as well as the Commission's work.[6]

Fr. Ted suggested that a radical change in the Commission's environ-ment would improve their mood and prospects for completing their fi-nal report. Hannah agreed. So on July 14, 1959, in a borrowed DC-3 provided by a Notre Dame trustee, the group flew to Wisconsin, where the Holy Cross order owned a beautiful lodge at Land O'Lakes in the northern part of the state.

"That first evening at Land O'Lakes was everything I had hoped it would be," Fr. Ted later said. In the crisp air, in the midst of the pine-scented forest, the Commissioners unwound and relaxed. Sitting on the front porch of the lodge, they drank martinis and ate steaks. All six Commissioners were ardent fishermen, and that evening they caught twenty fish while the staff worked on the final drafts of the report.

"[Hesburgh] was the penultimate host," said Berl Bernhard, a staff member. And a shrewd host. Before supper he had arranged for Battle to fish in the same boat with the new black Commissioner, George Johnson, who had replaced Ernest Wilkins. He wanted the pair together so they would build rapport and reach consensus on the report. "It was all calculated," observed Bernhard. "It gave the appearance of casual good fun, but it had a purpose . . . to accomplish as great a unanimity as was possible." Fr. Ted chortled at his scheme. "Look at them out there! We've got Gov. Battle and George Johnson [together]. They're fishing! We'll get those reports done!"[7]

With a full moon on the lake and an after-dinner glow on the Commissioners, at 8:30 P.M. they sat down on the front porch to work. In short order they unanimously approved a strong, clear finding that many Americans were being denied the right to vote because of race through "legal impediments, administrative obstacles, and positive discouragement engendered by fears of economic reprisal and physical harm." The report dramatically exposed the extent of disenfranchisement of black voters. In Lowndes County, Alabama, not one of the county's 15,000 blacks was registered; in Wilcox County, not one of 18,500. Concluding that legislation presently on the books was inadequate, the report recommended new proposals, the most far-reaching of which urged the appointment of temporary federal registrars to register voters for federal elections. The purpose was to cut through the administrative maze of recalcitrant local registration boards and to circumvent the lengthy and costly litigation required under existing remedies. While supporting the concept of federal registrars, Fr. Ted and the two other Northern Commissioners (Johnson and Hannah) pressed for an even more sweeping solution: a constitutional amendment to establish universal suffrage. They included their idea as a proposal in the final report (indicating that half the Commissioners supported it).

Astonishingly, the Commission had agreed on twelve recommendations, eleven of them unanimously. The next morning, while Ted was celebrating Mass, he overheard the three Southerners talking at the breakfast table. "What really happened last night?" asked Doyle Carlton. "I guess we were really taken in," replied Battle, "but everything was so nice . . . that we didn't have the nerve to fight about those recommendations. But we gave our word last night, and we're gentlemen. We're going to keep our word."[8]

In early September 1959, the Commission presented a 600-page report to the President. Eisenhower was dumbfounded: three Southerners and three Northerners had agreed on civil rights. After explaining the Land O'Lakes gathering, Fr. Ted told the President, "It's because we're all fishermen." Eisenhower replied: "Then we need more fishermen."

In response to the Commission's report, Eisenhower promised only one thing: to recommend that the Civil Rights Commission be extended for another two years. (Congress later granted the extension.) Overall, the Commission's recommendations were alien to Eisenhower's minimalist view of government. On the controversial proposals he said it would take time for them to be worked out.

Southern legislators condemned the 1959 report. Urging that the

Commission "be forced to die within 60 days of the filing of this report," Senator Olin Johnston of South Carolina promptly called it "one of the most devastating, unconstitutional documents I have ever seen." Senator Strom Thurmond charged that some of the Commission's proposals would have "the Federal Government further rape the rights of the states and the people."

The Commission was blazing new paths. An historian of the civil rights movement observed that the Commission was not "intimidated by southern intransigence and recommended proposals more far-reaching than those offered by either the civil rights groups or the [Eisenhower] administration."

The Commission's report was important because it had documented widely perceived injustices. "Everyone knew in 1957 that Negroes were being denied the right to vote," reflected a staff attorney, "but the Commission's 1959 report documented it in such a way that no one could challenge the conclusion."[9]

At every opportunity Fr. Ted used his new expertise to give speeches and interviews promoting the Commission's recommendations and the cause of civil rights in general. On June 13, 1960, his commencement address at the University of Rhode Island stressed that discrimination against the black was a national blight. "We have had enough of compromise, of gentlemen's agreements, restrictive covenants, of the myth of white superiority, of white citizen's councils."

He often challenged Catholic audiences to end their bigotry and to live up to the pronouncements of the Church and the hierarchy. "[There] is the matter of the Mystical Body of Christ, and the divinely revealed truth that all men—regardless of race or color—have the same origin, the same human nature and the same eternal destiny. Also, heaven is not segregated. God draws no color line when He comes to dwell through grace in the souls of men. What's good enough [for] Him should be good enough for us. . . . Christ said that all men shall know that we are His followers by the fact that we love one another. Again, if human beings of all races and colors are good enough for Christ, they should be good enough for all of us who profess to be Christians." (He later said: "I do receive a surprisingly large number of hate letters from Catholic ethnics every time I put in a good word for blacks or Chicanos.")

Following a Commission hearing in Mississippi, Fr. Ted took part in a seminar with religious leaders in the state. After reviewing the horrible testimony the Commission had heard, he said, "These acts of murder, arson, and brutality were committed by those who attend your churches and synagogues. Why cannot you get together and speak out . . . against this perversity?" One churchman responded that they would all be expelled from Mississippi if they spoke out forcefully.

Later, reflecting on the seminar in Mississippi, Fr. Ted described two great acts that made religious witness vital and forceful: prophecy and martyrdom.

Religious leaders must be perfectly clear in going against popular opinion when it is morally wrong—that is the essence of prophecy, to point out the blasphemy of prejudice *before* the tide has turned, not afterward, and to be willing to be a martyr for this most important religious truth. It calls for heroic courage at times, but if religion is to lead and not to follow, there is no other way than the courageous way of prophecy and martyrdom.[10]

He realized that publicity was potentially a significant power of the Commission, and he worried that the Commission's reports were being ignored. Therefore, in 1961 he sought to dramatize the problem of racism. "One man's indignation over man's inhumanity to man burst into vivid words," wrote a reporter *The New York Times*, referring to the close of the fifth volume of the Commission's 1961 report, where Fr. Ted had added an eloquent, sharply worded individual statement. The Commission was becoming "a kind of national conscience" in the matter of civil rights, Fr. Ted said. Yet Americans were apparently not getting the message. "As a conscience, its effectiveness depends quite completely upon whether it is heard, and whether the nation and national leaders act accordingly."

Why does America, the foremost bastion of democracy, demonstrate at home so much bitter evidence of the utter disregard for human dignity that we are contesting on so many fronts abroad? Americans might well wonder how we can legitimately combat communism when we practice so widely its central folly: utter disregard for the God-given spiritual rights, freedom, and dignity of every human person.

It was not enough to reject the inhuman communistic doctrine, he said.

We must demonstrate that we have something better to propose in its stead, and *that this something works better*, and is better for all mankind, here and everywhere. The most depressing fact about this report is its endless tale of how our magnificent theory of the nature and destiny of man is not working here.

Inherent in the depressing story is the implication that it is not working because we really do not believe in man's inner dignity and rightful aspiration to equality—unless he happens to be a white man.

Perhaps Americans could work up greater anger against the outrages against blacks if they meditated more deeply on the meaning of Christianity:

Could we not agree that the central test of a Christian is a simple affirmative response to the most exalted command mankind has ever received: "Thou shalt love the Lord thy God with thy whole heart, and thy whole soul, and thy whole mind, *and thy neighbor as thyself.*" No mention here of a white neighbor. There was another similar statement, "Whatsoever you did (good or evil) to one of these, my least brethren, you did it *to Me.*" We believe these truths or we do not. And what we do, how we *act*, means more than what we *say*. At least the Communists admit that they do not believe as we do. At least they thus avoid hypocrisy.

The nation was reaping the effects of its discriminatory practices, he contended:

We spend millions of dollars trying to convince the uncommitted nations of world (about 90 per cent nonwhite) that our way of life is better than communism, and then wipe out all the good effects by not even practicing "our way" in our own homeland. We are all excited about Communist subversion at home while we perpetuate a much worse and studied subversion of our own Constitution that corrodes the nation at its core and central being—the ideal of equal opportunity for all. What can we expect for the future, if one-tenth (and predictably at the end of this century, one-fifth) of our population are second-rate citizens, getting a second-rate education, living in second-rate houses in second-rate neighborhoods, doing all of the second-rate jobs for second-rate pay, and often enough getting second-rate justice?

Then, the most often-quoted portion of his statement:

Personally, I don't care if the United States gets the first man on the moon, if while this is happening on a crash basis we dawdle along here on our corner of the earth, nursing our prejudices, flouting our magnificent Constitution, ignoring the central moral problem of our times, and appearing hypocrites to all the world.

Some might regard his remarks as "intemperate," he conceded. But, unless there was some "fire" most government reports remained unread. "I have a deep and abiding faith in my fellow Americans; in their innate fairness, in their generosity, in their consummate good will," he concluded. "My conviction is that they simply do not realize the dimensions of this problem of civil rights, its explosive implications for the present and future of our beloved America."[11]

"Brilliant," wrote a Catholic magazine of Fr. Ted's statement. Both *Time* magazine and *The New York Times* quoted his appended remarks. It "was a declaration of conscience with significance for every American," *The New York Times* editorialized. "Father Hesburgh has done more than write a footnote to another government report. He has pointed a glowing road toward human betterment and decency."[12]

Fr. Ted deeply hoped that the racial situation would soon change, and he wanted others to share his view. In about 1960, as he stood at the 63rd St. Station in Chicago, waiting for the South-Shore train, a black woman waited next to him, and he struck up a conversation. After he broke the ice, the woman talked about her four-year-old son. She had recently given him a bath and told him to scrub himself hard with the soap. "Mommy, if I scrub myself hard enough will I be white?" the boy asked. And the woman said, "No, you're colored and you'll always be colored." The boy replied simply, "It's better to be white."

"Did you let him get away with that?" Fr. Ted inquired. The black woman answered, "Why shouldn't I let him? Isn't it better to be white in America?" Disturbed with her reply, he said, "Maybe on the surface it's better, but this isn't the way a youngster should think with a whole life before him. Because what is today does not necessarily always have to be, and, please God, it won't be the permanent pattern of our nation."[13]

Throughout the 1960s the Commission conducted field investigations, held public hearings, issued detailed reports, and lobbied for new legislation. Its first report in 1959 had concentrated on voting rights. Thereafter the Commission focused on education, employment, housing, public accommodations, and justice. The Commission issued its 1961 report in five volumes. By 1961 the Commission had built substantial popular support. Particularly in the North, it enjoyed an excellent press. In June 1961, the *Washington Post* endorsed its continuation with phrases like "extremely useful," "vital work," and "urgent need." Congress continued to extend its life.[14]

The Commission increasingly became an outspoken champion of civil rights. Instead of the Commission *on* Civil Rights, it became, in effect, the Commission *for* Civil Rights. Because replacements in Commission membership after 1959 were more sympathetic to justice for blacks, and because of the harsh and incontrovertible facts disclosed by

As chairman of the Civil Rights Commission reporting on federal civil rights enforcement efforts.

investigations and surveys, the Commission increasingly took forthright stands. Historian Foster Rhea Dulles, an expert on the early years of the Commission, thought the Commission's recommendations "helped to convince Presidents Kennedy and Johnson, the Congress, and a growing majority of the American people that the time for temporizing, compromise and accommodation had passed."

Berl Bernhard, the Commission's staff director from 1960 to 1963, expressed the Commission's view of its role. The Commission, he said, "established national goals, conceived legislation, criticized inaction, uncovered and exposed denials of equality, . . . prodded the Congress, nagged the Executive, and aided the Courts. Above all, it has lacerated, sensitized, and perhaps even recreated the national conscience."[15]

Despite the Commission's obvious support of justice for minorities, a major virtue of the panel was that it stuck to facts and was never found misrepresenting evidence. "That's a fine statement," Hannah told a staff member who wrote inflammatory prose. "Just take out all the adjectives and adverbs." Like Hannah, Fr. Ted insisted that the staff avoid polemics. "He was very determined to get to the facts," said Bernhard. "He thought if we did not exert the necessary discipline to get the facts, and not just our opinions of the facts, we would be discredited." He insisted on fairness. At one hearing he thought Bernhard had been too one-sided in cross-examining a witness. "[Hesburgh] was very direct and blunt with the staff that he was unhappy," recalled Bernhard, and he insisted there be more disciplined fairness. "We redoubled our efforts to be objective fact-finders."

Fr. Ted sought ways to bolster the stature and respect of the Commission. He told his colleagues that "ordinarily he preferred to hold hearings in courtrooms because it tends to establish better decorum."

Powerful forces in the South tried to discredit the Commission for allegedly swaying from the facts. Senator John McClellan of Arkansas sought to intimidate and harass the Commission. In a telegram to Commissioners on March 8, 1960, he noted that the Senate Committee on Government Operations, which he chaired, was responsible for studying the operation of government activities at all levels with a view to determining "its economy and efficiency." Then his chilling observation:

The Committee has received complaints concerning lack of efficiency and economy in the operation of the Commission on Civil Rights. Accordingly, I have directed the staff of the Senate Permanent Subcommittee on Investigation, a subcommittee of the Senate Committee on Government Operations, to conduct a preliminary investigation to ascertain if there is any basis for these complaints the committee has received and to report the results of such preliminary inquiry to the committee for its determination with respect to whether a full scale investigation should be made and executive or public hearings held in connection therewith.

McClellan asked to inspect the Commission's files and records "that may be pertinent and essential to this inquiry." The Commission, though, was able to sidetrack the inquiry.[16]

Fr. Ted earned respect because of his unique role. Because he was a priest, staff members and fellow Commissioners felt that there was no reward in the work for him except the cause of civil rights. Bernhard thought that Fr. Ted was fulfilling "moral [and] religious obligations" by serving on the Commission. Colleagues admired his controlled moral indignation. True to his calling, he was a preacher. Occasionally at hearings staff members would urge him to "give them a little theology," meaning they wanted him to put a Christian dimension into the proceedings. After Fr. Ted had denounced the un-Christian nature of segregation, Commissioner Battle approached him and said: "All my life I've been acting this way and today you told me it was un-Christian. . . . I can't argue with your theological reasons. I know you're right and I'm wrong; but I'm an old dog, and I can't change my stance now on things like integrating education."[17]

Friction with the U.S. Department of Justice was a recurring fact of life for the Commission from its creation. The Attorneys General were irritated with the Commission's role as gadfly critic and for interfering with the orderly process of lawsuits. The Commission and the Kennedy Administration were frequently at loggerheads, mainly because of the different missions of the Commission and President Kennedy's Department of Justice, headed by Robert Kennedy. "The strong personalities and convictions of both Robert Kennedy and Father Hesburgh were also important factors in the clash," Wofford thought.

Lacking an overwhelming mandate from the 1960 election, President Kennedy feared antagonizing the conservative Southern Democratic faction. He worried that pushing civil rights legislation would tear Democrats apart and jeopardize the rest of his legislative agenda. Therefore, he assigned low priority to pushing civil rights legislation. After the Civil Rights Commission issued its five reports in 1961, including a score of legislative recommendations, President Kennedy ignored most of them. Summing up Kennedy's first year as president, Martin Luther King stated that the White House had "waged an essentially cautious and defensive struggle for civil rights."

In an early meeting with the Commissioners, Attorney General Kennedy made it clear that he intended to handle voting rights. "You're second-guessers," he told them. "I am the one who has to get the job done." It seemed to the Commission that Robert Kennedy was jealously guarding his domain in the civil rights field and was trying to assure that credit for any success would go to his brother's administration.

The Commission thought the Justice Department was concerned only with voting rights, to the detriment of other equally important areas, and even there it was pushing its attack too slowly, case by case, through the difficult terrain of Southern judges. The Commissioners reminded the Attorney General that they had a statutory duty to investigate voting rights and argued that their hearings and reports educated the public. Kennedy's method of litigation would be insufficient, they argued; legislation striking down literacy tests and enabling federal registrars was necessary. But Robert Kennedy insisted that legislation wasn't necessary and was politically unfeasible, adding, "I can do it, and will do it, in my way, and you're making it more difficult."

The Commissioners saw themselves, as Fr. Ted often said, as a "burr under the saddle of the administration." But Robert Kennedy insisted on overall control. "His effort to bring the Commission under control turned the Commissioners against him, and made them more independent than ever," Wofford observed.[18]

The most serious dispute with the Kennedy Administration arose over the Commission's intention to hold politically sensitive voting hearings in Mississippi. Three times the Commission planned hearings and three times the Justice Department forced postponement. The Commission judged the situation in Mississippi so serious that the federal government ought to cut off federal assistance until the state granted basic civil rights. The Kennedy Administration strongly objected to such a tough proposal and continued to oppose hearings in Mississippi. "Fr. Hesburgh was among the most stalwart, if not the most stalwart, person of the Commission," in resisting the administration's pressure, said William Taylor, a Commission staff member. "We must do what's right in these circumstances," he told his colleagues. "We are here not to please any particular president, but to do a job of exposing conditions [in Mississippi]."

Although both John and Robert Kennedy respected Fr. Ted, they also felt he was causing them unnecessary trouble. Robert Kennedy complained privately that the Commissioners were second-guessers and irresponsible, adding, "And then there was always Father Hesburgh coming around the corner telling me what I was doing wrong."[19]

In retrospect, Fr. Ted has been sharply critical of the Kennedy Administration's civil rights record. President Kennedy was well informed on civil rights, he concluded ten years after Kennedy's assassination, but there was an "enormously strong myth" that President Kennedy was also courageous on civil rights. Quite the contrary. Kennedy didn't want to risk antagonizing the South, and his performance in pushing civil rights legislation was "miserable." After reading *Kennedy* (1965) by Theodore Sorensen, JFK's long-time confidant and speechwriter, which praised Kennedy's civil rights record, Fr. Ted asked himself: "Is he writing about the guy that I had to do business with?"[20]

Finally, in late February 1965, the Commission held its long-delayed hearing in Mississippi. The timing was propitious. Movement toward a new voting rights bill was gaining headway and the hearing's startling revelations of intimidation of blacks and denial of blacks' rights gave fresh ammunition to advocates of the new voting rights bill. "The Commission . . . hurried its Report and recommendations," noted Dulles, "in the hope of building up still further support." The entire civil rights movement reached a new peak in the spring of 1965, and the Voting Rights Act passed. The federal-registrar plan, incorporated into the 1965 Voting Rights Act, followed the suggestion originally pushed by Fr. Ted and the Civil Rights Commission in 1959.

When Fr. Ted had enough time, the Commission's staff preferred to bring him into a community early, before a hearing, for an extensive tour. "Then he could respond in a very empathic way," said William Taylor, the Commission's staff director from 1965 to 1968. In 1966 the staff took him on a tour of Hough, the rat-infested neighborhood of almost 60,000 people near the center of Cleveland. Despite federal urban renewal programs, Hough had undergone a steady decline. He toured streets and alleys littered with garbage and debris. Testimony before the Commission indicated that persons relocated by urban renewal and highway programs were often moved to worse surroundings, and the great majority of blacks were relocated in black areas. Upset with the poverty and poor housing he witnessed in Hough, he urged the Commission to "picture dramatically and brutally" the awful conditions in Northern cities. "If this could be done effectively," he told his fellow Commissioners on April 6, 1966, "the nation might commit $40 billion to do something about this, as it committed itself to land a man on the moon." In a widely publicized statement Fr. Ted condemned the federal urban renewal program: "[What] has happened is that people in the worst condition find their houses bulldozed from under them. The total program is immoral."[21]

Of the four presidents he eventually worked with on civil rights, he was most impressed with Lyndon Johnson. On issues of civil rights and poverty Johnson "really came from the heart," he thought. He gave Johnson major credit for the civil rights laws of the 1960s.

Historian Dulles thought the Commission "sometimes tended to exaggerate its own importance." Fr. Ted himself often praised the Commission and President Johnson but almost invariably overlooked the dramatic impact of civil rights demonstrations like those in Birmingham (1963) and Selma (1965).[22] Yet it is understandable that he took extraordinary pride in the Commission's work. In senatorial debates on legislation, repeated mention was made of the contributions made by the Commission. Senator Kenneth Keating of New York observed in

1964 that "were it not for the work of the Civil Rights Commission, the facts and figures which stand behind the affirmative case for the pending bill might not have been gathered." One study found that 60 percent of the panel's recommendations were adopted in some form.[23]

In the 1960s Fr. Ted developed other interests besides civil rights. One of the most satisfying endeavors of his life involved putting together an early Peace Corps project. After only a few weeks in office, President Kennedy took steps to fulfill a campaign promise to create the Peace Corps, a plan for voluntary service by American youth in countries overseas. On March 1, 1961, Kennedy signed an executive order temporarily establishing the agency (later accepted by Congress) and named his brother-in-law, R. Sargent Shriver, Jr., as director. Shriver, in turn, called upon a small group to draw up plans for the new agency. Fr. Ted was one of the first persons Shriver contacted.

With the Peace Corps only a few weeks old, Fr. Ted had already been to South America trying to develop a program and was reflecting deeply about the potential of the new agency. Most public discussion of the Peace Corps, he wrote Shriver on March 21, 1961, had neglected a major potential advantage of the programs: its beneficial effect on the young volunteers. Young people had generally greeted the idea of the Peace Corps with enthusiasm, he wrote Shriver.

[Is] it not slightly surprising that the younger members of this society should volunteer in large numbers for the hard work, discomfort, and sacrifice at no pay[?] What should one conclude from this fact? First, the nation can take new confidence from this reaction on the part of the young people. We may take some comfort and pride in the fact that the general softness and selfishness of so many of our elders have not been able to extinguish the native idealism, the generosity, and the pioneering spirit of our young people.

Every nation needed a dimension of greatness to which young people could strive, he told Shriver. It seemed providential that the Peace Corps would come along to provide it.

It might well be taken as more fundamentally prophetic that the young people who volunteer for the Peace Corps are, in fact, rebelling against the notions that have become so standard with their elders: that security, ease, comfort, and the soft life are important. The [opinion] of the young Americans of today would seem to say that these are not really important, that true greatness comes from choosing something quite different, something much more demanding, and something which alone can make America survive. If the Peace Corps has provided this dimension alone to our young people, it has done a great service to America and has contributed mightily to its survival. Whatever happens abroad, this is a great beginning.[24]

The first proposal Fr. Ted submitted to Shriver, however, was too elaborate and expensive. The Catholic Shriver and others close to the Catholic President Kennedy also worried about the "Catholic factor." It would be imprudent to have one of the first Peace Corps projects put together by Catholics at a prominent Catholic university.

Shriver asked, "Can you get other institutions to go in with you on this, and can you give us a scaled-down project we can afford?" Fr. Ted agreed and convinced the Indiana Conference on Higher Education (embracing all the universities and colleges in the state) to support a project. He also contacted the Institute of Rural Education, a private organization in Chile, which agreed to welcome a group of volunteers for service in their various schools. (The volunteers would train young Chilean men in carpentry, small animal husbandry, machinery, agriculture, and reforestation; the women were to be taught sewing, sanitation in the home, diet and nutrition, cooking, and health care.)[25]

Fr. Ted then waited impatiently throughout the spring of 1961 for the Washington office to approve his proposal. Too many bureaucratic roadblocks were holding up the fine project, he complained to Shriver in a long letter on May 4, 1961. "Sarge, I may have appeared brusque, but I know I need not tell you that my own interest in this project has been visceral and I am perhaps too deeply involved at the moment to discuss it without some deep feeling." Finally, the project was approved, and Fr. Ted convinced Walter Langford, professor of modern languages at Notre Dame, to direct the program for two years.[26]

On July 20, 1961, the trainees arrived at Notre Dame and plunged into a ten-week program, immersing themselves in the study of Spanish, Chilean history and culture, and community development. Since the project was Fr. Ted's brain child, from the moment the volunteers arrived he actively participated in their training. He had helped select the group, and he often joined them for meals, played soccer with them during their physical training, attended evening meetings, and practiced his Spanish. Langford thought that Fr. Ted's Spanish, not proficient at the beginning, improved more than anyone else's. "And his interest in and concern for the trainees quickly put him on the friendliest terms with every trainee," said Langford.

As soon as the volunteers arrived in Chile, letters began flying between Langford and Fr. Ted. (By the end of two years each had accumulated files several inches thick of letters, clippings, and reports.) Despite his grueling work schedule, Fr. Ted maintained a detailed interest in the volunteers, including the bottlenecks in shipment of supplies. "It's really criminal to be delayed on Winter underwear," he wrote Langford. "If the underwear doesn't get through soon, I think you should just go ahead and buy it locally, if possible."[27]

Fr. Ted customarily slipped away from Notre Dame for a week or two around Easter. In 1962 he wrote Langford that he planned to come to Chile for seven days near Easter and wanted to visit all forty-five Peace Corps volunteers. Langford was shocked. Because the volunteers were strung out over 800 miles north and south, many in remote rural areas almost out of touch with civilization, it normally took Langford a month to visit all of them. Langford told Fr. Ted that his planned itinerary was "impossible." Fr. Ted responded by telegram, saying in essence, "Impossible or not, we've got to do it. I can't see some of them without seeing all of them."

Fr. Ted arrived in Santiago on Sunday evening, April 8, 1962, and the following morning began seven days of nonstop travel by car, plane, train, bus, and jeep. In the diary he kept of the trip, Fr. Ted observed, "The road was just about as bad as any I've ever seen, and the jeep bounced all around as we plowed through clouds of dust." He visited Jim, a volunteer who lived in an austere small room with space for only a bed and a desk; rats often occupied the closet. He inspected everything—Jackie's kitchen and supply room, Gerry's new chicken brooder and rabbit hutches, and the furniture Larry had made. To each volunteer he presented a memento: a letter from President Kennedy thanking them for their generous work and wishing them a happy Easter. Whenever possible he took them to the nearest town and treated them to a good meal. "It always was rewarding to see the affection openly on display when the volunteers greeted and visited with Father Ted," Langford said.[28]

For a week he went without showering. He stayed up late at night discussing projects. (Because of his excitement, on several occasions he forgot to eat his evening meal.) He admired the esprit de corps and exceptional perseverance of the volunteers. "Anybody who thinks these volunteers have a picnic should take this trip and live with them for a while," he wrote in his diary. "Just the fact of these young people being here is an enormous demonstration that Americans have not completely gone soft and that we can take it if we have to."

Amazingly, after seven days Fr. Ted had achieved his goal. "We saw every single volunteer," said Langford. "He proved me wrong." "I really hated to leave when we returned to the airport," Fr. Ted wrote. On his first day back at Notre Dame, he phoned the parents of twenty-one volunteers, relaying messages and information.

Sargent Shriver was impressed with the Chilean group and especially with Fr. Ted's leadership. "The program run by Notre Dame in Chile was the best run, the most successful Peace Corps program managed by an outside agency." Unlike other college presidents, Fr. Ted engrossed himself in the effort. "Hesburgh did not just sign some papers and forget about it," Shriver observed. "He acted. He didn't fuss around and create 17 committees to advise him. He went down [to Chile]. He took a personal, as well as administrative, interest in what was going on. [Hesburgh] had more vision, more energy, more selflessness than most educators. . . . He was willing to risk his reputation, and Notre Dame's reputation, by getting involved in this rather visionary, useful, untried enterprise. It took guts."

After the Chilean volunteers returned to the U.S. in July 1963, they began writing Langford about their activities. The entire group maintained exceptional esprit de corps. Subsequently Langford published a newsletter which he sent out periodically for many years. Fr. Ted officiated at the marriages of some of the ex-volunteers, baptized their children, and helped them in other ways. "Fr. Hesburgh took a very special interest in that group," Chilean volunteer Tom Scanlon said. "It became a kind of family to him." Well-attended reunions took place at Notre Dame in 1981 and 1986. "Father Hesburgh was deeply involved in each weekend reunion from start to finish," recalled Langford. "It was one of the prime satisfactions of his life to put that Peace Corps program together." Overall, Fr. Ted made a deep impression on Langford. "I came to realize that he was truly a most remarkable man in his intellect, . . . in his perception of everything, in his quick grasp of a situation, in his organization. Most of all, I think everyone was astounded at his energy because he can keep a schedule . . . that would drive anyone else into the hospital in a couple of weeks."[29]

Far less successful than his Peace Corps role was Fr. Ted's attempt to stop a movie from besmirching Notre Dame. On December 7, 1964,

Notre Dame filed suit in New York to block the Christmas Day opening of the Twentieth Century Fox movie, "John Goldfarb, Please Come Home." The film's "theme" outraged Fr. Ted and Notre Dame's Board of Trustees, and the attempt to block the opening attracted extensive media attention.

The film, starring Shirley MacLaine and Peter Ustinov, tells the story of an American U-2 pilot named Goldfarb who crashes in the fictional Arab kingdom Fawzia and becomes a football coach. The addle-brained king of Fawzia decides to challenge and defeat Notre Dame in football, because his son could not qualify for the Notre Dame team. The king blackmails the U.S. State Department into sending the Fighting Irish to play Fawz. In the film's wildest and most offensive scene, Notre Dame players, plus U.S. officials, are feted at a pre-game banquet and are entertained by belly dancers and harem girls. On the football field the next day Fawz U.'s cheerleader, Shirley MacLaine, scores the winning touchdown against the astonished Notre Dame team. Most film reviewers judged the movie tawdry, tasteless, and incredibly dull.

Notre Dame also sought an injunction against the publishers of the hardback book, on which the film was based, and paperback editions of the book. Fr. Ted hadn't seen the film but had read the book. Several university officials, trustees, and influential alumni who had seen private screenings of the film recommended the legal action. The university's suit did not seek monetary damages, only an injunction.

The primary legal issue at stake was whether Twentieth Century Fox could appropriate the name, symbols, and prestige of Notre Dame without its permission and over its objections. The university's suit said it would suffer "irreparable and immeasurable injury." "Countless young people and their parents hold this university in high regard," Fr. Ted said. "They would never understand how we could in any way have allowed this casting of our good name in a context wholly inconsistent with the principles for which the university stands." The university has long been jealous of its rights to the use of "its reputation and prestige," he argued, "being concerned that they not be exploited and diluted for private gain by commercial enterprises."

Some of the university's arguments seemed overwrought and exaggerated. Notre Dame Attorney David W. Peck said the investment in the film was "puny" compared to what was at stake in the reputation of the university. "If they get away with this, nobody's reputation—no corporation and no education[al] institution—will be worth anything,"

Peck said. "It could be exploited just so long as it stops short of libel." Officials at Notre Dame consumed considerable energy worrying about the film. "You cannot believe how much time and attention . . . was devoted to whether we should enter into [the] law suit," observed administrator John Walsh, who sat in on the long deliberations.

Fox, which had invested $4 million in the film, defended the movie as "obviously a good-natured lampoon of contemporary American life and international affairs," and "in the long tradition of American comedy which enables us to laugh at ourselves." The issue was free speech, not commerce. The movie industry had a right to criticize and parody an institution so much in the public eye as Notre Dame.

Three courts eventually ruled on the tangled case. Initially a sympathetic New York Supreme Court Judge sided with Notre Dame, arguing that the script was "ugly, vulgar and tawdry" and that the film was a "clear case of commercial piracy" of Notre Dame's name. But the Appellate Court of New York reversed the judgment and New York's High Court of Appeals sustained the reversal. Notre Dame had lost, and the film went on to earn a small profit. Most observers judged as regrettable that Notre Dame took angry legal action against a silly film which, left unpublicized, the public would have ignored. Thirty years after the Goldfarb controversy, Fr. Ted seemed to agree. Although still convinced that the film insulted Notre Dame and violated its commercial rights, he reflected, "I would guess that today we would [not take legal action]."[30]

Meanwhile, in the 1960s Notre Dame improved rapidly, due largely to a dramatic breakthrough in fundraising. Suddenly, out of the blue, the university received a financial bonanza unprecedented in its history. In 1960 the Ford Foundation selected Notre Dame as one of five private, rapidly improving universities to receive a $6 million grant. The catch was that Notre Dame had to raise $12 million in cash (not pledges) within three years to qualify. (Before the Ford challenge Notre Dame's fundraising efforts brought in a meager $1.5 million per year.) The grant stimulated Notre Dame to increase the energy it put into fundraising. "My schedule has been knocked into a cocked hat this year," Fr. Ted wrote to a colleague in December 1960, "because of the necessity of traveling all over the country trying to raise money for our new Library." Challenge I (1960–63), as Notre Dame called its first capital campaign, raised more than $18 million, the bulk earmarked for a fourteen-story library, then the largest college library building in the world.

The Ford grant stimulated Notre Dame officials to set their sights much higher than they ordinarily would have set them. "It probably put us 10 years ahead of where we would have been had we been left on our own," said Fr. Edmund Joyce. Three years later the Ford Foundation pledged another $6 million if Notre Dame could again double the amount by 1966. Challenge II (1963–66) raised $16 million. A new Athletic and Convocation Center was the most visible result.[31]

"The task of a prophet," Fr. Ted said, "is to make comfortable people uncomfortable." Although he never referred to himself as a prophet, he sometimes spoke as one. In a widely publicized speech in 1961 he tried to make comfortable Catholic educators uncomfortable. Before the annual convention of the National Catholic Education Association, he bluntly censured Catholic parochialism in areas from science and theology to race relations.

He took a swipe at the ossification of Catholic philosophers and theologians:

The task for the Catholic higher learning will not be done if our philosophers and theologians continue to live among, work with, and speak to people and problems long since dead and buried.

Catholic educators must respond to modern times and modern problems:

What must future judges think of us if we live in the most exciting age of science ever known to mankind, and philosophize mainly about Aristotle's physics. We live today in the threatening shadow of cosmic thermonuclear destruction and often theologize about the morality of war as though the spear had not been superseded by the ICBM.

Having completed seven years on the National Science Board, he condemned Catholic parochialism on science:

We took the wrong turn in science as far back as Galileo, and while the roadmaps have been officially corrected since, we are still lagging far behind the main flow of traffic in the area of science and technology. I need not document this assertion for there has already been enough public breastbeating in the matter. Besides, I am interested here not so much in diagnosing the past as in charting a present day and future course. . . . Science is our potent key to the noble modern human quest to eliminate illiteracy, needless poverty and squalor, hunger, disease, and homelessness in our times. Science can help man achieve the basic material conditions essential to a life worthy of man's inner and God-given dignity.

He wanted Catholics in higher education to "mediate" between science and the humanities. This role was difficult:

The main reason that we have not mediated in the Catholic higher learning between science and the humanities is that we have generally neglected science and have not particularly distinguished ourselves in the humanities either.

"Personally, I have no ambition to be a medieval man," he said. "It is futile comfort for a Catholic university in the second half of the Twentieth Century in the United States of America to point with pride to the lively intellectuality and critical vitality of the Catholic University of Paris in Medieval France. Let the dead bury their dead."

His speech caused an uproar at the convention. "End this epidemic of self-criticism," some urged. Msgr. William McManus of Chicago asked for a "moratorium" on criticism of Catholic education and protested that "to keep it up is going to undermine public and Catholic confidence in a school system which is excellent from kindergarten through college." Undeterred, Fr. Ted snapped, "Piety is simply no substitute for scholarly competence."[32]

Notre Dame's system of controlling students was adapting to modern times but was not changing fast enough to suit some students. In 1960, the eighth year of his presidency, Notre Dame still had many regulations governing student life. On weekday nights the students' curfew was midnight and on weekends twenty-one-year-old seniors could stay out only as late as 1 A.M. Cars were forbidden for students on campus, as were parietal hours for women visitors. Many students were unhappy with the environment at Notre Dame and frustrated by the restrictions, the limited opportunities in South Bend, and inadequate dating opportunities.

The system was known as "in loco parentis," meaning Notre Dame assumed parental authority over students as long as they lived on campus. Molding character had long been an object of the university's education, and Notre Dame was proud of the results. "I can remember dozens of boys who griped all the time they were here and then came back to thank us," said Fr. Charles McCarragher, Vice President for Student Affairs in the 1960s. "It wasn't so much that we wanted [the regulations]," added Fr. McCarragher, "as the parents who demanded that we keep a close watch on their sons. In fact, that was one of the reasons why so many students were sent to Notre Dame. They were being kept out of trouble, both spiritual trouble and common mischief."

Periodically, the immaturity of students infuriated Fr. Ted. When Notre Dame students went on a "panty raid" to nearby St. Mary's College, and the local media embarrassingly publicized the incident, he was mortified. "Hesburgh was so angry that I thought he was going to explode," said an administrative colleague.[33]

"It was not the kind of thing you could change quickly," Fr. Ted later said of the restrictions governing students. He argued that Notre Dame had to improve academically before it could be better in discipline. With academic excellence "people would become a little more mature." Besides, the Holy Cross community controlled the rules. "I used to have a local council of priests," he said, "and every change I made I had to go to that local council and get them with me, or I'd be in trouble."

In 1961 Notre Dame did announce a major revision of the rules. Morning check at Mass was abolished; dorms would have all-night lights; officials would stop patroling downtown South Bend bars and off-limits areas; and the student manual was streamlined and rewritten "to convey a more positive attitude toward student behavior." Students rejoiced in their new freedom, but they wanted more.[34]

In the spring of 1963, student discontent boiled over. Fr. Ted endorsed academic freedom and freedom of speech, but he drew the line on some student freedoms. In 1963 the administration censored three articles in the student magazine *Scholastic*, and, as a result, three student editors resigned. The writers had objected to curfews, rules against cars on campus, and rules against women visiting dorm rooms. They also made derogatory remarks about priests of the Congregation of Holy Cross and urged Fr. Ted to resign as president. He should take a new post as chancellor because he was so often away from campus, and because a member of a religious order, subject to obedience to superiors, should not run an academic institution. He responded with a sizzling letter to each student sent to the parents' address. He denied that he was responding because of the suggestion that he be replaced, but he defended the restrictions and the honor of his fellow priests. His letter expressed both pain and heartache: pain that the student editors had been so harsh in their criticism, heartache that "the life-long dedication of hundreds of valiant priests and brothers over the course of 120 years since the birth of Notre Dame, was brushed off in several penstrokes." Discontent was not all bad. It affected any feeling person "and will not be cured this side of the beatific vision." But Notre Dame did not consider "students to be equal partners in the educative process." So "if anyone seriously believes that he cannot become well educated here without a car or girls in his room, or if he really thinks his personal freedom is impossibly restricted by curfew or state laws on drinking or the presence of priests in the residence halls, then I think the only honest reaction is to get free of Notre Dame, not to expect Notre Dame to lose its unique character." The primary responsibility of students "is to learn and not to teach," he bristled. "Students who think otherwise should go out and found their own universities and then take lessons from their students."[35]

Three hundred letters congratulating him for his stand poured into his office (plus a few dissenting ones.) Some of those who applauded were fellow presidents of universities. ("I guess they were in the same boat," he said.) The President of Valparaiso University endorsed his strong stand against the "heresy of freedom without responsibility. . . . Once the great virtue of obedience was central in Christian education, and it must return before we are completely true to our heritage."

However, *Commonweal,* the liberal weekly published by Catholic laymen, viewed the incident critically as the kind of drama that played itself out too frequently on Catholic campuses: "the censorship of a student publication, an indignant student protest, a defense of suppression by the administration." The finale was familiar, observed *Commonweal:* "The administration wins, the students lick their wounds, everything returns to normal." The magazine urged Notre Dame to come up with more creative solutions than "the traditional formula of suppression and admonition."

After the *Scholastic* incident, Fr. Ted complained that students were not transcending "petty concerns" of everyday institutional life, were not sufficiently concerning themselves with national and international issues. He wanted his Notre Dame students to take a more active interest in the Peace Corps, civil rights, the ecumenical movement, and "a host of similar burning questions." Ironically, students were about to begin concerning themselves ardently with burning national and international questions, and while doing so, they would severely complicate his life and the lives of hundreds of university presidents.[36]

Fr. John Walsh, Vice President for Academic Affairs at Notre Dame, often had long discussions with Fr. Ted about the future of Catholic higher education. How could Notre Dame be an open, academic, truth-searching institution and at the same time be rigidly Catholic? Fr. Ted wanted to move toward more openness. He worried that the university might become too clerically dominated or so rigidly Catholic that it would never become a university in the fullest sense. One way Notre Dame could become a university in the fullest sense was to transfer ownership and control from the Congregation of the Holy Cross to a predominantly lay board.

Since its 1844 charter of incorporation, Notre Dame had been governed by a six-man Board of Trustees composed of priests of the Congregation of Holy Cross. The university later established an advisory board composed of lay persons, but the clergy maintained power. Several factors led Fr. Ted to think a change was necessary. He had always shunned the idea of religious having material wealth. In any case, operation of Notre Dame was becoming too complex for the small number of priests in the Holy Cross order. Of the seven hundred members of the faculty in 1967 only fifty-five were C.S.C. priests or brothers. "We had reached the point where Notre Dame could no longer be run by a handful of Holy Cross priests," he said. With less administrative burden, the clergy would be freer to engage in pastoral work and teaching. Moreover, since lay people were already moving up the administrative ladder at Notre Dame, why not just extend the precedent?[37]

Most of Notre Dame's annual operating budget derived from secular sources. "Nondenominational foundations and government agencies often looked askance at Notre Dame's clerical domination," observed Thomas Schlereth. Some Catholic university administrators were worried that court decisions might make it increasingly difficult for religious institutions to receive federal grants. A Maryland court had declared unconstitutional the award of state funds to colleges wholly religious in character, and the U.S. Supreme Court might sustain the decision, jeopardizing Notre Dame's federal support.

The most compelling reason for change, though, was the directive of Vatican II which urged that lay people be given responsibility in the church commensurate with their dedication, competence, and intelligence. "Many people may not have taken that seriously," Fr. Ted reflected in his autobiography, "but we did." In fact, he had advocated a greater role for the laity ever since he wrote his doctoral dissertation two decades earlier.[38]

Initial discussion of lay governance took place in the summer of 1965, at the Holy Cross retreat at Land O'Lakes. Leaders of the Holy Cross order, Notre Dame's vice presidents, several key lay trustees, and Fr. Ted took part. A major impetus to change occurred when Fr. Germain M. Lalande, superior general of the Congregation of Holy Cross, agreed to lay control, stating that the principal commitment of the order was in sanctification of people in the Church and not in the administration of educational institutions.

Fr. Ted constantly consulted with anyone who had insight about the conversion to lay control. Fr. Paul Reinert, President of St. Louis University, was guiding his university through a similar process, and he and Fr. Ted exchanged many letters and phone calls. "We exchanged our thoughts, our arguments, [and] brought up objections we thought we would have to answer." It was a very delicate process. "To some it looked as though we were giving the place away," Reinert reflected. "There was a possessiveness that was very understandable."

Indeed, within the Congregation of Holy Cross some questioned the wisdom of converting to lay control. Why risk a great university like Notre Dame in an irrevocable experiment? The priests of Holy Cross built Notre Dame at a tremendous sacrifice, and Fr. Ted was selling out a heritage received as a trust; the Congregation would lose its influence at the university, and, smothered by a process of secularization, Notre Dame would go the way of other formerly church-related institutions, like Harvard and Yale.

Overall, progress went smoothly toward lay control except for one controversial issue: whether or not the president of the university should be a priest of the Holy Cross community. Some lay Catholics resisted adding the provision; Fr. Ted supported it, because he feared Notre Dame might otherwise slide toward secularization. The planners agreed that the president should be a Holy Cross priest appointed by the board of trustees.

As finally constituted, the new governing structure was similar to one established by Harvard: a small board of fellows and a larger board of trustees. The central controlling body, the twelve fellows, were divided equally between Holy Cross priests and lay people. They set up bylaws and statutes, amended them, and maintained the Catholic character of the university.[39]

In 1967 Fr. Ted announced the change. In effect, the Holy Cross order transferred assets with a book value of $133.5 million (and a replacement value of $192.5 million) to the new Lay Board of Trustees. Attorney Edmund Stephan, who had put the complicated legal documents together for the transfer of control, became the first chairman of the board. At the time of his appointment Stephan described the change as more "de jure" than "de facto" because the advisory board of lay trustees had recently been closely consulted on every major policy change at the university. "I don't see any radical change in the way in which the university is going," said Stephan. But the change delighted Fr. Ted. The "dramatic act," he would later say, was one of the accomplishments of his presidency of which he was most proud.

In 1969, after two years of lay governance, Fr. Ted added another virtue he saw in the new arrangement. The change had "solved once and for all time the problem of academic freedom within the Catholic university." Subsequently he said: "If the Church tries to interfere in a university like this one, which has a lay board, the board can say, 'We have academic freedom—we are autonomous'. . . . [When] your board of directors consists of cardinals, bishops and archbishops, like at Catholic University, then you might have to go along when word comes from headquarters."[40]

Has the transfer to lay governance made a significant difference at Notre Dame? In some respects the change was felicitous. A variety of talented lay people, with wide experiences and perspectives, felt a greater sense of participation and exercised real power; no serious friction occurred between Holy Cross priests and the lay trustees; the change protected the independence of the university from censorship and restrictions by papal authorities; and it freed Holy Cross priests for other duties.[41]

On the other hand, lay control was mostly a fiction under Fr. Ted's forceful leadership. He recommended (or was influential in selecting) the board members and most of them viewed him with admiration bordering on awe. Since the president and half of the fellows were Holy Cross priests, clerics still had substantial power. "We thought it was [a] big [change] at the time," reflected Walsh, who helped bring about the transition. "It turns out, it doesn't seem to have made a whole world of difference." Two years after the transition, an article in *The New York Times* called the change mostly "eyewash." Notre Dame was still a one-man show. "The day when a lay revolt might conceivably oust a Notre Dame priest-president is 20 or 50 years off, if it ever comes at all."[42]

Throughout the 1960s Fr. Ted was often praised and honored for his accomplishments at Notre Dame and for his generous and effective public service. On February 9, 1962, *Time* magazine dedicated its cover story to Notre Dame's president, describing him as the "most influential figure in the reshaping of Catholic higher education in the U.S."

On July 3, 1964, the White House announced that President Lyndon Johnson would present thirty distinguished Americans with the Medal of Freedom, the highest civilian honor the President could bestow. Two months later the recipients gathered at the White House to receive their awards. Fr. Ted's citation read: "Educator and humanitarian, he has inspired a generation of students and given of his wisdom in the struggle for the rights of man." Among the distinguished company who shared the honor with him were Dean Acheson, Aaron Copland, Edward R. Murrow, Reinhold Niebuhr, and Carl Sandburg. He prized the award and often wore a miniature of the Medal of Freedom on his coat lapel.

By 1967, twenty-five honorary degrees had been bestowed on him, including honors from universities in Canada, Austria, Chile, and the Philippines. Columbia University's citation, read by President Grayson Kirk, said: "Theodore Martin Hesburgh, C.S.C. Brilliant son of the Empire State you have given instinctively of your vision and energy, not merely to the church of which you are a cherished exemplar, but to all men, all races and all creeds. Under your resolute hand, the University of Notre Dame advances steadily toward its goal of high scholarship, productive research and wise teaching. Mediocrity and social injustice have long been your chosen adversaries; enlightened understanding your goal; and your armor, a determination to lift man's spirit to nobler things. . . ."[43]

4 ⌒ YEARS OF TURMOIL
1968–1972

IN THE LATE 1960s student protests at Notre Dame caused new and complex problems for Notre Dame's president. The first major U.S. campus protest had occurred at the University of California at Berkeley in the fall of 1964, when a number of campus groups united under the Free Speech Movement. Mass rallies, the takeover of university buildings, and police raids against demonstrators highlighted the student revolt. The unrest at Berkeley became the scenario that repeated itself on hundreds of campuses during the rest of the 1960s.

Like many college presidents, Fr. Ted underestimated the strength of the burgeoning student rebellion. In October 1967, he confidently pointed out that Notre Dame was having no serious problems with drugs, hippies or protestors—"just a few beards and I have nothing against beards." At first he thought the protest at Berkeley was an isolated incident. It wasn't until the Columbia University disturbances that he and other Notre Dame administrators started worrying.

In April 1968, the militant Students for a Democratic Society (SDS) ignited the uprising at Columbia, the largest campus confrontation since the Berkeley turmoil. In the course of the protest radicals broke into the office of Columbia's president, sixty-four-year-old Grayson Kirk, ransacked it, photographed his letters, drank his sherry and smoked his cigars. Pressured to restore order, Kirk summoned police, who responded by clubbing, kicking, and punching students, and arresting 698 persons.[1]

Meanwhile, student demonstrations were increasing at Notre Dame as well. In May 1966, only twenty-five students picketed the annual ROTC review; the following year the number of pickets had risen to 350. By the late 1960s students at Notre Dame were protesting against the university's opposition to a totally open speakers policy, disciplinary rules and parietal restrictions, the small number of minorities among the faculty and student body, the presence and accreditation of ROTC, on-campus recruitment by the Central Intelligence Agency and Dow Chemical Company (which produced napalm used in Vietnam) and, of course, against the Vietnam War.[2]

However, compared to the rebellion at large secular universities, like Berkeley and Columbia, Notre Dame experienced fewer protests, fewer activist students, and far fewer students who endorsed violence. They were less ideological compared to the committed New Left on other campuses and were tactical moderates who preferred peaceful demonstrations. The products of middle class, white, Catholic families, with many of their parents alumni of the university, they were tied to traditional values. "I don't think that by nature [Notre Dame students] are revolutionaries," said Fr. Joyce. "They [know] their families wouldn't like it." Notre Dame's protesters, observed Richard Rossie, student body president in 1968–69, "weren't liberals or radicals like at Berkeley or Columbia. We were still moderate when you put it in a national context. We wanted a sense of participation, but we didn't want control." Despite the different nature and scope of protests at Notre Dame, student and faculty activists were serious, persevering, shrewd protestors, whose demonstrations and sharp-edged rhetoric caused consternation to Fr. Ted and other university officials.

Activist students had a "love-hate" relationship with their president, said Rossie. They realized that his leadership had transformed Notre Dame in beneficial ways, and when he accepted a suggestion from students "he could be very supportive of it." But "we never perceived Fr. Hesburgh as liberal or as civil libertarian as he was perceived . . . in the broader community outside the university." Activist students viewed him as the "Great Establishmentarian."[3]

In light of Fr. Ted's monumental efforts for civil rights, the small percentage of blacks at Notre Dame baffled many people. There were only sixty-five black students at Notre Dame in 1968, about 1 percent of the total enrollment. Tokenism, cried black leaders on campus and their allies. The major problem was that the pool of academically qualified blacks who were Catholics and who wanted to come to Notre Dame was extremely small. "Do you understand how difficult it is to get blacks to come to a Catholic university in South Bend?" asked a Notre Dame law professor.

In addition, though, university officials had not ranked black recruitment as a high priority until the late 1960s. From 1952 to the mid-1960s Fr. Ted's priorities were new buildings, fundraising, curriculum reform, and faculty and student development. Had he concentrated more effort and resources on recruitment of minority students and faculty, Notre Dame might not have faced the embarrassing predicament in which it found itself. "It was a matter of commitment," contended David Krashna, the first black student body president at Notre Dame, who insisted that the university provide remedial assistance for blacks just as it did for its football players.[4]

At a Notre Dame conference on institutional racism black students baited Fr. Ted as he participated on a panel. A black graduate student contended that the contribution of the U.S. Civil Rights Commission to the black struggle had been minimal. When Fr. Ted interjected that the Commission had contributed substantially to the 1964 and 1965 civil rights acts, the graduate student dismissed the contention, arguing that the protests and sacrifices at Birmingham and Selma had forced the federal government to act.

A leader of Notre Dame's Afro-American Society also spoke up. Peering at Fr. Ted through his dark glasses, he snapped: "The Civil Rights Commission was created by The Man to study black people. Well, let me tell *you* something, Father Hesburgh; we've been studied enough! What we want now are deeds, and if you're committed to the cause of black people, then why don't you show it here at Notre Dame?"

When the program broke up, Fr. Ted found himself surrounded by vehement students demanding to know if he would commit himself to a goal of 10 percent minority enrollment. When Fr. Ted refused to accept that specific goal, he was told, "You're just puttin' us on, man!" Shaking his head, Fr. Ted retreated from the building saying, "You just can't talk to some people."[5]

Campus activists complained that Fr. Ted was too much of a gradualist. For them ROTC must go; parietal rules must go; Dow Chemical must go; fat-cat trustees must go; and the Vietnam War must go. Perhaps even Fr. Theodore Hesburgh, at least as a restrictive father, must go. They kept insisting that Notre Dame needed both a president and a chancellor, and Hesburgh should be simply a president who concerned himself mainly with outside activities and absented himself from day-to-day operations of the university.

At times students felt that he wasn't a good listener, that he tried to overwhelm them with his global experiences and views. "When someone talks about having met with the pope last week and the president this week, it is hard to come back," said Phil McKenna, student body president in 1967–1968.

Some complained that he was too often absent from the university and consequently had lost touch with students. A student grumbled, "In three years, I have seen him exactly once—going by in his car to the airport." Student activists sneered at what they called his "favorite ploy"—addressing a letter to them which began, "I am writing this high over the Andes. . . ." The most biting student joke asked: "What's the difference between God and Father Hesburgh? God is everywhere and Hesburgh is everywhere but Notre Dame." Much of the criticism was petty. *The Observer*, the independent student newspaper, often harshly criticized him, but, said two student observers, "it was so slanted that it had to be read at a 45-degree angle."[6]

Complicating matters were super-patriotic, right-wing students (some of them burley football players) who had to be restrained from physically confronting demonstrators. Moreover, a frequent and persistent complaint by conservative alumni held that the administration was too accommodating to rebellious students, and too permissive. The inmates were running the institution. They wanted Fr. Ted to act more assertively and throw out the rascals. "One man with guts is a majority," said an alumnus.

J. Peter Grace, an influential trustee, disgusted with the student radicals, urged Fr. Ted to punish them. "In my opinion, he was much too loose [with the student rebels]," Grace later said. "He didn't do anything to those people."

The media contributed to Fr. Ted's problems on campus. Undoubtedly he was correct when he observed, "If there's an article in a magazine saying Notre Dame students are docile, they'll spend the next week figuring out ways of being indocile, because they've been categorized in a way they don't like."[7]

To win concessions, student activists used a combination of negotiations and pressure tactics. Shrewdly understanding that the administration's Achilles heel was its sensitivity about its public image, they threatened to play havoc with that image. "Above all else," observed Joel Connelly and Howard Dooley, two student leaders who wrote a book about life at Notre Dame in the 1960s, "the university feared a public-relations catastrophe that would embarrass it with the general public, its alumni, and especially with its newfound foundation friends." Rossie agreed that pushing Fr. Ted to the brink often succeeded. "Direct action did work with him," said Rossie, because Fr. Ted and other Notre Dame administrators "were afraid of being [publicly] embarrassed."[8]

Effective in the fall of 1966, the university made additional changes in campus rules. Curfew was eliminated, restrictions on cars were eased, the position of rector was redefined as counselor, and student government was reemphasized. The only student demand that failed to get a hearing was parietal hours for women visitors. "When the students argued that a dorm room should be viewed as a student's home, where he could both study and socialize," observed Connelly and Dooley, "one of the clerics on the committee suddenly blurted the obvious: 'But can't you see? It's a bedroom!'"

In 1968 women still were not allowed to visit the dorms, and after the university suspended four students for violating the rule, Fr. Ted dashed off another letter to students. The men ought to be able to get along without women in their room, he insisted, and the rule would indeed be enforced. "If this makes me medieval, I'll live with that and ask you all to pray for my replacement by someone more modern."

Would the university relax its rules and allow female visitors? he was asked at a student government dinner in the fall of 1968. "Not in my lifetime," he bluntly replied. The same year he said over the campus radio that he would "expel a thousand students" before he yielded on the issue. "I despair at times at the possibility of having a really intelligent and meaningful discussion about parietals," he said in frustration on another occasion, "because it has become such an emotional code word—a red flag to anyone's bull. It becomes clouded with . . . challenges to masculinity, dangers to young and impressionable girls threatened by the strongest of social pressures when least prepared to meet them. The mere mention of parietals brings forth anguished cries of distrusted virtue on the part of students while the older generation, viewing their own past, still preserve ample distrust of themselves under appropriate allurements."[9]

Meanwhile, the intensity of protests on campus escalated. Notre Dame's largest student demonstration took place in November 1968, when 300 students engaged in a "sit-in" in the administration building to protest the presence of recruiters from Dow Chemical and the Central Intelligence Agency. Alarmed, Fr. Ted responded with a letter to all faculty and students on November 25, 1968. He believed the protesters "used their freedom of action to obstruct the freedom of others and to impose their own personal convictions on others." This was "completely out of order," he said, "whatever their motives."

The protesters argued that their demonstration had been nonviolent and should, therefore, be tolerated. Assuredly, sitting down in a doorway was not an act of violence, Fr. Ted conceded in an interview, but it was an act of force, and it did obstruct other people's rights. Student protestors had said, in effect, that anyone was "free" to walk into the room to visit the recruiters as long as they walked over twenty bodies. But this wasn't done in a civilized society, Fr. Ted thought. "I'm not going to walk on you to do it. I hope I'm more human than that."

In his letter Fr. Ted appealed to the Notre Dame community and its various committees to "declare" itself as to what action should be taken in the future. "I could have acted unilaterally, and many have accused me of weakness or lack of leadership in not doing so. However, I much prefer to appeal to you, for this is your community and your University and it cannot be what it should be without your support."[10]

Another major incident occurred at a conference on Pornography and the Law scheduled at Notre Dame February 5–10, 1969. Spectacularly underplanned, the university-sanctioned, student-organized conference on the touchy subject turned into a debacle. Members of the Citizens for Decent Literature, an anti-pornography group, objected to two "pornographic" films that were scheduled to be shown, and convinced the police department in South Bend to confiscate them.

In a letter to the student organizer of the conference Fr. Ted agreed that the two films were "hard core pornography" and banned their showing, while at the same time affirming that he had "no objection to a serious discussion of pornography which is a great problem in our day."

On February 7 a group of 250 students and nonstudents forced their way into the science building for an unauthorized viewing of one of the banned films. Local police, armed with a warrant, confiscated the film and then had to beat a hasty retreat from the angry, abusive crowd. On the retreat the police maced 15 of their pursuers.

Speaking of the action of the police, Richard Rossie contended, "It was really Gestapo [tactics]." The university's administration had been too embarrassed to defend free speech, he and other activists thought, because to defend "free speech would have put them in the position of defending pornography." The Pornography Conference, historian Thomas Schlereth observed judiciously, "had turned into a comedy of errors, unnecessary police harassment, and sophomoric embarrassment to everyone involved." For his part, Fr. Ted was shaken by the awareness that he almost had a major riot on his hands.[11]

The incivility of some students increasingly disturbed Fr. Ted, although he continued to be civil himself. One evening a dirty, smelly, unshaven student walked into his office with a beer can in his hand. "What are you doing here?" Fr. Ted asked. "F— you," the student shot back. During a confrontation in his outer office two shaggy-haired students refused to shake his outstretched hand. "We'll see about that after we talk," one sneered. Fr. Ted simply nodded and invited them into his office to talk. ("If that was me," said a young priest who observed the scene, "those guys would have been out on their ears. I couldn't take that kind of insolence. But Father Hesburgh is willing to put up with just about anything if he thinks it's for the good of Notre Dame.")[12]

In late January 1969, Fr. Ted had met with Representatives on the House Education and Labor Committee who warned him of a growing backlash against campus unrest, which was stimulating more support within Congress for restrictive legislation. He returned to campus worried about a major threat to higher education in the form of repressive legislation from federal and state governments.

Furthermore, the trustees had requested that he be prepared if the relative docility of students should end on the campus. With students rioting throughout the country, with universities under siege, what if the tumult spread to Notre Dame?

Rationality, stability, civility, and nonviolence—values central to a university—had to be restored. He understood why the students were demonstrating, but they shouldn't protest violence by being violent, shouldn't protest something that seems irrational by being irrational. Nor was there any excuse for being uncivil. Each incident at Notre Dame was more difficult to handle than the last, which meant to him that there was more to come and it would be worse. Because the whole university community was shaken and uncertain, he felt he had to do something.[13]

His response was to compose a stern eight-page letter and send it to all students and others in the Notre Dame community. In the letter, dated February 17, 1969, he stated that the central problem was what to do about student alienation and in what manner. Obviously society had many problems. However:

The last thing a shaken society needs is more shaking. The last thing a noisy, turbulent, and disintegrating community needs is more noise, turbulence, and disintegration. Understanding and analysis of social ills cannot be conducted in a boiler factory. Compassion has a quiet way of service. Complicated social mechanisms, out-of-joint, are not adjusted with sledge hammers.

After consulting with faculty, staff, students, trustees, and university committees, he believed he had a clear mandate from the university community to see that:

1. our lines of communication between all segments of the community are kept as open as possible, with all legitimate means of communicating dissent assured, expanded, and protected;

2. civility and rationality are maintained as the most reasonable means of dissent within the academic community; and

3. violation of others' rights or obstruction of the life of the University are outlawed as illegitimate means of dissent in this kind of open society. Violence is especially deplored as a violation of everything that the University community stands for.

Now comes my duty of stating, clearly and unequivocally, what happens if. I'll try to make it as simple as possible to avoid misunderstanding by anyone. May I begin by saying that all of this is hypothetical and I personally hope it never happens here at Notre Dame. But, if it does, anyone or any group that substitutes force for rational persuasion, be it violent or non-violent, will be given fifteen minutes of meditation to cease and desist. They will be told that they are, by their actions, going counter to the overwhelming conviction of this community as to what is proper here. If they do not within that time period cease and desist, they will be asked for their identity cards. Those who produce these will be suspended from this community as not understanding what this community is. Those who do not have or will not produce identity cards will be assumed not to be members of the community and will be charged with trespassing and disturbing the peace on private property and treated accordingly by the law. . . .

After notification of suspension, or trespass in the case of non-community members, if there is not then within five minutes a movement to cease and desist, students will be notified of expulsion from this community and the law will deal with them as non-students.

Probably influenced by the disruption at the Pornography Conference, he emphasized the importance of upholding the law:

There seems to be a current myth that university members are not responsible to the law, and that somehow the law is the enemy, particularly those whom society has constituted to uphold and enforce the law. I would like to insist here that all of us are responsible to the duly constituted laws of this University community and to all of the laws of the land. There is no other guarantee of civilization versus the jungle or mob rule, here or elsewhere.

If someone invades your home, do you dialogue with him or call the law? Without the law, the university is a sitting duck for any small group from outside or inside that wishes to destroy it, to incapacitate it, to terrorize it at whim. . . .

He claimed to have studied the cynical methods of confrontation: (1) find a cause, any cause; (2) force a confrontation at any cost of boorishness or incivility; (3) complain of police brutality; (4) then "call for amnesty, the head of the president on a platter, the complete submission to any and all demands." Must it be so? he asked. "Must universities be subjected, willy-nilly, to such intimidation and victimization whatever their good will in the matter? Somewhere a stand must be made."

He would continue to recognize the right to protest ("through every legitimate channel"), and he didn't want to have to expel any student.

We only insist on the rights of all, minority and majority, the climate of civility and rationality, and a preponderant moral abhorrence of violence or inhuman forms of persuasion that violate our style of life and the nature of the University.

His conclusion:

I truly believe that we are about to witness a revulsion on the part of legislatures, state and national, benefactors, parents, alumni, and the general public for much that is happening in higher education today. If I read the signs of the times correctly, this may well lead to a suppression of the liberty and autonomy that are the lifeblood of a university community. It may well lead to a rebirth of fascism, unless we ourselves are ready to take a stand for what is right for us. History is not consoling in this regard. We rule ourselves or others rule us, in a way that destroys the university as we have known and loved it.[14]

After his statement became public, a deluge of letters and telegrams swamped his office, backing his get-tough policy. The mail was probably the heaviest ever received at a Notre Dame president's office; it overwhelmed the university's two-man public information office. "Father Hesburgh really struck a nerve," sighed one of the officials. *The New York Times* thought the letter was "the toughest policy on student disruptions yet enunciated by any major American university in the course of recent disorders."

About 250 newspapers stormed into print, almost all of them praising his tough stand. *The New York Times* and *The Wall Street Journal* reprinted his letter. Dozens of television and radio stations rushed to arrange interviews. Finally, the newspapers, magazines, and broadcasters seemed to be saying, someone had the courage to "tell these twerps off." "Never before have we heard such clear and forceful rules laid down," applauded the *Orlando Evening Star;* "reasonable and commendably firm," said *The Indianapolis News;* a "brilliant exposition of the peril," the *South Bend Tribune* wrote. Even the liberal *Washington Post* thought it was "time to get tough." Supporters of his letter usually savored the warning of on-the-spot expulsion of any student who disrupted normal campus operations. Often they quoted the portion which warned that violators "will be given fifteen minutes of meditation to cease and desist" after which they would be disciplined.[15]

Predictably, student activists criticized his fifteen-minute rule, claiming he had exaggerated the problem at Notre Dame, was displaying his paternalism again, and had buckled before the pressure of conservative trustees and alumni. He was gone from the campus so much that he had lost touch with the students and the facts on campus, critics argued.

Some wondered if a Christian university really wanted to smooth the path of intelligence agents and napalm manufacturers by allowing them to recruit on campus. "Where was Hesburgh's Christian witness?" raged a Notre Dame professor sympathetic to the protests. "I thought Jesus was a radical."[16]

A few secular educators were unenthusiastic about Fr. Ted's approach. An administrator at California's San Fernando Valley State College observed: "If we had taken that stand, the place probably would have burned down." F. Donald Eckelmann, Dean at Brown University, said, "You need a completely intimidated student body to make that sort of statement and get away with it. I think that it will come back to haunt him."

Some made light of the matter. Senator Eugene McCarthy, who spoke at Notre Dame, was asked about Fr. Ted's hard-line statement on student disorders. With a mischievous smile, McCarthy opined that it was like warning an all-girl band not to chew tobacco. Notre Dame students might be hellish on weekends, he contended, but they would not engage in serious disruption. Some students said they planned to test the new ground rules by lying down at fourteen-minute intervals.[17]

Once again the most serious criticism came from *Commonweal*. The magazine judged his "threat" delusionary and one-dimensional. "Crises will loom so long as conventional policies keep Catholic campuses almost lily-white, so long as recruiters for questionable agencies and companies have free access to the student body, so long as ROTC units troop about campus training officers for dirty wars, and so long as ties are maintained with alumni and others that foster evils like institutional racism." Students should not be allowed to run wild on campus, conceded *Commonweal*, but "before the university administration lays down its fascist dicta, it [should] look to itself and the policies which justify the grievances, and therefore validate the confrontations of students."[18]

Fr. Ted quickly realized that the most intense champions of his statement were the hard-line crowd. To counteract their enthusiasm, he publicly reiterated that protest, even about university matters, was "reasonable" and "good." "Almost half the people I hear from are happy about that letter for the wrong reasons. They make me out anti kids and superhawk, and I'm not." Fr. Joyce agreed: "He got embarrassed by [all the praise] because he didn't mean it to be as strong as they were giving him credit for. He wasn't saying he would clobber these young kids." Fr. Ted spent much of the rest of 1969 trying to convince people that the students had legitimate concerns. "The last thing I ever wanted to do," he said shortly after issuing his edict, "was lose the kids. Because if you lose the kids you've got to get out of the business. You've got to love them, even if a few are not very lovable—but 98 percent are very lovable."

On the whole, though, the reaction pleased him. "It must have struck the right note somewhere," he said. "I'm glad I did it." Almost every place he went, people told him that "it was [his] statement that turned the corner."[19]

On February 22, 1969, however, he received an unwanted, four-page telegram from President Richard Nixon applauding his tough stance on student protests. A small, irresponsible minority of students had shown intolerance of "legitimately constituted authority, and a complete disregard for the rights of others," the President said. "Violence and vandalism have marked many of these protests, and the rights of the majority of the students have been grossly abused."

Nixon advised that Vice President Spiro Agnew would be meeting shortly at the White House with the nation's governors to discuss "what action . . . might be taken at the state and federal levels to cope with the growing lawlessness and violence on our campuses." The President asked Fr. Ted to convey his views to Agnew in preparation for the meeting.[20]

"My heart sank," recalled Fr. Ted of his reaction to Nixon's telegram. Nixon intended to recommend harsh federal measures to quell campus disturbances, he suspected, and wanted Fr. Ted's endorsement. "Repressive legislation was the last thing colleges wanted or needed. I certainly wanted no part of it," he said.

He received Nixon's telegram while he was enroute to a conference in Bogota, Columbia. With the national governors conference about to convene he hustled to write a recommendation to Vice President Agnew, and then asked Sol Linowitz, U.S. Ambassador to the Organization of American States, to hand deliver it when the ambassador flew from Bogota to Washington.

In his letter to Agnew on February 27, 1969, he emphasized the vital importance of maintaining the traditional independence of American universities. "The best salvation for the university in the face of any crisis," he said,

is for the university community to save itself, by declaring its own ground rules and basic values and then enforcing them with the widest and deepest form of moral persuasion for the good life of the university, and consequent moral condemnation with academic sanctions for any movement against university life and values—especially violence, vandalism and mob action which are the antitheses of reason, civility and the open society which respects the rights of each and all.

When moral persuasion and academic sanctions fail to work, then "outside assistance" may be necessary. However, he emphasized, the university "best judges its need for outside assistance and invokes this assistance, much as it would call for help in a three-alarm campus fire." Outside help was the "last alternative" and only the university should make that determination. He concluded by urging that there be no "repressive legislation, or over-reaction."

His letter arrived just in time to help convince the governors not to endorse repressive legislation. Fr. Ted probably exaggerated when he later contended that the governors did an "about face" on the issue mainly because of his letter, but on February 27, the National Governors Conference did refuse to call for a federal investigation of whether a national conspiracy was involved in student disruptions on campuses. After the governors had read Fr. Ted's letter, they defeated a resolution by Governor Ronald Reagan of California which would have urged the Justice Department to make "a full and complete investigation into the instigators, the causes and the effects of such violence."[21]

Early in July 1969, Fr. Ted left for a trip around the world. Exhausted, he wanted "to get away from it all" and regain his "equilibrium." Close friends and observers thought he was near the end of his rope. "He looked terrible before he went," said Fr. McCarragher, and photographs of the time confirm the judgment. Deep pouches had formed beneath his eyes; worry lines etched across his face. "The president's color was pale, and a testy expression was often worn during public appearances," observed Connelly and Dooley. Earlier he had checked into the Mayo Clinic, where doctors said he suffered from angina pectoris, a thickening of the heart muscle and a symptom of incipient heart disease.

He may have feared that, like other college presidents of the era, he would be a victim of the students' protests. He kept a list of all the major university presidents who were driven from office during the student rebellion, and when reporters inquired about the list, he pulled out a handwritten sheet of yellow legal paper and read off the names of the victims, like fallen heroes. Early in 1970 there were nineteen college presidents on his list. "It was sickening," he remarked about Grayson Kirk of Columbia, "the way no one spoke a word in his defense. Yet when you look at what that man accomplished for that school, where it was when he became president in 1953, and where he took it. . . ."[22]

Occasionally he vented his frustration to reporters. Asked early in 1970 what the administration would have done to student protesters in the 1930s during his undergraduate days, he snapped, "They'd have been out of here in three seconds." Then he quickly resumed a placid tone.

He felt the students were slipping away from him. Student editors repeatedly lashed out at him; student activists pressured him and sapped his energy. Since he had declared his availability to any student, a few took him at his word and showed up at his office at 1 A.M., consuming his precious time. "You find yourself spending 70 percent of your time talking to 1 percent of the students," he said.[23]

Potentially explosive problems remained to be faced. After Notre Dame's director of public information, Richard Conklin, talked with a reporter for *The New York Times*, who had been interviewing on campus, he related the reporter's information. "Pat told me," Conklin wrote Fr. Ted on September 10, 1969, "an unmistakable consensus was evident at Notre Dame: the most likely source of serious trouble is from our black students, who do not feel the issues they raised last year have been satisfactorily met."

Notre Dame administrator George Shuster had been trying to get Fr. Ted's attention to discuss a proposal concerning population control, but student protests occupied too much of the President's time. "Over the past months he has been so concerned with student problems that it has literally not been possible to get him to think about other matters," Shuster wrote a friend. "This concern has taken a great deal out of him."

It wasn't just the student rebellion that caused excessive demands on Fr. Ted's time and energy. He had to perform a balancing act between "five or ten different constituencies" in an increasingly complex job with more and more details to look after. Besides the normal administrative tasks, he complained, "We're expected to achieve peace, clean up pollution, educate twice as many students, reform the corporations and extend the frontiers of knowledge." He found the university's bureaucracy stifling. Everybody wanted to "talk, talk, talk." He spent too much time putting out fires and consequently had minimal time left for educational reform. "Unless things are simplified, I would guess that before long no intelligent guy in his right mind would want to be a university administrator."

The multiple pressures affected his normally calm demeanor. He woke up in the morning with a knot in his stomach and would say, "What's going to happen today, and what am I going to do about it?" He was forced to make a series of quick decisions. "You can make six good ones in a row but one bad one will cost you everything."

When asked if he ever regretted taking the Notre Dame presidency, he grinned broadly and quipped: "About ten times a week." A few faculty members wrote encouraging letters of support, and he could walk across the hall where Fr. Joyce offered him words of consolation. Not all of his late-night visitors had an axe to grind. Just before Christmas one year a group of students climbed the fire escape after midnight and serenaded him with Christmas carols. "It was wonderful," he said.[24]

After being quiet about the Vietnam War, Fr. Ted began speaking out on the pressing issue. He had been a staunch supporter of World

War II; it never crossed his mind to object to the effort against Hitler and Tojo, because they were monsters. "We were trying to put justice back in the world and achieve world peace," he later said. Initially, he thought the Vietnam War was a similar situation, but he eventually came to view the Vietnam conflict as different and much harder to justify.

Up to 1968 he thought it was morally permissible for the United States to use force in Vietnam. One person with whom he had privately debated the issue was Notre Dame theology professor Fr. John Dunne, who rejected the use of force. By 1969, however, Fr. Ted had come closer to Fr. Dunne's position. "It was a dramatic switch," said Fr. Dunne. The course of the horrible war undoubtedly influenced his change. So did the moral fervor of anti-war students on campus. "They gave him his conscience," said an administrative colleague.

On October 14, 1969, the eve of the nationwide Vietnam moratorium protesting the war, Fr. Ted announced that he had signed a letter with other college presidents calling for stepped-up withdrawal of U.S. forces from Vietnam. "Were I in a position to do so," he said, "I would end this war tonight before midnight." The following day he was conspicuous in his presence on the sideline while 2,500 students gathered in front of the library to celebrate a peace Mass. "I thought that was a courageous move for a university president," theology professor Fr. David Burrell later said. In an interview with the student newspaper, *The Observer*, Fr. Ted urged a stand-still cease fire and agreement on free elections supervised by a mutually acceptable international organization. Then if South Vietnam's government refused to cooperate with the proposal, he said, the U.S. would have an acceptable reason for ending its participation in the war. His stand impressed student activists. "A college president, *their* college president, had spoken out against the war," Connelly and Dooley observed of some campus sentiment, "and Notre Dame students cheered him and endorsed his stand." [25]

The only time Notre Dame enforced the fifteen-minute rule occurred on November 18, 1969, when ten students were suspended after they lay down in front of the office where recruiters for Dow Chemical and the CIA planned to interview. (Nine later returned to the university and graduated.) Fr. Ted noted that the suspensions marked "the end of the challenge to the university's right and ability to govern its students." [26]

He was one of the few college presidents who survived the tumultuous student rebellion of the late 1960s. How did he do it? While walking a tightrope, he maintained contact with all his constituencies and won their respect. For the most part he dealt with students in an adroit and sensitive manner. He made it clear that he stood for law and order, but at the same time he built rewarding liaisons with most student leaders. David Krashna, a harsh critic of Fr. Ted, nonetheless had many productive meetings with the president. "They were [almost] always very affable and calm meetings," conceded Krashna. "Something in him appealed to the students," observed Thomas Stritch. "He was ready to talk to them, visit them in their dorms, reason with them, and above all be candid with them. Yet he never got down on all fours with them."

Many students supported him throughout the turmoil. "He's done more for Notre Dame than anybody;" "I've known students to call at his office past midnight and talk with him all night." He earned their trust. Even many of the student journalists who clamored for his resignation knew that he stood for freedom and dignity. "This undercurrent of trust," said Stritch, "this link between Hesburgh and his students never failed him. Moreover, it was based in part on Hesburgh's sympathy with some student causes, much as he deplored their lawless pursuit of them."[27]

Unlike public universities, Notre Dame channeled some frustration into the liturgy. (Draft cards were burned during the offertory at Mass.) In order to isolate the radical, anarchistic left that threatened violence, Fr. Ted built a valuable bridge to nonviolent, Christian pacifists. "Hesburgh realized it was important to keep these students from going over to the [radical] side," said Richard Conklin. "Whenever the core of anarchistic left would get rolling, it would meet the solid resistance of the nonviolent group." The strategy, added Conklin, "was one of the reasons Notre Dame came through that era without some of the tragedies that happened on other campuses."[28]

Fr. Ted was determined to keep an open mind and made major efforts to win over critics. The university donated $25,000 to the Robert F. Kennedy Institute for Social Action, even though the institute's leader had been the organizer of the ill-fated Pornography Conference. When a group of student critics met with him and requested a new course on nonviolence, plus programs on nonviolence and new library materials to support the innovations, Fr. Ted embraced the idea. To the astonishment of the students, within twenty-four hours he had secured a $100,000 pledge for the program from the Gulf Oil Company.[29]

Although he deplored most of the methods of the student activists, he sympathized with many of their goals. He promoted several proposals that he thought would alleviate the alienation of youth, including National Service, the eighteen-year-old vote, and elimination of the draft. During the Nixon Administration he served on the Gates Commission on an All-Volunteer Armed Forces, a concept legislated by Congress after the Commission's report. The change alleviated tension on campus caused by the military draft. ("I had an easier time in the University once the draft was dropped," he later said.)

He tried to get others to understand youthful idealism. He was constantly being asked, What's happening to this generation? Why the unrest, the protest, the revolt? Why bother to educate a bunch of kooks? He admitted to a certain amount of "unpriestly impatience" at the line of questioning. He recalled a New York press conference where he released his frustrations on a reporter. "What you're really saying is that unless students are nice fellows like you, we shouldn't be interested in trying to educate them." "I didn't say that," the reporter countered. "Then what are you saying?" This drew silence. Fr. Ted started over again. "What is so good about you or your world?" he asked the reporter. "Is there nothing to be uneasy about, nothing to protest, nothing to revolt against?" Another silence. Fr. Ted explained: "We might begin by trying to understand what causes the unrest, the protest, the revolt of the young people today."

Beginning in the fall of 1967, Fr. Ted acted with minimal prodding on several fronts to improve Notre Dame's record on minorities. He ordered that 11 percent—the level of the black population of South Bend—of university employees be minorities. (Four years later minority employment had risen from 45 to 345.) He also actively sought funds for minority scholarships, was the driving force to involve alumni clubs in minority recruiting, and dispatched student government leaders and black students to the banquet circuit to explain minority recruiting techniques. He even personally recruited academically exceptional black high school students. Although the Afro-American Society on campus had berated Notre Dame's civil rights record, it was given $18,000 for a Black Culture Week in the spring of 1969.

Some thought he conceded too much. They thought he was lowering admissions standards, allowing admittance of some disadvantaged blacks. The critics charged that the blacks admitted were academically unqualified, formed themselves into militant groups, and led protests on campus. "People complained that Ted was responsible for attracting that kind of student," said Fr. Ernest Bartell.

Finding funds for minority scholarships was Fr. Ted's principal goal, and he came up with an important new source. Until 1969 he had agreed with Notre Dame's traditional policy of not allowing the football team to take part in post-season bowl games. What if Notre Dame reversed its policy and earmarked the money earned from the game for minority scholarships? In one of the meetings on the subject of bowl participation, Fr. Walsh observed, "I could almost see [Hesburgh's] brain cells revolving. It was almost as if a light went on in his eyes." With Fr. Ted's prodding, in 1970 the university broke its forty-year tradition of not participating in post-season bowl games and permitted the football team to face Texas in the Cotton Bowl. The university invested the proceeds ($300,000) in minority scholarships.[30]

By 1969 Fr. Ted had modified his views on restrictions governing students. He was willing to concede students more of a "real" instead of a "fictitious" part in the university community. New structures should give students involvement and voice without conferring on them the instant competence that characterized faculty or the ultimate responsibility that was the prerogative of the trustees. Catholic higher education had always been paternalistic toward its students. "This will no longer wash," he said.

Therefore, in 1969, when the newly formed Student Life Council (made up of faculty, students, and administrators) voted overwhelmingly in favor of women visitation in the dorms, Fr. Ted yielded without a murmur. Diehards on the faculty and within the Congregation of Holy Cross saw his action as another in a long series of disastrous concessions to win the affection and support of students. However, Fr. Ted explained that universities must establish "communities" in order to stem violent forces and emotions. "If the Student Life Council, which I regard as the authentic voice of this university community, tells me something, I've got to listen to it, otherwise I don't belong in this job."

Some of Fr. Ted's associates said that he was uncomfortable with the parietal hours situation, opposing it privately but supporting it publicly. "He walks a tightrope on this as on many other issues," said a reporter for *Chicago's American* in March 1969, "balancing off the interests of the students, the alumni, the faculty, and the church. . . . [He] has managed to maintain the confidence of the majority in each constituency, by keeping in constant touch with all of them."[31]

One last convulsion of protests rocked college campuses in early May 1970. In a belligerent, provocative television speech on April 30,

1970, President Nixon justified sending troops into Cambodia in order to attack key North Vietnamese military targets. The invasion further polarized domestic opinion in the United States. On May 4, a torrent of protest erupted when Ohio national guardsmen shot and killed four students at Kent State. The reaction on campuses to Cambodia and Kent State eclipsed all previous protests. Disruption occurred at 415 campuses, and more than 250 had to close before the end of the semester. On the weekend of May 9–10 more than 100,000 protesters descended on Washington D.C.[32]

Shock and outrage swept the Notre Dame campus as well as students reacted to the Cambodian invasion and the deaths at Kent State. On Friday May 1, 1970, about thirty-five students invaded the building where the University's board of trustees were meeting and pounded on the doors, disrupting the meeting and forcing it to be cut short. Further tense confrontations and discussions took place over the next two days and by Sunday night Fr. Ted was exhausted. "It had been a horrible weekend," he recalled. Arriving at his office at midnight, he learned there would be a "blow-up" on Monday. One student passed along a rumor that the ROTC building would be firebombed. At 3 A.M. on Monday (May 4) David Krashna asked him to speak early Monday afternoon at a large rally on the mall. Fr. Ted distrusted Krashna's intentions, having learned from other students that Notre Dame's president was to be embarrassed or humiliated at the rally. But he agreed to speak. "Almost always I talked off the cuff, but this was one time I sensed that I had better prepare carefully what I wanted to say. I wrote out the whole talk, including a list of recommendations that I thought would defuse the situation." He finished the speech at 4:30 A.M., left it for his secretary to type, and went to bed.[33]

On Monday, before a crowd of 2,000, he delivered one of the most important speeches of his life. With the whispered first reports of the Kent State deaths circulating in the crowd, he read his speech from wind-swept pages. He came down hard against the Vietnam War, urged students not to strike classes, and proposed a method to end U.S. involvement in the war. U.S. participation was a "mistake," he said. The 40,000 U.S. deaths and billions of dollars spent on death and destruction had not won anything of real substance and were not worth the cost of "so many lives and so much of our resources that might have been more humanely and more fruitfully expended elsewhere."

He credited President Nixon with "sincerity" and "courage" in sending troops into Cambodia, but disagreed with his decision. "One great need of this nation today is for unity of purpose, clear priority of values, lofty vision regarding where we might go together. Vietnam runs counter to all of these present desires."

He defended the dead who had fought in Vietnam, and he committed himself to the safe return of U.S. war prisoners. Nonetheless, he continued, "I have tried to understand the recurrent military logic that the war must be widened to be narrowed, but . . . I fail to follow a logic that has grown more barren, more illogical, more contradictory, and more self-defeating in promising victory through defeat." There comes a point when "moral righteousness is more important than empty victory."

"All of us want to be loyal and patriotic—but we also want to be morally clean in the process. . . . Our real power and strength bear on spiritual values, justice, and honor. If our national conscience bothers us, we must stop, look and ponder our future."

What should be done? he asked. Violence was totally unacceptable. Striking college classes was also counterproductive. "Striking classes as some universities are doing, in the sense of cutting off your education, is the worst thing you could do at this time, since your education and your growth in competence are what the world needs most, if the leadership of the future is going to be better than the leadership of the past and present."

He then put forth a six-point declaration which "I would be proud to sign with you and transmit to our President." Among other measures, his proposal called for the "withdrawal of our military forces at the earliest moment and the designation by the Congress of an ultimate date for complete withdrawal." It also declared that the nation's priorities "are not military, but human," and that the nation should dedicate itself "to justice, to equality of opportunity, and to renewing the quality of American life." The declaration concluded by calling for a commitment "to help work for a better America and a better world in a peaceful and non-violent manner."[34]

Thunderous applause greeted his speech, but the same reaction greeted the next speaker, Krashna, who offered a more radical proposal. Ignoring Fr. Ted's expressed wish, Krashna urged the student body to boycott all classes for an indefinite period. Students should "stop, look, and listen—and absolutely say 'stop' to the education we're getting at this time." A "new education" must begin, one that studies militarism, racism, and sexism at Notre Dame.

When Fr. Ted returned to his office a group of students awaited him. They wanted copies of his speech. "How many do you want?" he asked. "Thousands," they said. They wanted students to circulate it as a petition throughout the South Bend area. "I'll tell you what," he responded. "You guys do that and when you get all of the signatures I'll make sure [President Nixon] gets them." (About one thousand students took up their president's suggestion and in the next two weeks circulated their petition and collected 23,000 signatures from residents in South Bend endorsing the "Hesburgh Declaration.")[35]

On Monday evening Krashna went to Fr. Ted's office to discuss the student strike. They had talked on many occasions, but this time Fr. Ted didn't greet him with the usual pleasantries. "This was the first time," recalled Krashna, "that I had ever encountered Fr. Hesburgh . . . stressed, tense, [and] irritated." He was irritated because Krashna had called for the student strike. As they talked, however, Fr. Ted "lightened up" and regained his normal disposition. He wanted to make certain the strike was a constructive educational experience and, most important, he wanted to know when it would end.[36]

Notre Dame's Student Government, joining thousands of other students at hundreds of universities, voted to strike; on Tuesday morning (May 5) strike posters were slapped on buildings and bulletin boards. Striking students passed out handbills, but there was no disruption or coercion. Estimates varied on the success of the strike—from an absenteeism of 50 percent in Arts and Letters to 20 percent in Business Administration.

Fr. John Walsh, Vice President of Academic Affairs, cancelled Wednesday's classes (May 6) and Thursday was the Feast of the Ascension, a traditional holiday. The administration asked the Notre Dame community to "set aside Wednesday and Thursday . . . as days for speeches, teach-ins and liturgical ceremonies to express the deep feelings and reservations about our government's recent actions in Indochina."[37]

On the Wednesday of suspended classes a thousand people took part in a Mass on the Main Quad and a special faculty meeting, after robust debate, endorsed the Hesburgh Declaration by a vote of 211 to 134. Late in the afternoon a long line of 5,000 student marchers snaked through the campus and marched peacefully to a rally at Howard Park in South Bend. Fr. Ted asked faculty members and administrators to abide by the student strike and to let it be an opportunity for teaching. He wanted the faculty "to be quietly present but not dominantly so," said Fr. Burrell.

At Notre Dame apathy and division were being replaced by a spirit of solidarity. "Many people at Notre Dame who had shown no previous interest in doing anything to oppose the war now looked at Cambodia and Kent State with dismay," wrote Robert Schmuhl, who chronicled the turmoil at Notre Dame. "The events of May enlarged the ranks of those opposed to the war—in just a few days, many in the mainstream center found common cause with those in the anti-war left."[38]

One of the most impressive events during the seven days was the community liturgy held on Ascension Thursday (May 7) with Fr. Ted as the principal celebrant. Every element of the campus—faculty, students, clerks, secretaries, alumni—crammed into Sacred Heart Church to hear Fr. Ted eulogize the slain students at Kent State and plead for a society in which "ballots replaced bullets" for American youth. The liturgy, said an observer, "illustrated the continuing power and value a shared symbolism holds for a community." Fr. Ted later commented that he saw "more praying in those two days on campus than I had seen all year long."[39]

At the time of the protest the Notre Dame alumni presidents from a hundred clubs happened to be on campus for an Alumni Senate meeting. They altered their planned agenda to allow maximum time to interact with the demonstrating students. Some lived in the residence halls; others took part in formal meetings where student strikers argued their positions. At least half of them, according to Alumni Association President Donald O'Brien "probably did not fully approve of [Fr. Hesburgh's] statement." That included O'Brien, who thought the U.S. invasion of Cambodia was wise and necessary. However, reflected O'Brien, "I think the majority of alumni feel Father Hesburgh had a personally stabilizing effect on the university in that week. . . . Those at the meeting expressed their admiration for what he had done." O'Brien thought the majority of the alumni not only supported Fr. Ted, but "are very proud of Father Hesburgh and support him in virtually all of his activities."

Classes resumed Friday (May 8) although attendance was still below average. By Monday (May 11) the campus was beginning to return to normal. That evening students at the Stepan Center gave Fr. Ted a one-minute standing ovation when he appeared on the platform to introduce a speech by Indiana Senator Vance Hartke.[40]

On May 18 Fr. Ted wrote a long letter to President Nixon and attached the text of the Hesburgh Declaration. "I have seen a moral rebirth on this campus during the past ten days," he told Nixon. He hoped the President would not be angered by his critical comments. "[The] best part of friendship is honesty and frankness, and I send this to you in that spirit." He assured the President of his "sincere friendship" and continued prayers.

Notre Dame emerged from the seven days of protest without damage, violence, or national guardsmen, and even without bitterness and confrontation. It was a tribute, said an observer, "to serious student leadership, maximum faculty cooperation and administrative flexibility." Fr. Ted was delighted with the results of the May protests. "All around us in other universities there were students killed, buildings burned, acts of violence and lawlessness, while here there was a serious discussion of issues carried on in an atmosphere of peace and without any violence whatever," he responded to a prominent alumnus, angry at the student protests. "As a matter of fact, the few radicals who do exist here were completely neutralized during this period, and there never has been a time in the life of the University when the faculty, students, and administration came as closely together as we did during May of this year."[41]

Although pleased with the results of the May protests at Notre Dame, the constant pressure had left him exhausted. On June 4, he wrote a friend in Europe, "It's been a very difficult year here in all American universities, and I am more tired than I have ever been before."

Over the next few years the university made notable changes partly as a result of student complaints. "[A] pass-fail system was . . . instituted," said historian Fr. Thomas Blantz, "the office of provost was created, the Student Life Council was set up, wider student rights were incorporated in the student manual, the number of students in each residence hall was significantly reduced, a new team was appointed to the Student Affairs area, and the university began admitting undergraduate women to its student body in 1972."

On reflection, Fr. Ted held ambivalent memories of the student uprising. Writing in *Daedalus* in 1974, he assessed the results of the campus protests. In some ways, it was a most unfortunate and unpleasant experience.

Everything became unhinged at once. Support was nowhere. The unheard of and unprecedented happened daily. Nothing seemed right and everything wrong. Moreover, almost nothing one tried worked, and one had the feeling in the pit of one's stomach of being perpetually the small boy with his finger in the dike, holding back the flood, precariously. The great university virtues of civility and rationality were replaced overnight by boorishness and unthinking emotion. In the name of putative student rights, the rights of real students were flaunted by nonstudents. Into the peaceful atmosphere of universities, violence and even killing entered. Overnight universities passed from one of the most respected of American institutions to an institution in which few had any faith at all.

He also worried that universities took a backward step in the quality of their residential communities:

In the name of scrapping the age-old attitude of *in loco parentis,* most universities not only gave up all and every measure of adult supervision of student mores, but also gave students the impression that they do not care how students live, what their real values are as regards drugs, sexual activity, drinking, and the disciplined life in general. . . . One should be able to eliminate petty *in loco parentis* discipline without abandoning *in loco parentis* caring for students and their inner-life values. This is not easy. It does require dedication, imagination, skill, and patience on the part of nonacademic educators in the whole area of student life, but it can and is being done in some quarters. One would hope that student anomie or moral rootlessness will not be another permanent result of the student revolution.

On the other hand, he endorsed the increased role of students in university policymaking, their presence on most departmental committees and the councils of each college. He thought students improved the level of discussion. More importantly, in Hesburgh's eyes, the national student rebellion helped turn the nation around on the war.

When the student revolution began, most adults had unthinkingly gone along with the Vietnam misadventure, since it cost them little personal sacrifice. It was not many years before these students—who were, after all, sons and daughters as well—began to confront their parents with the moral issues to a point where the great majority of adult Americans turned against the war and joined the young in pushing for its early conclusion. This was possibly the first time in the history of the republic when the young educated their elders so convincingly in an essentially moral national concern.

On another moral front, he credited the student rebellion with enhancing educational social justice:

I would credit student participation in the civil rights movement for some of the progress that was made throughout higher education during the sixties in opening the universities to members of minority groups in significant numbers.

His conclusion:

One should not exaggerate either the good or the bad results of the student revolution, but on some presently quiet evenings—when the library fills up as students study and seek security for the future and are not greatly concerned, as they once were, about festering world problems—one might ask whether it would not be helpful to have a touch of continuing revolution in the educational process. We have learned that universities can certainly be too noisy. But they can also be too quiet.[42]

While Fr. Ted's problems with campus rebels started to wane in 1970, another major tense confrontation, this time with the President of the United States, was just beginning. Shortly after President Richard Nixon's inauguration, the entire Civil Rights Commission paid a courtesy call at the White House. When their chat ended, Nixon asked Fr. Ted to remain for a private discussion in the Oval Office.

"What would it take for you to come with this government full time?" Nixon inquired.

"What do you have in mind?" Fr. Ted replied.

"I'd like you to take over the poverty program," the President said.

Fr. Ted told him he didn't think that was a good idea. "The poverty program is a mess, and I think I know how to clean it up and make it work, but it would make you the most unpopular guy in the country because it's turned into a patronage program for all the big city mayors who've got all their buddies making $30,000 a year on the poverty program. The first thing I'd do is fire the whole kit-and-caboodle and every mayor in the U.S. would be unhappy beginning in Chicago and going to Atlanta. The further south you go the more unpopular you'd be because I'm a priest." He then suggested that the two should just forget the President's proposal. "Well," Nixon replied, "it seemed like a good idea, but I guess you're right."

A few days after their meeting, Fr. Ted wrote the President, thanking him for his "generous thoughtfulness." The job offer was "theoretically possible for me," wrote Fr. Ted, but would be "potentially troublesome" for the Nixon Administration. "The growing openness of our society is leading towards this kind of service by clergy in the future," he told Nixon, "but my instinct tells me that you are ahead of the times at the moment, and I would not want for the world to be any cause of embarrassment for you and your administration."[43]

Fr. Ted had known Nixon since 1952, when the newly elected Vice

With Vice President–elect and Mrs. Richard Nixon on the 50-yard line.

President and his wife attended a Notre Dame football game, and they had enjoyed a cordial relationship ever since. A few weeks after their meeting in the White House Nixon asked him to accept the chairmanship of the Civil Rights Commission. (Hannah had stepped down.) Reluctantly, Fr. Ted agreed. "I told him I would take it for a year and see how it went," he recalled, "but that I really thought I should get off and make room for somebody else." At first he assumed that the new President intended to support civil rights, and he outlined proposals he thought Nixon would endorse. But he misjudged Nixon's intentions. Ironically, by agreeing to become chairman he was embarking on four years of confrontation with the man who appointed him.[44]

In 1970, in a government filled with huge bureaucracies, the size of the Civil Rights Commission was small—140 people on its staff. Its budget hovered around $3 million. The Commission struggled within a vortex of social and political forces, relying on aggressiveness, persistence, and deep faith in its goals of justice and equality. Civil rights advocates often praised its efforts. "I have great faith in the Commission," said Clarence Mitchell, chief lobbyist for the NAACP. Veteran civil rights activist Joseph Rauh, Jr., former president of Americans for Democratic Action, described the Commission as "the moral conscience of the nation."

Initially, the Commission had applied the phrase "civil rights" almost exclusively to blacks. By 1970, however, it was studying Chicanos, Puerto Ricans, and Indians as well. At a Commission meeting in Denver, discussion focused on another form of discrimination. One Commissioner worried that if the Commission moved into the area of sex discrimination, people would assume that it had exhausted its efforts for racial minorities. Fr. Ted disagreed, pointing out that the line of reasoning would never have allowed the Commission to get into Chicano affairs. At first the Commission had looked only at the problems of blacks; it could have been argued that if it had started looking at the problems of Chicanos, it would divert the Commission from black problems. "Father Hesburgh said that there should be expansion into new areas," the secretary recorded in the minutes; "we should say that we have not completed all we have to do for minorities, but there are also other segments we have not gotten into."

Fr. Ted wanted to go even further. At the same Denver meeting he urged the Commission to "look ahead with vision" and move into the broader area of human rights. The recording secretary summarized his argument:

Chairman Hesburgh said that as we approach the 200th anniversary of our nation the greatest thing the United States could do would be to proclaim its dedication to human rights. This might set an example for other nations of the world. Chairman Hesburgh said he understands the objections to our attempting this and he understands the feeling that people might think that we are deserting our civil rights efforts. However, he thought that we could say that the civil rights job is far from done and we will continue that effort, but that the human rights job also has to be undertaken. Chairman Hesburgh felt that either the President or one of the Presidential candidates would have to take this up as an issue in order to make the move successful.

A few observers credit President Nixon with some success in the field of civil rights. For example, his administration's "Philadelphia Plan" required lily-white construction unions involved in federal contracts to open their ranks to black workers. For the most part, though, soon after taking office Nixon began a calculated retreat in the area of civil rights. He charted a political route that moved him away from black voters toward white conservatives in the South. (In this course he had stiff competition from conservative Alabama Governor George Wallace). While enthusiastically pursuing his Southern strategy, Nixon played on the racial antipathies of Southern whites, criticized busing to promote school desegregation, and nominated conservative white Southerners to the Supreme Court. (During Fr. Ted's four years as chair of the Civil Rights Commission, President Nixon would spend only fifteen minutes with the Commissioners.)

On July 3, 1969, Attorney General John Mitchell and HEW Secretary Robert Finch announced that HEW would shift its enforcement emphasis on school desegregation from cutting off funds to bringing suits in federal court. The Commission opposed the substitution of legal action for fund cutoffs in dealing with unyielding segregated school districts, because the experience of the civil rights movement from 1957 to 1964 indicated that legal action was too slow and cumbersome. Fr. Ted was livid. In view of the effectiveness of both approaches, he thought the administration's action was like trading a Cadillac for a pair of roller skates. (He wrote a vigorous dissent but, he later said, the "result was so incandescent that I never published it.")

Late in the summer of 1969, the Nixon Administration, seeking support from white Southerners, joined the state of Mississippi in a lawsuit to delay the integration of schools in the South. Full compliance with desegregation, Justice Department lawyers charged, would mean wholesale busing of school children (*white* school children).[45]

The Civil Rights Commission was the first group to react to Nixon's new policy. In action unprecedented for the Commission, Fr. Ted publicly criticized Nixon's strategy of delaying school integration. The Administration had circulated "an overly optimistic, misleading and inaccurate picture of the scope of desegregation actually achieved." The nation must keep up the momentum on civil rights, he said. "We need manpower. We need fund cutoffs. But first we need commitment," inferring that the Nixon Administration wasn't committed to civil rights. "Every kid in the country stands up and says, 'One nation, under God, indivisible, with liberty and justice for all.' But for the Negro, there's neither liberty nor justice."

Administration officials, led by Attorney General Mitchell, privately denounced the Commission and its chairman, though everybody in the

Administration was careful what they said publicly about a priest. Others endorsed his stand. "Hesburgh has guts," commented a reporter in *Look*. "If a thing needs to be said, he'll say it."[46]

Civil rights workers assailed the Nixon Administration's civil rights record. "Some charge there is no administration leadership at all," noted the *Christian Science Monitor;* "others, that it is leading a retreat."

The minutes of the Commission's meeting on March 8, 1970, reflected the sad commentary Fr. Ted presented to his colleagues about the deteriorating climate for civil rights progress.

Chairman Hesburgh said that in view of recent developments in the civil rights area, the apparent change in the climate of the country, and the concern of the Commissioners and the staff members about what is happening, he thought it would be useful if we took time for everyone at the meeting to express his opinion, very briefly, about what the Commission should be doing to "turn things around."

After a year as chairman Fr. Ted would have preferred to resign from the Commission to pursue other interests, but because he was butting heads with the Nixon Administration, he couldn't bow out. "I really was staying on only because tough things had to be done, and I knew I was prepared to do them." He thought that Nixon probably assumed that the new chairman of the Commission would be easy on his Administration. "But I don't believe in being friendly when it's a question of law or right or human dignity," Fr. Ted later stated.[47]

On October 12, 1970, just three weeks before the 1970 congressional election, the Commission issued a 1,115-page report, "The Federal Civil Rights Enforcement Effort." The report criticized the federal government for failing to enforce civil rights laws. For six months the Commission had surveyed the federal government in its multiple role as employer, purchaser of goods and services, financial patron to state and local governments, and regulator of airlines, railroads, radio, television, and other industries. Wherever the panel looked, it discovered mostly failure. Rating forty departments on their effectiveness in complying with the laws, it gave almost all of them a "poor" rating. For example, the Equal Employment Opportunity Commission relied passively on injured parties to file a complaint and rarely initiated an attack on employment discrimination on its own.

Staff Director Howard Glickstein likened the failure of the federal government to implement the new civil rights laws to "building a beautiful library and not putting any books in it." The Commission urged President Nixon to exercise "courageous moral leadership" in behalf of racial justice and to set up a White House committee to oversee enforcement of civil rights laws.

When the Commission first readied its report, Administration officials urged postponement until after the 1970 congressional elections. Len Garment, special consultant to President Nixon and the Commission's contact at the White House, phoned Fr. Ted and exclaimed: "My God, what are you trying to do to us?" The report was devastating, he said, would hurt the Administration, and should be postponed until after the midterm election. But Fr. Ted persisted, telling Garment that he would not postpone the report, the Commission's action was not political, and the facts spoke for themselves. If the facts hurt, then the Administration should do something about them. "If the White House had not suggested we hold the report," a staff member later observed, "the Commissioners [might] have decided on their own that it might be prejudicial to the election to release it. But once they were asked not to, they had to release."[48]

Fr. Ted told his colleagues that "follow-up and monitoring" the effect of the report was very important. The favorable media response delighted the Commission. "We are particularly encouraged by the large number of editorials and 'think' pieces," Glickstein informed the Commissioners. To publicize the report further, Fr. Ted appeared on several television programs and held several news conferences.

At a press conference shortly after the 1970 midterm election, Fr. Ted urged the Nixon Administration to make civil rights compliance a top priority. The President should withhold funds from departments and agencies that failed to enforce civil rights laws. A decision had to be made as a nation. "We're going to have equality of opportunity, or we're not," he said. "We're either for it, or we should tell the world we're not—that we're really two countries. Let's stop being hypocritical about it."

Release of the report embarrassed and angered the Nixon Administration. An Administration spokesman criticized the Commission for its "absolute and unyielding position," and Nixon's domestic advisor John Ehrlichman snapped, "This is nothing but another sermon from Father Hesburgh." More and more clashes took place between Nixon Administration officials and the Hesburgh-led Commission. "We would say something in [a] press conference," recalled Stephen Horn, vice chairman of the Commission, then "the press would run over to Ehrlichman, and he'd say something."[49]

Len Garment and Fr. Ted shared a mutual trust. (As time went on,

Garment was about the only person in the White House Fr. Ted did completely trust.) But Garment also disagreed with Fr. Ted's criticism of the Nixon Administration. President Nixon felt strong pressure from his conservative followers to curb affirmative action, busing, and school desegregation. Garment reflected: "The tensions were inherent between the Commission . . . and myself as the political officer of the administration trying to move things along in the civil rights area, but also mindful of the very, very powerful countervailing pressures on the President from more conservative elements."

Garment thought the Commission was "politicizing" the race issue in a "brazen" way at the time of an election. "The political [problem]," observed Garment, "was that Fr. Hesburgh was a very powerful name, and when he called a press conference, when he issued a bulletin about the [Nixon] Administration and civil rights, if it wasn't a front page story, it was a page two story." The negative publicity upset Nixon and his advisors. "Every president hates to be criticized," said Garment. "[Fr. Ted] was very much a burr on the saddle of the administration."

Although he consistently maintained his civil rights convictions and issued strong indictments, Fr. Ted tried to maintain good relations with the Nixon Administration whenever possible. After a reporter for the *Washington Star* misrepresented remarks he had made, making it appear he had personally attacked President Nixon, he wrote a blistering letter to the *Star* chastising the reporter and correcting the record. He met regularly with Garment to talk about problems. He effusively praised the infrequent civil rights initiatives of the President. In May 1970, when the President asked Congress for $500 million to assist schools facing the stresses of desegregation, Fr. Ted lauded his "forthright statement." The President, he said, "has brought to bear the prestige and leadership of his office on the side of ending . . . the problem of school segregation which has been allowed to linger far too long."

In May 1971, the Commission found some progress in enforcement by the Nixon Administration. "The dinosaur finally opened one eye," Fr. Ted told a news conference on May 10. Nonetheless, the Commission also found substantial "regression" in civil rights activities in some federal agencies. Fr. Ted again blamed the slow pace of civil rights enforcement on a "lack of moral commitment" on the part of the majority of Americans and the federal government. He promised that the Commission would continue to be a "burr under the saddle" of the federal government. Meanwhile, his calls for an end to the Vietnam War and his sympathizing with peace demonstrators added to the animosity of Nixon Administration officials.[50]

"With minorities giving Mr. Nixon a mere pittance of votes in 1968 and no likelihood of much change in 1972, there just isn't any political incentive for this administration to do the things the Civil Rights Commission is demanding," observed columnist Carl Rowan. "Father Hesburgh seems to think morality, sense of justice, national interest should override the issue of personal political gain," Rowan continued. "Which may explain why priests head colleges and commissions, but they never get to reside at 1600 Pennsylvania Avenue."

In 1972 the Commission and its chairman directly took on the issue of school busing. In the wake of George Wallace's victory in the spring primary in Florida in 1972, in which opposition to busing earned Wallace much support, the Nixon Administration sought to make political capital with the issue. President Nixon announced his opposition to busing and a score of anti-busing bills and constitutional amendments were introduced into Congress.

Fr. Ted stood up for busing. In testimony before the House Judiciary Committee on March 1, he cited a staff study conducted in five cities where busing was proceeding relatively smoothly. "Outlandish activities of parents" often accounted for trouble at the start of busing, he argued, but the children usually got along well "if their elders [did] not provide them with too many disgraceful examples to follow." Busing was necessary, he said, because communities refused to abolish dual school systems and because segregated housing patterns kept minority group children in the worst schools.[51]

Busing was a "phony" issue, he kept repeating. "Busing never aroused emotions where it was done for all the wrong reasons—like the black youngsters in Wallace's Alabama who were bused 100 miles a day from Selma to Montgomery and back to attend a black vocational school when there was a lily-white vocational school where the buses left from in Selma," he said. "I remember Medgar Evers saying that his first recollection of busing was the new school buses passing him and other black children on the way to school . . . splashing them with mud as the white children on their way to a good school yelled out the window, 'Nigger! Nigger!' No objections to busing then." The issue was not busing for the sake of busing, he contended; or even busing solely to achieve racial balance. "The major issue is the kind of education available at the end of the trip."

On July 28, 1972, in trenchant testimony before the House Committee on Education and Labor, Fr. Ted criticized President Nixon's anti-busing legislation in the guise of the Equal Opportunities Education Act. It "burns the last bridge out of the ghetto," he said. It was a "racially reactionary policy which will end inevitably in disaster for all." The bill's title misrepresented its true nature. "If this measure is designed to implement the 1954 decision requiring desegregation of schools, it fails. If it is designed to move the nation towards justice, it fails. But if it was designed to [factionalize] the nation along racial lines, it succeeds."

Much of the passion generated about busing stemmed from the fear of white suburbanites that their own children would be bused into poor-quality, inner-city schools. Fr. Ted tried to address the fear. "I don't want kids bused into bad schools," he said. In July 1972, he proposed a compromise. To reduce the fears of parents who felt busing meant an inferior education, he favored a legislative provision prohibiting the busing of any child to an inferior school.[52]

Impassioned appeals for civil rights, which stirred millions in the 1960s, was now being met with a stifled yawn. "Black is boring" seemed to be the pervasive attitude among whites, and politicians carefully read the times. In 1972 Fr. Ted often sadly admitted that things were not going well for civil rights. "The country is taking a very bad turn at the moment," he said in June. "A lot of the steam has gone out of civil rights efforts. A lot of Northern liberals have become very illiberal. The fact that more than 100 congressmen can even discuss a constitutional amendment considering reversing the decision on busing is a straw in the wind that the enthusiasm of the 60s is lacking."

Civil rights was easier to support in the North in the 1960s because changes were being forced on the South. When the focus shifted to the North—to open housing, desegregation of schools by busing, equality of opportunity in employment in Northern cities and suburbs—then Northern politicians objected as strongly as Southerners had. Fr. Ted observed of the Northern position: "Not *my* neighborhood, not *my* child's school, not *my* university, not *my* club, not *my* job."[53]

By 1972, as the civil rights movement languished, the Commission itself, which included some new members appointed by President Nixon, also appeared languid. Fr. Ted raised the possibility of resigning in order to bring new initiatives and direction to the Commission, but staff members worried that if he resigned, President Nixon would replace him with someone unsympathetic to civil rights.

"When he was just a member of the Commission, he gave us a portion of his time," said a colleague. "Now, as chairman, we really feel his strength, his personality, his philosophy. He takes over. And when he speaks as a priest about conscience—about how we should be the conscience of the country in this matter of civil rights—then you feel he really knows what he is talking about. He is a priest who carries weight." John Herbers, who covered the Civil Rights Commission for *The New York Times* while Fr. Ted was chairman, agreed. "It was a matter of conscience for him," said Herbers, "and he made it clear that he was acting completely without political motivation. For example, he never used any elaborate public relations mechanism as most politically motivated individuals do. He was concerned about the institutional wrongs and believed the government must do what is right."

Fr. Ted's efforts aroused another type of reaction as well. When he pointed out that horrible social conditions in urban ghettos often caused black crime, he received scores of hateful, racist, and sometimes threatening letters reproaching him for being soft on crime. "Why are you urging crime, violence and burning?" demanded one anonymous critic. Continuing:

You no doubt have learned what happened to John Kennedy, Robert Kennedy, and Martin Luther King. It's time for you to get lost—but fast. We want to live like decent Americans and crime, violence and burning will never remedy the situation.

Wake up you stuffed toad and start reading books that will educate you. You will never make it to heaven.[54]

Fr. Ted continued to deliver strongly worded speeches. Just before the 1972 election, in an address at Union Theological Seminary, New York, on the occasion of receiving the Reinhold Neibuhr Award, he made perfectly clear his belief that America had an unfinished agenda, and the agenda was being ignored. At the "heart" of America's domestic problems was racial injustice. And "no one likes to look at the heart of darkness."

Despite all of its success, America's melting pot failed to function in one critical area: color. "Reds were murdered like wild animals. Yellows were characterized as a peril and incarcerated en masse during World War II for no really good reason by our most liberal President. Browns have been abused as the new slave labor on farms. . . ."

And the blacks. Fearing them, running away from them, isolating them, refusing to accept them, had complicated our domestic scene and given politicians the impetus to promote fear instead of faith. Political leadership was the key. "We must be willing to shuck the status quo when it is retrogressive, unjust and going nowhere. . . . We must put an end to expedient political compromises that stifle progress to gain votes."[55]

He sensed that his days were numbered as the Commission's chairman. As Nixon's first term drew to a close, he was the only original member of the Commission still serving. If Nixon replaced him, though, he indicated it would not bother him: "I've been on [the Commission] a long time, and at times have been a thorn in the administration's side."

A few days before the presidential election between Nixon and George McGovern in November 1972, *The New York Times* published Fr. Ted's long article entitled "Father Hesburgh's Program for Racial Justice." Once again he labeled busing a "phony" issue and set forth his solutions to discrimination in education, housing, and employment. For the Nixon Administration the article was the last straw.[56]

After Nixon's triumph over McGovern, the President asked for the pro-forma resignations of 2,000 high government officials, to give him flexibility to shake up the government after the election. On Monday, Nov. 13, 1972, the Commissioners were meeting in executive session. It was the 138th Commission meeting Fr. Ted had attended and his last. At 10:25 A.M. the phone rang. John Buggs, the staff director, answered. The caller, a woman secretary to Fred Malek, special assistant to the President, conveyed the message that the President was demanding the resignations of all the Commissioners (although he might not accept all the resignations). Buggs added, "He wants a letter of resignation, especially yours," nodding his head at Fr. Ted. Buggs recalled Fr. Ted's reaction to the news: "I don't think I had ever seen him get so angry. He was remarkably quiet but his face and manner revealed how he felt inside. He was deeply hurt and disturbed."

After the meeting Buggs informed Fr. Ted that the message included a demand that Hesburgh be out of his office by 6 o'clock that evening. "That got my dander up," Fr. Ted recalled in his autobiography. "I asked John to call the secretary back . . . and tell her that I had worked for four Presidents and that I understood that the President could dismiss me as chairman, but not as a member of the Commission." He was not going to leave his office by 6 P.M. He would try to be out at the end of the week.[57]

The President and his advisors were caught in an awkward dilemma.

They specifically wanted Fr. Ted's resignation, but they didn't want the adverse publicity of firing a renowned Catholic priest. If all the Commissioners resigned, then the President could select the resignations he wanted to accept and disguise his reasons for doing so. The Commissioners did resign, but the only resignation accepted was Hesburgh's.

On Thursday, November 16, Fr. Ted drafted his formal letter of resignation. White House press secretary Ronald Ziegler left no doubt that Fr. Ted had been ousted. "I am told that during the campaign he said he would resign if the President were reelected," said Ziegler. He apparently was referring to a remark Fr. Ted was quoted as making in October 1972 that he could "not survive if the President is reelected—either by his wishes or my own." Fr. Ted denied making the statement. On the evening of November 16, Fr. Ted wired the White House, refuting Ziegler's contention:

Despite recent irresponsible news articles to the contrary, I did not—repeat not—say that I would resign if President Nixon were re-elected. When asked to comment about this story at the time, I simply denied it. What I did say was that if I were asked to resign by the re-elected President, as is his privilege, I would. He did ask, and I did resign. After 15 years of service on the Civil Rights Commission, I would appreciate having the record honestly stated.[38]

In effect, Fr. Ted had been fired. Now he won praise for standing up for his principles. It was an instance of the "good guy" winning after appearing to have lost. In a letter to the *Washington Post* praising his fifteen years of service, three former staff directors of the Commission joined in saying, "A judgment from Father Hesburgh combined the intellectual and moral and the pragmatic in rare combination. His analysis always was disciplined and he realistically appraised what *could* be done as well as what *should* be done."

Commonweal thought it ironic that President Nixon, "the person in whose office are enshrined the body of the nation's ideals should sweep out first the individual who came to epitomize so many of the nation's ideals in the areas of justice, human rights and equal opportunity."

The black journal *The Crisis* saluted his "courage and dedication." *Christian Century* thought the forced resignation not only "exposes the hypocrisy of the administration's 'commitment' to the enforcement of civil rights, but also illumines the remarkable character of the president of Notre Dame University." Another "good man" had been eased out of Washington because he was a "burr under the consciences" of powerful men, Carl Rowan wrote in his syndicated column. "This is no great surprise to anyone who knows that Father Hesburgh has been wise, compassionate and courageous—unwilling to bend to the mob on issues like busing to break up Jim Crow schools, unafraid to criticize this administration for its weak civil rights efforts, or to speak loudly about the lack of moral leadership offered by President Nixon."[59]

In the weeks after his ouster Fr. Ted maintained an unaccustomed silence. He declined more than forty requests for interviews, including a network news crew that flew to Notre Dame to record his parting words. "I think it's best to leave with a little grace," he did say two weeks after the dismissal. "I suppose I'll have to hold a press conference to satisfy everyone, but that can wait a little while."

On December 20, 1972, he received a florid "Dear Ted" letter from the President in which Nixon expressed his "deep gratitude" to him for having "worked courageously and tirelessly to advance the civil rights of every American." When Nixon's letter was made public, Fr. Ted's friends and supporters were incredulous. Stephen Horn wondered if the President knew that the White House staff had sought to remove him. "I broke out in laughter when it was read during a Commission meeting," Horn said. "Ordinarily, you don't write a letter like that to someone you have just summarily dismissed."[60]

On February 12, 1973, the Civil Rights Commission held a reception at the Ambassador Hotel in Washington to say goodby to their chairman. The commissioners were wary about talking to reporters concerning his dismissal; Commissioner Maurice Mitchell came closest to addressing his ouster: "We would be happier if you were retiring because of old age instead of because somebody doesn't like what you say." Fr. Ted gave a big bearhug to Len Garment, the White House civil rights advisor, who made a brief appearance. Garment came, he said, "to say goodbye to my friend."

The Commission's staff gave Fr. Ted a neon orange hunting jacket "so your enemies will see you and know whom to shoot, and your friends will recognize you and know not to shoot." His emotional farewell speech drew sustained, standing ovation. "All of us . . . in this room [have] tried to make America a leader of nations in what nations desperately need—justice and peace," he said. "Let's do it. Without bitterness, without rancor, with firmness and courage, but especially in our heart of hearts with love for one another. Because then, somehow, peace will come."[61]

After Fr. Ted's dismissal, the Nixon Administration left the chairman's position vacant for sixteen months. His dismissal weakened the

Commission's moral and political influence. No one else on the Commission could match his stature; no one else could galvanize public opinion and influence Congress the way he did. "In the absence of Hesburgh," said Commissioner Manuel Ruiz, "the Commission was leaderless for a great period of time. Naturally, there was confusion."

Subsequently, Fr. Ted did comment on his dismissal. From 1957 to 1972 he had spent about 700 days working on civil rights for the federal government. He was ready to retire from the Commission. "I was delighted to have a little peace for a change," he said. He thought he could have gotten along better with President Nixon had it not been for the key advisors to the President. "They were pretty nasty, at least in my dealings with them." Key people in the Nixon Administration did not have a "heart" for the poor, he thought. "They bent over backwards to help the milk industry, ITT, Vesco . . . but if you happened to be poor or black they'd say, 'What can he do for us?'" He understood why he was fired. "I was pushing [Nixon] very hard," he said with a smile. "I think if I were President, I probably would have fired me, too."[62]

His fifteen years of work on the Commission won applause at Notre Dame. Faculty with widely diverse political views nonetheless agreed in assessing his civil rights career. "I'm really proud to be part of a university with a president who [showed] that kind of leadership," said liberal Professor John Houck. With respect to civil rights, commented conservative Professor Ralph McInerny, Fr. Ted "was a great leader—a hero." Fr. Ted was a good example for Notre Dame's students as well. By spending fifteen years on the Commission he taught students far more about the need to be concerned with human rights than if he had lectured them on the subject.

For liberal Democratic Congressman John Brademas, who represented the South Bend area, it was vitally important to have his most prominent and respected constituent as an ally in the civil rights cause. Although Brademas's district was only 6 percent black, he voted consistently for civil rights bills. Because Fr. Ted was a "moral conscience" in the civil rights field, Brademas felt more confident supporting crucial civil rights bills, which "otherwise would have been very difficult."[63]

A spell of coldness set in between Nixon and Fr. Ted, and after the Watergate scandal surfaced, Fr. Ted publicly branded Nixon's cohorts as "a bunch of hucksters." For some years after Watergate Fr. Ted had perched on his desk a plastic coffee cup that someone had given him. Inside the plastic liner of the cup was a three-dollar bill with Nixon's picture on it. "We had to remove it every time we took a picture in his office because we didn't want it to show up," said Richard Conklin.[64]

However, when a researcher called and asked for a list of embarrassing questions on civil rights that television personality David Frost could ask Nixon during his first in-depth interview after Watergate, Fr. Ted declined. "Nixon was down and out," he explained, "and I don't believe in kicking somebody who's down." Subsequently, he extended an olive branch to Nixon, and their relationship became more cordial. When Fr. Ted spoke at a dinner at the Waldorf-Astoria in New York, Presidents Nixon and Ford were both in attendance. Ford had many friends and speaker after speaker began, "President Ford, President Nixon . . ." "It did not seem right to me," Fr. Ted reflected in his autobiography. "When I approached the podium, I paused to shake hands, first with Nixon, then with Ford, and when I began my talk, I addressed Nixon first." It was a minor gesture, but Nixon seemed gratified. From then on Nixon sent Fr. Ted copies of his books, and Fr. Ted responded with gracious letters. In 1985, after receiving a copy of Nixon's new book, *No More Vietnams*, Fr. Ted commented: "[All] of us appreciate the fact that you continue to address these thorny problems without ducking the tough issues that must be faced." In closing he added: "I have heard that Pat is having some health problems. Do tell her that I keep both of you in my Mass daily for all blessings."

Fr. Ted didn't believe he had the option of holding a grudge or not forgiving. "I think I've got to love everybody. I don't have to like everybody because that's kind of hard to do." As one gets older, he wrote in his autobiography, "it becomes more apparent that forgiving and forgetting is much better than holding grudges. Besides, it is more Christian."[65]

5 ⌒ BECOMING A LEGEND, 1973–1987

IN 1968 a study of 6200 Notre Dame undergraduates found that more than half came from all-male Catholic high schools and had not been in day-to-day casual contact with young women since they were thirteen years old. Notre Dame's all-male atmosphere sometimes produced crude, raunchy behavior. Walking across campus with a young woman on a Saturday night caused embarrassment. "[Students] yell obscenities from dorm windows," a senior physics student complained in 1969. "Somehow they prove their masculinity by insulting women." Fr. Ted was disgusted when a woman walked across the mall and students acted like it was "feeding time at the monkey house—all those whoops and hollers!"

Until 1965, the few women who had studied at Notre Dame had been members of religious orders or in the Graduate School. In 1965 a Co-Exchange Program started with nearby St. Mary's College. Notre Dame students could take some courses at St. Mary's, and St. Mary's students could do the same at Notre Dame. But this involved only a small number of students. By the late 1960s male students at Notre Dame were pushing for coeducation, arguing that it was a more normal environment for learning. Hoping to ease the strained social life of the students, Fr. Ted blessed the movement to bring more women onto the campus. "All-male education is a thing of the past," he said in 1969. "In the last century practically all the colleges that have been started have been coeducational."

The most logical step to implement coeducation was to merge with St. Mary's College. By the fall of 1970, the merger of the two schools seemed probable. A joint committee was busily studying the integration of faculty, curricula, and building space, and in May 1971, the trustees of both schools ratified proposals for unification. However, six months later both institutions changed their minds and announced that they were breaking off merger negotiations. (Financial and logistical factors were the primary reasons the merger fell through.)[1]

Notre Dame still proceeded with its decision for coeducation, and on December 1, 1971, Fr. Ted officially announced that Notre Dame would admit women the following academic year. In the fall of 1972, the university admitted 365 women to a student body of 6357. The three major television networks were on hand to record that the "male bastion" of Notre Dame had given way. The ratio of men to women dropped from 17:1 in 1972 to 4:1 in 1975 to 3:1 in 1987.

Taking on the role of leading advocate of coeducation, Fr. Ted sold it successfully to the alumni from coast to coast. "The integration of women into an all-male institution," observed Notre Dame historian Thomas Schlereth, "previously run by men for men, went remarkably smoothly." There were a few problems. Efforts to revise the famous Notre Dame Fight Song to "sons and daughters" were met with boos and laughter. More important, some female professors complained about alleged salary inequities, a patriarchal administration and bureaucracy, and discrimination in hiring, promotion, and tenure. A group of female faculty filed a sex discrimination case against the university, which was settled out of court in 1981.[2]

For the most part, coeducation provided wider dimensions of intellectual and social experience for both men and women students. The women at Notre Dame evolved from a novelty to partners with men in learning. "Stereotypes between the sexes are still cited as a social problem at the university," said an article in the student newspaper in 1987, fifteen years after the change, "but they are a social problem of society itself, and not unique to Notre Dame." Living and studying together, the men and women increased their sensitivity and insight.

"Coeducation has had a marvelous effect on Notre Dame," Fr. Ted believed. The university had broadened its commitment to educate "the other half of the human race." The admission of women substantially increased the number of applicants, enabling the university to raise its admission standards and improve the quality of its students. "Our women students brought a good measure of gentility to the campus and enhanced the family feeling of it," Fr. Ted thought. "With women actually there, the men could stop thinking about them as a breed apart. It soon became clear that the presence of the women created a much more normal and healthier atmosphere on campus."[3]

In 1970 the Board of Trustees, to provide Fr. Ted with administrative support, created the new position of provost, the second-ranking executive officer of the university. Upon Fr. Ted's recommendation, the Board appointed Fr. James Burtchaell, C.S.C. to the post. Fr. Burtchaell had joined the Notre Dame faculty in 1966 and had been chairman of the Department of Theology from 1968 to 1970. Energetic, dynamic, a brilliant and enlightened teacher and writer, Fr. Burtchaell seemed an ideal choice. He was to be Fr. Ted's protégé and, most assumed, after sufficient seasoning would succeed to the presidency. But the plan went badly awry, causing embarrassment and bitterness.[4]

While in the post from 1970 to 1977, Fr. Burtchaell attracted talented scholars, tightened tenure requirements, and inaugurated new academic programs, winning respect from some at Notre Dame. Increasingly, though, influential trustees and Fr. Ted were uneasy with him, particularly with his abrasive personality. Regarded by some as arrogant, condescending, and undiplomatic, Fr. Burtchaell alienated many faculty and trustees. The last straw occurred in 1977. When faculty members pushed for unionization, the Board of Trustees sought to bring in anti-union specialists from a Chicago law firm to fight the move. Fr. Burtchaell objected, insisting he could handle it himself. The Board of Trustees disagreed and insisted on his resignation. The Board wanted him to remain in his position through the 1977–78 academic year, but the forty-three-year-old priest, not wanting to be a lame duck, resigned suddenly on August 25, 1977.

Fr. Ted felt terrible about the Burtchaell tragedy, since it had been his idea to install him in the first place, but he kept mum publicly except to praise Burtchaell for his service. "It was an awkward situation for everyone involved," concluded a trustee, one of many reluctant to discuss publicly the sensitive dismissal. "It was a very painful, difficult situation, and the scar tissue is borne by everyone."[5]

Throughout the 1970s and 1980s Fr. Ted spent considerable time running to airplanes, working for foundations, boards, presidential commissions, and a variety of humanitarian causes. In 1961 he had been elected to the Board of the Rockefeller Foundation, and his twenty years of service on the board stimulated his interest in development. The foundation had been incorporated in 1913 by John D. Rockefeller, Sr., and given a sweeping mandate to "promote the well-being of mankind throughout the world." At first the foundation emphasized health and medicine, leading to programs attacking infectious diseases (such as malaria and yellow fever), through health education, research, and training. It also pioneered in working for population control and supported the humanities and the arts. One of the country's wealthiest foundations, in 1979 it listed assets of $776 million.[6]

The foundation's support of agricultural research most impressed Fr. Ted. Begun in the 1940s, the research had led to the development of high-yielding grains and the "green revolution" of the 1950s and 1960s. Several times he visited the International Rice Research Institute at Los Banos in the Philippines, an exceptionally successful Rockefeller Foundation project. The institute gathered 250 of the best species of rice and genetically crossed them to get the best hybrids for different climates and water conditions. He marveled that the scientists were able to completely re-engineer the plant genetically so it didn't grow too high and fall over, and even shortened its growing period so it yielded two or three crops instead of one. The result was a spectacular increase in rice cultivation in Asia.

He much preferred the self-help approach to problems in developing nations and fondly quoted Mohandas Ghandi on development: "Give me a fish and I eat today. Teach me how to fish and I eat every day." It was common sense to adopt the self-help approach: "We just can't consider that the world will always be waiting on American handouts. That's not the way to run it." Secular foundations were more realistic reformers than the Catholic Church, he said. For years the Church thought that charity was "giving out things." The rich gave their old cast-off clothing to the poor and handed out extra food. "Poor people weren't getting much more than crumbs." But the Rockefeller Foundation used more effective methods. Instead of giving away food, as the Church did, they sought to multiply crops five or six times with better seed, fertilizer, and insect and rodent control. The best thing a person can do in development, he said, "is do yourself out of a job."[7]

When David Rockefeller, CEO of the Chase Manhattan Bank and grandson of John D. Rockefeller, Sr., asked him to serve on Chase's Board of Directors, Fr. Ted laughed. Never having had a course in economics, or money, or banking and not even owning a bank account, what could he contribute? "We don't want you on the Board to teach us about banking," explained Rockefeller. The bank sometimes encountered complex moral and ethical problems, Rockefeller told him. "I would like you to represent the conscience of the Board." Fr. Ted accepted and served on the Board for nine years (1972–81).

As a board member, he received generous fees—amounting to about $12,000 in 1975—which he put into a special fund to assist people in need, particularly students at Notre Dame. Since he knew nothing about the maze of banking regulations, he appreciated legal assistance from Chase officials. "As the latest babe in the woods," he worried to an official in 1972, "I trust you are keeping me legal with the SEC."[8]

Some liberals accused him of cozying up to the corporate world. It was "unwise" for Fr. Ted to become a member of Chase's Board, charged Professor Peter Walshe of Notre Dame. "Such a degree of intimacy with mammon was bound to compromise the prophetic witness a Christian university should be giving." On the other hand, when David Rockefeller explained that Fr. Ted had renounced material wealth, a critic grumbled, "We stockholders have not taken a vow of poverty."[9]

Once on the board, Fr. Ted sought to learn more about money, particularly its enormous importance in the process of development. In order to establish a more just economic order, he needed to understand international monetary policy. "I've always been a little skittish about many religious reformers who are naive about the thing they're trying to reform. They don't know as much as they should know about economics, finance, or development policy." He didn't want to be naive. "The problems of the world are too complicated to hand over to amateurs just because they have good motivation."

Although a neophyte on banking, Fr. Ted's extensive knowledge of foreign countries allowed him to give incisive advice to bank officials and fellow board members. "He had a better knowledge of international activities of all kinds [political, social, and economic] than probably anyone in the United States," observed a fellow board member. "He was highly respected by David Rockefeller."[10]

As anticipated, Fr. Ted did address moral and ethical issues. His overall effectiveness is unknown, but he did attempt to be the board's moral weather vane. When David Rockefeller referred a moral or ethical problem to him at a board meeting, his first response was to gather and understand the facts. "Is this the problem?" Then he would try to define the moral principle that applied to the specific situation. "I didn't claim any infallibility," he reflected on his role.

He understood that bankers were oriented toward what bankers were supposed to be oriented toward—profitability. But he also found them open to moral and ethical suggestions. At one meeting discussion emphasized the services the bank provided; then, offhandedly, members made a final point about the bank's social responsibility. "You better make that statement of social responsibility very, very strong, very pointed, and very specific," he interjected, "because the other preceding points could apply just as well to the Mafia." The Mafia also tried to jettison unprofitable businesses, enhance profitable ones, and maximize business opportunities. "The fact is that you get your whole character from the final point—it says what kind of corporation you are, that you're interested in social responsibility, that you're going to be a responsible citizen both here and abroad."[11]

Besides providing moral input, Fr. Ted sought to educate as well. On September 22, 1978, he enclosed his most recent travel diary for David Rockefeller's inspection. He specifically asked Rockefeller to note in the diary the deplorable human rights violations he witnessed in South Africa and South Korea. The diary was long, he advised in his cover letter, "but the first part on South Africa may be a special interest to you. Also, the part on [South] Korea and the poet Kim, of which there is a paragraph on Page 142 and a continuation on Page[s] 146 to 149."

A vice president at Chase regularly solicited Fr. Ted's evaluation of articles on business ethics and values. On business trips with Chase officials, Fr. Ted invited them to his daily Mass and preached his homily on the importance of maintaining high ethical standards in business and banking.

Not defensive about his role with Chase Manhattan, he observed in 1976: "Our many New York branches have 36 percent minority employment, high for a bank, and we are involved in about a dozen international development funds overseas." The projects generally were not profitable, but were enormously helpful.

When critics charged that his association with American business legitimized activities of multinationals, Fr. Ted responded that while he supported U.S. foreign aid to help develop poor countries, the U.S.

contribution was far too small, and he deplored its frequent misuse for political gain. In his view multinational corporations helped underdeveloped countries by providing jobs, organizing corporations, marketing expertly and operating efficiently. A "good" multinational with the right motivation could do more for world development than most governments, including the U.S. But multinationals should pay a fee to the host country, he believed; the people who own the resources ought to get a fair share of the profits.[12]

From 1971 to 1982 Fr. Ted was Chairman of the Board of the Overseas Development Council (ODC). There he worked closely with James Grant, an economist, lawyer, and the founder and the president of ODC. A private, nonprofit foundation formed in 1969 and headquartered in Washington, D.C., ODC acted as an advocate in the United States for development in the Third World. Through research and education, it sought to influence U.S. policymakers and all citizens not to neglect the pressing problems of underdeveloped countries. Initially focused mainly on foreign aid issues, ODC broadened its scope by 1980 to include energy and the environment. Research projects in 1980 included an analysis of the World Bank, alternative policies toward population growth, and a multi-year interdisciplinary analysis of Mexican-U.S. relations. Authoritative, widely respected, the ODC was one of the most effective institutions in the United States as a source of information about Third World countries.

Fr. Ted was expected to be the "political executive," the person with prestige and clout. To advance the ODC agenda he inspected projects, gave speeches, wrote articles, held news conferences, and appeared on television. In April 1974, on the "Today Show," reporter Frank McGee asked him why Americans should assist underdeveloped countries. "[We] ought to do it because it's the right thing to do," Fr. Ted replied. "It's being human; it's being Christian. . . . [It's] doing the kind of thing that human beings ought to do, being compassionate toward each other."[13]

In 1974 he warned that a world food crisis was emerging in poor countries that would make the simultaneous energy crisis seem like a picnic. An energy crisis in the United States was an inconvenience; a food crisis in a poor country was a catastrophe. "If you run out of gas," he said on April 9, during a luncheon speech that received extensive publicity, "you can't go on a picnic in the country but if you run out of food, you die." Overfed Americans should look ahead, start using "a little moral leadership." The forty poorest nations of the world needed an additional $15 billion to pay for more food, fertilizer, and fuel. The food crisis was the "moral imperative of our day."

"I thought he did a superb job," reflected Grant on Fr. Ted's role. "He clearly is a person dedicated to the concept that this rough, tough world we are in must become—and can become—a better and more humanistic world."[14]

On the U.S. Civil Rights Commission, Fr. Ted had dealt with domestic injustice, and the effort stimulated his interest in global injustice. For him it was a small step from justice at home to justice abroad. Justice was the name of peace, he often said. "You'll never have peace without justice."

In the late 1950s, during his early years on the Civil Rights Commission, Fr. Ted had supported equality of opportunity when he addressed basic human needs and rights. Two decades later he had modified his view. When there was a very wide separation between groups of people or between nations, some affirmative action was needed to close the opportunity gap.

Otherwise, equality of opportunity means equal opportunity to start a race in which everyone is well trained, except the poor fellow who has never run before. He now has an equal opportunity to compete, but he is simply not competitive because of past prejudicial practices. This would certainly argue for some concessional help and preferential treatment on the part of the very poorest of the poor, either among nations or within nations. I should think that would be understood and supported by any concept of American fairness.

During the primary elections in the spring of 1976, Fr. Ted publicly charged that the presidential contenders in both parties had been seriously remiss in not discussing global economic and political issues. It was shocking, he said at an ODC press conference, that the only discussion of foreign issues focused on detente with Russia "and the personality of Henry Kissinger." Asked by a reporter what he wanted the candidates to say, he responded: "I'd like them to speak to the idealism of the American people and demand some sacrifices." He cited a study showing that U.S. foreign aid in 1974 totalled $3.4 billion, about equal to the $3.3 billion Americans spent on flowers, seeds, and potted plants, and about one third of the $9.2 billion spent on toilet articles.

Most of the people of the world were not free. Some were not free politically, governed by regimes that denied basic liberties. But there were other ways in which freedom was denied.

Others were so economically poor that freedom was meaningless. Their real problem was to get enough food to survive, or a house for shelter, or meaningful work to earn enough to provide for food and shelter when it was available for a price. Then there were a billion people who were not free because they were illiterate, cut off from all the human culture and learning of centuries of human development in literature, history, science, and art. Ignorance for them was a very real kind of slavery. Last of all, to be perfectly honest, there were those who lacked even elemental justice regarding their lives—political outcasts. They were killed, imprisoned, tortured, exiled, and mistreated in every inhuman way.

He strongly preferred reform to revolution. Capitalist institutions were very difficult to reform, but violent revolution usually made matters worse. In the 1960s, he argued, the great civil rights laws reformed U.S. apartheid.

Assessing Fr. Ted's thoughts on development, the writer Gary MacEoin observed: "Even if one has reservations at times about the profundity and accuracy of the analysis, the sincerity and the level of achievement are impressive. Here is a man who illustrates the continuing value of commitment, openness, civility, readiness to serve, and profoundly humane integrity."

While traveling throughout the world he had often observed hunger and famine at close range. Anguish almost overwhelmed him when he saw the emaciated children and adults in Senegal, Mauritania, and Mali. "I looked into the faces of hungry men, women, and children living on the edge of the desert. After four years of practically no rainfall, their animals had all died, depriving them of milk and meat and their whole nomadic way of life. Here one learns that behind the dismal statistics there is a human condition that demands a solution. . . . There are few sights more heart rending than human beings without food or drink. One understands, in seeing them, the premium the good Lord placed on feeding the hungry and giving drink to the thirsty."[15]

Developed nations tolerated incredible injustices, he thought. "We in the northern part of this globe worry about overproducing Ph.D.'s; many children in the Southern Hemisphere never enter a school. We speak of heart and kidney transplants; they never see a doctor from birth to death. Half the children already born in the poorest countries will die before the age of five. We are often overfed and overweight; they are undernourished from birth. . . . We travel anywhere on earth, now supersonically, in hours; they are trapped for a miserable lifetime in urban or rural slums. We spend more annually on foolish armaments, devilishly devised to destroy life, than they have annually available to maintain life."[16]

Mountains of injustice did not leave him wringing his hands. "One gets the feeling," wrote the *Chicago Tribune* in 1978, that "he would grab his perpetually packed satchel and head for the door if he suspected some mover and shaker would implement the plan he has." He was preaching the need for international human rights long before Congress or President Jimmy Carter discovered it, and he strongly endorsed Carter's human rights campaign. In turn, early in his administration President Carter was an unabashed supporter of Fr. Ted, seeking his counsel, offering him a place in the State Department, and appearing at Notre Dame three times in slightly more than a year.

Notre Dame's spring commencement ceremony in 1977 was a deliberate endorsement of Carter's human rights program. Notre Dame awarded honorary degrees to Bishop Donal Lamont, who had been ousted from Rhodesia; Stephen Cardinal Kim, who fought against the repressive policies of the South Korean government; and Paul Cardinal Arnes who criticized human rights violations in Brazil. (Soviet dissident Alexander Solzhenitsyn had also been offered an honorary degree but politely declined.) President Carter was the commencement speaker and delivered a strongly worded endorsement of human rights around the world.[17]

Fr. Ted defended Carter from the charge that applying human rights to U.S. foreign policy was naive and impractical. The U.S. was not founded by pragmatic people, he insisted. For the first time since World War II, the U.S. had the Soviets on the defensive. "And for the first time in ages, Americans are giving young people around the world a new ideological choice they cannot get from Communism—mainly freedom and respect for human rights. . . . It may be troublesome at times, but so was the Declaration of Independence in 1776, and we were a poor and impotent newborn nation then. Should we be less idealistic and courageous now?"

He blamed "cynical people," particularly in the media, for labeling Carter's ideas as simplistic, naive, and counterproductive. "I don't think the Declaration of Independence is counter-productive. I think it's a great idea and I think [Carter is] bringing it back to life again and I think he's right and the people that are criticizing him are dead wrong."

Fr. Ted's human rights positions received mixed reviews from foreign policy experts. In 1979 Professor John P. Armstrong, an Asian expert from Bowdoin College, hoped "Father Hesburgh will climb down from his pulpit long enough to show us how we might apply his moral principles." But Kenneth W. Thompson, political scientist and foreign policy expert, contended Fr. Ted spoke for a respected tradition in American thought, "that of moral idealism." (On reflection Fr. Ted said of Jimmy Carter: "I do not think he was a good manager, and that probably is what did him in. He had very good ideas and I think he was a very sincere person.")[18]

One of Fr. Ted's least successful endeavors hopelessly embroiled him in divisive national and international politics. For two weeks in August 1979, Vienna played host to the U.N. Conference on Science and Technology for Development. The conference, the last in a series of U.N. "megaconferences" held in the 1970s on food, housing, women, and the environment, attracted 4000 delegates from 160 countries. Included among the seventy members of the U.S. delegation were scientists, university presidents and deans, business leaders from major corporations, federal government officials, and two dozen Senators and Representatives.

President Carter selected Fr. Ted to head the U.S. delegation to the Conference and appointed him as an ambassador. When he was sworn in as U.S. ambassador, someone remarked that he was the first priest to serve in the role. Because he believed that a priest was a mediator, he felt comfortable. True, he was not mediating between God and humans, his normal role; but an ambassador mediates between humans. "Mediation is a frame of mind, as well as a professional task," he said. Unfortunately this time in his mediating role he would confront unsurmountable barriers.

Jean Wilkowski, former ambassador to Zambia, was assigned as Fr. Ted's coordinator. She and her staff collected recommendations from U.S. interest groups and supervised the writing of the U.S. position paper. During three years of preparation for the conference, Fr. Ted attended meetings throughout the world and at the U.N.; he also made about twelve trips to Washington, D.C. As usual, he won the respect of his chief assistant. Wilkowski thought her boss was organized, supportive, and imaginative. "We got along famously," she said.

The conference encountered numerous problems. A worldwide economic recession faced developed nations, making them less likely to accommodate developing countries. In the U.S. several pitfalls emerged, including the apathy of the U.S. public, the declining credibility of the U.N. with the American people, and fears by organized labor that the conference was a big giveaway at its expense. Through no fault of Fr. Ted, friction developed within the U.S. delegation. The scientific members complained they were along for window dressing.

The conference issues were almost impossibly complex, contradictory, and intensely political. Rich developed countries overwhelmingly controlled science and technology; poverty characterized the developing countries. Anti-American attitudes dominated the conference. The developing countries, represented by the so-called Group of 77, made strong economic demands on the U.S. and other developed countries, demands that the U.S. Congress would never accept. At Vienna they sought $2 billion in aid immediately and $4 billion within a decade, plus establishment of a science-and-technology-for-development office at the U.N. General Assembly, where their voting power lay. Through two weeks the conference played itself out amid a "drifting smog of skepticism, cynicism and rhetoric."

Fr. Ted was one of the major "spiritual" presences at the conference. "The choice of Hesburgh was a deft one for the U.S.," a reporter observed, "whose unhappy group . . . needed as its chief negotiator a person bound by holy oath to seek and tell the truth."

"Why did you send your Father Hesburgh to Vienna?" a Middle Eastern correspondent demanded of an American reporter. (A French journalist had earlier asked the same question.)

"He is not representative of U.S. attitudes. He is not committed to U.S. policies.

"Your Father Hesburgh *believes* in a better world," said the Middle Eastern correspondent. "He knows the sacrifices that are required. If we demanded that he tear his heart out—and if it would make a difference—he would do it.

"But surely one man—not even an angel, not even Father Hesburgh—cannot turn around U.S. positions."

At the conference Fr. Ted eloquently expressed his personal concern about the problems of developing nations:

Science and technology are not the guarantors of civilization; they only guarantee the possibility of civilization. Fast cars or fast breeders, synthetics or cybernetics, do not a civilization make. Unless our existence reaches beyond the frivolities of materialism and becomes a life enriched with meaning, science and technology will not be hallmarks of progress; they will only be the trappings of modernity. The pursuit of scientific excellence must be based upon the pursuit of human goals.

Can the world call itself civilized, he asked, "When one-fourth of this earth's population lives in abject poverty, starving, idle and numbed by ignorance? When in this century alone over one-hundred million people have fallen victim to wars? When millions today are denied their basic human rights because of their political convictions, religious beliefs, ethnic origin or economic status?"

Nonetheless, the conference ensnared Fr. Ted in a major inconsistency, caused by his normal role as critic and his current capacity as defender of U.S. interests. For two decades he had indicted the U.S. for its meager assistance to undeveloped countries; now Ambassador Hesburgh was forced to defend U.S. foreign aid from the harsh criticism of the Group of 77. The U.S. was, indeed, committed to foreign aid, he stated at the conference, arguing that since 1950 the U.S. had put up more than $100 billion for the cause and therefore had nothing to apologize for.

President Carter did not make the conference a priority, not sensing any political advantage in it. Fr. Ted complained privately that Carter's statements about the conference were mere "banalities." That Carter spent only fifteen minutes with Fr. Ted discussing the conference infuriated Wilkowski. "I thought President Carter treated him shabbily," recalled Wilkowski. "[Fr. Ted] had taken this appointment, given so much of his time, and done it so well, under lots of hardships, and Carter gives him fifteen minutes!"

Despite protracted negotiations, the conference failed to agree on crucial points, such as a code of conduct for multinational corporations producing goods in foreign countries. The result was a disappointment to Fr. Ted. Politics in the U.S. and politics within the U.N. had ruined it.[19]

Far more successful was Fr. Ted's intense and heartrending effort to improve the plight of the miserable Cambodians. In late December 1978, the Vietnamese government launched a lightning military offensive against the brutal Pol Pot regime controlling Cambodia (Kampuchea) driving Pol Pot and his Khmer Rouge to seek safety in the remote jungle near the border of Thailand. A new pro-Vietnamese government headed by Heng Samrin was established in Cambodia. A year of unprecedented movement of people followed the military offensive, causing severe refugee problems. In Cambodia homes were devastated, the countryside was barren, and towns were without functioning services or administration. Said one authority: "Masses of people, undernourished and worn out by [Pol Pot's] four years of slavery, criss-crossed the nation seeking reunion with their families. Stocks of rice, including seed rice, were eaten and food supplies ran low."

Thousands sought refuge and food on the border of Thailand. Worried about the potential for immense disruption, the government of Thailand closed its borders. In April 1979, thousands of Cambodian refugees were returned or forced back at the border, where many died from hunger, neglect, or violence. By late October 1979, it had become apparent that the fanatical Pol Pot had exterminated millions of Cambodians, targeting the educated and professional population, and that millions more were dying from starvation, disease, and the ravages of war.

Nightly television brought the plight of Cambodians to Americans. Telecasts featured starving Cambodian women and children—"wide-eyes, shrunken, bones draped with sagging flesh"—struggling to cross mined borders to the relative safety of Thailand. The President's wife, Rosalynn Carter, making Cambodian relief her special cause, visited refugee camps along the Thai border. While there she was photographed with a dying baby in her arms, thereby dramatizing the urgency of the crisis.[20]

At James Grant's urging, Fr. Ted assembled forty religious and relief organization leaders in the board room of the Overseas Development Council. Within two hours they agreed on a relief plan for Cambodia, and the entire group went to the White House, where they met for twenty minutes with President Carter in the Cabinet Room. On October 24, 1979, with Fr. Ted appearing at his side, President Carter pledged $69 million for the relief effort; that was later increased to $106 million by various acts of Congress and the Administration. At an international conference in November, other Western countries pledged another $210 million.

While urging President Carter to act, Fr. Ted starkly compared the Cambodian crisis to a similar crisis earlier in the twentieth century:

In the thirties and the early forties, a Holocaust took place, a brutal effort to exterminate a people, in which millions suffered torture and death. Many of us stood by then, excused ourselves later on the ground that we did not know the extent of what was going on, and vowed that we would never again concur passively in the attempt to destroy a nation. But what has taken place in Cambodia is nothing less than a mass assault on the basic human right to life. We cannot say that we do not know this, and we cannot let this suffering continue. We must not permit political, financial, or technical difficulties to bring about another Holocaust.

Fr. Ted became co-chair of the National Cambodian Crisis Committee, an umbrella organization of more than thirty private voluntary groups, which raised an additional $70 million from private sources in a few months. Cambodia was, in Fr. Ted's words, being forced "back to the Stone Age." Pol Pot's regime had executed over one million of the eight million living in the country; 100,000 orphans roamed about; schools hadn't operated for four years; transportation had broken down; medical facilities were nonexistent, and no rice seeds had been planted.

Determined, resolute, and zealous, he urged assistance for the desperate Cambodians. "I'm perfectly willing to ride the lead truck and get shot at in the process," he said, "rather than sit back and have it on my conscience that I did nothing to stop a second Holocaust."[21]

He wrote hundreds of letters requesting support from leaders in government, business, and the media. Seeking a "high level of national visibility," he contacted the editors of leading magazines, trying to solicit their support for a multi-magazine project for simultaneous articles on Cambodia. Offering suggestions to Lenore Hershey, editor of the *Ladies Home Journal*, he wrote:

The psychological conditions of an uprooted people, eyewitness accounts of the genocide and starvation of the past five years, heroic relief efforts underway, the forecast of another famine to come—these are but a few of the angles from which stories can be drawn.

In July 1980, Fr. Ted journeyed to Cambodia to judge for himself the effectiveness of the ten-month international relief effort. On Sunday, July 20, he arrived in Bangkok, Thailand, and the next day joined an Australian Air Force relief flight into Cambodia, a perilous journey few Americans had made in recent years. In Cambodia he carefully analyzed the food and nutritional situation, food distribution, the care of orphans, widows, and the handicapped, health care, and educational supplies. He coordinated his efforts with officials of UNICEF, the Red Cross, and various American and European Christian organizations.

He traveled about the country in a Land Rover and was protected by two young Vietnamese soldiers carrying AK-47 Russian automatic rifles. "I have never been on a worse road in my life," he wrote in his diary on July 22. "It used to be a good macadam, but due to the war passing through here, the road literally was destroyed about every 100 yards. This means a continual series of ditches and bumps and potholes, so that it's impossible to go more than five or ten miles an hour most of the time." A reporter was astonished at the fortitude he displayed as their entourage traveled the rough roads: "Father Hesburgh . . . doesn't complain of the length of the journey or of the chaos, thirst or lack of food provisions. He only expresses admiration for the wounded Kampuchean people and his indignation as we cross devastated towns and villages."

Fr. Ted visited a Pol Pot extermination camp where thousands of women and children had been interrogated, tortured, and executed, but he offered no reflections or commentaries to reporters. Back in Bangkok, though, a reporter witnessed his "saintly anger" explode at the brutality of Pol Pot's regime. He was angry and mystified that the U.S. and other countries continued to support Pol Pot's regime as Cambodia's official representation in the United Nations. "Whether or not we support the present [pro-Vietnamese] regime in Phnom Penh," he argued, "at least we should not have anything to do with the Khmer Rouge who have proved themselves to be as bad as Hitler." He hoped the U.S. would be on the side of "justice and redevelopment" and would not use children as "bargaining chips."[22]

He publicly disagreed with U.S. diplomats, including the U.S. ambassador in neighboring Thailand, who had contended that the food and seed sent to Cambodia had been commandeered by the Vietnamese army and was not getting to the needy. He had seen plenty of evidence that supplies were being delivered. "Anyone would have to be blind to travel this road, which few people have done, and not to see that not only are the people beyond the starvation stage and fairly well fed at present, but are striving mightily to put in the crops which will assure their feeding the months ahead after the November harvest."

In the course of his tour he had an encounter with King Bhumibol of Thailand, who told him that there were "political" obstacles to solving the refugee problem on Thailand's border. In his diary Fr. Ted described his reaction to the king's fears. "I responded that when politics rise above humanitarianism, then civilization faces disaster." The King had noticed in the newspapers that Fr. Ted had urged rescinding recognition of the Pol Pot regime by the U.N. "He asked me why I said this,"

Upon receiving the Jefferson Award from the Council for Advancement and Support of Education, Fr. Hesburgh accepts a bouquet of thanks from a Cambodian girl for his fundraising efforts to ward off starvation in her country.

Fr. Ted wrote. "I told him that if Hitler were to be reincarnated and re-instated in the political order, we should not do business with him and I felt the same, if not more strongly, about the Pol Pot regime." With a twinkle in his eye, the King responded that Fr. Ted was accusing him and others of insanity for supporting Pol Pot's recognition. "I said that there was another kind of insanity with which I agreed, namely, being just and right, no matter what the opposition or the criticism."[23]

A reporter quizzed him about his controversial conclusion that America's recent enemy, the Communist Vietnamese, were effectively cooperating with the giant international relief effort. "As a Catholic, aren't you afraid . . . of being accused of supporting the setting up of a Communist regime?" asked the reporter. Fr. Ted replied: "If Christianity means anything, I think it means helping our brothers and sisters who-ever they may be. When someone is hungry, you don't ask him what his political beliefs are, you give him something to eat."

On his return to the United States, he lauded the international relief effort. "I returned from Cambodia full of hope," he wrote Lane Kirk-land, president of the AFL-CIO. Food and supplies were being distrib-uted; rice seed provided by relief agencies was planted and growing; star-vation and epidemics had been avoided. Much still needed to be done, he wrote in the *Los Angeles Times* on August 28, 1980. "But, whereas last fall despair permeated this small and once-gentle land, now there is hope. And where there was near total devastation, now there is rejuvena-tion." He was intensely proud of his efforts for Cambodian relief. "We literally saved that people from extinction," he later wrote a colleague.[24]

Fr. Ted also accepted presidential appointments to tackle two thorny problems: amnesty, and immigration and refugee policy. In September 1974, President Gerald Ford appointed a nine-member Presidential Clemency Board to decide on a case-by-case basis what to do with civil-ian and military personnel accused of violating the law during the Viet-nam War. Ford named Fr. Ted as one of the board members.

"I was always in favor of an unconditional amnesty," Fr. Ted later said, "simply because the war was ill-begotten in the first place." He also thought that President Richard Nixon got off scot-free for the crimes of Watergate, and so did Vice President Spiro Agnew despite accepting kickbacks. "If those at the heart of [the war] escaped with impunity," he thought, "why should those who got caught in its tentacles down the line be punished?"[25]

As the most liberal board member, he had frequent verbal exchanges with its most conservative member, General Lewis W. Walt, the retired Assistant Commandant of the Marine Corps, who had served in World War II, the Korean War, and the Vietnam War.

"I'm against amnesty," Walt declared, "and if one person out of a hundred gets amnesty, I will think we're doing badly."

"Well, if ninety-nine out of a hundred do *not* get amnesty," Fr. Ted retorted, "I'm going to think we're doing badly, because I'm in the forgiving business and amnesty means forgiving."

"If ninety-nine out of a hundred get clemency, what do you think the American people are going to call this board?" Walt demanded.

"They'll probably call it the Presidential Clemency Board," Fr. Ted shot back, "which is what we are."

Working on the Clemency Board was one of the most grueling assignments he ever undertook, because of the enormous amount of personal time and effort it took to study the individual cases. He devoted the better part of an entire summer studying individual applications in Washington, D.C. "Keeping up with the caseload was brutal," he later said. "In order to dispose of a hundred appeals every day, we had to stay up half the night reading documents, then start the next meeting at eight o'clock the next morning. Many of the files on these cases, especially those involving military courts-martial, were an inch or two thick."

A total of 15,468 persons applied to the Clemency Board. Of that number, 4,620 military deserters and 1,432 draft evaders received outright pardons; 7,252 deserters and 299 evaders received clemency, contingent on performing alternative service; only 911 applicants received no clemency.[26]

In October 1978, Congress established the Select Commission on Immigration and Refugee Policy. A rising influx of illegal aliens from Mexico and increasing refugee pressure from Southeast Asia had made immigration and refugee policy reform imperative. After a personal plea from Vice President Walter Mondale, Fr. Ted agreed to chair the blue ribbon commission. He worked with sixteen commissioners: four Cabinet members (including the Secretary of State and the Attorney General), eight members of Congress of both parties, and four public service members.

The issues were exceptionally complex and politically sensitive. Organized labor, for example, pushed for employer sanctions against hiring illegal aliens, but Mexican-American advocacy groups, civil libertarians, agri-business, and the Chamber of Commerce opposed the move. Agri-business and the *Wall Street Journal* endorsed a guest worker program, but labor unions, Mexican-American groups, and many liberals opposed it.

Fr. Ted tried to rise above all the bickering and sought to make the country's policy fair, racist-free, intelligent, open, and systematic. "He was just a wonderful boss," said the Commission's executive director, Larry Fuchs, who thought Fr. Ted had a clear sense of priorities, delegated effectively, supported the staff, and spoke clearly and forcefully.[27]

In 1981 the Hesburgh Commission submitted an exhaustive report to the White House. In the end, the Commission recommended "closing the back door to undocumented/illegal migration" and "opening the front door a little more to accommodate legal migration." It took five more years of congressional action for most of its recommendations to become the Immigration Reform and Control Act of 1986. The act provided for employer sanctions against companies hiring people without proper working or immigration papers; acceptance of the principle of a secure system of employee eligibility; amnesty for aliens who had illegally entered the country before a certain date; and a guest worker program with labor standards and strong protection for the rights of the employees. (Fr. Ted had unsuccessfully urged that a law be passed requiring all American citizens to carry identity cards that could not be counterfeited.)[28]

Fr. Ted loved to travel and especially savored adventurous travel experiences. He had sailor blood in his veins. ("I never feel better than when I'm aboard ship.") He was thankful he was born in the airplane age. A century earlier, he couldn't have done the things he did. "It wouldn't be possible for me to start the day in Los Angeles and finish it in Peking." Never a licensed pilot, he logged over three million miles as a passenger, mostly in commercial flights. Fast military planes and highly sophisticated surveillance aircraft fascinated him. Shortly after World War II, he accompanied a pilot who flew off the deck of an aircraft carrier; later he rode in a supersonic F-14 Tomcat, the same type of advanced fighter used in the movie, *Top Gun.*

His most thrilling ride occurred in 1979 when he soared in the SR-71, the supersonic reconnaissance plane. At age sixty-two, he endured three days of grueling physical and psychological tests at Beale Air Force Base in Sacramento in order to qualify for the flight. ("I don't know any-

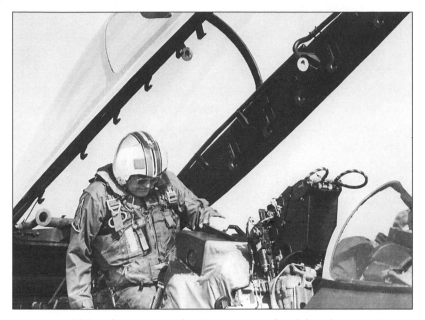

Pursuing a lifelong fascination with aviation, Fr. Hesburgh boards a U.S. Navy F-14 swept-wing jet for a test flight.

one else who would bother," mused Richard Conklin.) He was anxious to break a speed record, not just go sky riding. In his autobiography he described the last portion of his flight with Major Tom Allison:

I watched the Machmeter as we went through Mach 1. Then Tom pulled the stick back and, just as he said, we started climbing straight up, faster and faster. The rate-of-climb indicator on my instrument panel turned to a blur. We blasted through Mach 2, then Mach 3. I could feel the flesh on my face pulling against my cheekbones and trying to move around to the back of my head. I could hardly believe the instrument panel. As we roared through seventy-six thousand feet we were climbing at the rate of four thousand feet a minute. Tom had the plane into a climbing turn as we passed through eighty thousand feet. We were still climbing. The Machmeter was registering 3.35. My eyes were glued to the needle, watching for the instant that it passed that mark. At last it did, and I was exultant. Major Tom Allison and Father Theodore Hesburgh had just set a new world speed record!

They had flown about 2200 miles per hour. "At that speed, we could have flown from Sacramento to Notre Dame in forty-five minutes," he noted.[29]

He fantasized about riding in the space shuttle and celebrating Mass in space. He even managed to get himself on the list of civilians who volunteered to go up in the space shuttle, but the Challenger disaster in January 1986, which killed seven astronauts including civilian Christa McAuliffe, put an end to civilian space travel.

On his trips he took everything in stride—uncomfortable accommodations, delays, cancellations, even danger. He had a cast-iron stomach and wholeheartedly attacked native food. "As for jet lag," observed Walter Langford, "he just doesn't seem to understand how that's supposed to work."

From 1937, when he first sailed to Europe from New York, until 1989, he visited 131 countries. On a single trip he sometimes wore multiple hats. In July 1980, during a whirlwind journey around the world, in Alaska, Hawaii, Guam, and Manila he primarily met with Notre Dame alumni; in American Samoa, Guam, and Saipan he studied immigration policy for the U.S. Select Commission on Immigration and Refugee Policy; in Bangkok, Thailand, he worked on a project for the Rockefeller Foundation; and in Cambodia he wore the hat of the Cambodian Crisis Committee.

While in Australia on another trip, a reporter asked him when he was returning to South Bend. "I'm not going there right away," he explained. "I have a conference in San Francisco tomorrow. Then a meeting of the Rockefeller Foundation at Williamsburg, Virginia, on Wednesday. On Thursday I have a Civil Rights Commission hearing in Washington. Maybe I'll be home for the weekend."[30]

Because he had been the Vatican's representative to the International Atomic Energy Agency from 1957 to 1970, he had become friends with several Russian officials. In 1975, at a meeting of the International Association of Universities in Moscow, his diplomatic contacts allowed Kingman Brewster, President of Yale, and Richard Lyman, Stanford University's President, to meet with key Russian officials. Brewster recalled: "Who should put President Lyman and myself in touch with the Minister of Higher Education, the director of Tass, and the former head of the Russian atomic energy program? None other than Father Ted. It struck me as very amusing that these secular progressive university presidents from Yale and Stanford should have to find that their best ambassador in the precincts of the Kremlin was this Catholic priest who was the president of Notre Dame."[31]

Fr. Ted made his first trip to China in 1979 to discuss science and technology. As always, he carefully cultivated friendships with important officials. "It takes some time to develop a special relationship with someone from a completely different culture," he wrote in his diary on June 25, 1979, after meeting a Chinese official, "but I think we crossed that bridge tonight and at the end of the reception were calling each other good friends." Any remnants of Catholicism in atheistic and communistic China intrigued him. In 1979 he saw several churches—empty buildings no longer used—and he talked briefly with two priests, but he came away with only minimal information.

On his second trip, in 1984, he led a Notre Dame contingent as guests of the Chinese Academy of Sciences. He sought to promote educational and scientific collaboration between Notre Dame and China, and to discuss the nuclear threat with Chinese officials. But he had another, highly personal and informal goal as well: to make more extensive contact with Chinese Catholic clerics.

"I was ready for another great adventure," he wrote in his diary on July 4, 1984, as he set out to visit a Catholic Church, determined to talk to the clergy there. "He was like a little boy," observed Francis Castellino, Dean of Science at Notre Dame and a member of the entourage; "he was quite excited." He located a Catholic bishop who was wearing a gold chain and pectoral cross dangling in front and an episcopal ring, which Fr. Ted duly kissed. To break the ice, he hauled out a picture of Notre Dame and explained the buildings and presented the history and statistics of the university. He was most interested in the status of Catholics in China and pumped the bishop for information. After exchanging gifts, Fr. Ted suggested they visit the nearby church and pray together to confirm their cordial meeting. "We knelt in the front pew and prayed silently, and then I asked if we might say a prayer together out loud. Grasping his hand, we went through the Our Father, the Hail Mary, and the Latin Mary Immaculate, pray for us."[32]

Commentators often facetiously and affectionately described his far-flung travel and extensive public service. "For a few perilous moments last month the federal government was left dangling without the services of the Rev. Theodore Hesburgh," wrote columnist Colman McCarthy on November 14, 1979. "When his work on the President's Commission on the Holocaust ended, a full 48 hours passed before he was appointed to head the Commission on Immigration and Refugee Policy."

By the late 1970s Fr. Ted had earned a reputation among politicians in Washington as the man who was willing to tackle hard problems: civil rights, human rights, global hunger, immigration, and amnesty. In 1980 he simultaneously held six appointed chairmanships, some of them difficult, complex, time-consuming assignments.[33]

He drew sustenance and energy from dealing with a variety of issues at the same time and relished the synergy that flowed from the combined effort. His outside experiences overlapped, and he developed a national and a worldwide network of friends, colleagues, and coworkers.

He had a burning desire to serve the "common good," an ideal he sadly confessed was declining in America. We lacked a "total" view of crises and problems. "There are probably between 30,000 and 50,000 lobbyists in Washington and they have no regard for the common good," he said. "What they are working for is a particular good. You have to ask yourself how many laws are promulgated for the common good—not many."

How did he engage in so many different activities? "I could always do three or four jobs at the same time," he said in 1988. "I can't remember when I only had one job. So I became fairly good at balancing them." Some questioned if he was being "used" by the secular organizations, such as multinational corporations. "If I thought I was being used, I wouldn't be there," he responded.

He approached his assignments with dedication, optimism, and zest. He did his homework and didn't ask for special privileges. Asked why he did all the extra service work and what it meant to him, he responded: "You've got to have meaning in your life. You've got to get up in the morning with some sense that today is not going to be just an exercise in drudgery or routine, but something is going to happen because you're living that day. . . . We can't all be presidents, but we can all do something in our own ways to make a difference. Meaning in life comes from making a difference."

Public service also warded off boredom. "I'd have been bored to death if all I did was be the president of the university," he said candidly; "once you've been through it six times you pretty much know where all the holes in the road are."

Fr. Ted estimated he was on campus 60 percent of the time, off campus 40 percent. Fortunately, his religious superiors were understanding and supportive. He was almost always the first priest and the only Catholic in his various public service roles. Naturally, most of the friendships that grew out of his service were with non-Catholics. "He was very acceptable to the . . . WASP establishment, largely because he rarely contradicted them," a former Notre Dame administrator remarked, referring primarily to Fr. Ted's work with the Rockefeller Foundation. "And when he did, he did so graciously, so smoothly, that they couldn't associate him with the stereotypes of Catholics, which were almost entirely negative."

He always operated as a priest, never disguising himself as a layman. He wore his clerical garb, offered Mass, prayed his breviary every day, but he never flaunted his priestly role. Most of the problems he dealt with had a moral dimension—civil rights, poverty, war and peace, development in Third World countries, science and technology—and he didn't want all dedication and proposed solutions to come from those who had "at best merely humanistic or, at worst, purely materialistic interests." Dedicated Christians must work toward solutions.

For critics within the Catholic Church who didn't think a priest should be involved in public or governmental service, he retorted that none of his activities compromised his priesthood or the Church. On the contrary, his activities enriched his priestly apostolate and placed him at the cutting edge of modern moral problems. "In my judgment, without the government service, . . . both my priesthood and my Church and my educational apostolate, and the Good News of Christ and the common good of my fellow citizens and the world would have been less well served."

Columnist McCarthy thought Fr. Ted was "one of the few idealists we have who aren't being ground down by the times. Consistency of fervor can be the hardest of all virtues, because when others give up or burn out the one who insists on pushing ahead is dismissed as going 'overboard.'" Fr. Ted had been successful, McCarthy thought, because he shrewdly judged how hard to press for what is humane and fair. "Figuring it out, while still being effective, demands mother wit. Go too far and you become the predictable radical; lie back and you are the kept liberal of the powerful."[34]

Not everyone was pleased with his views, his extensive traveling, or his administration of Notre Dame. He angered leftists by inviting President José Napoleon Duarte of El Salvador to give a commencement address. (Duarte was a Notre Dame graduate and a former student of Fr. Ted's.) They also disliked his lack of criticism of Nicaraguan contras; his friendship with contra leader Adolfo Calero; his support of Notre Dame's large ROTC program; and his administration's opposition to the attempt by the Teamster's Union to organize the groundskeepers who worked on the campus.

On the other hand, a conservative Catholic writer, Frank Morris, complained that Fr. Ted's Notre Dame was far too liberal and was not producing "real Catholic leadership," meaning "effective, knowledge-able scholars and defenders of the faith of Rome. I am speaking about Papal loyalists who can answer the attacks, both new and old, on the re-liability of the Church's tradition and doctrine."[35]

The problem of low minority enrollment at Notre Dame persisted. The same limitations against increased black enrollment remained: competition from Harvard and Stanford and other schools with larger endowments and more scholarships; and Protestant and urban blacks were not attracted to Catholic Notre Dame and its fairly rural setting. "I can perhaps excuse our lack of success in attracting black students," Thomas Swartz, professor of economics, said in 1987. "But I cannot ex-cuse our lack of success in attracting Hispanics for that reason. We need to be doing better." Fr. Ted acknowledged the problem and responded the best way he knew how: to raise $10 million for minority scholar-ships. "It's a matter of money," he said. "We'll get there."

The number of minority faculty members also remained small. In 1981–82 the figures were fifty-nine minorities of whom sixteen were black. Critics charged that the university had a "poorly organized" and "ineffectual" affirmative-action plan and offered "limited upward mo-bility." However Nicholas F. Fiore, a white former chairman of the De-partment of Metallurgical Engineering and Materials Science, claimed that his department worked hard on affirmative action and that Fr. Ted encouraged those efforts. At one point, Fiore recalled in 1982, Fr. Ted said: "There won't be another engineering faculty member hired unless he's black." "I am satisfied that they are sincere and that they try very hard," said the *South Bend Tribune's* editor, John Powers, of Notre Dame's attempt to recruit minorities.[36]

One of the most controversial issues Fr. Ted faced in the 1980s was the university's investments in white-dominated South Africa, where five million whites ruled twenty-one million blacks through the brutal system of apartheid, enforced segregation.

Fr. Ted had made his first trip to South Africa in 1958 and another twenty years later. In the summer of 1978, he closely inspected the coun-try with a group of American educators. In discussions with white

South African officials, members of the American entourage took turns "being heavies." Taking his turn, Fr. Ted praised the South African physical resources—gold, platinum, diamonds—and the generous hospitality the Americans had received on their tour, but he criticized the essence of the South African system. "Apartheid is an immoral philosophy, and should be eliminated root and branch," he told his hosts. He was seldom depressed or pessimistic, but because of the South African system "I find myself at this moment somewhat obsessed by sadness, pessimism, and depression."

"It seems to me," he continued, "that there will be no peace in this country without justice. . . . There can't be any peace in a country that is obsessed by fear, abuse of power, hatred between ethnic groups, monumental frustration at the lack of participation, paranoia regarding any criticism from the outside, a basic humorlessness of the leaders, constant drift and confusion regarding policies for the future, in summary, a kind of hopelessness that seems to pervade every conversation. If one talks to whites and blacks concurrently, there is a diametrically opposed view of the actual reality of this country. It seems to me that the time has come to bite the bullet. The challenge is really between liberation for the blacks and survival for the whites. Another challenge is that the rich cannot go on becoming richer while the poor become poorer. The have's and the have-not's are in constant conflict because justice is at stake and justice is being abused. It would seem that the time has come to try to make this country a more unified one by the practice of justice and humanity."

As a result of the 1978 trip, Fr. Ted joined the board of the Committee for Educational Opportunity, which sponsored the college education of South African blacks in the United States. He estimated that by 1986 three hundred South African blacks had received their degrees and that almost all of them had returned to South Africa.[37]

In the mid-1970s the divestment movement erupted and by the mid-1980s, twelve states, more than thirty large cities and sixty colleges and universities had divested their holdings in South Africa. Some black civil rights leaders in the U.S. also supported the movement. Notre Dame's Board of Trustees began considering the issue in 1978. At that time it did what many universities were doing: required all companies which invested in South Africa to adhere to the emerging Sullivan Principles, a set of guidelines created by Rev. Leon Sullivan of Philadelphia, which mandated that American companies in South Africa desegregate.

Behind the scenes Notre Dame conscientiously applied its criteria and pressured companies to abide by the Sullivan Principles in letters signed personally by Fr. Ted.

In 1986 Notre Dame had approximately $30 million of an overall endowment of $340 million invested in twenty-nine companies in South Africa. Gradually Notre Dame had added more qualifications to be met by American companies. In October 1985, officials announced tightened guidelines but still rejected student activist's demands for immediate divestment. The new policy stipulated that Notre Dame would not invest in firms that sold goods or services to the South African police, military, or government, or in companies involved with loans to the South African government or its agencies, or in banks or institutions selling or trading South African Krugerrands. The university labeled its new guidelines "selective divestment." Between 1985 and 1990 Notre Dame quietly divested itself of about fifteen companies that did not meet its criteria.[38]

Throughout the 1980s there was extensive discussion on campus about the right policy to adopt toward South Africa. Students debated the issue and protested. The Board of Trustees continually placed the issue on its agenda. In 1986, while a reporter questioned him about his South African position, Fr. Ted picked up a piece of paper on his desk. "I have here an open letter written by one of our professors who calls me 10 kinds of a skunk."

Notre Dame's Peter Walshe, a native South African and professor of government and director of African Studies, was Fr. Ted's most vociferous critic on campus. "An investment policy that refers to some vague possibility of divesting at some unknown future date will not do," argued Walshe. "It is unworthy of the leading Catholic university, and it is likely to tarnish Notre Dame's image as an institution committed to the pursuit of truth and justice."

Notre Dame, argued Walshe in May 1986, was placing a considerable slice of its endowment at the disposal of the South African oppressors. "What has happened to the Father Hesburgh of earlier civil rights days?" asked Walshe. "Why is he now totally out of step with civil rights leaders in America and deaf to the voices of South Africa?" The answer, concluded Walshe, was that Fr. Ted had embraced corporate leaders— like J. Peter Grace and David Rockefeller—to entice them to grant funds to Notre Dame, and had distanced himself from his colleagues of his civil rights days. "Nevertheless, he uses his reputation gained in the early civil rights struggle to legitimize his current political commitments." Walshe thought it was sad that there was "not much prophetic spirit in [Hesburgh's] administration. And Hesburgh's recent track record on justice is not impressive; he has not discomforted the establishment." Alexander Cockburn, the prominent, abrasive, leftist columnist, used Walshe's arguments for two attacks on Fr. Ted in *The Nation.* Cockburn concluded that Notre Dame's president was "odious."[39]

Fr. Ted countered that the controversy was not about apartheid—almost everyone at Notre Dame was against apartheid. His and the Board's position was "pragmatic" because it hoped to keep pressure on American companies in South Africa to combat apartheid and eliminate it from their working conditions.

Divestment was "phony," he contended. "It might make you feel good, but it doesn't help them over there." Notre Dame's divesting wouldn't subtract from the capital invested in South Africa because someone else would buy the shares Notre Dame sold. Full divestment would mean a loss of moral leverage. "If we do sell stock we'll lose all influence with these companies. If American firms pull out, they'll be bought up at 50 cents on the dollar by Japanese and German firms that couldn't care less." Business would continue but under leadership that didn't care. "Because we have stock, we have influence. I write these CEOs and I get long letters back."[40]

"I swear I could leave this place today without notice and be gone for two weeks, and the place would be running like a top on my return," Fr. Ted often said. "Everybody is doing his own job." That might have been true, but some at Notre Dame thought he was away too much. Some probably would have preferred that he be in his campus office all the time to handle every detail of the university's business, from textbooks to tenure disputes. Franklin Murphy, a friend and fellow university administrator, heard only one criticism of Fr. Ted as president. "I think [he] may have tended to be gone too much, and tried to do too many things," said Murphy. "He wasn't there a lot in the later years. . . . I heard echoes of grumbling: 'We never see the president.'"

Some faculty complained that Fr. Ted's extensive outside interests and global perspective left him too remote from the day-to-day functioning of the university. "The [outside work] more and more preoccupied him," thought Fr. Ernan McMullin. "The concerns that he would mention became more and more distant from [the faculty's] concerns."

Professor Vaughn McKim agreed. "He was not much in touch with what was happening here," and was more of a "figurehead." Yet, conceded McKim, Fr. Ted "was living out an incredibly important lifestyle of his own."[41]

Although some complained and joked about his being away from the university so much, many accepted his being gone and applauded his outside work. In 1979 when the campus newspaper grumbled that he was off to Vienna for a conference when he should have greeted freshmen and their parents for orientation, a student countered that it was "foolish to request that Father Hesburgh neglect the millions of poor and hungry in the world in order to please a handful of white, upper middle-class, well-fed parents." "I have heard all the jokes about him being off-campus so much," said a junior from Cleveland. "But it also makes us [students] feel proud when our president is out there advising presidents or being questioned on TV about a hostage crisis."

The notion that his extensive travel led him to ignore Notre Dame irked Fr. Ted. "He rightly points out," Fr. Joyce observed, "that he's away a lot, but when he's here, he's working double time, which is true. He hasn't neglected anything back here as a result of these other outside obligations." Fr. Ted's mentor and advisor George Shuster had told him that a university president not worth seeing outside the university was also not worth seeing inside it. His travel and public service stimulated the development of numerous foreign programs at Notre Dame, attracted scholarships and grants, and lured distinguished persons to the campus and to the annual commencement ceremonies. "I can get the best of them to come [to Notre Dame] because I do things for them," he said. "I've been able to approach this job with a lot more savvy because of what I've learned in all these other jobs."[42]

In April 1977, black leaders on campus staged a protest on the steps of the administration building, protesting what they called racism on campus and Fr. Ted's alleged inattention to human rights. He met with the students and then issued a statement in which he implored everyone to be mindful of the "worm of prejudice that we all have within us." Some critics alleged in letters and speeches that the former Chairman of the U.S. Civil Rights Commission was a practicing hypocrite.

The university's chaplain, Fr. Robert Griffin, rushed to defend him. "Petitioning Ted Hesburgh to be attentive to human dignity, for God's sake!" he wrote in disgust. "While you are bad-mouthing him," Griffin reminded campus critics, "you might think there are children he is worried about in the world's cities, lest they die in their sleep tonight of hunger, or perish as the victims of war. It is hard to remember there are people who daily face such global concerns; but Father Hesburgh is one of them, and we must share him with the human family."

Griffin did not expect the campus community to have blind faith in Fr. Ted. Their president was not a saint, superman, or the Sistine Chapel. "He is Father Ted Hesburgh of Notre Dame; a man who must sometimes grow weary of being a father to the world; a man who—for some of us—is the greatest man we will ever meet. There is nothing I can write that will add to his greatness. But sometimes, when I have been with him, and he seems tired, or especially gray around the temples, I think: he doesn't deserve to be splattered with mud."[43]

John Gilligan's rebuttal to critics was all inclusive. Gilligan, former Governor of Ohio, was special assistant to Fr. Ted. "Out of the 150 year history of the University of Notre Dame, who has done more for the University or its students, or its faculty, or its graduates than Theodore Hesburgh? Name one person. Usually that ends the conversation," said Gilligan. "Few critics," a writer for the *National Catholic Reporter* said, "would openly question either the integrity or motives of Hesburgh."[44]

Fortunately, Fr. Ted received far more praise than criticism. "There is seldom a figure in public life that can match him in integrity or virtue," said Fr. Griffin. "Somewhere in the 70s, there was a turning point where he just passed into the hall of fame," reflected Notre Dame Professor Frederick Crosson.

In 1978, in a poll conducted by *U.S. News and World Report*, Fr. Ted's peers selected him the third most influential man in the country in education and second most influential in religion (the only person selected in more than one field.) Most students were too intimidated by his presence, too awed by his reputation, to bother him with their problems. In 1977 Student Body President Mike Gassman said he would not dare interrupt Fr. Ted with mundane school problems because "he's too important now."[45]

Of all the good causes he espoused in his long career, none seized him more suddenly and more fervently than the threat of nuclear annihilation. On November 11, 1981, "Nuclear Day" at Notre Dame and hundreds of other campuses, Fr. Ted offered Mass and preached a homily on the nuclear danger. Then one of Notre Dame's alumni, Dr. James Muller of Harvard, co-founder of the anti-nuclear organization Physicians for Social Responsibility, spoke to students and faculty on the effect a one megaton nuclear bomb would have if exploded over South Bend and Fr. Ted's beloved Notre Dame. Suddenly the dire facts became clear in a localized scenario. Dazed, as Fr. Ted walked alone back to his office, it occurred to him that all the good projects he had worked on for thirty years would become irrelevant unless some solution could be found for the threat of nuclear catastrophe. "I thought of my long involvement with human and civil rights, world hunger, development in the Third World, education, immigration and refugees, illiteracy, housing, and health—all of these would be irrelevant if there were no more human beings left to have problems. All the progress I had worked so hard for could be obliterated in a few minutes if the nuclear weapons, now existing, were unleashed."[46]

He had long been aware of the danger of nuclear weapons, and had spoken about the problem as far back as the 1950s. But Muller's warning was different. Suddenly the threat grabbed him with a "passion." He worried about President Ronald Reagan's hard-line policy toward the Soviet Union. Reagan seemed to envision defeating the Soviet Union in the Cold War, and described the U.S.S.R. as the "evil empire."

After the revelation of November 11th, Fr. Ted traveled to Vienna over Thanksgiving and met with Franz Cardinal Konig, with whom he had worked for fifteen years when he was the Vatican Delegate to the International Atomic Energy Agency in Vienna. He and Konig contacted associates around the world to organize against the nuclear threat. Clearing his schedule, he resigned as chair of the Rockefeller Foundation, left the board of the Chase Manhattan Bank, finished his report on immigration, and convinced Robert McNamara, former Secretary of Defense, to take over his spot as chair of the Overseas Development Council.

The nuclear problem was not just a political, military, and diplomatic problem, he argued during the next few years in scores of speeches, articles, and interviews. It was inherently spiritual and moral as well. He reformulated his thoughts about the theological principle of reconciliation. Everyone was forgivable, even the Soviets. "[Now] we need to learn how to sit down and talk with the Russians, to try to draw their humanity out of them, . . . and have them see that we are all up against a common evil. Reconciliation—the ability of one human being to talk to another even after being burned, to be able to say, 'Oh, it is terrible and I wish it hadn't happened but I forgive you'—maybe we can learn that now." He constantly warned against a pessimistic or fatalistic attitude. "There is nothing worse . . . than a fatalistic world. We need hope to go on living."[47]

Nuclear annihilation was not some vague danger, he repeatedly pointed out. Fifty thousand warheads, with a million times the power that obliterated Hiroshima and Nagasaki, hair-triggered and targeted, were positioned on sophisticated delivery systems and could be launched, possibly by accident or computer error. If the weapons were launched, in a few moments they could "reverse God's good creation and our own, by wiping out for all time all that is good and beautiful on Planet Earth."

Like his approach to the Cambodian tragedy a few years earlier, Fr. Ted's comments often had a terse spiciness. "I don't think of nuclear weapons as weapons. They're suicidal. A weapon is something you use to defend yourself and then you are still alive. With this, you defend yourself and you're dead." He continually referred to nuclear war as a blasphemy, "the worst sin since Creation."

In 1983 he wrote that the American people were being told that the Russians were escalating the arms race wildly ("which they have been doing"), while the U.S. had presumably been sitting on its hands. He rejected the contention. "[While] we have been sitting on our hands, we have developed the MX with ten warheads, the Triton submarine with new super accurate missiles, the Pershing II, the cruise missile, the B-1 bomber, and the upcoming Stealth bomber. What would we have done if we were not sitting on our hands?"[48]

"The world has a new arms controller: a cocky, urbane American who takes no orders from Washington," a correspondent wrote for the *National Catholic Reporter* in 1983. "He appointed himself. He finances himself. He sets his own agenda." The correspondent was referring to Fr. Ted's personal crusade to end the nuclear threat. He had decided to bring together two groups which had not made common cause "since Galileo"—the religious and scientific leaders of the world. Why? When scientists spoke against nuclear war, he contended, they were accused of acting in poor grace because they created the scientific technology that produced nuclear weapons. Similarly, when religious leaders opposed nuclear weapons, they were accused of being naive and ignorant. But together? The scientists could clearly elaborate the nuclear situation; then the religious leaders could pass moral judgment on the facts. He called his campaign Science and Religion Against Nuclear War.

It was an ambitious project, but he had already convinced himself that no enterprise was too difficult if he worked hard, organized the right people, and maintained hope. He raised $100,000 for his campaign, including $30,000 from an institution or a foundation he wouldn't identify. ("They told me to submit a grant application," he recalled. "I told them to stuff it." He received the check the next day.)

From 1982 to 1984 he helped organize a series of meetings in Vienna, London, the Vatican, and other locations, bringing together scientists and religious leaders from most of the major nuclear powers, including representatives from the Soviet Union.[49] At one of the meetings in Vienna, Fr. Ted took a walk outside his hotel with the most prominent Russian representative, Yevgeny Velikhov, Vice Chairman of the Soviet Academy of Sciences in Moscow. The two had earlier struck up a friendship. On their walk Fr. Ted candidly explained his fear of a nuclear conflagration. There were certain things that needed to be done even though doing them was difficult, Fr. Ted told him. Like peace in the world. He painted a horrendous picture of nuclear destruction. "We have the capacity to take this beautiful world that God created, the beautiful people that He created, plus everything that we've created—culture, art, music, science, human institutions—and wipe it all out, turn this beautiful planet into a cinder," he told his Russian friend.

Velikhov wondered why he should be as worked up about the problem as Fr. Ted. "Because you have a grandson," responded Fr. Ted. "That's the reason you ought to be concerned. Our lives are mostly lived, but these people are coming along, and people after them. Do you want to wipe out the whole process?" The next day, at their final meeting in Vienna, Velikhov said to him: "You know, I've been thinking about what you said yesterday. And I am convinced that the problem is not out there somewhere, but in here, inside ourselves. Until we can purge the evil within, we won't get rid of the evil without." A few months later, at a meeting at the Vatican, Velikhov reached into his pocket and pulled out a photo of a little boy sitting in a field of yellow flowers and showed it to Fr. Ted. "My grandson," Velikhov said, "the one you talked to me about."

At the close of a meeting in Vienna in 1983, Fr. Ted publicly revealed a bit of his method of diplomacy. Sitting in the lounge off the lobby of the Hotel Intercontinental on a Saturday afternoon, he enjoyed a beer with Velikhov. Sensing the skepticism of several reporters sitting at the table, Fr. Ted said to Velikhov, "These guys don't think it does any good for the two of us to talk, but I do." Fr. Ted continued: "As I read the literature on arms control, I found that every single breakthrough came about initially at an unofficial level." Turning to Velikhov he said, "It would be hard to meet officially in Moscow or Washington the way you and I can meet here and have a beer. And if we don't get our two governments together on this issue somehow, we're all going to be blown up."

Reporters observed an awkward imbalance in their conversation. While Fr. Ted criticized the Reagan Administration's policy of nuclear deterrence, Velikhov parroted the hard-line Soviet view. "Frankly speaking, I think the problem is in Washington," said Velikhov. Fr. Ted conceded the imbalance, but insisted that discussions should not be ruled out. "Okay, so I can get on the phone and tell Reagan he's crazy," he told Velikhov, "and you can't do that with Andropov." The Soviet scientist acknowledged the distinction, saying, "It's not so simple" for Soviet citizens to criticize their leaders. Eventually, Fr. Ted and Velikhov came to believe that there was little to gain by posturing in public. They agreed to work together for positive, constructive change.[50]

The highlight of Fr. Ted's efforts was a meeting at the Rockefeller Conference Center in Bellagio, Italy, on the shores of Lake Como in November 1984. Twenty-three of the thirty participants came from five major nuclear powers—China, France, Great Britain, the United States, and the Soviet Union. Roald Sagdeev, the Director of the Soviet Academy of Sciences' Space Research Institute, represented the Soviet Union. The participants agreed on a 600-word statement, which was released jointly in South Bend and in Moscow.

Broadly worded, the statement condemned the nuclear danger, and warned of the "hideous and unimaginable" consequences of nuclear war—calamitous climatic and other environmental changes, plus the dreaded "nuclear winter," the cold and darkness around the world spread by smoke and dust. The statement urged a reduction in the world's nuclear arsenal and in international tensions. "Our central purpose and proximate endeavor must be to reduce international tensions (particularly between the Soviet Union and the United States), to develop more effective cooperative efforts for dealing with our common human problems and interests, and to bring a greater measure of justice and peace to the whole world." The group published their statement in *Science* and in the *Bulletin of the Atomic Scientists,* and reproduced three million copies in the Soviet Union's most popular scientific and technical magazine.[51]

At dinner one evening in Bellagio, Roald Sagdeev rose and, with his arm around Fr. Ted's shoulders, made a toast. "Being raised in a Communist society," he said, "I was taught that religion is the opiate of the masses. Having spent some time with Father Hesburgh, I think, 'I'd like a little more of that opium!'" The Harvard astronomer Carl Sagan witnessed the remarkable scene. The incident "struck me," Sagan recalled, because Sagdeev's remarks were "so at variance with official Soviet ideology."

The extreme danger of nuclear catastrophe dominated Fr. Ted's thinking. Asked by a magazine in 1983 to name the books he had recently read, he named four,—three of which focused on the nuclear threat. He didn't have faith in the U.N. to find a solution because it was a "cave of the winds" and largely unworkable when it came to finding solutions and implementing them.

In his more whimsical moments, he fantasized about an invasion from outer space uniting all humans into one family to defend the common home. "However, this invasion is difficult to organize, so perhaps the greatest of evils, the nuclear threat, may help us transcend our differences and become what we truly are: brothers and sisters over all the earth."

He didn't want his crusade to be confused with unilateral disarmament, passivism, conventional weapons, the abolition of war, or nuclear power reactors. "The threat of total nuclear disaster transcends all of these problems," he said, "and is the one problem that will eliminate all others unless solved in our time." Some of the scientists he talked with urged de-emphasizing the nuclear threat and stressed controlling conventional armaments. Fr. Ted disagreed. "I would . . . say let's eliminate the nuclear and take our chances on the conventional. At least that way we won't destroy the world."

Because he didn't know President Reagan but wanted to influence him, Fr. Ted met with Reagan's closest associates and wrote long letters to them, trying to convince them to approach the President on behalf of Fr. Ted's plan for peace. He and Norman Cousins, the magazine editor and freelance peace ambassador, met with Vice President George Bush on the Monday after Easter, 1982, and outlined their ideas for the Vice President. Writing to Senator Paul Laxalt of Nevada, a close advisor to Reagan, Fr. Ted insisted that his approach to nuclear disarmament was "verifiable and not pie-in-the-sky, practical and not naive, and . . . politically viable." "I would assume," he optimistically told Laxalt,

that once the religious leaders have accepted the statement of the scientists, passed their own moral judgment upon the principles involved, and then communicate it to their followers all over the world, there might very well be a new ground swell of opinion regarding the elimination of the nuclear threat to humanity. Following this raising of consciousness, hopefully in a valid and rational manner, I would assume the next move would be to enlarge the discussion to include some groups already organized, the physicians, the academicians and artists, students, lawyers and professional people. . . .

He asked Laxalt's assistance in getting into the White House to present his plan to Reagan. The President was "in a rather unique position to be a force for peace, just as President Nixon was in a unique position to open up China," he said. Fr. Ted never succeeded, however, in gaining access to President Reagan.

Would any of Fr. Ted's efforts do any good? Was it all well intentioned but futile? Would political leaders listen to the religious leaders and scientists? Was he hopelessly naive? Some diplomats and other observers expressed skepticism about his activities. "There is a danger of oversimplification," said one diplomat. But Fr. Ted thought the greater danger was to do nothing. "You have two options in life. You can sit on your can and let the world go to hell, or you can take a few small steps forward. . . . I'm a meddlesome priest. I stick my nose in other people's business. . . . I think things can happen if you make them happen." "I'm not naive," he insisted, and "I'm not a pacifist." Although outspoken, he was not among the radicals in the anti-nuclear movement; most of his energy was spent on his low-key effort to unify religious leaders and scientists.

While Fr. Ted was arranging meetings on the nuclear danger, American Catholic bishops were in the process of drafting a major pastoral letter on nuclear war and disarmament, *The Challenge of Peace: God's Promise and Our Response* (1983). The document's "reasoned" and "courageous" stand against the nuclear threat delighted him, and he touted the letter as the "finest document that the American Catholic hierarchy has ever produced." He also encouraged the creation of a new course at Notre Dame, "Nuclear Dilemma," and helped establish a new Inter-Faith Academy of Peace at the Ecumenical Institute for Advance Theological Studies at Tantur, Jerusalem.[52]

"It's some kind of Christmas present," said John Gilligan. He was re-

Addressing students during a prayer service aimed at calling attention to the nuclear arms race.

ferring to the announcement just before Christmas 1985 that Joan B. Kroc was donating $6 million to Notre Dame for the Institute for International Peace Studies. Mrs. Kroc was the widow of Ray Kroc, the wealthy founder of the McDonald's Restaurant chain. The institute had been operating informally for over a decade but was living a hand-to-mouth existence. Mrs. Kroc had begun her own disarmament crusade in 1984, and after hearing Fr. Ted speak on the need to find peaceful solutions to global problems, she made the large donation to the institute so it could greatly expand its programs. Gilligan was the director. The institute sponsored graduate and undergraduate courses and a year-long graduate seminar for students from a dozen countries, including China and the U.S.S.R. Its main focus was prevention of nuclear war, disarmament, conflict resolution, and world order.[53]

In the summer of 1986, Fr. Ted journeyed to Russia and China to enlist the cooperation of the Russian and the Chinese Academies of Sciences. In Moscow he met with Sagdeev and Velikhov, and urged the two

Russians to serve on the International Advisory Board of the Peace Institute. Velikhov had checked himself out of a Moscow hospital to meet with Fr. Ted. "As I embraced him," Fr. Ted wrote in his diary, "I noted that he still had a fever." Fr. William Beauchamp, a Notre Dame administrator traveling with the entourage, witnessed Fr. Ted's relationship with the Russian officials, particularly with Velikhov. "It was clear that these [Russian officials] had made special efforts to make sure they saw Fr. Hesburgh because they considered what he was involved with important." Both Sagdeev and Velikhov agreed to join the International Advisory Board.[54]

In 1980 Fr. Ted announced that he would retire as president in June 1982. A search committee was formed to look for a successor, but no qualified candidate emerged because none had been groomed. Therefore, the Board of Trustees asked Fr. Ted to stay for another five years. "We have in Father Hesburgh a man who is in vigorously good health and who is as intellectually alive as I've ever seen him," Edmund Stephan said on October 24, 1981, while announcing the decision. "The conviction finally came to us that we should not change the leadership when we have such a winning situation."

After the October press conference four young Holy Cross priests were moved into executive positions to gather experience and train as Fr. Ted's possible successor. Why, with Fr. Ted approaching 65 and concluding his third decade in the presidency, had the Board of Trustees waited so long to groom a successor? "I suppose we could be faulted for not having more people ready to go," said Stephan, "although we continually surveyed people we thought showed promise." He added a bit sheepishly: "But I guess that down deep in our hearts, we really didn't want Father Ted to quit."[55]

Fr. Ted remained in excellent health. Since 1945, when he first came to Notre Dame, he hadn't missed one day of work because of illness. However, on Saturday, September 20, 1986, he participated in the inauguration of Yale University's new president, Benno Schmidt, Jr. About 7 o'clock that evening, as he was waiting for a cab outside his hotel, he for no apparent reason fainted. He lost consciousness for less than five seconds, but bystanders summoned an ambulance, which rushed him to the Yale–New Haven Medical Center. Fr. Ted, 69, was hospitalized while doctors tested him and ruled out a heart attack or a stroke. (He apparently had experienced a fainting episode known as syncope.)

The next morning, over the medical staff's objections, he insisted on leaving the hospital. "It's a free country," he said. "I'm leaving." (Before he left, he celebrated Mass in the intensive care unit.) After hopping a plane to Washington, he gave a speech at a ceremony honoring the twentieth anniversary of the Peace Corps, flew back to Notre Dame, and a little more than twenty-four hours after collapsing, was sitting in his office sifting through papers.[56]

In the mid-1980s, as Fr. Ted approached retirement, Notre Dame still had noticeable academic weaknesses. Few of its programs ranked in the top twenty among universities. John Gourman, author of the *Gourman Report*, which annually rated undergraduate and graduate programs, placed Notre Dame's law school thirty-fifth in the country and its undergraduate business program thirty-ninth. In 1986 the median Scholastic Aptitude Test score of entering freshmen at Notre Dame was 1220 of a possible 1600, impressively well above the national average of 906 but still well behind Princeton's median score of 1339. In 1986 Notre Dame ranked only fortieth in attracting freshmen National Merit Scholarship winners.

Notre Dame excelled in undergraduate education but was still not a major research institution. A 1982 assessment of universities offering doctorates ranked Notre Dame highest among Catholic universities. "Nonetheless," noted historian Jay Dolan, "its highest-ranked programs, philosophy and chemical engineering, were considered to be slightly better than average." "Notre Dame is making a determined effort to move into the top rank of universities," concluded Fr. Ernan McMullin in 1986. "But it's nowhere near there yet."[57]

On the other hand, from 1952 to 1987 average faculty salaries jumped from $5,400 to $50,800, placing it near the top rank among universities. Student financial aid rose from a scant $20,000 to $40 million, and forty new buildings were constructed. The proportion of undergraduates who ranked in the top 10 percent of their high school class increased from 30 to 95 percent. In 1984 Notre Dame's endowment ranked nineteenth in the nation, far ahead of its nearest Catholic competitor, Loyola University of Chicago, which ranked fifty-first; by 1987 money for one hundred endowed chairs had been raised.[58]

"Whether it's Hesburgh or the nurturing atmosphere he has created on campus, the 7,500 undergraduates appear to cherish their school," wrote columnist Colman McCarthy in May 1987. "The retention rate for freshmen is an astonishing 99 percent, with 92 percent over four years."

"What [Fr. Hesburgh] has accomplished is that he has transformed this university over his lifetime from a university that emphasized teaching to one which emphasizes both teaching and research," said Notre Dame's Provost, Timothy O'Meara. "And doing this . . . while maintaining the Catholic character of the university. The wholeness of it all is what dominates the campus."

Fr. Ted's main achievement may have been the new prestige he brought to Notre Dame. "Whatever its merits—and they were considerable—the Notre Dame Hesburgh took over in 1952 simply did not have the prestige of the Notre Dame of 1987, when he retired," observed Thomas Stritch. "Hesburgh inherited a college that had just turned the corner to university status. He left it a full-fledged university, on its way to the top."[59]

6 ∽ PROFILE: PERSONALITY, INTELLECT, VALUES

F R. T E D O N C E L I S T E D his personal traits as "good health, a cast-iron stomach, a gift of gab, a generally optimistic and an unflappable nature, a non-violent tendency, a readiness to forgive and forget, [and] the skin of a rhinoceros for personal affronts and subtle insults. . . ." Although accurate, his brief, simple list was far from complete.

He combined exceptional qualities of intellect, character, personality, and spirituality, as well as a flair for management. Not succumbing to the weaknesses of mortals (alcoholism, illicit sex, avariciousness, intemperance), his character flaws were minor. "The closer you come to people, the more flaws you [ordinarily] see," said his friend and special assistant Fr. John Egan, but with Fr. Ted, "the more I got to know him, the greater [he seemed]. The myths about him aren't myths; they're really true."[1]

Usually even-tempered, seldom in an ugly mood, serene and tranquil, Fr. Ted seemed impervious to agitation or turmoil. "I don't know that I have ever seen him angry," said the university's chief fundraiser, James Frick. "He has a great toleration for almost anything."

Fr. Ted's disposition changed slightly but noticeably during Lent. For the forty days before Easter he refrained from drinking any alcohol and stopped smoking cigarettes and cigars. "It will be good to have some scotch and cigars again," he wrote in his diary as Easter approached. The austerity he imposed on himself affected his personality, making him moody. Tim O'Meara, who became Notre Dame's provost in 1978, normally found his boss even-tempered and easy to gauge. Except during Lent. "You'd have to stratagize," O'Meara observed. "You didn't know how he would react." Robert Gordon, Vice President for Advanced Studies, agreed. "He got a little more irritable. He would be aroused by things more easily." His secretary Helen Hosinski said she didn't give up anything for Lent; her sacrifice was to tolerate her boss's crankiness. "I have to put up with him in Lent when he quits smoking his cigars and having his Manhattans."[2]

Fr. Ted's calling seemed to require that he submerge his inner feelings. "For all his heartiness," said *Time*, "the inner Hesburgh seldom surfaces." Only a handful of people got behind his strict reserve. "You rarely see him with the full extent of his humanness showing," said an observer. "It's that priest training—guard emotions, keep confidences."

In public he sometimes appeared coolly efficient. "When he would walk into lunch at the Morris Inn," observed O'Meara, people saw only "a power machine going through the dining room without much warmth." But O'Meara thought this demeanor a protective device. "I think he was protecting himself . . . from saying the wrong thing and being misquoted."[3]

Actually, he was a man of enormous good will. He tried to embody the compassion of Christ. "He is great-souled," said a former Notre Dame administrator. In the ten years that James Grant knew him, "I never saw him do a mean or selfish act." Exceptionally loyal and devoted, he remembered people in his prayers, often visited hospitals, and served at hundreds of funerals. When he returned from a trip, and Marty Ogren, his chauffeur, met him at the airport, Ogren occasionally informed him that someone in the Notre Dame family was hospitalized. "Let's go to the hospital," Fr. Ted instructed, sometimes delaying a university meeting. Because of his stature and fame, any attention he gave to the bereaved, humiliated, or crushed had extraordinary impact.

Many who knew Fr. Ted had an "imagine that" story. There were many small, intimate acts of kindness. After a befuddled blind man attracted his attention at O'Hare Airport, Fr. Ted helped the man find his gate. As Fr. Ted passed the desk of the Morris Inn and learned that a guest was ill, he summoned a physician and stayed with the sick person until the doctor arrived.

A Notre Dame student body president was returning with Fr. Ted from a banquet when the pair stopped at a gas station. The student recalled: "Father Hesburgh knew the Hispanic attendant, spoke to him in Spanish, boosted his spirits and encouraged him to enroll in continuing education classes on campus. He talked to that man the same way he would talk to a vice president."[4]

Anyone connected to his beloved Notre Dame was an object of special concern. "It never fails," said S. L. Montague, the janitor in Notre Dame's gold-domed administration building. "He always has the time to talk to me, to ask me how my work is going and how I feel. He is the type of guy you could go to with a problem."

When the wife of staff member Roger Valdiserri was dying of cancer, Fr. Ted visited her at the hospital, wrote notes to her while he traveled, offered a special Mass for the couple, and finally buried her. "It was so comforting," said Valdiserri. "My wife admired him so much."

Several times he went to extraordinary lengths to assist Notre Dame friends who were leaving the priesthood, helping them through the maze of Vatican regulations to successful laicization. "He was a wonderful friend," said Neil McCluskey. "The advice he gave me was very sound."

Fr. Ted had a discretionary fund (earned from speaking fees and from serving on boards), which he used to assist others. Often he helped foreign students with financial problems. When a nun ran out of money to complete her Ph.D. and her religious order couldn't continue to support her, he dipped into his fund and provided her with assistance. "No fanfare," observed James Frick who witnessed the incident. "That was not unusual at all."

In the 1960s two Notre Dame undergraduates, returning to school, were involved in a serious auto accident in Maryland. The university dispatched John Twohey and another student to the small-town hospital to comfort the families. At about 2:30 A.M. Fr. Ted rushed into the intensive care unit carrying his suitcase. He had been in Washington, D.C., learned of the accident, and hopped a Greyhound bus to the Maryland hospital. Seeing "Hesburgh burst in there in the middle of the night gave everyone a terrific lift," Twohey recalled. On another occasion, while enroute to the airport in Washington with Frick, Fr. Ted learned that a Notre Dame student had been injured in an auto accident. He directed the cab driver to go to the hospital instead, and he visited the young man and his parents. "We missed the plane," said Frick.[5]

Gracious and charming, he welcomed interviewers with a smile and a hearty handshake. "You would think the only thing he had to do that day was talk to you," wrote a reporter. He charmed students, faculty, and trustees. "He can talk with the maids in the hall and charm them," said Fr. Robert Griffin. "He could go to a convention of janitors and probably have an insight on the problems of janitors." The wife of Dean Francis Castellino often attended social gatherings at Notre Dame, and she appreciated the personal attention Fr. Ted paid her. Castellino thought Fr. Ted tried to pay attention to all the spouses in the university community. "He makes the whole family feel part of the place, not just the person who has the job."[6]

Fr. Ted could also be critical and tough. When he and Frick visited an alumnus, hoping for a large donation to the university, the alumnus shocked them with a harangue against the university's decision to become coeducational. Afterwards, Fr. Ted said to Frick, "Jim, trying to talk to him is like trying to talk with an open fire hydrant. . . . He is a first-rate, second-class guy." Reflecting on the remark, Frick observed: "You couldn't condemn a person worse than that."

In 1973 General Augusto Pinochet overthrew the government of Chilean President Salvador Allende. When the new Chilean dictator threatened to expropriate a Catholic high school in Santiago owned by the Congregation of the Holy Cross, Fr. Ted flew to Santiago, met with Pinochet, and warned him of the consequences. He told Pinochet that he would make sure that the dictator's relations with the Catholic Church worldwide as well as in Chile would become severely strained. Pinochet backed down and took no action against the school.[7]

He often got his way, usually in a graceful and diplomatic manner. "He is always very much in control of himself and of the situation but without appearing to be in control," observed Jean Wilkowski. "You always knew that whatever the conversation he was having, he was going to steer it and get the outcome that he wanted but without looking heavy handed, or acting heavy handed."

Asked if he ever thought of becoming a salesman like his father, Fr. Ted reiterated that he never wanted to be anything except a priest, but then added significantly: "I *am* essentially a salesman. I sell the university and the good news of the Lord."

Sometimes he used a persistent, determined sales approach—and got his way. In 1981 he wanted former Secretary of Defense Robert Mc-Namara to replace him as president of the Overseas Development

Council. "Let's give Bob McNamara the full court press," Fr. Ted wrote an ODC official. "I'm confident he'll say 'yes' if we keep his feet to the fire." McNamara accepted the position.

In 1985 Notre Dame's Board of Trustees was searching for a new chairman of the board. The Nominating Committee's first choice was Donald Keough, a trustee and the President of the Coca Cola Company in Atlanta. Because of other commitments and the long commute from Atlanta to South Bend, Keough turned down the offer, clearly and finally. Or so he thought. Two weeks later Fr. Ted phoned him and arranged a luncheon meeting with Keough and his wife in Atlanta. Even before the first course was served at the luncheon, Fr. Ted began his sales pitch to convince Keough to accept the important Notre Dame position. "Let me tell you something," Fr. Ted told him. "One of these days, in the not too distant future, you will be confronting St. Peter at the gate. When you get there, he is going to say, 'Don, what did you do?' If you . . . say, 'Well, I did very well. I was the President of the Coca Cola Company' he won't even know what you are talking about. If you say, 'Among other things, I served as Chairman of the Board of Trustees of the University of Notre Dame,' you'll walk right in." Fr. Ted kept pressing him. "By the time we got to the dessert," Keough reflected, "[My wife] and I looked at each other and we knew that it was the right thing for me to do." Keough accepted the position.

Fr. Ted moved in and out of various worlds with the ease of a career diplomat, comfortable with himself in widely different environments. With theologians he talked theology; with scientists he talked science. In the afternoon he'd speak on options for the poor at the Catholic Worker House; the same evening he'd mingle among wealthy guests at a cocktail party at an exclusive home. "He talks to the Pope the way he talks to a bunch of kids in my kitchen," marveled Edmund Stephan, who accompanied him on a papal visit.

David Rockefeller appreciated Fr. Ted's tact and graciousness at elegant social functions sponsored by Chase Manhattan. If the bank held a function which included, in Rockefeller's words, "entertainment at a fairly generous level," Fr. Ted mingled and enjoyed himself. "That," said Rockefeller, "was a very appealing characteristic. He took very strong public stands on issues . . . of the poor and downtrodden, but it was nice that he was also . . . perfectly understanding of other people enjoying things."

At social gatherings, said an observer, he stopped "to talk with nearly

With honorary degree recipients at the 1960 Commencement: Fr. Hesburgh is flanked by President Dwight D. Eisenhower and Cardinal Giovanni Battista Montini, who was later elected Pope Paul VI.

everyone, calling some aside for a private conversation, leaving a group so gracefully when he felt he should move that there was no impression that he had left abruptly." Yet his presence sometimes overwhelmed; people became nervous after learning they were to be in the same room with him. Nonetheless, he had the great facility to make people feel at ease.

He remained crisply cool under adverse conditions. Amid all the turmoil of 1969, he said candidly, "If I'd lose my cool, I'd be dead." Even intricate problems didn't unduly perturb him. In tense situations he urged people to "relax." His poise was contagious. "His quiet confidence that there had to be a solution had a soothing effect on all of us who worked with him," said Fr. Edmund Joyce.[8]

Fr. Ted's friends and colleagues enjoyed his sense of humor. "He is able to laugh at the crazy things that happen—our own foibles," said Fr. Joyce. Fr. Ted often told the story of becoming President of Notre Dame not through his choice but because of the vow of obedience. When he wanted to be a chaplain, he was sent on for his Ph.D. When he completed his Ph.D. and wanted to enter a chaplaincy, he was ordered to teach. After he began to like teaching, he was ordered into administration. "The next time they ask me what I want to do, I'm not going to [tell them]," he said grinning. As he struggled to fix a screeching microphone, he told the audience that it was like trying to kiss a screaming woman, adding quickly that, of course, he had no experience with that kind of thing. His humor was often dry. On a tour of archeological ruins in Mexico, he understood the guide to say that hundreds of years earlier people played a ball game on a large field. The main problem with this competitive sport, though, was that the one who put the ball through the circle was killed. Commenting in his diary, he wrote: "This really must have cut down on the competitiveness." At a hearing on immigration problems, an Irish-American witness had two recommendations: (1) that the U.S. allow more Irish into the country, and (2) keep out the homosexuals. Fr. Ted turned and whispered to his staff director, "What do we do about Irish homosexuals?"

Occasionally he told a humorous joke. One of his favorites was about the poor boy who broke his mother's heart by praying all during December for a new bicycle at Christmas which she knew she couldn't afford. When Christmas came with no bicycle, she said to him, "I hope, son, you are not disappointed that God didn't answer your prayer." The boy responded, "He answered my prayer. He said no."[9]

Overall, he was not noted for his humor. He seldom cracked jokes; his conversation was more interesting than humorous. "Ted enjoys humor," observed Fr. Egan, "but humor doesn't often creep into his conversation." Conklin agreed: "He tends to be on the serious side." Nor did he insert much humor into his speeches. "They are all pretty serious," said Fr. Egan. "He doesn't give light talks."[10]

Conklin often teased Fr. Ted about his perpetual optimism. "Of faith, hope, and charity, he has always come down on the side of hope," said Conklin. "I've never seen him in a mood of . . . black depression, saying he was 'giving up.'" Walter Langford agreed: "He doesn't like the word 'impossible.' That is a word he doesn't accept." There were no insoluable problems. If a new library was needed on campus, the money to build it would be found; people with apparently fundamental differences could reason together and find common ground.

The bane of our age was hopelessness, he believed, especially in the face of great problems and evils, whether it was lack of confidence in government, the threat of nuclear destruction, or poverty and hunger in the world. "I spend my time trying to get people stirred up—stirring up hope," he said. History was filled with examples of people who zeroed in on a problem, remained hopeful, and stirred up others. The U.S. abolished slavery, he believed, primarily because individuals complained about it, "over and over again," until it was banned.

In reviewing Fr. Ted's book *The Hesburgh Papers*, a critic for *National Review* parodied Fr. Ted's extreme hope: "He faces the future hopefully, deals with the present hopefully, and even reserves hope for the past, since it may be redeemed by the future it has begotten."

Nothing discouraged him for long, and he advised others to persevere despite odds. After quoting Scripture, "God has chosen the weak of this world to confound the strong," his own advice was: "So we are weak. No matter."[11]

Colleagues learned quickly to avoid him early in the morning. "Anyone who signs [Fr. Ted] up to give a talk at seven in the morning ought to ask for [a] rebate," teased Helen Hosinski. "You learn quickly not to discuss things with him [in the morning]," said James Frick.

He developed an unusual work schedule. On a typical working day on campus he awoke about 10 A.M., did some exercise, showered, shaved, and prayed. Then it was off to celebrate Mass and more prayer, followed by a light breakfast. He arrived at his office at noon, always in his black suit with Roman collar. His afternoon was taken up with conferences, phone calls, visitors, and mail. By late afternoon, while other people were winding down, he was winding up. At 5:30 P.M. he joined his community for prayers. After dinner with the community in Corby Hall, he went back to his office, where he worked another eight hours. Half-listening to classical background music—Chopin, Tchaikovsky, Beethoven—he waded through more correspondence, wrote memoranda, letters, speeches, and reports, read magazines and books, met with his staff, and phoned friends and colleagues. Sometimes a student who saw his light on would come up the fire escape to talk. ("That's ok," he said. "They just want to see if you're real.") He seldom quit before 3 A.M. "He is here until 4 in the morning sometimes," confirmed S. L. Montague. When Helen Hosinski arrived in the morning, she found the prodigious output of his evening's work. Sometimes he turned out several hundred letters a week.[12]

Administrators who worked with him found themselves (sometimes reluctantly) adapting their work schedules to his—that is: late-show-up and late-stay-up. Fr. Joyce commented wryly, "I usually quit at around 1 or 2. I need more sleep than he does." When Philip Faccenda was asked to talk with Fr. Ted about his new position with the university, the time was 2 A.M.

Did he have enough time to sleep? Fr. Ted was occasionally asked. "Yes," he replied; he worked long hours, but he could "turn it off," leave problems behind him, and sleep. "I've found that people who say they only need a couple of hours of sleep are half asleep most of the time. If I'm up late, I catnap, or I catch up over the weekend. I sleep."[13]

His office suite in the administration building had high ceilings, built-in bookcases, dark-wood furniture, a private bathroom, and plenty of elbow room. Filled with comfortable clutter, there were lines of books, sculptures, Easter Island wood carvings, photos of friends and relatives, plus signs of his glamorous life off campus—photographs with presidents and popes, an inscribed silver plate from Jacqueline Kennedy, and an ornate ring given to him by Pope Paul VI. On his desk an ashtray overflowed with small coins from foreign countries, a bounty he used to keep the hands of young children off his real treasures.[14]

"Notre Dame," said his advisor George Shuster, "was a university trying to catch up with its president." Fr. Ted's energy and endurance inspired awe. "You can't help but be impressed by his . . . vigor, his vitality, and willingness to work twenty hours a day," Fr. Joyce marveled. "I don't think he'll ever be relaxed," observed his sister, Betty O'Neill. "I think he is a compulsive doer."

In long meetings he gathered strength while others faded away. One reason he so often got his way was that he could absolutely outsit any group. "He might want some result out of some council or board," observed Fr. Charles Sheedy in 1977. "The meeting will go on and on. At some point that would normally be the end, Father Hesburgh will say, 'How about us just knocking off for a half-hour and getting something to eat? Then we can start again back here. I think we're on to something.'"

The sequel would go on and on as resistance lowered. "At the end of a session like that," continued Sheedy, "when they are all stumbling out of the room, Father Hesburgh might mutter to some friend, 'Oh, boy, I'm dead; that's 14 straight hours.'" The group would adjourn to the nearby Morris Inn for a nightcap. There in the lobby, Fr. Ted would meet an alumnus and chat with him for half an hour. "People see this as incredible," Sheedy concluded.

After a long trip by Fr. Ted, Marty Ogren waited for him at O'Hare Airport with a car and an attaché case full of mail that had accumulated in his absence. Fr. Ted excitedly dove into the mail and read half of it on the two-hour drive back to Notre Dame. "He just could not wait to open his briefcase and get into new business," said Ogren. "It revived him." After a quick shower, he often worked in his office for 3 or 4 hours to clean his desk before he returned to his room. "I read until about three o'clock Tuesday morning," he wrote in his diary after returning from a trip to China, "and by that time, since I had been up for over fifty hours, [I] decided it was time to get to bed."[15]

He traveled to New York City for one day, performed three different tasks, jumped back on a plane at 6:30 the next morning, and immediately returned to his desk at Notre Dame. Although he traveled to New York City many times, he didn't take time to see a movie or a Broadway play. "You can get a lot done, but you've got to keep at it," he said. "You can't play around, and I haven't had much chance to play around." Contemplating his schedule sometimes overwhelmed him. "Every time I look at my calendar, I am driven to despair," he wrote a colleague in 1979.

Early on as Notre Dame's president he decided never to run for political office, never to identify with a political party, and never to endorse a candidate. To do anything partisan would alienate a portion of the alumni and violate his strong conviction that a priest should mediate and reconcile, not divide. Partisan politics would also mean owing favors. "I don't like anybody to have a piece of me—I like to be independent of everybody except God."

He turned down offers from President Johnson to head the National Aeronautics and Space Administration (NASA); from President Nixon to direct the anti-poverty program; and from President Carter to fill a high post in Latin American affairs. In the early 1960s a group in New York State promised to take care of all financial expenses if Fr. Ted would agree to run for the U.S. Senate. He rejected the overture. In 1972, after Thomas Eagleton was jettisoned as the running mate of Democratic presidential nominee George McGovern, and a number of prominent Democrats rejected offers to replace Eagleton, Sargent Shriver phoned Fr. Ted and asked, "Would you run for Vice President with

McGovern?" Fr. Ted politely refused. He didn't think it was wrong for a priest to run for elective office; but "I think it's wrong for me to run for elective office." "He could have been a very successful politician," said Shriver. "Certainly he could have been elected to the United States Senate."

At a dinner in Fr. Ted's honor in South Bend, Congressman John Brademas said that Fr. Ted was his candidate for President of the United States. There was only one problem, added Brademas, tongue-in-cheek. "I'm not sure that the American people are ready yet for an upstate New York, German-American bachelor."[16]

Although nonpartisan and uninterested in seeking political office, he was politically astute and used political means to advance his causes. He had the affability one expects in a high-class politician. He had his own ideas, agenda, and moral standards and had no hesitation about promoting them. Not content to hold his position quietly, he wanted others to understand, to accept, and to support his point of view. John Gilligan observed that this goal led him into "what is generally described as political activity."

While testifying before Congress, he won respect for his refreshing candor and for avoiding carefully couched, carefully qualified positions. "Everybody else, whether they were politicians or academicians," said Gilligan, who observed his testimony, "were all busy covering their backsides, and he wasn't . . . [and] that was the great source of his power and influence." He also personalized and humanized his messages. "He came across as a person and not a stick, a mouthpiece, or a robot," said John Powers. Like a good politician, he was a wily negotiator. He compromised on some tactics, but he kept his eye on his final goal. Derek Bok, former President of Harvard, thought Fr. Ted uniquely combined the qualities of practicality and idealism. Fr. Ted understood the "practical problems" of the world and was not a "dreamy visionary," too far removed from the real world to understand it. Yet he possessed "obvious conviction and principles and considerable . . . strength in expressing them."[17]

The last Catholic clergyman to gain wide publicity in the U.S. political arena had been the notorious anti-Semite and Nazi sympathizer Fr. Charles Coughlin. Fr. Ted was different. "Hesburgh's public forays into the centers of power gave Catholics a real ambassador to pluralistic America who reflected back to them who they had already become and could be," observed Kenneth Briggs in the *National Catholic Reporter*.

"Hesburgh became a stalwart Catholic celebrity who visited the tents of the most high and returned telling intriguing stories about what had happened. He was more than a token. He was a forerunner."[18]

As Fr. Ted walked through an airport in Moscow, Shanghai, Tokyo, or New York, former Notre Dame students pushed their way through the crowd to introduce themselves, and he responded warmly. "He has become a virtual prince among priests," said *Time* in 1977. Wherever he went, he made an impressive entrance. "You can feel him coming in," said an acquaintance. "He had a lot of charisma," said Clark Kerr, former President of the University of California. "And I don't use that word very often."

He wore the mantle of greatness easily. He had a knack for making the most of the spotlight while appearing disinterested. "Marshall McLuhan would most probably rate him highly as a 'cool' subject for television," said an observer, "having ambitions without seeming to for a moment."

"He could absolutely inspire people," said James Frick who often witnessed his speeches to potential benefactors. "You really wanted to help this man. A leader," added Frick, "is one who has the ability to get others to do his will willingly for a common cause. If there is anyone that could do this to the nth degree it is Theodore Martin Hesburgh."

"After my parents, Father Hesburgh was probably the single most important influence on my life," said Bruce Babbitt (ND, 1960), former Governor of Arizona, candidate for the Democratic nomination for president in 1988, and Secretary of Interior in the Clinton Administration. "I learned the ethics of public service and the relationship between values and the obligation of individuals to apply those values in the name of social change," said Babbitt. "His influence led me into the civil rights movement, the war on poverty and ultimately into politics."[19]

Because of Fr. Ted's integrity, avoidance of partisan politics, and indefatigable work for human rights and the poor, he developed exceptional moral power. "That exactly describes it," said Thomas Carney, former chairman of Notre Dame's Board of Trustees. "That is where he gets his influence—from his moral power."

His prestige, energy, and moral power translated into exceptional clout. On short notice he arranged major conferences with influential people for important causes. After Fr. Ted had arranged a conference at Wingspread, which included the president's cabinet members and major national political leaders, Congressman Brademas observed, "There are only two people in the country who could get a group of people like this together on such incredibly short notice for a meeting like this: Fr. Ted Hesburgh and whoever happens to be president of the United States at the time." [20]

Close friends and colleagues were reluctant to comment on Fr. Ted's weaknesses and limitations. "Of course he had limitations," Timothy O'Meara told an interviewer, "but I'm not sure I'm going to tell you." "I don't want to be criticizing this man," said a friend. "I love this man!"

Fr. Ted often exaggerated. His claim to have been a "counselor for four Popes and six Presidents" since 1952 was inaccurate. ("I have had long conversations with all the presidents from Truman up to the present day," he said in 1987.) Some of the Popes and Presidents he barely knew at all; others he gave occasional advice on a specific issue. Pope Paul VI and President Jimmy Carter were the only ones he actually "counseled." [21]

He often embellished his stories. On February 28, 1979, courtesy of President Jimmy Carter, Fr. Ted flew in the SR-71, the supersonic reconnaissance plane. (In his autobiography he wrote more than eleven pages about the exciting adventure.) Commenting on Fr. Ted's description of his flight, a friend observed: "It seems to me that the plane goes faster every time he tells the story." He molded stories into parables. "Historical accuracy is not always there," said another friend. "But the truth of the parable is there."

He exaggerated the fundraising success of Notre Dame. "When our endowment would be $75 million," said Frick, "he might very well say our endowment was $100 million—not because he didn't know it was $75 million, but because he was already at $100 million in his own mind." Conklin agreed. "He was always kind of looking ahead. He would always give the goal rather than the reality. Those of us who were keepers of accurate figures had to do some nimble dancing every once and awhile." [22]

When Fr. Ted had been traveling for several weeks, he enjoyed returning to his Holy Cross community at Notre Dame and relating his stories. "We would try to be home for him," reflected Fr. Chester Soleta. "That meant very often that we would just have to listen and he would talk." Like many people who have had the limelight thrust on them, he assumed he was the leader in any social gathering and should dominate. "He has always found himself—even when he doesn't want to be—the center of attraction," said John Walsh. "He assumes he has to . . . carry the conversation." He was a marathon conversationalist; the problem was to get him to *stop* chatting. (Fr. Joyce occasionally needled him. "You were sure long-winded tonight.") He related his anecdotes and views because he thought they were informative, interesting, entertaining, or inspiring. He told stories about the people he met, the exotic places he visited, and the exciting things he did.

Many people, especially those who were hearing his long anecdotes or commentary for the first time, were mesmerized. "If you sit at the table with Fr. Hesburgh," observed Fr. John Dunne, "you know who will do the talking. I sometimes deliberately sit where he is [seated] because it's fun to hear his stories." Notre Dame trustee J. Peter Grace didn't mind that Fr. Ted dominated conversation. "Whenever he speaks, you learn," said Grace. "It's hard to squeeze in a single word," said a student government leader. "But he's so fascinating, his experiences are so amazing, that you don't usually mind." On the other hand, some people didn't like to get too close to him because they were overwhelmed by his presence and experiences. A trustee who knew him well asked not to be seated at his table during a dinner because he was intimidated by Fr. Ted's conversation.[23]

Others, especially those who worked closely with him and heard his stories many times, were sometimes irritated and bored. "Critics could probably draw from [his marathon talking] that he has egotistical tendencies," admitted Walsh. "It is hard to sit at a table with him because he dominates the conversation the whole time," said a former administrator at Notre Dame. "He tries to get you in and you say one sentence and that reminds him of a story and away we go. He is not the most social person in the sense that it is two-way sociability. . . . People who haven't heard all these stories love it. . . . The rest of us who heard them twenty times are dying." At social gatherings he often retold the story of his flight in the SR-71. "I've heard him tell that a million times!" complained the former administrator.[24]

"Sometimes he would drive you mad with his [marathon talking]," said O'Meara. "You'd get the impression he wasn't listening." Yet, added O'Meara, "You would love him for the whole person," and at the next social gathering, if he was absent, "you'd miss him. [Then] the next time that he was there, he would overwhelm the whole table." "[In] most conversation," observed Fr. Griffin, "people try to match each other in anecdotes and experiences, but there is no matching him. It doesn't work that way."

Partly because he gave so many speeches, Fr. Ted fell into the habit of name-dropping, particularly at public dinners and before alumni groups. Often he referred to the famous and powerful. "I had lunch with the President last week;" and "Recently, while I dined with the Pope;" and "I'm walking across Red Square and who do I meet but" . . . ("I've heard the Red Square story a hundred times," said the former administrator.) "He even city-drops," said a staff member. "When I was in Vienna last night," he would say.

Students caught on to his habit. At a spring commencement exercise, he spoke about an inscription he saw on a memorial to Mohandas Gandhi in India. He began to explain by saying, "Every time I'm in New Delhi . . ." but incredulous students drowned him out with a burst of laughter. Some thought his name dropping was inappropriate for a man in his position; others were impressed and found his stories fascinating. Indeed, his world was populated with the famous and powerful. Accusing him of name dropping, contended theology department chairman Fr. Richard McBrien, was "like accusing Julia Childs of talking too much about food, or Johnny Carson of telling too many jokes, or Pope John Paul II of saying too many prayers."[25]

Some people thought he was vain, judging that he arranged to be in positions of power, attention, and notice. "He is vain," a Notre Dame faculty member bluntly said; "there is a strong streak of vanity there." A reporter for *Time* thought he had a "healthy ego." Others disagreed, contending that what appeared to be vanity was actually self-confidence.[26]

"He is a very humble man," insisted Thomas Carney. Francis Castellino stood behind Fr. Ted at the airport counter. "When he hands his coach ticket to them, they bump him to first class. Everybody pays so much attention to him [that] you'd have to be a person of enormous strength not to let a little vanity creep in. But as a priest, he is an extremely humble individual." "You see little flashes of ego," agreed newspaperman John Powers, who observed him for the *South Bend Tribune*. "And you'd have to have an ego to be president of Notre Dame for three decades. But he has kept himself in perspective."[27]

He expressed modesty about his accomplishments and credited others for successes. Compliments were wonderful, he often said, quoting Adlai Stevenson, "so long as you don't inhale them." He often retold the warning against arrogance given him by Fr. John Cavanaugh: "The cemeteries of the world are full of indispensable people. Five minutes after you're out of here there will be someone in your place doing a better job."

He took accolades in stride. Inscriptions and awards did not find their way onto the walls of his presidential office. In 1972 visitors inquired about the Meiklejohn Award granted him by the American Association of University Professors two years earlier. "You want to see it?" he said. He walked across the room and pulled the sofa away from the wall. Stacked against the wall were about fifteen plaques and awards. "It's a nice award," he said, holding it up and reading from the plaque's inscription. Then he put it back with his other trophies.[28]

His private world was modest and simple. When he came to Notre Dame as a student in 1934, he was assigned a laundry number (00652); almost sixty years later he still had the same number. He didn't have a checking or savings account. "After all these years, I haven't got a nickel in the world," he often said, "and I like that."

Like his fellow Holy Cross priests, he lived in two small rooms with a bath in Corby Hall. His suite was no larger or more elaborate than any of the other priests. His location in Corby was a bit noisier at times, though, because his room was located over a dumpster, and the garbage truck made its morning rounds two floors below.

For years he slept on the same iron cot, amid stacks of cans of orange juice and Campbell soup, a sharp reminder of his almost monastic life. "It is the mark of an asceticism that Ted Hesburgh seems to impose on himself," *Time* wrote in 1977, "almost as though he felt a need to reassure himself that he still is a priest." Usually, when he was on campus, he dined with his fellow priests at Corby Hall. "I am sure he could be wined and dined every night of the year if he wished," observed Fr. Griffin, "but instead he recognizes his need to keep in touch with his roots in the community and to talk to people in the community and share his mission with them."[29]

He cultivated his excellent mind. He had wide intellectual interests and read extensively. "[Hesburgh] is more knowledgeable on more subjects and up to date on them, and in depth on them, than any person I've ever come across," said Walter Langford. He became very proficient (in some cases an expert) about religion, theology, philosophy, science and technology, geography, higher education, Catholic education, civil rights, underdeveloped countries, nuclear warfare, immigration and amnesty. He was curious about many other subjects as well. "You start him on airplanes, and he'll dazzle you by all he knows about that," said Fr. Joyce. "You can't name a subject that he doesn't have an interest in," marveled Gilligan. A classic introduction to Fr. Ted was: "He's equally at home explaining the split atom, split T, or split infinitive." (Of the three he would have had the greatest difficulty explaining the split T.)

Partly because he had been an administrator since 1949, Fr. Ted seldom displayed the probing, meticulous mind of the scholar. His mind was more intuitive than logical (although he was not illogical) and more active than reflective. ("Ted is a doer," said a close friend, "not a tormented intellectual seeking some kind of truth.") His mind worked on a "horizontal level," across subject matters, rather than in a "vertical way," thought Clark Kerr. He was very perceptive. When Notre Dame trustee Newton Minow helped search for a new president of Northwestern University, he requested Fr. Ted's analysis of the final two candidates. "He gave me an absolutely perfect, succinct, perceptive, insightful rundown of their strengths and weaknesses," said Minow.[30]

"Analysis of a sustained sort drives him nuts," observed Fr. David Burrell; "he wants to go right to the point." He tackled complex subjects, gathered vast amounts of information, synthesized it, and tried to reduce the subject to simple terms. His knowledge of atomic energy and radiation was limited—more than the popular understanding, but less than the physicist. Yet he was able to articulate his understanding to the public better than a withdrawn scholar-physicist.

He carefully avoided spending his time frivolously or unproductively. "If you go into life [striving to be productive]," he advised students, "I grant you that you won't play much golf, and you won't play much bridge, either. But you may find . . . that you're getting more educated every day of your life because you are involved with very exciting people and very exciting projects."

He kept stimulating himself by learning more each day. "If I go through a day and don't learn something, I've wasted a day." Enormously curious, in Latin America he toured a large citrus factory with Donald Keough, President of Coca Cola Company, and he kept probing the guide for information about the factory as though he intended to buy it.

When he cared about something, he had a passion to know the subject exceptionally well. For him knowledge was usually linked to passion. When Pope Paul VI asked him to spearhead the creation of an ecumenical institute (one eventually built at Tantur, near Jerusalem), he had been a university administrator for fifteen years and out of touch with current theology. But the project rekindled his passion for theology, and he began to read voraciously on the subject. "He got very excited . . . about what was going on in theology," observed Fr. Burrell.[31]

He did his "homework" close to the event (often on an airplane), trying to avoid an interval that would cause him to forget what he had studied. To avoid confusion, repetition, and turmoil, he focused on one thing at a time, blocking out all distractions. "Right now I'm interested in talking to you," he explained to a reporter, "and I'm not worried about what's coming up next or what I just got through doing."

He cultivated his memory as well, gathering information and knowledge and storing it in his mental data bank to be pulled out and used at a later date. He developed a keen memory for conversations and names.

In a speech to an audience in Latin America, he quoted a conversation he had three years earlier: "As a Peace Corps volunteer said to me in Chile . . ." Walter Langford, who listened to the speech, was astonished. "My God. I was there," he reflected. "I heard that. I know the [volunteer] said that. But I would never have recalled it again in my life! He didn't forget anything! He has a built-in computer in his mind."

While distributing communion at a liturgy for major benefactors of the university, most of whom he rarely saw, he called each person correctly by name. In the summer of 1965, about sixty-five Peace Corps volunteers began training at Notre Dame. Langford, who directed the training, printed a booklet containing the name, brief biography, and photo of each volunteer and sent a copy to Fr. Ted. After having the booklet only three days, Fr. Ted met the volunteers for the first time at an outdoor barbecue. "He went down the food line," Langford recalled, "and he greeted each [volunteer] by full name and missed on one name out of sixty-five."

While walking across campus, Fr. Ted encountered a faculty member and for five minutes engaged in conversation, remembering details of the person's life.

"How is Mary Ann?

"How is her mother?

"Are the children all right?

"Is Mike ok? What is he doing?"

How did he do it? It helped to have a "reasonably good memory," he said, but the most important factor was "paying attention" and "working" at improving the memory. When he was rector of Farley Hall in 1948, he had 330 students. "I . . . just made it a point within the first week to know all 330." He mixed up six students, but by concentrating he had 324 names "down cold." The reason people do not remember names, he contended, "is because they don't work at it." At a conference in Louvain, a friend sat behind him while a participant read a long paper. Instead of listening to the presentation, Fr. Ted concentrated on remembering names of persons in the audience. "He had a list of all the people who were there, and I could see him looking around the audience to find a person and then checking [off the person] on his list."[32]

"He can't stand it when he can't communicate directly with people," said Gilligan, "so he's constantly studying languages." "I like to communicate with people," agreed Fr. Ted. "You can communicate best when you are speaking their language. I like to understand different cultures, and you get that best in their own language." Once he learned a few languages, he wasn't intimidated about learning others. "You just barge in," he said. "If children can learn them, you can learn them."

He was fluent in five foreign languages: French, Italian, Latin, Spanish, and German. (He was best in French.) He also developed a limited but still impressive knowledge of six other languages: Russian, Japanese, Chinese, Portuguese, Greek, and Hebrew. He delivered commencement addresses in four languages. In 1977 Langford accompanied him to the Dominican Republic, where Fr. Ted delivered a commencement address in Spanish. Langford was impressed by Fr. Ted's pronunciation and accent. "He talked 45 minutes and didn't miss a beat. It was fluent Spanish all the way," said Langford. (Fr. Ted had a different recollection of the afternoon in the Dominican Republic. "I was speaking from a text, whereas in most languages I speak from the heart," he said. "But I never took a class in Spanish and didn't feel confident enough to extemporize. The ceremonies started late and it was getting dark before I was halfway through. It was a race between darkness and the light of my message. The last three pages may have been the fastest they ever heard an American speak Spanish.")[33]

On vacation aboard the giant French oil tanker *Esso Picardi* in 1982, Fr. Ted had to speak French all day to the French crew. "I find myself thinking in French now," he wrote in his diary on July 31. "As thoughts go through one's mind when one is alone, they tend to be cast in a certain language and, right now, it is French."

He constantly worked at increasing his proficiency, listening to records to improve his Russian, German, and Spanish; reading the *New Testament* in foreign languages; bantering with interpreters. "I finally finished up my trip through the French-English dictionary," he wrote in

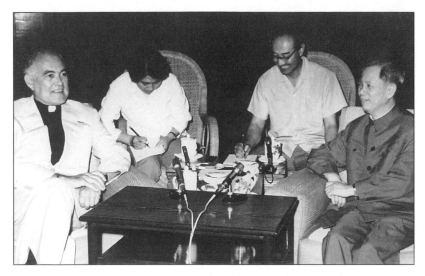

Meeting with governmental officials on one of his several visits to China.

his diary. "I covered more than 5,000 words and find that I know about 90% of them."

Learning Chinese provided a special challenge. "[Every] word is a monosyllable, and since that leaves so few possibilities for words, they differentiate between each word by four different tones which gives them four words for the same spelling. If you miss the proper tone, they simply look at you with a complete lack of understanding." Throughout his visit to China in 1979 he practiced Chinese with his interpreter. "By the time we had left China," observed James Grant, "he had several hundred phrases that he could communicate."

Overall, his proficiency with languages was critically important for the success of his public career. "Probably a third of the things I've done in my life," he estimated, "I couldn't have done if I hadn't known other languages."[34]

If something interested him, he read his way through it, sometimes consuming three books a week. From age twenty he regularly read *Time* and *Newsweek*. Usually he glanced at another fifteen magazines per week. Major newspapers were clipped for him. "I've always got a pile of clippings on thirty subjects I'm interested in," he said. He studied reams of reports to keep abreast of current projects. "We have fifty different projects in operation now," he told a reporter in 1970 of his work for the Rockefeller Foundation, "and I have to be familiar with each of them."

He read many popular novels ("idiot reading," he called them) because, he said, he wanted to understand the mores and values of the modern world. He read every night before going to sleep. (Someone teased that he would die tired but not illiterate.)

He treasured his free time and never was without something to read. "It kills me when I get on an airplane to go to Africa or Europe and a guy comes in and sits beside you and expects you're going to amuse him. He's got nothing but his passport; I get on there with stacks of stuff I must get through because I've got to do something when I arrive.[35]

He read clusters of books on the same theme to avoid shallow understanding. "You just can't be on the surface of things," he said about his reading style. In July 1982, while vacationing aboard the *Esso Picardi* enroute to the Arabian Peninsula, he explained his reading schedule. "To get myself in the mood, I had picked up a book by Frederick Forsyth called *The Devil's Alternative*, a story about the high-jacking of a super tanker. I'll have to give it to the Captain to give him bad dreams at night, but I finished it Sunday aboard ship. Then I began to read some of the books I brought aboard to get myself organized for my first trip to the Arabian Peninsula. The first day I read *Mohammedanism*, a historical survey by H. A. R. Gibb. . . . It's a fine book which gives a useful overview of the whole history of the Mohammedan religion, about which I knew all too little. Having finished that, I embarked a day or so later on Bernard [Lewis's] book *The Arabs in History*. . . . These two books got me off to a good start in thinking about where I was going and how to understand it. Having finished them, I began a third book as we entered the harbor on Wednesday. This is a more modern description of Saudi Arabia by Robert Lacey, entitled *The Kingdom*."

He read critically. In his diary he explained the aggravation one writer caused him. "All day long, I've been reading about *Arabia without Sultans* by Fred Halliday. It's one of those books that really gets my goat, since it involves a writer who is very talented and very well-informed and very journalistic, and yet who romanticizes anything revolutionary. Like so many others, he is always comparing the ideal of socialism with the reality of capitalism. He wouldn't think of doing it the other way around, contrasting the ideal of capitalism with the reality of socialism. One should be willing to admit that there are faults in capitalism as well as faults in socialism and then compare the two realities in a balanced, disinterested way. Halliday does not do this. . . . Anyway, I am reading him, and it took several hours of virtue today to keep myself moving from chapter to chapter. Unfortunately, I still have about 150 pages to read, so that will mean practicing a lot more virtue."[36]

For a solemn occasion like a commencement address, Fr. Ted wrote out his speech and spoke from a typed manuscript. Otherwise he spoke extemporaneously or with a few notes. Increasingly his formal speeches were "mix and match"—parts of previous commencement speeches would make up a new one. "He was given to borrowing from here and there," said Conklin.[37]

He often said privately, "Change the audience, not the speech. Why rewrite Hamlet?" For twenty years at the Freshman Honors Assembly he gave almost the same speech—on the importance of competence, commitment, and compassion. The faculty, who had heard it before, were bored, but the honored freshmen were impressed.

Each immersion in a new area of public service stimulated a fresh theme for scores of speeches and articles. Special events also energized him. In preparation for the 1976 Bicentennial, he dove into one of his weakest fields of knowledge—American History. He prepared three speeches—on justice in America, religious freedom, and American idealism—and delivered them on twelve major occasions during the Bicentennial year. "Whatever its faults," he concluded optimistically in one of the speeches, "America is still the most exciting human experiment in all the world."

He often challenged his audience. After indicting a group of business leaders for being self-centered, he urged them to use their resources to attack poverty and racism and to improve the urban jungles. The leaders might retort and say that the problems were none of their business. "Then I ask, whose business is it if not of those most endowed with the growing knowledge, the great leverage of local power, the affluence and security to govern one's time and the use of one's talent? If such as we, the young, the intelligent, and the energetic, are not interested, how will the problem ever be solved?"

Many university presidents avoided controversy and divisive issues, not wanting to alienate potential benefactors or split their various constituencies. "As a result," observed Derek Bok, "they come across as rather bland. That was conspicuously not true in Ted Hesburgh's case. I think it had a lot to do with the respect which he eventually came to command."

During his extemporaneous speeches Fr. Ted had poor eye contact with his audience. Rather than looking directly at them, he looked over the crowd. He also developed the habit of licking his thumb as he spoke. Because he was so busy, he sometimes spoke without adequate preparation and thought. On these occasions he rambled—a fifteen-minute speech became forty-five.[38]

Although he looked at the ceiling, licked his thumb, and sometimes rambled, when he prepared his speech he was usually impressive. In both speaking and writing he used various stylistic devices to enhance the impressiveness of his presentation, such as alliteration ("violence, vulgarity," "conflicting convictions," "abused and abandoned"); rhetorical questions ("Where do we go from here?" "What really was wrong within colleges and universities?"); parallelism ("It took us the better part of two centuries to make it come true for most Americans, *women as well as men, black as well as white, young as well as old, poor as well as rich.*); and repetition ("When I am sick, I want an *elite* doctor, when on an airplane, an *elite* pilot, when in a difficulty with the law, an *elite* lawyer . . .").

Clark Kerr thought most audiences were impressed by Fr. Ted's ability to develop themes that featured new and interesting information. Listening to Fr. Ted keynote the annual meeting of the Catholic Press Association on May 11, 1960, a reporter for *America* noted: "Suddenly I realized that I was hearing a great address and I leaned forward attentively." The reporter concluded that Fr. Ted's message was "apt, urgent, quietly eloquent." At a gathering of mostly non-Catholic philosophers at Notre Dame, Fr. Ted impressed the group with the conviction, intelligence, and eloquence of his speech. "They were just absolutely struck by it," reflected Fr. Ernan McMullin. "I remember afterwards being very struck by how struck they were. He obviously had reached them."[39]

He often delivered forceful, moving homilies at funerals and other special occasions. Notre Dame alumni groups found him warm and inspiring. "He is a hypnotist," said Thomas Carney; "I have never known him to give a poor speech. [The audience is] completely enthralled by what he has to say." He inspired some faculty at Notre Dame, as well. Robert Gordon walked out "three feet off the ground" after hearing Fr. Ted's annual address to the faculty. Other young biology professors were equally impressed, Gordon thought. "You'd walk out of that [annual] meeting really elevated, and it would take you a year to come back to earth, and then it would be time for another meeting with the man."[40]

The one group that objected to Fr. Ted's speeches was the faculty at Notre Dame. Especially in the 1970s and 1980s, they thought his speeches were long, rambling, repetitious, and not directly germane to the educational mission of Notre Dame. "He tended to repeat the same symbols," said theology professor Josephine Ford. "We used to smile when he said, 'A beacon, a bridge . . .'" They objected to his litany of the famous and powerful, and his constant references to his travels and to his service outside the university. Some faculty would mutter, "I wonder what travelogue we are going to get this time?" When he began describing obscure cities in Chile or Central Africa, some faculty snickered. Preoccupied with being Chairman of the U.S. Select Commission on Immigration and Refugee Policy, he stressed in a speech to the faculty that everyone should have an identification card that couldn't be counterfeited. "I just thought to myself that this is ludicrous!" reflected Prof. John Houck. "That was the low point."[41]

He wrote at a rate that would stagger most people, putting forth millions of words. By 1990 he had written four books; edited or co-edited two others; issued nine volumes of speeches and essays; published two hundred and six articles for journals; turned out thirty-six newspaper articles; and written the introductions for sixty-five books. In addition, he composed hundreds of unpublished speeches, sermons, and papers, plus thirteen (some lengthy) travel diaries which he photocopied and distributed to friends and colleagues. Finally, he was an extraordinary letter writer, dictating tens of thousands of letters during his presidency. Notre Dame archivist William Cawley, who organized Fr. Ted's papers, observed: "Hesburgh kept in touch with cardinals, archbishops, bishops, and monsignors, with admirals, generals, and members of Congress, with scientists, philosophers, historians, and theologians. He personally responded to letters from ordinary people, answered their questions, dealt with their criticism, and helped solve their problems." (He tried writing poetry many times, but quit. "I just don't have the talent," he said.)

The recurring themes in his writing were the moral aspects of education, values, and the importance of inculcating a sense of justice and service to mankind. Except for his autobiography, on which he had assistance from a freelance writer, he wrote all of his own material. He admitted to the "usual judicious thievery of ideas from many sources." He enjoyed writing but found it difficult to get started. "I never know quite where I am going until I get into it," he said in 1982. "The things begin to take shape and the very act of writing somehow leads the way to form and substance." Once he got started he wrote very fast.[42]

His four books were: *The Theology of Catholic Action* (1946), originally his doctoral dissertation; *God and the World of Man* (1950), a theology textbook; *The Humane Imperative: A Challenge for the Year 2000* (1974); and his autobiography, *God, Country, Notre Dame* (1990). Of the published collections of his speeches and essays the most noteworthy is *The Hesburgh Papers: Higher Values in Higher Education* (1979).

The Humane Imperative, the 115-page published version of the Terry Lectures he delivered at Yale in December 1973, was his most impressive book. Broadly interpretive, cautiously optimistic, he urged that theological and philosophical principles become operative in a wide variety of human affairs. In a strong, confident voice, he offered solutions to some of the world's problems. The most original and provocative essay outlined a plan for global education. Instead of spawning more conventional classrooms with hordes of teachers, he proposed launching three satellites into space, each with an educational data bank. The technological possibility existed for the program, he insisted, and the specter of thirty million illiterates could be destroyed. Sure it would be expensive, but so were the ills of ignorance and illiteracy. Reviewed mostly by Catholic newspapers, *The Humane Imperative* earned plaudits. "Exciting," "refreshing," "the voice of a statesman" were typical comments.[43]

Less successful was *The Hesburgh Papers*, a collection of eighteen addresses and essays, some of them Fr. Ted's command performances before the likes of the American Council on Education and the National Science Foundation. His themes were vision, values, change, higher education, Catholic higher education, student unrest in the 1960s, and civil rights. Most reviews were critical. Writing in the *Los Angeles Times*, Jack Miles, an editor at the University of California Press at UCLA, described the book as "invincibly bland." It "conceals rather than reveals its author's remarkable personal history. . . . It may have been a nice gesture to publish Hesburgh's speeches, but the old man *must* have more to say than this." Some of the pieces were "interesting" and "practical," said the review in *Library Journal*, "but most are lofty and above-it-all, the values they espouse too broadly defined to make exciting reading."[44]

Some reviews were downright hostile. Fr. Ted and two others edited *Patterns of Lifelong Learning* (1973), essays on continuing and lifelong education. "The text represents another pathetic attempt to dignify a foundation's study by associating it with leading educators," said the reviewer for *Choice*, the important library journal. "In general, this text is written in the deadly prose of commission reports and is filled with those inane and bromidic comments that insult the reader's common sense."[45]

Fr. Ted's thirteen travel diaries chronicled his activities with the detailed precision of a movie camera. He described his daily routine; the sights seen, meals eaten, and gifts purchased; the name and brief description of almost everyone he met; and, inevitably, the endless encounters and chance meetings with Notre Dame alumni. He also provided historical and geographic descriptions of each place he visited. "I can't close today without a few words about Ecuador. . . ."

"Do not expect a literary gem," he wrote friends in his cover letter for his insightful Cambodian diary in 1980, "since this diary was dictated late at night (usually after a long and busy day). It is also a rough draft, hastily corrected by hand so that I could share it with you quickly before it is dated. At least it's a new look at a rather dramatic recovering from death and destruction, averting total holocaust for the Khmer people in their ancient land. I share the story with a sense of hope and a glimmer of success, although much remains to be done."[46]

His writing was usually thoughtful and timely, often provocative, and always sincere. Fr. Andrew Greeley, the columnist and critic of the Catholic Church's hierarchy, praised Fr. Ted for writing "simple declarative sentences" unlike the "clericalist language which most church leaders used." He wrote most effectively when in an emotional state of controlled anger or when deeply felt beliefs were under siege or being ignored. Examples were his letter to *Sports Illustrated* in 1959 defending the dismissal of Terry Brennan; his individual statement in the Civil Rights Commission's 1961 Report; his 1969 Letter to Students; and his articles on science and values.

"He has one regrettable tendency," observed Richard Conklin, "the long sentence. He is apt to go a paragraph with a long sentence." Actually, he had a few other regrettable tendencies. Sometimes his thoughts were murky and verbose. The "modern Christian," he wrote, "refuses to confine part of his activity to time and part to eternity. He realizes that we must travel to eternity through time, and that the light of our faith must somehow illumine and suffuse all temporal activities." His greatest deficiency, however, was the hurried manner in which he wrote and published. "If someone could get me a couple weeks off, I'd give them a book," he glibly told a reporter. He wrote two papers in two days. One evening he composed an article on the Bible for the *University of Michigan Quarterly.* Commenting in his diary later, he said, "I think it only took me about an hour-and-a-half." He did his own research, seldom revised, didn't send out drafts for review, and usually did not receive the benefit of criticism and editing from a skilled editor.

Despite its huge volume, Fr. Ted's published material has had only small impact. "None of his writings have had particular effect," Notre Dame professor Michael Crowe correctly observed. "People who know of Hesburgh do not refer to his writings." "Nobody remembers anything he wrote," added a former Notre Dame administrator. "He is not incisive on the permanent record."[47]

He advanced a host of ideas for solving world problems and then promoted them with the passion of a crusader. Most were not original, but they were unconventional and appeared fresh and new to many who read and heard them. Examples include his proposal for a common market for South America and the educational satellite program that would wipe out illiteracy. He repeatedly pushed for a Human Development equivalent of the Reserve Officer Training Corps (ROTC). Students would receive college scholarships, like ROTC candidates, but instead of studying military science, they would study foreign languages and history. In the summer, instead of sailing on Navy ships or going on Army maneuvers, they would work with underprivileged people in the U.S. Then, after graduation, they would have a four-year commitment to the Peace Corps, VISTA, AID, Save the Children, or some other human development agency, and would be leaders for development, comparable to the ROTC's second lieutenants. "Imagine what we could do with 200,000 college graduates each year," he said.[48]

Often he studied an expert's concept, simplified it, applied it to a specific problem, and then promoted his new, hybrid proposal. In 1967 he listened to a speech by Alvin Weinberg, director of the Oak Ridge National Laboratory, for nuclear reclamation of agricultural resources. He reworked Weinberg's ideas and in an op-ed piece for *The New York Times* on October 1, 1970, he proposed his own Mideast peace plan to solve the "nightmare" and "horror" in the region. Fast-breeder nuclear reactors should be built in both Israel and Egypt which would feed into a common electrical and water grid irrigating the Sinai, opening it up to agriculture and industry. Palestinian refugees would be given the first choice for the newly fertilized land. Arabs and Israelis would literally be working on common ground, establishing mutual interests required for the negotiation of a peace settlement. When told that his idea was not economically viable, Fr. Ted shot back, "Well, is a war economically viable?" and added that it was crucial that Arabs and Israelis develop a common interest in the Sinai to avoid another war.[49]

An idea particularly close to his heart—one he promoted indefatigably for two decades—was dual citizenship. For him the greatest result of the space program was the striking picture of the world from the moon. "There we are, on a perfect jewel of a globe, blue, brown, and flecked with white clouds. No artificial boundaries, no political or ideological differences, no hatreds, no power struggles, no military strategies visible. Just one earth, the human habitat, home."

Nationalism was a major contributor to international injustice and war, he believed. Yet it was deeply lodged in our bones. Rather than fight nationalism, he preferred to circumvent it. He wanted everyone to consider themselves not only citizens of their own country but citizens of the world. "I do," he said. World citizenship as well as national citizenship "would require that we not only feel compassion for all who suffer everywhere, but that we commit ourselves, our lives, whatever talent or time we possess, to do something about the monumental injustices that exist, in our own countries and elsewhere. Unless we do this, the world has little hope for peace."

In order to qualify, one had to certify one's belief in the unity of mankind, in the equal dignity of every human being regardless of nationality, race, religion, sex, or color. One also had to work for world peace and "do something" to prove the sincerity of one's beliefs, something to promote justice, peace and the well-being of fellow humans at home and abroad.[50]

He condemned communism for its materialism and atheism. It viewed man as simple material reality with no destiny beyond time, "the pawn of deterministic causality, bereft of innate spiritual dignity, and, therefore, a creature of the state with no inherent or inalienable rights." But the subject of communism was not a major theme of his speaking and writing.

He welcomed change, not for its own sake, but because "it is a sign of life in a non-eternal, imperfect world." Centuries without change were usually centuries of stagnation. Changes were ruinous, however, if not related "to the changeless principles that give meaning and direction to human life."

A consistent, firm advocate of a liberal education, he personally exemplified its value with the extraordinary breadth of his knowledge and interests. Vocational training was fine, but it was not enough to make life rewarding. One should learn how to be an accountant, a businessman, a doctor, a lawyer, a priest, or a teacher. "But everyone should, I think, have some liberal education. If all I learn is how to do one thing—to put this screw in this wheel in this automobile—then that means for the rest of my life I'm going to be doing just that. It seems to me that is a terrible prospect for any human being."

He deplored the trend away from "thoughtful" courses. At Notre Dame, more and more students were opting for "corporate management, financial planning and accounting, and that's not education," he complained in 1980. An administrative colleague remarked: "I am sure he has great respect for businessmen, but I don't think he has [respect] for business courses."

A liberal education freed a person from ignorance, and cultivated clear, logical thinking, which enabled a person to judge and evaluate. "One of the beauties of a liberal education is that it permits you to move into almost any field and learn about it quickly because you've learned how to study, to read, to express yourself, and to ask the important questions." He had many different jobs in his life with different sets of rules and procedures for each. "[Yet] I find if you can read and learn and think you can pick up a brand new job . . . knowing almost nothing about it and, after a year or so, be fairly conversant with the whole field."[51]

He envisioned a social dimension to scholarship and wanted to use the tools of the social sciences for the benefit of the poor and disadvantaged. The thought of a small group of elite economists constructing elegant mathematical models—partly to impress others—bored him. "He always saw . . . economics as a kind of social service," observed Fr. Ernest Bartell, an economics professor at Notre Dame. "I [reminded] him that economics was an academic discipline."

He disliked democratic antagonism toward "elite" higher education. There was a difference between equality and egalitarianism and a bottomless gulf between quality and mediocrity. "When I am sick, I want an elite doctor, when on an airplane, an elite pilot, when in difficulty with the law, an elite lawyer. Who does not want elite doctors, elite lawyers, elite teachers, elite artists, elite scientists, elite engineers, elite architects? And where will they come from if not from elite education, open to the highest talent of every nation and race?" American higher education should always reflect both quality and equality, rather than settle for being mediocre and egalitarian.

The cliche of "relevancy" received little hearing from him. Moreover, it was foolish to tie one's conception of knowledge merely to facts. "The whole of human knowledge is doubling every 12 to 15 years. You'd better learn how to *think* today, how to cope with new knowledge and with evolving situations, because that's the kind of life you're going to face."[52]

The liberal arts, he believed, also helped teach values. "Learning values has always been a difficult task," he observed. "Without liberal education, it is an impossible task." Language and mathematics stressed clarity, precision, and style; literature provided insight into good and evil, love and hate, peace and violence; history recorded man's success and failure, hopes and fears, virtue or the lack of it; music and art purveyed a sense of beauty seen or heard, "a value to be preferred to ugliness or cacophony."

It was much easier to exemplify values than to teach them directly. He wanted teachers to be examples in their own lives of the kind of values they taught students. "The world won't be saved by education and intelligence alone. It's going to be saved by character and heart."

Value-free education wasn't "worth a hoot." It prepared a person for strictly professional competence, but would not suffice in the long run. "Lawyers without a commitment for justice, doctors without compassion or priests without piety or teachers without a passion for learning—those are all values." To have a university that was professedly concerned about human values was critical. "If you don't have that you have a gaping hole in society."

By contrast, the Watergate scandal during the Nixon Administration exemplified the failure of some universities to inculcate values. Almost everybody involved in the scandal was college educated; many were professional people with three years of post-graduate training. They were brilliant political manipulators, he conceded, but "by their own admission, many of them confessed that they had not learned to ask the right questions, such as, "Is this the right thing to do? Is it honest, just, or fair?" They made ends of means, substance of shadows, rights of wrongs. "In a word, they were hucksters."[53]

He was discouraged with the poor quality of leadership everywhere. When asked by a reporter in 1976, "Who are your heroes?" the question caught him flat-footed. After thinking awhile he asked, "Living or dead?" The reporter wanted living heroes. "I have to say I don't have any," he answered sadly.

He couldn't find leaders with vision. The top priority for any leader, he believed, was "great vision." Intelligence, honesty, decency, wisdom were all qualities needed in leaders, but vision came first. "Without vision the people perish." John Kennedy failed as a champion of civil rights, Fr. Ted believed, but Kennedy conveyed an inspired vision. "When Jack Kennedy stood up at his inauguration, he gave a vision, which, though it failed in many ways, was still a vision that got people excited." People joined the Peace Corps, marched for civil rights, and challenged poverty.

A new global vision was needed if man was to create on earth the beauty the planet manifested from space, he said on June 13, 1973, in his commencement address at Harvard. "The vision must be one of social justice, of the interdependence of all mankind on this small spacecraft. Unless the equality, and the oneness, and the common dignity of mankind pervade the vision—the only future of this planet is violence and destruction on an ever increasing scale, a crescendo of man's inhumanity to man that can only result globally in the extermination of mankind by man."[54]

Another major theme in his speeches and writings was the misplaced priorities in the use of science and technology. Both the Soviet Union and the U.S. placed far too much emphasis on using science and technology for military purposes, using human talent and brain power to destroy man. Almost as disturbing was the trivial use of science and technology. In an article for *Saturday Review* in 1963 he indicted scientists for producing luxuries:

To a hungry world we give the image of stored surpluses, better dog food, more esoteric dishes, how to eat more and still lose weight, how to have more appetite and then alleviate the effects of over-eating, how to stimulate and then sedate. Better soap, better deodorants, better beer, better cigarettes, better heating and cooling, better barbiturates, better cars, better chewing gum: these seem to be the ultimate blessings that science and technology have afforded us, the highly visible trappings of our American society, the most widely advertised contributions of science and technology to modern day America and to the world.

He understood that the trivial use of science brought great personal profit. "The noble is rarely profitable," he said. He also understood that science and technology were committed to tasks other than war and luxuries. There were exciting adventures in space. "But even here the pressured pace and the resulting escalated costs would not be so extreme if we were not operating under the exigencies of cold war competition and military possibilities."

At a dinner in honor of the National Science Foundation in 1962 he criticized scientists for prostituting science to something far below its capacity and for not seeking to abolish hunger, disease, and illiteracy in the world. "Should we pioneer in space and be timid on earth; must we break the bonds of earth and leave man in bondage below?" *The New York Times* stated that Fr. Ted's complaint was familiar, "though rarely stated more eloquently."[55]

"He doesn't relax in the true sense of the word," said Fr. Ted's brother James. "Very few people have relaxed with Fr. Hesburgh," echoed Conklin, adding that most people probably wondered "What Hesburgh does to relax." He enjoyed classical music, attended a few movies, and visited with friends. Except for news programs, he had little interest in television. Because of his life style, he didn't have time to play golf, tennis, or softball. He liked to play bridge, but gave up the game, except on vacation, because it took too much time. Although he knew remotely what was going on, he didn't follow teams in the National Football League or the pennant races in baseball. "You have to grab every free moment there is," he said.[56]

One of his favorite leisure activities was fishing in Northern Wisconsin. "That's my fishing cabin right there," he told a visitor to his office, pointing to a photo on his wall. The hideaway was at Notre Dame's retreat at Land O'Lakes, 5,500 acres of emerald-green forest and a ten-hour drive from South Bend. For about two weeks a year, in the solitude, away from telephones, schedules, and deadlines, he hauled in bass, pike, and an occasional muskie. He read and he wrote speeches, essays, and books. "It is always difficult to know where to begin," he reflected at Land O'Lakes as he started to write. "Especially when one sits at a long porch table covered with papers, distracted by the beautiful, tree-fringed lake out beyond, birds singing, clouds floating, water lap-lapping, and all the rest."

It was one of the few places he didn't dress in his clerical garb. When the pressures of his office work became intense, he looked at the photo on the wall and said, "I'll be up there one of these months." To his visitor he added: "That's what keeps me going." After a summer vacation, he wrote a colleague that he was "rested, informed, and ready to face the dragons of the new year."[57]

Another favorite vacation spot was Mexico. For fourteen years he spent a ten-day Christmas vacation at Rancho Las Cruces in the Baja

Peninsula of Mexico with C. R. Smith and Charles Jones. Smith was the founder and president of American Airlines, a pioneer in civil aviation in America, and former Secretary of Commerce. Jones was president of the Richfield Oil Corporation.

Fr. Ted had met Smith in the mid-1950s when the business executive attended a meeting at Notre Dame, and Smith convinced Fr. Ted to join him and his friend Jones on vacation in Mexico. It was an odd trio. Smith and Jones were raised Southern Baptists but neither went to church. "They were rough and tough Texans, self-made men, highly successful business executives," said Fr. Ted.

At Las Cruces the hunting and deep-sea fishing were spectacular. Fr. Ted bagged a lot of ducks and geese, and in a little more than two hours, he caught seven marlin and sailfish, some of them weighing 250 pounds. "It was a great ten days," Fr. Ted reflected of the carefree joy. Besides hunting and fishing the trio played bridge, drank margaritas, smoked cigars, joked, and told stories. Jones later told him: "Here we were going to take vacation and Smith just tells me with no warning that he's bringing a Catholic priest along. I figured you wouldn't drink, wouldn't smoke, wouldn't play cards, wouldn't fish, wouldn't hunt. And I knew you wouldn't cuss like we did. You really surprised me. Except one thing. You never cussed." In his autobiography Fr. Ted commented, "Well, nobody is perfect."

At a remote village Fr. Ted said midnight Mass on Christmas Eve and a week later on New Year's Eve. Villagers built a small church on a commanding cliff overlooking the sea, and Smith and Jones donated money to furnish it and even attended the two Masses.

After Christmas vacation Fr. Ted returned to Notre Dame rested and renewed. "What renewed me," he reflected, "were the beauty and tranquility of the place, the fresh air and the slow pace, and, of course, the company of two men who differed so markedly from the clerics, academicians, and government types I associated with the rest of the year."

After Jones died in 1970, Smith and Fr. Ted continued to vacation together at Christmas for sixteen more years, but at places far from Las Cruces. They went to Durango, the Yucatan Peninsula, Argentina, Kenya, Spain, the Amazon, and Barbados. Smith died in 1990.[58]

"It never hurts to be good looking," commented Philip Gleason of the advantages of Fr. Ted's appearance. He inherited the black Irish good looks of his mother. At 5'10", 175 pounds, with his graceful carriage, black hair, dark, deep-set, piercing eyes, and massive jutting jaw, he had what *People* magazine called "matinee idol quality." As he approached retirement he remained handsome, even though he added a few pounds, grey hair, and some facial wrinkles. His dress was severely clerical, but well-tailored and immaculate. "[Hesburgh] is one of those people who looks dressed up even in a rowboat," said Thomas Stritch.[59]

He had occasional small illnesses and periodically underwent a physical exam, but, for the most part, he paid little attention to his health. He exercised moderately by walking, "running to airplanes," or riding several miles on a stationary bicycle. For the most part, he was unambitious about exercising. Watching a woman demonstrate Nautilus equipment in the gym of a cruise ship, he wrote in his diary: "I got tired just watching the athletic young lady illustrate it all. There must be an easier way of staying healthy." He never returned to the gym.

For twenty-five years he smoked Lucky Strike cigarettes, finally giving them up and replacing them with an occasional cigar. He almost never took a drink during the day, but he liked a mixed drink before dinner and often one before going to bed "because it relaxes me and I go to sleep right away." After a strenuous day in Central America, he shared a bottle of Cutty Sark with his two male traveling companions. "At least all three of us went to bed this night with a nightcap, a reward for a full day," he wrote in his diary. But he was always careful not to drink too much, and no one ever reported him inebriated.[60]

He tried to watch his weight, eating about half the food put in front of him, and keeping away from sweets. For the most part, eating was a mere necessity. "Eating was functional for him," said Fr. David Tyson. "He didn't get a big charge out of [eating]." "He doesn't think about a good meal," agreed Fr. David Burrell; "he just thinks about gasing up."

Helen Hosinski efficiently took care of many of his personal needs. One Christmas Fr. Ted gave Fr. Tyson a new blue cashmere sweater. Later Fr. Tyson talked with Hosinski about returning the sweater for Fr. Ted's own use. "He won't wear it," Hosinski responded. "He always wears a green and gray sweater. As a matter of fact, when he gets holes in the arms of that sweater, I just take it off the clothes tree and throw it out and go out and buy another one just like it. He doesn't even realize it's a new sweater."

Fr. Ted was always deeply respectful of women, but until late in his career he assumed a woman should be a mother, a partner with her breadwinning husband in raising a family. Because of his background, male profession, and inexperience in dealing with professional women, he often put his foot in his mouth, causing some women in his audience to shudder. He referred to the "men and the girls" and even after Notre Dame began hiring female faculty, he absentmindedly spoke of the "faculty and their wives." He referred to women as "dear." "In this day and age [dear] doesn't wear too well with some [women]," observed Richard Conklin.

Still, he tried. He asked people to correct him when his language was sexist or not inclusive. "He stumbled his way through in the early years," said a female observer. "There was a lot of growth and a lot of movement over the years." Fr. Ted's niece, Mary [Hesburgh] Flaherty also defended her uncle. "[For] any man of his generation, there are some views of women that might be viewed as chauvinistic. However, I don't think he is a chauvinistic person. He feels that it is very important for women to have family, although in later years, he has come to respect the fact that not all women were meant to have children."

His views did change. He was sympathetic to the movement to grant women a larger role in the church, and supported the woman's right to have a career outside the home. In the mid-1970s he endorsed the Equal Rights Amendment, mainly because he found parallels with discrimination against racial minorities. "[Everything] comes down to the fact women should have the same rights as men," he said in 1976. "To me, it is a great satisfaction to see that our women are moving up," he added a decade later.[61]

Most women found him exceptionally attractive and charming. "All of our wives . . . have been absolutely infatuated with his personality," said a colleague on the U.S. Civil Rights Commission. "Women thought he was just so darling and cute and wonderful," commented John Schneider. They would say, "Oh, that divine Fr. Hesburgh." Schneider thought women had "crushes" on him. Indeed, some did. The wife of a prominent university president kidded her husband: "If Ted weren't a priest, I'm not so sure I would continue to live with you. I think I would run away with Ted if he'd have me."

Although always charming and chivalrous, he was very guarded in his friendships with women. After bad weather grounded their flight, Fr. Ted and Jean Wilkowski were stuck together in Hong Kong. "I'll meet you for supper," he gallantly told Wilkowski. Yet both were very guarded. "Both of us were very careful not to show any affection with one another," said Wilkowski. "It was just second-nature to him. And yet he was a regular guy."[62]

He accepted his vow of chastity, but nothing in canon law prevented a priest from becoming a foster parent. He enjoyed his experience as a foster parent. "I just wish that priests could have children and grandchildren as I do," he wrote in his autobiography.

In 1956, on a tour of South America, he met Charles and Victoria O'Grady at a party in Buenos Aires. The couple convinced him to watch over their children while they attended St. Mary's College and Notre Dame. Unbeknown to Fr. Ted, this new and unique responsibility would become exceptionally rewarding.

Anne, the oldest of the O'Grady children, enrolled at St. Mary's College in August 1956, at the age of 19. Her sister, Virginia, who was fourteen months younger, entered St. Mary's at the same time. Mary O'Grady, the third O'Grady to come under Fr. Ted's wings, enrolled at St. Mary's in 1959.

Fr. Ted took the young women to movies and to dinner at the Morris Inn; they visited his office and attended his Masses. He advised them about their careers, scouted their boy friends, and helped select their college courses. They joked and teased, talked about Argentina, discussed current events, and reflected on the last dance at Notre Dame. A safe haven, he helped them overcome many small problems and a few major ones. When one of the O'Gradys became seriously ill, Fr. Ted helped arrange medical attention. "We knew if there were any problems, he would be there," said Anne.

Although he advised and counseled, he didn't adopt a heavy-handed parental role, a decision the O'Gradys appreciated. He never told them they were wrong or ordered them to do something. "He was never preachy," said Mary.

Eventually five O'Grady girls and one boy made their way to South Bend. On January 28, 1963, Fr. Ted wrote to Anne, who was then working in the Peace Corps in Chile and planning to marry. He presented his up-to-date assessment of the young O'Gradys:

I had the O'Grady clan over to dinner last night and we discussed the usual set of crises. I tried to talk Mary into taking your job with the Peace Corps, but apparently she likes it in the United States and wants to stay. I told her she was lacking in the spirit of adventure, but I'm afraid I made no sale. Bob seems inclined toward graduate study, although I think his mind is pretty fuzzy on what he really wants to do in the future. Anyway, we gave him a hard time, too. Carol is more or less fed up with St. Mary's and would like to go to the University of Cincinnati to study interior decorating. I think I managed to get her to hang on until the end of the year so that all of this can be discussed en famille when you all arrive. Maybe we can get her to talk herself out of it by then.

I talked to Ginnie last week. She seems busy with exams, but otherwise happy and still desirous of going to Ecuador to work with the Indians. . . .

I am delighted that all goes well on the plans for the wedding. At least we have one O'Grady home safe, and I trust we'll get the rest around first, second, and third base before the game is ended.[63]

Anne thought Fr. Ted greatly benefitted from their relationship. During their conversation he listened intently. "By the way he looked and the way he [steered] the conversation," observed Anne, "he was getting a lot of information. We brought a whole lightness and charm about being a woman," Anne concluded. "Yet it was safe. It was nice for him to be able to be seen with us . . . and no one would say anything."

The O'Gradys admired Fr. Ted because of his values, his character, and his kindness. "He was so inspiring," said Mary. "He brought out the best in us. For most of us, even our friends don't do that. It's more 'take and not give.' With Fr. [Ted] it was always all 'give'. He didn't 'take' from people. That is extraordinary. Having that friendship is a blessing which happens to few people."

Subsequently, Fr. Ted married his O'Grady "children," baptized their offspring, and stayed informed about their lives.

Fr. Ted played a special role in the life of another young woman as well. He first met Hely Merle in January 1956, when he traveled to Chicago to pick her up and bring her back to South Bend. Fr. Ted's friend, Frank Freimann, chief executive officer of Magnavox, had made it his avocation to bring relatives to the United States who were displaced during World War II. Freimann asked Fr. Ted to take Hely under his wings. Orphaned at three, Hely had been living in Yugoslavia until Freimann brought her to Chicago. When Fr. Ted met her, he later said, "she looked like a plucked chicken who needed a course in makeup." Hely spoke no English, so on the trip from Chicago to South Bend they struggled to communicate in German. "We did use a dictionary an awful lot," she recalled.

Merle posed a new and difficult challenge. The O'Gradys had parents; Hely did not. The sophisticated O'Gradys had been well educated in Argentina; the unsophisticated Merle came from a deprived background. "He was much more of a protector when it came to guiding me through life," Hely said.

"He was always very good at telling me what I should wear," she recalled. "He did not like the fact that I was not as sophisticated as some of the girls who were born here. He gave me orders to go buy clothes. He made dates for me to go to the prom and concerts." Fr. Ted also helped her to adjust to the U.S., supervised her education, confirmed her in the Catholic faith, checked out her boyfriends, and married her. He continued to advise and assist her into the 1990s, even after she had seven children. "He has always been my protector," she said. "No matter what I asked him, he had the right answer for me."[64]

By 1990 Fr. Ted had thirty "grandchildren." Three of the boys were named Ted. "It was both a wonderful education and a wonderful relationship," he said in his autobiography. "Having had it, I just wish there were some way that more priests could have this kind of experience. If there were some way that priests could adopt children, at least in the kind of temporary way that I did, I think they would be better for it, not only as priests but as human beings."[65]

He enjoyed being part of family life, like his visits to Edmund Stephan's family in Chicago. "Our kids worshiped him," said Stephan. "They just loved to have him come and sit around [and talk]." During Thanksgiving festivities at Stephan's home, Fr. Ted helped make the gravy in the kitchen. "He'd have a big, long cigar in his mouth," recalled Stephan. "There would be ashes hanging perilously on the end. He'd be stirring the gravy, and we'd be wondering if the ashes would end up in it."[66]

He kept in touch with his sisters and was especially close to his brother, James. When relatives died or were injured in accidents, he was at the bedside. He married his sisters, nieces, and nephews, and baptized scores of their children and grandchildren. For many years, during the week before Easter he visited his brother in Pacific Palisades, California, and performed Holy Week services at his brother's parish, acting like a "normal" priest, preaching and saying Mass.[67]

Some of Fr. Ted's nieces and nephews attended Notre Dame, and he visited with them and took them out to eat. Of all his nieces and nephews he was closest to Mary Hesburgh, James's daughter. For a while, until he moved his family to California, James Hesburgh had lived in South Bend, and Fr. Ted often stopped in for birthday parties and cookouts. When Mary invited classmates to her thirteenth birthday party, Fr. Ted cooked the hamburgers on the grill. "He rolled up his sleeves and became part of the group," Mary recalled. Mary attended Notre Dame from 1976 to 1979. On the spur of the moment, Fr. Ted would phone her dormitory and say, "Let's go get some Chinese food together." At the restaurant he talked about his work and foreign travel, and they laughed and joked. After she graduated, married, and started a family in California, Fr. Ted visited her and his brother. With children attending, the family gatherings often focused on Fr. Ted's Mass, which he celebrated on Mary's dining room table. "He has a strong sense of family," Mary related. "He likes to keep everyone together."

In the late 1980s, Mary Flaherty underwent surgery for breast cancer, the same disease that had killed Fr. Ted's beloved sister Mary. "Naturally, when he found out about it, he was concerned," said Mary. Shortly after the surgery, Mary returned to Notre Dame for her class reunion. Fr. Ted invited her and a few others to a Mass in a small chapel. "It was one of the most special Masses I've ever been at," Mary recalled. "I just felt him spiritually and emotionally reach out to me at that Mass. It was a special bond. I think he did overtime in the prayer department for me. That was special."[68]

7 ⌒ PROFILE:
THE PRIEST

"WHEN THIS man committed himself to the priesthood he wasn't kidding!" said Fr. John Egan; "[Hesburgh] is *really* trying to walk in the footsteps of Christ."

When asked how he viewed himself, Fr. Ted's response was straightforward, constant, consistent, and simple. No matter what his activities or duties, he always viewed himself as a priest of the Congregation of Holy Cross. He always acted as a priest, thought as a priest, believed as a priest, and prayed as a priest. "If you said to me, 'What are you?' I wouldn't say 'university president.' I wouldn't say 'educator.' I wouldn't say 'world traveler.' I wouldn't say, 'I'm involved in government or foundations. . . .' I'd say, 'I'm a priest.'"

He said that, if he had the choice between being President of the United States and celebrating the Eucharist, the choice would be easy: he would celebrate the Eucharist. "If the only way I had to celebrate the Eucharist tomorrow morning was to walk 20 miles," he told an interviewer, "I would start walking tonight."[1]

He loved to tell priesthood stories and relished liturgical hardship. He told of long, treacherous jeep rides in the Chilean Andes to celebrate Mass for Peace Corps volunteers, and dusty drives in the Baja to perform the same service for Mexican villagers.

He found much joy in being a priest. Asked in 1963 to list the greatest satisfactions he experienced as a priest, he responded with the two most satisfying: offering the Mass and giving absolution to penitents. But his list was much longer. It included having Russian scientists inquire about God; being in St. Peter's Square at the election of Pius XII and talking with him and Pope John XXIII; meeting Notre Dame alumni everywhere in the world and seeing the "goodness of their lives;" hearing confessions and saying Christmas Mass for Mexicans who hadn't had a priest for twenty years; seeing the growing families of the Vetville couples to whom he had been chaplain after the war; the many happy occasions of marriages and baptisms; the "friendly faces, good lives, and great future promise of our Notre Dame students of today"; the kindly friendship of many non-Catholics and non-believers and experiencing their appreciation of spiritual values when presented to them; the heartwarming first months of the Second Vatican Council; visiting Peace Corps volunteers in Chile, Ghana, and Nigeria; and seeing missionaries at work around the world.[2]

The central focus of his faith was that God revealed himself in Christ. The Incarnation of Christ was the most important event in history. Everything before led up to it; everything after resulted from it. The Incarnation made God a reality "through the life he lived, the words he spoke, the message he gave us, and the salvation he promised, especially eternal life." After God became man, nothing human could ever be strictly human again. That belief was the "very central thing in my life; without it I don't think my life would have much purpose."

Fr. John Walsh (who later left the priesthood) and Fr. Ted had many long, stimulating theological discussions. "He really takes the Incarnation as a fact—that the son of God, the second person of the Blessed Trinity, *literally* became a human being," recalled Walsh. In Fr. Ted's mind there was no room for doubt on this key point of Catholic teaching. Walsh's position was considerably different, and they argued. "He reiterated that the greatest thing that ever happened in this world is the Incarnation," Walsh said. "The world would be an entirely different world if that hadn't happened." But it did happen, Fr. Ted believed, and we are in a new, Christian era. Although Walsh disagreed, "I knew that [Hesburgh] was totally sincere, completely convinced of his position and that he lived [his] convictions in a way I just totally admired."[3]

In the Mass, Fr. Ted vicariously experienced daily this great historical event. He and the congregation were doing what Christ did, they were reenacting the life and death of Jesus. When he was ordained in 1943 he made a personal pledge to himself that he would celebrate Mass every day of his life (even though it was not required by the Church). Daily Mass would serve as an act of gratitude for being accepted as a priest and bring him closer each day to the Holy Spirit.

He more than fulfilled his pledge. In over fifty years as a priest, he has offered Mass about 18,000 times, in front of large audiences and in solitary places. Excluding Good Friday, when the priest can't say Mass, he has said Mass every day since his ordination. (Except one day. He was in a hospital after midnight visiting a woman who was having a caesarian. After he baptized the child, he walked by a drinking fountain and, not thinking, took a drink. In those days the priest had to fast from midnight in order to say Mass, abstaining even from water. Although he couldn't celebrate Mass that day, he attended one.)[4]

Wherever he traveled he carried with him an old-fashioned Mass kit with miniaturized vestments, linen, chalice, paten, crucifix, candles, cruets for wine and water, and even a tiny altar stone. Therefore, no matter where he said Mass, he said it fully vested in the traditional, though cut down, setting. "I love to travel with him," said Thomas Carney. "He would say Mass early in the morning . . . in his hotel room. . . . One of the great experiences of my life. He would give a homily to me."

"He'd say Mass if he had pneumonia, or stomach flu, or the bubonic plague," said Edmund Stephan of Fr. Ted's legendary fidelity to the Mass. In 1963, with only four hours of sleep in twenty-four, he said Mass in three different locations in Antarctica: "at sea on a pitching icebreaker, within a mile of the South Pole, and half a continent away at an even more remote place, Byrd Station."[5]

In his autobiography he described the range of his Mass experiences: "I have said Mass with atheistic Russian Communists standing around the altar; with readers such as Rosalynn Carter and Robert McNamara; in an Anglican church that had not seen a Catholic Mass since the middle of the sixteenth century; in a dining car aboard a lurching railroad train; on all kinds of ships; in the middle of an African jungle; in thousands of hotel rooms in more than a hundred countries; and in all five languages that I speak." He even figured out a way to spread out a portable altar and say Mass in space if he was ever chosen to ride the space shuttle.

On a day trip that took him from the U.S. to Rome and then to Jerusalem, Fr. Ted realized that his only chance to celebrate Mass was

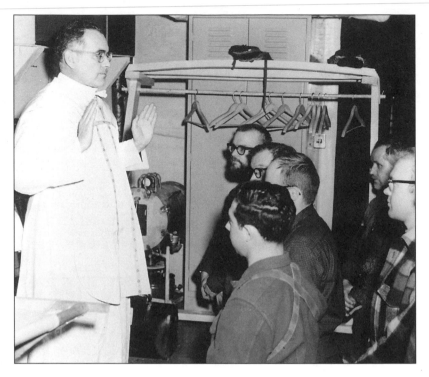

Celebrating Mass in the Antarctic.

during a short stop in Rome. He discovered a small, seedy hotel near the airport, but when he asked the hotel manager for a room "for just an hour," the manager reacted suspiciously. "I told her if she had any bad thoughts about it, she could come up and watch me offer Mass," he later said laughing. When Fr. Ted paid the bill, the manager said, "[Now] you have sanctified my hotel." Fr. Ted responded, "It sure needs it."

On campus he usually said Mass in a small, private room off to the side of the crypt in the basement of Sacred Heart Church. Starting in the 1970s he tried to visit each student dormitory at least once a year to say Mass in the chapel, followed by an informal reception in the lounge. (In 1978 there were 25 dorms.) Occasionally, with his student congregation he punctuated his sermon with slang as if he thought his youthful audience would relate to him better. He referred to himself as "Ted, old boy," mentioned something was "for the birds" and a chap who had made "an ass of himself."[6]

Modern liturgies varied, adapted to group celebration, and emphasized participation by everyone, even in preparing the liturgy. By contrast, Fr. Ted's liturgy was traditional and always the same. A critic, a younger Holy Cross priest, thought the way Fr. Ted said Mass was "just awful." It was only his "germanic dedication" that compelled him to say Mass every day. Rather than an extemporaneous liturgy, Fr. Ted sounded as if "he was reading it off a page." People enjoyed his intimate Masses in homes and hotel rooms only because they were overwhelmed by his famous "persona," concluded the critic. For whatever reason, most people said they enjoyed attending Fr. Ted's Mass.

Regular religious retreats kept him focused on his inner spiritual life. Almost every day for nearly half a century, he read his breviary, the Divine Office or prayers of the Church. Reading it was "a bit of a drag" when the prayers were in Latin, but after the change to English, he found it a "delight." Other people had to adjust to his prayer schedule. "He'd go off for 45 minutes in the morning in the middle of a very interesting conversation, and say his Office," Stephan observed. "I think he'd say his Office if he were on his death bed."

Every night before going to sleep he underwent a ritual self-examination, seeking forgiveness from God for his mistakes and vowing to do better. Usually he went to sleep praying the rosary. Occasionally he stayed overnight at Stephan's home near Chicago. "I have gone into one of our bedrooms to awaken him in the morning," said Stephan. "He'd be lying on his back, his arms folded on his chest, and rosary beads still in his hands." With his fidelities to the Mass, the breviary, and the rosary there was a graciousness and innocence about his priesthood, said an observer, that was as "old-fashioned as Barry Fitzgerald playing the role of an Irish pastor."[7]

When he was a seminarian and a young priest, he had been seized by the logical arguments for God's existence he found in his study of theology and philosophy. His early speeches as President of Notre Dame presented a highly abstract view of God. "Our aim," he told students and faculty in September 1953, "must be a Christian humanism born of the Incarnation of the Son of God, a humanism embracing all the wide dimension of the world and the human spirit, a humanism that is adequate to the designs of God for Notre Dame."

His view changed over time. The older he became, the more he experienced, the more he was convinced that knowledge of God and the sense of God came from the "realities of life" more than a lot of "logical arguments." He found God in life itself, in justice, in helping the poor.

He saw God in special moments, such as "great heroic virtue being practiced." He discovered God in the beauty in the world—in music, art, and especially in human beings. People incarnated the perfection of God by loving each other, by giving of themselves totally for the good of others, and by acts of magnanimity. "There are so many ways to find God," he believed.[8]

Prayer was the "direct line of communication" with God. In his own life he thought his two greatest needs were for wisdom and courage: "The wisdom to know what to do in the face of many possible decisions, and the courage to carry out the right decision . . . even though it might be very difficult." When he needed enlightenment and courage, he prayed to the Holy Spirit.

God was made real to him every day in a special way in the Holy Spirit, his "friend." When the Lord was about to ascend into heaven, he said he was going to send the Holy Spirit. "God did not leave us orphans in the world," said Fr. Ted. "So praying to the Holy Spirit is our big chance." The short prayer, "Come, Holy Spirit," was his favorite while he made difficult decisions. "And the Holy Spirit has never failed to show me the way, and to give me the strength of purpose to struggle on in the face of all kinds of adversity."

The Gospel of Saint John was his favorite gospel; St. Paul was his favorite apostle. He often prayed to Mary, the mother of God. When he spoke about the Blessed Virgin, he expressed conviction and fervor; he believed his work at Notre Dame was assisted by the Blessed Virgin. "I believe that this place is a shrine to Our Lady," he said. When Fr. Robert Griffin walked his dog at 3 A.M., he occasionally saw Fr. Ted praying at the Grotto of Our Lady, Notre Dame's replica, on a smaller scale, of the famous shrine at Lourdes, France. "When he talked of Our Lady, he was kind of sentimental," said a priest colleague, "[like] a child talking fondly about a mother."

He claimed he was prepared to die for his faith: "I am not afraid to say to you, openly and simply, that the Faith is my most precious possession." In a speech in 1967 he added:

It is the only reality which I am prepared, unequivocally at this moment, to follow, even unto death. Till they point the gun or begin the torture or accumulate the temptations that follow all of us in daily life, this must be a qualified testimony, since no man knows the limits of his endurance until he is tried. But, as of this moment, I am prepared to say, "For this Faith, I am ready to live differently each day, and to die for it if I must."

Fr. Ted enthusiastically endorsed a new Catholic symbol—service.

What has always bothered me is that in my youth many people prayed the Rosary, went to church regularly, performed acts of devotion, stuck little prayers in their prayer book to say every day, and never did anything to right the injustice that was around them. In their conversation, they often used racist terms and never felt there was anything un-Christian about that. In other words, I think it's quite possible to have all the symbols and still be quite un-Christian.

Nonetheless, he was disturbed that some Catholics relied exclusively on service, and didn't pray.

I don't think you can be involved in deep service on a continual, constant basis without having a fundamental commitment to the Kingdom of God, God himself, and Christ—which means some relationship to prayer, supplication, adoration, and all the rest. So we're always between the rock and the hard place: too much spiritual symbolism and not enough Christian service or a great deal of Christian service with very little prayer. You must have some of both.[9]

His passion for justice and concern for the poor were rooted in his interpretation of Christ's message. When asked for the biblical image most basic to his vision of the world, he referred to Christ's admonition: "Love the Lord your God with your whole heart and your whole soul and your whole mind and your neighbor as yourself." Even more basic was: "What you do to the least of my people you do to me." How different was the state of the world compared to what the Beatitudes said about man, he stated in a sermon. Christ said, "Blessed are the poor"; he did not exalt the rich as they seem to be exalted in the world. Treating the Beatitude as a truly revolutionary message, Fr. Ted banged his hand on the lectern and said with a smile, "I did not make this up. This is what the Lord Himself said."[10]

It was not easy loving the poor, because the least brothers and sisters were often not the most attractive humans.

They are often old and smelly, ugly and uncaring, twisted and ungrateful. How much easier to mediate God and His blessings to attractive, successful, caring, fun-filled young men and women. Besides, they respect us, love us, lionize us, and massage our egos. Well, a priest has some of each, but must take care that the poor, the powerless, the outcast and the lost souls get his prime attention whenever possible. They need God most of all and we need to find and serve God in them most of all.

In 1954 President Eisenhower asked him to join the National Science Board, and for the next twelve years he was immersed in frontiers of science and technology. Before the appointment he knew little about science and technology, having spent a good part of his life studying philosophy and theology. "It occurred to me that this immersion in modern research projects might challenge my faith in God and His Word as we find it revealed in the Bible."

Not only did his faith never waver, it deepened. The more he learned about science and technology the more he saw the need for God and His Word. Science neither supposes nor denies God's existence; it merely studies what is. "Philosophy and theology alone can tell us how the world came to be this way, what values should govern the use of the power that science and technology gives us, what the destiny of man and this world ultimately is." Science and technology were morally neutral. It was the scientist and engineer who were good or evil, depending upon how they used their knowledge and power.[11]

One of the greatest dangers, he believed, was confusing godlikeness with being our own god. "We are still accountable to Someone greater," he believed. "He, not we, is the Beginning and the End, the Alpha and the Omega. He, not we, is the goal of our efforts, the Maker of the rules of life, the destination of our lives and our help along the pilgrim way."

He thought other priests better than himself. Others were "more learned, certainly holier, [and] more capable in many ways." Despite his best efforts, he expressed concern that he still didn't know God well enough. He profoundly believed in Him, prayed to Him, and was grateful that He revealed Himself as Jesus Christ. "Even so," he wrote in his autobiography, "as I get older, it is increasingly clear to me that I know God all too little."[12]

Despite a few worries and infrequent feelings of inadequacy, in general, Fr. Ted never experienced a traumatic spiritual crisis, never seriously doubted God. Nor did he experience the serious identity crisis that many priests faced—an ambiguous role, loneliness, the need for intimate human love, a feeling of uselessness. "At the risk of appearing square, simplistic, insensitive, or out-of-touch," he said in 1971, he just hadn't experienced those problems. "He doesn't question [his faith]," said Anne O'Grady. "He is not personally turbulent."

He thought of the priesthood primarily as a work of mediation, a concept which had been a major theme of his Ph.D. dissertation. St. Thomas Aquinas had argued that the proper role of the priest was to mediate between God and man. Christ was the "perfect mediator," Fr. Ted believed, because he united the all-Holy God and sinful humanity.

Christ "has divinity in common with God and humanity in common with man," he wrote in his theology textbook in 1950.

Everyone participates in Christ's priesthood, but the priest stands in for Christ, stands between God and man. A difficult role. "If you are standing between God and man, you've got to be close to God and close to men," he thought. It was much easier to be close to men than close to God. Being close to men "comes naturally if you have any compassion . . . in your soul." To be close to God the priest has to pray and sacrifice. "Of course, the essential prayer is the Mass," he said. "That is the greatest thing a priest can do."[13]

Everything he did as a priest must bring people closer to God and make God more of a reality to man. The priest held a special role as a mediator in a secular society. In all the roles and jobs he performed, he wanted to bring the insights of the priest to the problems of the world. "My role has been to see the moral dimensions of a problem, something which we need since you see so many people viewing problems exclusively in a technical sense."

Other priests believed in mediation, but few applied it to all aspects of life on a global scale. The world was disjointed and fragmented, he thought. Mediation was needed between blacks and whites, Russians and Americans, science and the humanities, the ignorant and the wise, religious persons and secularists.

However, when he applied his concept of mediation to the complex world of Catholic higher education, his ideas sometimes became murky and vague. He was most successful as a personal exemplar of the concept. Being a mediator meant being a visible sign or a walking sacrament in the world. "If you're doing your job, people should look to you for things godly, the Good News, the grace of God." He thought he should act as a bridgebuilder. "I try to spend most of my life building bridges, through knowledge and through persuasion, and at times through preaching."[14]

In another sense he acted the role of a mediator during his long tenure at Notre Dame, especially during the turbulent 1960s, when he dealt with constituencies with different ideas and values. Pacifying both alumni and impatient students was described by *The New York Times* as "one of the most spectacular balancing acts in the history of American education."

"I wouldn't think of him as a theologian," said Fr. Ernan McMullin. He was too busy as president of Notre Dame to keep up with the scholarship in theology. Although he regretfully admitted that he was no longer a theologian, he read extensively on theological subjects, keeping abreast of some current theology. "His theology is rather like his liturgical practice," commented Fr. Sheedy. "[That] is personally conservative and traditional, but open and hospitable to new ideas, out to some line which he can draw where he thinks rationality and/or faith have been exceeded."[15]

"[He] would not be Father Hesburgh if he were not a missionary," observed George Shuster in 1972. Fr. Ted read extensively about missionaries and his desire to travel the world partly stemmed from his missionary impulse. In effect, he acted as a missionary on his Christmas vacation when he celebrated Mass in a remote village in Mexico and heard confessions for the impoverished people.[16]

Disturbed that few Catholic priests and religious were prominent in intellectual endeavors, he urged them to dedicate themselves to the greatest human instrument which God had provided—our mind. "Why," he asked bluntly in 1963, "have only two American priests been elected Fellows of the American Academy of Arts and Sciences—and no brothers or sisters? Why are no priests, brothers, or sisters, elected to the 600 member National Academy of Sciences, if we claim education as one of our greatest works? Why is only one priest a member of the Board of two great educational foundations, and none on the others?" Through priests and religious Christ must penetrate the world of the intellect and be at home in the house of intellect. It was not enough to be good priests and religious; "we must be competent scholars, cherishing the intellectual virtues and values, and understanding in its depths, the contribution that Christian wisdom has to make to our particular art, or science, or intellectual discipline."[17]

"We should never stop trying to become a saint," Fr. Ted stressed in a sermon in 1980. "We should never stop trying to love." Fr. Griffin wrote of Fr. Ted's saintly qualities, yet realized that to talk of him as a saint would embarrass him. "If he's not a saint, it's because he's too busy doing the saints' work for them," Fr. Griffin remarked. "Why bother to ask if he's a saint, if you can see the visible manifestations of wellsprings of grace from the depths of his soul?"[18]

Trying to emulate Christ, Fr. Ted adopted a saintly attitude toward forgiveness. His favorite parable was the Prodigal Son, the "greatest story on forgiveness." The child hurt his father by wasting his inheritance, yet when he returned home, seeking forgiveness, the father ran down the road to greet him. "He wouldn't allow a speech of apology," Fr. Ted observed; "he simply gave forgiveness and surrounded the child with love and kindness." Fr. Ted's conclusion: "There's not enough forgiving in the world."

He forgave easily. He forgave Richard Nixon for his callousness. In the late 1960s a columnist for a campus newspaper attacked Fr. Ted. "Privately," recalled Richard Conklin, "[Fr. Ted] could not have helped but be hurt, and letters from the campus community indicated that it, too, had sensed a violation of ground rules which had tolerated some rather vitriolic criticisms of University officials." Later the same student critic, now graduated, wrote Fr. Ted a letter requesting support for conscientious objector status. Fr. Ted supported his request. "It's called turning the other cheek," remarked a person who knew of the incident.

"I can think of people at the University of Notre Dame," observed John Gilligan, "who have been extremely critical of him for one thing or another, and he refuses to respond in kind, and instead treats them very generously, very openly, very warmly—when he would have every possible excuse to shun their company, to publicly embarrass them, or humiliate them. He just won't do it."[19]

He said he loved all facets of being a priest—the preaching, counseling, baptizing, marrying, absolving, and instructing. Care of the dying was a special grace because the priest boosts "the worried soul into eternity in peace." Before he first started hearing confessions, he worried that he might become disillusioned with his fellow human beings. Quite the opposite occurred. "I soon learned that they were inspiring me by their honesty and humility. I have never spoken a harsh word to any penitent and never will." A large portion of his daily mail brought cries for help. "I've saved people from suicides," he said. He took seriously his pastoral responsibilities. Despite his burdensome work load, before marrying a couple he spent several hours counseling them, particularly on the responsibilities of marriage. "I don't know how he does it and gets his work done," said Fr. Egan.

In airports, train depots, and other public places, he invariably wore his Roman collar. That way people would be more likely to ask his spiritual counseling and not pass him by. "If I've got that Roman collar on and they need help," he told a colleague, "they'll come to me. . . . I've been able to help a lot of people because I have that Roman collar on."

He was inspired by a French cardinal who described pastoral counseling as the "apostolate of one's presence." In Rome he encountered an auto accident where a young man was dying. He administered the Final Absolution right there on the street. Commenting on the incident, he wrote in his diary: "I often speculate, when these things happen, about the person arriving at the Gate and having St. Peter say, 'Oh, it's O.K. You were taken care of by a passing priest.'"[20]

"A lot of people, far more than anybody expects, go to Ted Hesburgh for advice," Fr. Egan observed. Fr. Ted tended to drop everything, no matter how important, to counsel someone. "The easiest way for a student to get to see Hesburgh," said Conklin, "would be to simply call him up and say, 'I've got a personal problem. I want to talk to you.'" Philip Faccenda agreed: "[If a] student came in with a hard luck story, Fr. Ted would have a very hard time saying no." In counseling sessions he listened, questioned, and responded, offering his wisdom and common sense.

He became personally involved when priests and lay faculty suffered from serious personal problems, like alcoholism. Quietly and compassionately, so as not to cause embarrassment or ruination of character, he arranged for professional assistance and counseled the family. There were many other people around who could have performed the service—colleagues, a department chair, a dean, a vice president—but he did it himself. "Fr. Hesburgh felt a kind of pastoral responsibility for the community as a whole," said Frederick Crosson, Dean of Arts and Letters from 1968 to 1976.

At a meeting in Hawaii of the Carnegie Commission on Higher Education, a staff member became ill and had to be rushed to the hospital. Fr. Ted and Clark Kerr visited him. "In a very moving scene," Kerr recalled, "Fr. Ted said a little prayer over him . . . and you could just see . . . life coming back into [the staff member's] face and his eyes sparkling more. It lifted up his spirits."

Occasionally he gave spiritual advice to the famous and powerful. When Ann Landers, the syndicated newspaper advice columnist, endured a painful divorce in 1975, she twice sought the counsel of Fr. Ted. Particularly worried about her career, she thought editors would not look kindly on a divorced woman giving advice. "He gave me tremendous support," she said. At a forum in Scottsdale, Arizona, executives and CEOs of Fortune 500 companies—powerful businessmen from Ford, General Motors, Kodak, and General Electric—came to him seeking his ethical advice or thanking him for previous assistance.[21]

The religious vows Fr. Ted took were essential to all that he was able to accomplish in his adult life. He seemed to thrive on his vows of poverty, celibacy, and obedience, viewing them as spiritual blessings. He encountered few problems living up to the vow of poverty. In 1968 he helped draft a revised constitution for the Holy Cross order. He and another priest wrote the section on the vow of poverty. Christian poverty was not the poverty of destitution, a circumstance that degraded man. Rather, wrote Fr. Ted and his colleague, the vow meant that the religious renounced his right to use material goods for himself, in order to free himself to do God's work on earth. "This interior disposition must be expressed externally in personal, social and apostolic activity." The religious expressed his renunciation by a life of simplicity and personal sacrifice. "As Christ gave himself for all, so by his poverty the religious gives himself totally—time, talents and resources—for others." Although available to all people, the religious should show "special care for the destitute, the hungry and those suffering from social injustice not only in attempting to relieve their immediate needs, but to eliminate the causes of that poverty which is evil."

He found it liberating to remain unattached to material possessions which occupied the time and attention of most people. Living out of a common purse, not having material worries, having enough for living but not for amassing, was a "great relief." He always had enough to eat, clothes to wear, a simple room, and money for books, clothes, and transportation. Most of the world was "shackled" by bank accounts, houses, clothes, and cars, but he felt as "free as a bird." He had what he needed and needed nothing more. Ironically he raised and spent huge sums of money, not for himself, but for "good causes," like Notre Dame and those in material need.[22]

The Church had often viewed women as a real and present danger to the celibate priest. It was best to avoid them. Seminary training and priestly spirituality, observed one authority, "called for control of the eyes, training of the thoughts, denial of impure feelings, and a double-check of intentions when it came to sex and women." While alert to the temptations that endangered the celibate priest, Fr. Ted, nonetheless, regarded celibacy as a "liberating experience" in his own life.

He unapologetically viewed celibacy as the ideal for the priest and often defended the advantages of a celibate clergy. On March 15, 1971, he endorsed an unmarried clergy in his keynote address at the Annual Convention of the National Federation of Priests Councils in Baltimore. "This will seem unduly harsh," he told the gathering (which supported optional celibacy), "but the present crisis is such that we will not be able to do what must be done if we cannot count on total dedication in the evangelical tradition. I do not discount the possible contribution of married priests, particularly in certain areas of contemporary life, but they will not be the shock troops that will carry the day against the monumental powers of darkness that presently threaten the people of God."

In Fr. Ted's case, celibacy did not seem to be a burden, or lead to severe loneliness, or cause sexual discomfort—problems that many priests faced. Celibacy seemed unnatural or inhibiting to many, but he felt comfortable. Celibacy was no great virtue in itself, but a "free and loving gift to God." The gift was to surrender the possibility of a loving wife and children in order to fully and lovingly give of himself to others. Rather than being dehumanized by the vow, the celibate priest gave up a particular love to exercise a universal love. By not belonging fully to one person, he could be called "Father" by everybody. He enjoyed having tens of thousands of people call him "Father." "I know the caller owns me and has a call on me for anything needed, especially compassion and understanding in a real spirit of Christian love." If the priest did not accept the spiritual and loving dimension of celibacy, "he is just a selfish bachelor."

Fr. Ted thought that women felt less inhibited with him because they instinctively understood and appreciated celibacy, "the fact that by choice we priests are out of circulation." True, celibacy required self-discipline and fidelity to the vow and made the priest more vulnerable. The vow did not automatically shut off the roving eye or the errant desire. "But we were not promised a rose garden," he said. Perhaps even Fr. Theodore Hesburgh occasionally had a roving eye or entertained an errant desire, but there was never a hint of sexual indiscretion in his long, celibate career.[23]

By the late 1970s he sounded more ambivalent on the advantages of celibacy, conceding the possibility that a married clergy might be best in some circumstances, while still strongly defending celibacy in his own life. "I don't have any problem in permitting priests to marry," he now said. There may be situations where a priest was better off married—for example, a priest in the upper Amazon, where desolate conditions and loneliness might cause mental and physical deterioration. Even in less extreme conditions in the United States, such as remote parishes, the quality of life in the rectory might be so impoverished that "marriage might be a solution to the isolation priests must endure."

He was eighteen when he first vowed celibacy. Would he do it all over again? Make the same vow at age eighteen? Yes, he said more than half a century later, "but only on the same premise that led me to do it the first time: that vowing celibacy would make me a better priest. . . . Without the bright promise of priesthood, I am sure I would not want to be celibate."

Celibacy, however, limited his insight about sexuality. He addressed the subject in highly abstract, often vague, philosophical and theological terms. He deplored America's "sex-drenched civilization." Sex should have "real dignity and importance within the dimensions of the truly human," he said, and must be placed within a scale of Christian values. It was "not unimportant," but neither was it "all-important."[24]

The vow of obedience was the most difficult commitment for him, because he gave up the precious gift of freedom. He did what he was assigned to do. His life as a priest would have been much different had he been able to do what he wanted to do instead of what he was assigned to do. However, in his case everything worked out, for two reasons. First, he found that he liked what he was assigned to do and probably was more productive. Second, in a curious way, he still ended up with substantial freedom. As long as he performed his primary assignment at Notre Dame, the Congregation of Holy Cross allowed him extraordinary freedom to serve in a wide variety of national and international tasks.

In some ways living in the Holy Cross community was easy and comfortable. The bell rang and he went to eat. On Sunday night he tossed out his laundry, and it came back clean on Thursday. For him the most attractive feature of life in a vowed community was everyone's dedication to the same goals. They all served the Church together, not separately; they all engaged in a common ministry and common prayer. A community like Holy Cross provided "a base, a circle of friends to live with and to depend upon for challenge and support." He also realized the presidency of Notre Dame came to him through his membership in the Holy Cross order.[25]

When he traveled out of the country, he preferred to stay at places run by Holy Cross priests and missionaries. "After seven weeks of hotels and the boat, it is good to feel at home for a change," he wrote in his diary of his simple room at an institution run by the Holy Cross in South

America. "He has great respect for the traditions," observed Fr. Griffin. "When he is home, he always comes to the community meals and community prayers. He makes his friends from among community people." Not surprisingly, his community also appreciated him. "The [Holy Cross] community is very proud of him," observed Fr. William Beauchamp.

He made a point of being kind to older, retired priests. "I am a nobody here," said an aging Holy Cross priest living in Corby Hall, "but I can feel very close to him when I meet him because he respects me." He was an inspiration to other priests. "He is for me," said Fr. Griffin. "His word is constantly encouraging, like a shipmate telling you all is well. I'm a better chaplain after saying hello to him, because I want to be worthy of belonging on his crew."

George Shuster worried that fame might ruin Fr. Ted, might undermine his exceptional priestly qualities. "[Not] a day has passed since I first came to know him that I have not prayed that he would never surrender to pride, intellectual covetousness and conceit," Shuster wrote in 1972. "I really thought that neither Notre Dame nor the Church in the United States could flourish if he did succumb."[26]

In October 1958, Pope John XXIII ascended the throne of Peter and set in motion events leading to a profound revolution in the Church. Shortly after his election to the papacy, he announced plans to convene an Ecumenical Council. Called the Second Vatican Council (Vatican II), its goal was to bring the Church up to date, to open windows and let in fresh air. One of the most important religious events of the twentieth century, Vatican II brought 2500 Catholic religious leaders together for four three-month sessions starting in 1962 and concluding in 1965.

As the Council opened, Fr. Ted didn't know what to expect. He vaguely hoped for a more open Church and the abandonment of repressive measures. Like most Catholics used to traditional ways, though, he didn't have a specific vision of what should happen or would happen.

The Council produced sixteen documents, some quite ordinary and others brilliant. One of the most revolutionary revised the liturgy, radically changing the way Catholics prayed. "Equally important," said church historian Jay Dolan, "was the new understanding of the church as the people of God. Gone was the judicial, institutional image of the church, and in its place was a more biblical understanding first captured in the concept of the mystical body of Christ." The Church was to be a "servant" Church, putting itself at the service of the human family. Ecumenism was a major goal. Seeking union with, not separation from, other churches, Vatican II encouraged Catholics to enter into dialogue with other Christians, to engage in common prayer, and to cooperate with them on social problems. Another key document, incorporating many ideas of Jesuit John Courtney Murray, called for religious freedom.[27]

The Mass underwent visible changes, which seemed earthshaking at the time. "In 1960, Mass was said in Latin," observed Dolan, "the priest faced the wall and prayed the prayers of the Mass silently and alone; occasionally the tinkle of a bell or the sound of the organ would break the spell of silence; . . . people knelt in reverent silence, separated from the altar by an imposing guardrail; they prayed the rosary, recited prayers, or followed the Mass in an English-language hand missal; no one except the priest was supposed to talk in church." Gradually the rules for celebrating Mass changed, and by the end of the 1960s a new vernacular Mass had replaced the Latin Mass.

The Second Vatican Council also helped topple the elaborate scholastic synthesis enforced since the late nineteenth century. Generations of Catholics had been assured by the Church's authoritative leaders that matters of faith were settled. "But," Philip Gleason observed, "the spectacle that presented itself during and after the Council of theologians, bishops, and curial officials in almost furious disagreement over the most fundamental questions of discipline, worship, and doctrine forced even the dullest Catholic to realize that these matters [of faith] *weren't settled at all.* In these circumstances the Neoscholastic synthesis came down like a house of cards."

In sum, there were major changes in theology and church life. The Council turned the Church on its head and caused serious disagreement. The genius of John XXIII had been to cut through tradition, simply and decisively. Gone was the aloofness, imperial splendor and harshness toward people of different religions. "In their place," said Dolan, "stood warmth, concern, openness, simplicity [and] an urbane, modern style."[28]

Fr. Ted had grown up immersed in the values and beliefs of the pre-Vatican II church, and he had accepted, mostly without question, its tenets. In his 1950 theology textbook, *God and the World of Man*, he often referred to the Catholic Church's dogma as "truth," as "certain," because it was based on "fact" and "real evidence." In his account the

University Club Dedication Mass celebrated by Fr. Hesburgh.

Catholic Church had a monopoly on the correct interpretation of God and his teaching: "[Many] people in the world today rebel against what they call the 'dogmatism' or 'authoritarianism' of the Church. In reality, they are rebelling against God and His word, for the Church represents nothing else."

His book confidently critiqued "Protestant errors" and "heresies." Without providing any evidence, he suggested that the Protestant's "overly pessimistic view of man" was a dangerous forerunner of modern socialism and totalitarianism. He wrote uncharitably of Martin Luther, contending that Luther's "personal problem" with inner corruption unfortunately led to his "dreary," pessimistic view that good works avail us nothing and only faith can save mankind. He lampooned the Lutheran "preoccupation with sin" by quoting approvingly a critic of Reinhold Niebuhr after the prominent American Protestant theologian had spoken in England:

> At Swanwick, when Niebuhr had quit it
> Said a young man: "At last I have hit it.
> Since I cannot do right
> I must find out tonight
> The best sin to commit—and commit it."[29]

Vatican II did nothing to destroy his long-time love for the Church, the Holy Father, the bishops, the priests and the nuns. On reflection, he particularly appreciated his elementary and secondary education. "I definitely feel positive about my Catholic rearing," he said, forty years after graduation from high school. "There were some very good, wonderful priests and nuns around. I must say that, for their own lights and for their own times, they did a very good job. And I'm grateful for it."[30]

In 1974, however, when he reflected on pre-Vatican II, he presented a harsh and powerful indictment of many of the values imposed by church leaders, a period he now described as the "closed church." He spoke partly in "caricature," he admitted, "but not altogether so."

When I grew up the church had all the answers to every conceivable question and the answers were always black and white. We were right and everyone else was wrong. There was no partial truth, no tentative searching, no intellectual modesty—the leadership simply said yes or no, right or wrong, and that was that. Authority was a force to be reckoned with in the closed church. The reckoning was simple: authority commanded and you obeyed; no questions asked; no reasons given; only the statement, "You do it because I say do it; do it or get out."

If the state wanted to progress, it had better listen to the Catholic Church's advice.

If there was evil in these secular worlds of politics, business, or societal life, it was because they were not listening carefully enough to what the church, the perfect society, was saying. If culture was degenerating, again the church could give the reason why. Evil books, that is, evil in the church's judgment, were put on the Index, not to be read by faithful Christians without special permission, even in the university. The church would tell you what movies to see or not to see as well. Again, these judgments, aesthetic and intellectual as well as moral, were made peremptorily, finally, with unfailing certitude and enforced rigidly up and down the line.

This was the church Ted learned at home, at school, and later in the seminary. It was a law and order church, little doubt was expressed, and dissenters were shown the door.

It was peaceful in a way, superobedient and faithful, easy to govern, and for all of these reasons, triumphalistic in style, medieval monarchic in governance, as safe and secure as the gilt-edged government bonds of the time, and about as exciting as a graveyard in its easy victory over the world of the flesh and the devil.

By opening Vatican II, Fr. Ted thought, Pope John had in fact "opened" the church, opened it to other Christian churches, and, he added approvingly, "apologized to the Jews for centuries of anti-Semitism."

Happily, Vatican II meant the end of the *Index* and the modern Inquisition. There would be

no more suppression of university theologians who speculate on the frontiers of theology; no more quiet exiles for those who dare to question; no more secret and hidden agenda of the powerful clerical few; no more triumphalistic lording it over other Christian communities; no more arrogance of "our" truth or suppression of "their" error; . . . no more insensitivity to immense problems like poverty, population, racism, global justice; no more one-man rule on every level of authority; no more unconscious assumption that the church is a male preserve, or a Roman one either; no more unconcern for the voice and presence and will of the people of God in the church which is to say, the laity.

Openness was here to stay, he said, thank God.

The church is not more secure, safer, more peaceful, more orderly, but it is more modest and less triumphant; more Christlike and less worldly and wealthy; more conscious of its central apostolic mission and less cluttered by interference in secular affairs that are none of its business; more involved in the world's growing problems of justice and peace and less immersed in politics; more concerned with ecumenical "oneness in Christ" and less conscious about others finding us; more ready to learn, less sure of teaching everyone, everything; more ready to serve than to control others; praying for forgiveness for ourselves and pardoning all others; more totally dedicated to Christ and his Kingdom; more open to the Spirit—the most fundamental openness of all.

As a consequence of Vatican II, he thought, Catholics had deeper interior motivation and were doing Christ's work because of dedication, concern, and conviction instead of rote, routine, and habit. The Holy Spirit had been working overtime through John XXIII, he believed; Vatican II was just what the church needed. "John XXIII did more for the church, the faith, the cause of reform, and the acceptance of Catholicism than anyone since the Reformation," he reflected in his autobiography. "Having lived about half my life before Vatican II, I much prefer the half that I have lived since then."[31]

Quickly, easily, enthusiastically, he embraced the ecumenical spirit inspired by Vatican II. Catholics and Protestants should emphasize their similarities, not differences, he urged. Both believed in Jesus as the Savior, eternal life, prayer, and the primacy of things spiritual over things material.

"Not long ago," wrote a reporter for the *Chicago Sun-Times*, "what happened [at Valparaiso] Wednesday would have been unthinkable." Times had changed and so had Fr. Ted's views on Luther. On November 1, 1967, Fr. Ted stood in the Memorial Chapel at Valparaiso University, a Lutheran-affiliated institution, where he received an honorary degree, and praised Martin Luther. The ceremony marked the 450th anniversary of Luther's tacking his 95 theses to the door of a church in Wittenberg, Germany. In preparing his talk, Fr. Ted studied Catholic attitudes toward Luther and discovered "harsh and very often unfair condemnation of Luther on the part of Catholic historians and writers." The purpose of the "slanderous" attacks on Luther, he told his mostly Lutheran audience, was to disabuse any Catholics who might think Luther to be upright or virtuous in any way. "Like most Catholics," he admitted, "my personal view of Martin Luther was largely shrouded in myths." Recently, though, Catholic scholars had taken a more judicious, understanding, and charitable approach to Luther. Consequently, Fr. Ted now judged Luther to be a man of deep faith and prayer, a man almost overcome by the almightiness of God. "The first Reformation, unfortunately, separated us," he concluded. "Let us hope and pray that this present reformation will unite us as we face together the great modern challenges of Christianity." After his speech Fr. Ted told a reporter, "I think it certainly is a sign of the times that I'd be invited to give a talk on this subject on this occasion at this place."[32]

He and others made a valiant and successful effort to bring ecumenical influence into the previously traditional and rigid Department of Theology at Notre Dame. He urged that the major religions return to the "transcendental" center. "If we could get back to that center," he said, "we would be amazed how close Jews and Muslims and Christians would be because we are all sons of Abraham, we all worship the God of Abraham, Isaac, and Jacob. We are all religions of the book—the Word of God impinging on human history. That is the vital center which draws us together, the common center which calls us into unity."

While saying Mass at Notre Dame, he spotted an Episcopal bishop in the congregation and invited him to the altar to an honored place. When it came time for the final blessing, he turned to the bishop and asked him to deliver it. "[Hesburgh] is very sensitive to things like that," said an observer.

He respected evangelist Billy Graham, and the pair prayed together on one occasion. But Fr. Ted judged Graham's approach as too limited. The word of Christ was something that one was going to be inspired— not harmed—by hearing. "I have never heard [Billy Graham] say anything that I would say theologically is wrong or that I would disagree with as a Catholic theologian," he said in 1977. However, "There are things that I would say over and above what he says."

When Graham planned a crusade in Eastern Europe, he asked Fr. Ted to write Catholic archbishops and cardinals in Hungary, Romania, Bulgaria, and Yugoslavia to smooth the way for his venture. Graham wanted Fr. Ted to introduce him and testify that Graham was a "good man" who preached "the Gospel of the Lord." Fr. Ted wrote the letters of support, and after Graham returned from his crusade, he phoned Fr. Ted to thank him for his useful assistance.

Fr. Ted won several awards from Jewish groups, spoke to Jewish audiences, preached at Jewish funerals, and paid homage to Jewish traditions. He initiated a dialogue between Christians and Jews at Notre Dame and invited Elie Wiesel, the well-known Jewish author (and subsequent Nobel Peace Prize winner), to deliver a series of lectures on four Hasidic masters.[33]

His most extensive involvement with ecumenism started in April 1964, when Pope Paul VI asked him to spearhead a special project: an ecumenical institute in Jerusalem where top Christian scholars—Catholic, Protestant, Orthodox—could study theology together. Fr. Ted pursued the project zealously, traveling 250,000 miles on behalf of the institute, setting up an advisory committee, and overcoming financial problems, the Six-Day War, and widespread skepticism about building a $2 million institute in Jerusalem. Eventually the Vatican bought property, and Fr. Ted raised funds for a building from a generous Notre Dame benefactor (I. A. O'Shaughnessy). In November 1971, the Ecumenical Institute for Advanced Theological Studies opened its doors to a pilot program for 34 scholars from 11 countries. The institute's beautiful building sat on the top of Tantur, an ancient hill covered with olive and pine trees, between Jerusalem and Bethlehem. In October 1972, as he took reporters on a tour, he told them, "What you see here is the realization of a very great dream." Afterwards he extended his dream by ar ranging and attending conferences to achieve more cooperation and unity among Christians, Jews, and Moslems.[34]

Until 1982 he knew little about Islam. But on a month-long voyage to the Arabian Peninsula in the summer of 1982, he plowed through the best books he could find on the religion. "I just read them one right after the other," he said. The effort further convinced him of the many points of contact in the development of all religions.

On a trip to Phnom Penh, Cambodia, he visited the silver pagoda at the Royal Palace, bowed before the Buddha statue, and offered sticks of incense and jasmine flowers. Teased by a reporter as he was putting on his shoes at the temple door, he explained simply, "I venerate the spirit and pay homage to local traditions."[35]

Ironically, Fr. Ted's ecumenical spirit also extended within the Catholic Church itself as he tried to overcome petty rivalries. Jesuits ran most of the major Catholic universities in the United States other than Notre Dame, which gave rise to some jealousy and even hostility. Neil McCluskey, a Jesuit, worked at Notre Dame and advised Fr. Ted. "I got in trouble with my Jesuit peers," he said. "They accused me of disloyalty. Why wasn't I working at some Jesuit school rather than Notre Dame?"

Displaying no signs of jealousy or hostility himself, Fr. Ted sought cooperation with Jesuit officials. He hired many Jesuits, and he and Mc-

Cluskey tried to establish an inter-university graduate center that would include Notre Dame and the Jesuit universities Loyola and Marquette. But their proposal never materialized. "The obstacles, of course, were pride, tradition, envy, jealousy," McCluskey thought. "It floundered on the narrowness of some Jesuits." By contrast, McCluskey concluded, Fr. Ted had "breadth of vision" and an exceptionally "open mind."

Fr. Ted adopted a tolerant attitude toward nonbelievers. A priest friend inquired why so many of the finest people he knew practiced no religion. "How can they be that good and not be [Catholics] like us? No belief in God, no faith, no church, no sacraments." Fr. Ted responded, "You can't be exclusive and think that all good people are in the clergy or belong to a certain religion. Somewhere along the line you were told something that isn't true: that only those who have the faith are really good."

He made one exception to his ecumenical spirit. "I really get turned off by pop religion." In 1978 he witnessed an example in Africa when he watched a witch doctor perform his ritual. It was the nadir of his trip, pure fraud. "He was about as much of a witch doctor as I am," Fr. Ted complained.[36]

He came to know four popes. He respected Pius XII (1939–58) but judged him too stiff, stern, and remote. "I didn't really cotton up to him that much," he said. He enjoyed Pope John XXIII (1958–63) because of his courage in calling for Vatican II, because he didn't take himself too seriously, and because he "really loved people."

He became particularly close to Pope Paul VI (1963–78) and often consulted with him. With Paul VI he was always respectful, but he didn't have to be overly deferential. He could be candid and disagree. Occasionally, when the Pope expressed an opinion, Fr. Ted repled, "Well, your Holiness, it isn't quite that way. It is more like this . . ." Paul VI insisted that Fr. Ted always visit him when Fr. Ted was in Rome. After the Pope died in 1978, whenever Fr. Ted was in Rome, he tried to visit St. Peter's to say a prayer at the tomb of Paul VI. "He had said that he wanted to see me whenever I was in Rome," Fr. Ted explained, "and so in a way I am still honoring his wish." He talked occasionally with Pope John Paul II (1978–), but their relationship was distant.[37]

Irv Kupcinet, the Chicago columnist, promoted Fr. Ted for pope. So did priest-columnist Fr. Andrew Greeley, who wrote from Rome in October 1978: "A papacy under the president of Notre Dame could be a delight, however unlikely it may be."

Although most of the American Catholic hierarchy seemed to admire Fr. Ted, strangely they never honored him. Disturbed by the oversight, Fr. Egan complained to two members of the hierarchy. "Do you realize," wrote Fr. Egan, "that the man I consider the most distinguished priest in this century has never once been recognized by the American hierarchy?"

Rumors circulated that he would be appointed bishop, archbishop, or cardinal and assigned to a major post, like Chicago or Washington, D.C., but nothing happened. The editor of Notre Dame's Ave Maria Press sarcastically remarked that Fr. Ted would probably never be appointed a bishop because he was "overqualified." "Why," Fr. Greeley demanded to know in 1981, "is Theodore M. Hesburgh not an archbishop or a cardinal? Why is a man of such extraordinary charisma excluded from the American hierarchy? I use the word 'excluded' advisedly."

Fr. Greeley expressed cynicism that Catholic Church leaders would ever recognize Fr. Ted's effective leadership. Fr. Ted was "good enough for the United States government, for the United Nations, for the Rockefeller Foundation, the Ford Foundation and the Chase Manhattan Bank," but "not good enough for the Roman Catholic hierarchy." Appalling? "Sure," Fr. Greeley contended, "but the way leadership is selected in the Catholic Church is appalling. In no other human organization, at least in the free world, is ability of such little importance and sycophancy of such great importance as it is in institutional Catholicism."[38]

Neil McCluskey thought that Pope Paul VI wanted to bestow major recognition on Notre Dame's president—making him archbishop of Chicago, New York, or Washington, D.C.—but was advised by the Curia not to make the appointment because Fr. Ted was too outspoken and too liberal on social issues.

If Fr. Ted was disappointed at not receiving a high ecclesiastical post, he never showed it. It was honor enough to be a priest. "The real price of freedom is to be free of ambition for secular or ecclesiastical preferment," he said. "The day one starts thinking and acting with an eye to impressing the right people so as to get advanced, that day one's life becomes artificial, false, and worst of all, unfree." Ambition among churchmen was corrosive. "I've seen it ruin so many," he said.

In fact, Fr. Ted did have two modest opportunities for promotion to bishop, but he refused both offers. During the papacy of Pope Paul VI, he was extended functional appointments as chaplain of the U.S. armed forces and director of Catholic relief services throughout the world. Both appointments would have included a promotion to bishop. He turned them down because neither appointment was as important or prestigious as being President of Notre Dame. Besides, both would have required him to resign as President during critical stages of fundraising drives at the university.

Some thought any post in the American hierarchy would limit his talents. If he were the Archbishop of Chicago, his focus would be Chicago. "As it is," observed Fr. Griffin, "his parish is . . . the world. He is kind of a world minister."[39]

Probably one reason for the failure of the hierarchy to honor him was his outspoken and blunt criticism of the Curia, the Vatican bureaucracy of congregations, tribunals, and offices through which the pope governs the Catholic Church. In his autobiography he referred to the Vatican bureaucracy as a "bureaucracy like any other, or maybe I should say, unlike any other." Because all bureaucracies, including the clerical bureaucracy, tended to become solidified, conservative, and unimaginative, he adopted a maverick sense of independence. He would not accept appointment as the Vatican Ambassador to the Atomic Energy Commission until he obtained authority to vote his conscience. "I didn't want some two-bit monsignor from Rome calling me up at 5 in the morning and saying, 'Vote for the Portuguese because it's a nice Catholic nation.' I wanted to be able to do what I thought was the right thing."

In March 1971, when he spoke to the Annual Convention of the National Federation of Priests Councils in Baltimore, he criticized the selection of bishops who were "safe, uncontroversial, favorably disposed to Rome and preferably Roman-educated, seminary rectors or canon lawyers or episcopal secretaries, in a word, generally those who will not make waves. It is objected that a majority of such men will give us a bland leadership in a Church that was founded to cast fire on the earth." Perhaps he was thinking of himself when he added: "Put in the opposite focus, it will assure that those priests who have manifested dynamic leadership, who, therefore, are controversial or liberal, or especially intellectual and committed to a broader sense of academic freedom, stand almost no chance of ever assuming leadership in a Church that is led by those chosen to be bishops." Acknowledging some specific exceptions, he nonetheless argued for the choice of bishops by the priests and people of a diocese.

Being blunt in expressing his views made him unpopular with some in the Vatican. "That's why they don't like him over there," said Fr. David Burrell. "He is very forthright and candid." Fr. Ted agreed. "I have a very simple way of dealing with that [bureaucracy]," he said. "I am simply totally honest . . . [but] it doesn't make you terribly popular with the bureaucracy." After Fr. Ted had criticized Vatican officials during a face-to-face meeting in Rome, a colleague remarked, "You really can't have much ambition if you insist on speaking like [that]."

He could not stand incompetence parading as power. Occasionally he had to deal with Vatican officials who had major responsibilities for Catholic higher education. "He . . . is forced to talk with some Jesuit who didn't get tenure at Marquette who is going to write this document which is going to affect them all," observed Fr. Burrell. "It just drives him nuts."[40]

In September 1975, Dr. S. Thomas Greenburg, director of the Institute of Catholic Higher Education at St. John's University, Jamaica, N.Y., was quoted in a newspaper article agreeing with the Vatican's Sacred Congregation for Catholic Education that there must be more Church control over "religious studies" taught in Catholic colleges. Greenburg was in Rome to talk with the Prefect of the Sacred Congregation for Catholic Education about the problem. Fr. Ted was irritated. He didn't want Catholic theology departments in the United States controlled by Vatican bureaucrats. On the bottom of the clipping Fr. Ted wrote: "Jack Greenburg is still at work with his private crusade. Too bad he's welcomed in Rome, and taken seriously."[41]

He was also irritated when critical public remarks he made about the Vatican bureaucracy were relayed to Rome and misinterpreted as criticism of the Pope and the Church. In his autobiography he complained that "little old ladies in tennis shoes and the ultra-right-wingers" sent his comments to Rome "with nasty letters saying that Hesburgh was picking on the Church again." Fortunately, he had a direct line to Pope Paul VI. "When the Curia goes after him," said a theologian at Notre Dame in 1969, "he just forwards the whole thing directly to His Holiness. That usually shuts them up."

Nonetheless, his outspokenness may have made him a pariah among some in the Church's hierarchy. "I've just been outspoken on too many issues," he reflected. "I've been out in front of the pack too many times. [Members of the hierarchy] like a certain amount of stability. I'm sure some of the things I said have upset conservative people at times."

Privately, he joked with friends about how Vatican officials viewed him. "Occasionally he can be slightly irreverent when talking about Rome," observed Jean Wilkowski. "I am in trouble with the Curia," he said to a friend. Half-jokingly he told Congressman John Brademas that when the Vatican bureaucrats saw him coming, they said: "Oh, Oh. Here comes trouble again!"[42]

Despite his occasional criticism of the leadership of the Catholic Church, particularly for bureaucratic fumbling, he was the farthest thing imaginable from a rebellious priest. He might criticize a particular move or edict of the Vatican, but his basic devotion to the papacy and the Church remained unquestioned.

His support for Vatican II, the ecumenical movement, justice, and human rights placed him on the liberal side of the Catholic spectrum. But on major Church doctrines he remained traditional. The Incarnation was a fact; Christ was really present in the Eucharist; prayer and daily Mass were important; the sacraments were a method of obtaining grace; the ideal priest should remain celibate. "I think if you read the old Baltimore Catechism to him, he'd still nod at it," said Stephan. "There is not a basic doctrine of the Church that he disagrees with."[43]

In morality he thought of himself as rather straitlaced. "I think I'm rather conservative when it comes to values," he said. When moral questions came to him in the mail, he sometimes farmed them out to someone else he thought trustworthy but more lenient.

He was asked how a committed Christian should confront a world that was confusing, threatening, challenging, and changing. What the Christian needed was a system of values, he responded. In the case of the Christian there was satisfaction in having a philosophy of life based on a "fixed revelation from the Lord" that involved certain basic values. The committed Christian could, therefore, "have confidence in time and eternity. We're not confused each day. Each day is not a fright. Each day we have a goal in life and we're conscious of it."

The "Christian ideal" was indissoluble marriage. He was proud of one study indicating that 93 percent of the marriages of Notre Dame's alumni held together. Young people should not live together before marriage. Divorce was wrong and one should not remarry after a divorce. (Still, he adopted a "pastoral" attitude toward divorced persons and didn't refuse them communion, although it was against the normal rules.)[44]

In the 1940s, in speeches and in his course on marriage, Fr. Ted railed against the evils of birth control and endorsed large Catholic families. The family, he lectured in 1947, was critically important and yet was "fighting for its life." Young couples were being "deluged" with "filthy literature telling them twenty new ways of practicing birth control." Besides being immoral, birth control was unnecessary and damaging to the family. Twenty-five percent of U.S. couples did not have any children, he said, and twenty percent had only one. Another twenty percent had only two children, "which is not even enough to balance our population." The consequences were disastrous, he claimed. "Eight-six percent of our divorces come from couples who have no children, or only one or two children. On the other hand, couples with five children represent less than one percent of the divorces granted in this country."

It was obvious, Fr. Ted glibly concluded, that big families were the happy families. "The reason is that you have to be big yourself to live and grow in a big family. And if you are big yourself, you are kept too busy finding things to do for other people, to have time to find fault with them." Besides, a "husband and a wife work best together as a father and a mother." He added:

The world today may go its way, turning away by the millions babies that could and should be born for the glory of God, but let them not call themselves Christian for it was Christ who said: "Suffer the little ones to come unto Me, for of such is the kingdom of heaven." Heartless modern people who are wedded to the dollar may go on, closing their doors and making life difficult for couples with children, but they too will one day face the Christ who said: "Whatsoever you did unto one of these my least brethren, you did it unto Me."

My dear friends, never forget that God is not mocked. The world may make and break its own rules about marriage, but it cannot find happiness in marriage apart from God and God's way.

In 1960 Fr. Ted still accepted uncritically the Catholic Church's controversial stand on birth control. Catholics believed that the rhythm method—abstinence during the few days in twenty-eight that a normal woman was fertile—was the only morally acceptable method of contraception. (Most Jews and Protestants believed that artificial contraception was equally moral.) Catholics were always being asked, he observed, why the Church didn't change its position. He answered by endorsing the traditional stance. "We cannot reverse our position," he said, "because it is based on unchanging philosophical and theological principles regarding the nature and destiny of man, of marriage and of sexuality, too."

In the 1960s a commission set up by Pope Paul VI could not agree on the issue of birth control. A majority favored changing the Church's teaching, but the Pope rejected the majority's opinion, and on July 25, 1968, he issued his encyclical *Humanae Vitae*, creating a storm of controversy. The encyclical reaffirmed the Catholic opposition to artificial methods of contraception, including the pill. Leading theologians and priests and much of the Catholic press criticized the papal declaration. "For the first time in modern history," observed Fr. Richard McBrien, "wide-ranging dissent greeted an official church teaching, dissent not from skeptical non-Catholics but from Catholics themselves."

By the late 1960s Fr. Ted had modified his position, and encouraged discussion of the Church's intractable stance. He also hoped that research in reproductive biology and the biochemistry of reproduction would provide additional moral means to control population. Nonetheless, he believed that the prevalence of concern for family control in the U.S. had led to a deplorable contraceptive mentality. Young couples were choosing to replace children with double-income lifestyles. "This kind of contraceptive mentality makes selfishness and promiscuity popular," he said. He did not even refer to artificial birth control devices by their proper names. To him they were "gadgets."

Increasingly, the Church's position on birth control became unpopular among Catholics, including large segments of Fr. Ted's Notre Dame constituency. Critics charged the rhythm method was ineffective—"Vatican roulette." After 1970 Fr. Ted said little publicly on the subject, prompting a reporter for a Catholic magazine to observe in 1987 that on Vatican teachings on sexuality, "Hesburgh has been virtually silent."

In recent years he has become even less inclined to support the Vatican's position on birth control, but still seldom talks about the issue publicly. He wants the Church to modify its position. "As I got more deeply into the whole question of development in the world," he reflected during an interview in June 1994, "it became obvious we had a real problem with population. We just can't go on doubling every few years. [Overpopulation] is a terrible strain on economics, education, food [and] housing. . . . I began to see that in the long run [the Catholic Church's position on birth control] was not really a sustainable policy for the good of all humanity. I became more and more unconvinced by the arguments that I myself used when I was teaching the marriage class."

He thought the Vatican had become obsessed with sexuality and facetiously urged in private that the Vatican make no official pronouncement on sex for ten years. "He thinks that is probably the place where we have messed up the most [and] have done the most harm," observed Fr. McBrien.[45]

On one aspect of sexuality, Fr. Ted's uncharacteristic private opinion shocked some of his associates. Normally tolerant and supportive of minorities, the disadvantaged, and the victims of discrimination, Fr. Ted adopted a decidedly different attitude toward homosexuals. In the early 1990s, during the national debate about whether to admit homosexuals into the U.S. armed forces, he became privately agitated about the issue and astonished listeners with his critical comments. "He just absolutely blocks completely on any kind of discussion of homosexuality," said a priest colleague. "He is extremely traditional [on homosexuality] to the point where he cannot even carry on a serious conversation." During an informal discussion with other priests about gays in the military, Fr. Ted aggressively interjected his opinion and told a story which ended with a naval commander saying, "Any guy who makes a pass for one of my crew gets thrown overboard." Commenting on the commander's policy, Fr. Ted added: "That solved the issue."

A second priest colleague, who heard Fr. Ted express disparaging remarks about gays, was dismayed. "I was surprised," the priest said. "It was almost a kind of emotional response." The priest thought Fr. Ted's attitude was wrong, that homosexuals and lesbians suffered greatly, and that the Catholic Church should make a sincere effort to help them.

For the public record, when asked in 1994 about the approach the Catholic Church should take toward homosexuality, Fr. Ted responded that the issue was a "tough one" and "very complicated," partly because genetic factors may be involved. On the one hand, he opposed "discrimination." However, "There is no way the church can come out and say that the practice of homosexuality is a normal thing in Catholic theology. I think it will always be considered abnormal." As for his personal views, "I try to be decent in my own dealings," he said.[46]

Fr. Ted consistently opposed abortion, but in the 1970s his inattention to the issue, his distaste for the methods of some Catholic anti-abortion groups, and his affiliation with the allegedly pro-abortion Rockefeller Foundation embroiled him in major controversy, bringing down on him the most intense criticism since the student rebellion of the late 1960s. On the issue of abortion, observed Professor Ralph McInerny, a pro-life advocate, "Some people are disappointed in [Hesburgh]."

He had occasionally criticized abortion. In a lecture at Yale in 1973 (published the following year in *The Humane Imperative*) he spoke on behalf of rights, including "the unborn children who are so cavalierly deprived of the most basic right of all, the right to life." Three years later he criticized the controversial Supreme Court decision, *Roe v. Wade* (1973), which he said practically allowed "abortion on demand for whatever frivolous reason during the first trimester."[47]

For the most part, though, as the Catholic pro-life movement grew in intensity after the *Roe v. Wade* decision, Fr. Ted was preoccupied with other matters and failed to gauge the depth of Catholic feeling on the subject. Trouble began in 1973. In an open letter, released on October 11, Bishop Leo A. Pursley, head of the Diocese of Fort Wayne–South Bend, publicly charged that "pro-abortion positions have been publicly advocated on the campus of Notre Dame University," adding, "I have seen no adequate explanation of these events by the representatives of the University." Subsequently letters and telegrams criticized Fr. Ted for permitting an abortion advocate to speak at Notre Dame. But Fr. Ted defended the right of "speakers of all persuasions" to be free to express their ideas at the university, especially in a pluralistic society. Critics retorted, though, that he was more sympathetic to free speech in a pluralistic society than in stopping the "greatest atrocity of our times."

In 1974 Fr. Ted sent pro-life supporters into paroxysms of rage when he bluntly criticized some Catholic anti-abortionists. In a speech to the Catholic Press Association, he said many "forces for good" did not want to be identified with "mindless and crude zealots who have neither good judgment, sophistication of procedure, nor the modicum of civility needed for rational discussion of disagreements in a pluralistic democracy."

Catholic anti-abortionists had been "selective" in their moral indignation: "We cannot be loud in condemning abortion after being silent about napalmed Vietnamese children or seemingly unconscious of the horrible present fact that 60 percent of the children already born in the poorest countries, with more than a billion inhabitants, die before the age of 5. We can and must do something about abortion, but it must be one of several equally horrendous problems that we are doing something about."[48]

His charge that Catholics were loud about condemning abortion but silent about napalmed Vietnamese children aroused the wrath of Catholic pro-life advocates. An alumnus responded in a Notre Dame magazine:

One wonders why Father Hesburgh assumes that every prolife advocate is a supporter of napalming Vietnamese children. Did he protest every North Vietnamese atrocity? If not, does this mean that he approved of the atrocity? Of course not.

There are many ills in the world. Can we not protest one crime unless we simultaneously file a brief documenting and condemning a dozen others?

Catholics are working against abortion. They should be praised for their efforts, not scolded because they haven't the time to work for all the other good causes.

Far too many clergy are giving lip service to the prolife movement but dragging their feet rather than join or support any real effort to counteract abortion.

After serving on the Rockefeller Foundation for sixteen years, on January 14, 1977, Fr. Ted was elected chairman of the board of the prestigious foundation, replacing Cyrus Vance, who became Secretary of State under President Jimmy Carter. He must have felt proud to lead an institution which donated nearly $50 million annually to worthwhile projects throughout the world. But after assuming his new post, he had to confront angry pro-life critics who charged the Foundation with supporting abortion.

A month after his selection, Fr. Ted responded to critics, denying that the Foundation ever supported abortion. "The Foundation has nothing to do with abortion." In fact, he added, "You'll never find the word 'abortion' in the report of the Foundation." His remarks turned out to be impetuous and inaccurate, providing ammunition for critics to lambast his leadership of the Foundation.[49]

On April 20, 1977, in a widely publicized 2,000 word article in *The Observer*, the university's student newspaper, Notre Dame law professor Charles Rice rebutted Fr. Ted's claim in detail. Trying to demonstrate that the Rockefeller Foundation had quite a bit to do with abortion, Professor Rice cited publications of the Foundation itself which described grants to groups working for the spread of abortion. Two examples: In 1975 the Foundation's *Report* listed a $5,000 grant to the American Civil Liberties Union Foundation "for distribution to American obstetricians-gynecologists of the educational brochure, 'The Abortion Controversy—A Doctor's Guide to the Law.'" Rice also drew connections between the Foundation and organizations that helped bring about the famous abortion decision in 1973. He pointed out that the Foundation granted the James Madison Constitutional Law Institute $50,000 in 1972 to handle the appeal for the pro-abortion side in the Supreme Court case of *Roe v. Wade* and a companion case.

Fr. Ted's contention that the word "abortion" never appeared in Foundation reports was simply untrue. The 1977 Rockefeller Foundation report listed the following grants:

The Alan Guttmacher Institute, Washington, DC, for a study on the impact of the restriction of Medicaid funding for abortion—$25,000; the Transnational Family Research Institute, Bethesda, MD, for support of its International Reference Center for Abortion Research and publication of Abortion Research Notes—$10,000; and the Roger Baldwin Foundation of the American Civil Liberties Union, Chicago, for litigation on the constitutional issues involved in the Illinois Abortion Law of 1975—$13,500.[50]

A Benedictine priest and pro-life leader from Collegeville, Minnesota, castigated Fr. Ted for accepting chairmanship of the "anti-life" Rockefeller Foundation. "Fr. Hesburgh's words and acts of the past clearly liken him to the pre-Hitler intellectuals who, lacking courage, wisdom, and foresight, failed to speak out."

An editorial in a Catholic periodical accused him of being the "house chaplain in an abortion mill." The Rockefeller Foundation had sponsored "monstrous evil" and it was shocking that Fr. Hesburgh would lend his name "to a foundation that has become almost synonymous with our American abortion ethos." The editorial concluded: "Very plainly, Fr. Hesburgh should resign."[51]

The volley of attacks left Fr. Ted reeling, awkwardly needing to recheck his statements. He did not respond directly to the charges of Professor Rice or to other pro-life critics. He probably felt that his main argument held true: that he personally was on record as opposed to abortion and that the pro-abortion grants referred to by critics were for minuscule dollar amounts (which the board itself did not have to clear) compared to the $50 million per year in grants to prevent disease and hunger and to improve education.

As a member of the Foundation's board, he claimed he constantly argued against "the 'Fuller brush' approach to population control, whereby objectionable means of every variety are pushed upon large populations without the slightest regard for their cultural, religious or psychological characteristics." One-issue people, he charged in December 1979, "would say that if one percent of what you are doing is wrong and 99 percent is good, you should disassociate yourself. That is very simplistic, especially if you are on record as against the one percent that is wrong, which I certainly am."[52]

Ordinarily Fr. Ted sloughed off criticism, but he was thin-skinned about attacks from pro-life groups. Associates warned him of impending danger. After one newspaper's account of his attack on the pro-life movement, Richard Conklin, Notre Dame's public relations director, sent him the clipping and a note, warning "We'll hear from the anti-abortionists."

When the National Right to Life Committee, Inc., criticized Fr. Ted for his connection with the Rockefeller Foundation, John H. Knowles, President of the Rockefeller Foundation, wrote to him and apologized for the attacks by "paranoid" groups. Added Knowles: "I . . . feel badly that you have to take such an unseemly licking periodically." Fr. Ted reacted far less tolerantly than usual. "I agree with you in your judgment about [the National Right to Life Committee, Inc.] and the wisdom of not getting into a frontal argument with them," he wrote Knowles. "You certainly recall the old story about not wrestling with a pig. You both get dirty and he enjoys it."

After Professor Rice wrote him, offering unsolicited advice on abortion, Fr. Ted responded with unprecedented impatience and sarcasm. "I appreciate all the good instructions you send me, . . . but I would also appreciate it if you would allow me to make a few decisions for myself," he wrote. "In other words, I think you have advised me enough on this subject for the time being." Later, when Rice again criticized his position, Conklin sent the clipping to Fr. Ted with the notation, "Any comment on Rice's latest? We'll get calls."[53]

As the 1980 election approached, Catholic pro-life advocates argued that abortion was such an overriding issue that any political candidate not strongly opposed to it should be opposed on those grounds alone. Fr. Ted strongly disagreed, arguing that politics should not be black or white or focused on one issue. What if politicians supported by pro-life groups were wrong on twenty issues of equal importance? "We say [abortion] is overriding," he said in December 1979. "What is so overriding about this when there are a million children dying this year in Cambodia." That, too, was important. "You are talking about living human beings, not human beings in the womb. So, I say to start making a distinction on the dignity of life."

Michael Schwartz, executive director of the Catholic League for Religious and Civil Rights, rejected Fr. Ted's argument against "single issue" voting on abortion. Writing in *Our Sunday Visitor*, Schwartz argued that the "difficulty with that position is finding any issue in contemporary American politics that is as serious as that of legalized abortion." Fr. Ted's assertion that everyone should be equally concerned with the genocide against the Cambodian people was merely a strawman. "No one on the American political scene . . . is in favor of killing Cambodians. But there are very many people, including a majority of the United States Senate, who favor the continued killing of American babies."

Schwartz quoted Fr. Ted's remark concerning Cambodia: "You are talking about living human beings, not human beings in the womb." Surely, Schwartz retorted, Fr. Ted was not seriously contending that "human beings in the womb" are not "living human beings." Fr. Ted's insensitive remark showed "that the Notre Dame president has failed to grasp the gravity of the human life issue. This, perhaps, explains his lack of sympathy for the political judgments of pro-life leaders."[54]

Beginning in 1981 Fr. Ted's position on abortion noticeably changed, and he moved closer to the views of Catholic pro-life advocates. Heightened awareness of the morality of the issue, dismay at the large number of abortions in the United States, and probably the criticism of him by pro-life groups accounted for his new stance. He stopped criticizing pro-life groups, resigned from the Rockefeller Foundation, and often harshly indicted abortion and vigorously defended the right to life.

Helping persuade him of the basic immorality of induced abortion was a sign he saw in Chinese above a cemetery in Hong Kong. It said, "What you are I once was; what I am you soon will be." A fetus, contended Fr. Ted, could well say to us: "What I am you once were. What you are I soon will be, if you let me."

"The fundamental civil right is a right to life," he now contended. Abortion was a moral "abomination." The fact that Americans were snuffing out 1,500,000 human beings a year, "overwhelmingly for the convenience of the mother," was an awful indictment of our society. He called *Roe v. Wade* "probably one of the worst blunders the [Supreme Court] has ever made." Disagreeing with those who said the Catholic bishops had placed disproportionate emphasis on abortion, he argued that the issue was "hard to get out of proportion: 1,500,000 deaths [a year], that in itself is an extraordinary proportion of evil."[55]

In 1984 New York Governor Mario Cuomo addressed a standing-room only crowd in Washington Hall on the Notre Dame campus. He confessed his personal difficulties in being true to his Catholic faith while carrying out his sworn obligation as an elected official to uphold the laws. He focused on abortion. "I accept the church's teaching on abortion," he told the audience. "Must I insist you do?" He offered this solution: "To assure our freedom we must allow others the same freedom, even if occasionally it produces conduct that we hold to be sinful."

Fr. Ted offered a different solution to Cuomo's dilemma: create and mobilize a new consensus for more restrictive abortion to reverse the Supreme Court's ruling. He used the analogy of civil rights to illustrate his strategy. In 1896 the Supreme Court in *Plessy v. Ferguson* sanctioned the separate but equal doctrine for blacks, allowing apartheid in the American South. Although *Plessy* was the law of the land, opponents worked against the law from within the law. Fifty-eight years later, in 1954, with a new national consensus, in *Brown v. Board of Education* the Supreme Court reversed *Plessy*. "Neither the consensus nor the change just happened; both were made to happen," he argued. The same approach should be used to restrict abortion—even though an absolute ban was not currently possible. "If it was patriotic, just and noble to work for the repeal of *Plessy v. Ferguson* and apartheid, why should it now seem un-American to work for fewer legally sanctioned abortions when there is already a moral consensus in our country that finds our present legal permissiveness on abortion excessive and intolerable?"[56]

Overall, Fr. Ted expressed dismay at the way the media covered Catholic religious issues. The media, he contended in 1980, overemphasized the "sexy six" subjects: divorce, homosexuality, birth control, abortion, women priests, and marriage for priests. "I don't think your average garden variety Catholic wakes up in the morning and says, 'I want to see women become priests,' or 'I want to see priests get married.'" The "sexy six" were not the essence of Catholicism. Most certainly, they were not the essence of Catholicism for Fr. Theodore Hesburgh.[57]

8 ∽ PROFILE: THE PRESIDENT

F R. TED WAS A VISIONARY who wanted others to
share his vision, especially for Notre Dame. "He had [vision] to
a degree that was unusual," thought Professor Ernan McMullin.
"He was always thinking about the future," agreed Edmund Stephan.

He urged Notre Dame's faculty to be exemplary, not just as teachers
and scholars, but as human beings. "Perhaps I am being too idealistic,"
he told the faculty on October 4, 1983, "but I do believe . . . that students do react positively to a great vision of what they and their world
might become. If we really want to shape the future, the operative question is: Do we want to shape it in truth, justice, beauty, the good and,
yes, in love, too? If we are unclear or less than enthusiastic about this,
who will follow the uncertain trumpet? Certainly not our students."[1]

He tried to formulate a consensus and galvanize the university community about the future direction of Notre Dame, specifically that it
should strive to be the most outstanding Catholic University in the
world. "Everybody seemed to have the same vision," Robert Gordon
thought. "Personally, I desire one quality for Notre Dame," Fr. Ted insisted, "dedicated excellence in all the broad educational endeavor that
goes on here—intellectually, spiritually, physically. I would rather see
Notre Dame die than be educationally mediocre. . . . We will be the
best, or please God, we will cease to exist here."[2]

Thinking big occasionally met resistance, a problem he faced when he pushed for enough money to fund one hundred endowed faculty chairs of at least $1 million each. (An endowed chair moved a professor's salary from general operating expenses to a special account funded by the benefactor.) "He would adjust," said Timothy O'Meara, "but the ultimate goal was to get those endowed chairs to bring in the best professors in the country. That is how he would improve the university." Some faculty worried that they wouldn't get an endowed chair; others objected that only a few people would be rewarded while the rest would suffer lowered morale. Nonetheless, Fr. Ted persisted. By the time he retired the university had raised enough funds for the one hundred endowed chairs. "They have had a very significant effect on raising the quality of the university," reflected O'Meara. "But if all people had been pleased in the beginning . . . those resources would have been dissipated. [Hesburgh] endured to the end. . . . That is where his vision paid off."[3]

The proliferation of international programs, the peace institute, the emphasis on academics over athletics, hiring excellent faculty, building an outstanding Department of Theology, all reflected his vision. In 1980, after hiring Fr. Richard McBrien to head the Theology Department, Fr. Ted gave him six endowed chairs and told him to hire "the best people in the world." "He has one of the broadest visions of anybody I've ever known," said Fr. McBrien. "He thinks *big*."

As the president of Notre Dame, Fr. Ted dealt with complex problems and was often subjected to intense, sometimes conflicting pressure. At the core of the university was the independent-minded faculty, which often regarded itself as the heart of the university and frequently disagreed with the administration. In addition, he had to placate students, trustees, alumni, donors, and townspeople. Besides major teaching, learning, and research centers, Notre Dame had police and fire departments, restaurants, libraries, art galleries, a major health center, and scores of residence halls. "We spend a lot just to keep the place green and looking beautiful," he pointed out.

In running the institution some universities give disproportionate power to faculty; some give it to deans. Notre Dame has always been a university dominated by the president. After 1970 Notre Dame was organized so that the president had two senior university officers reporting directly to him: the executive vice president who handled finances, buildings and grounds, university relations, and athletics; and the provost, who directed all academic and student affairs. Fr. Edmund Joyce, C.S.C., served as executive vice president throughout Fr. Ted's presidency. Fr. James Burtchaell, C.S.C. (1970–77) and Timothy O'Meara (1978–) were the provosts.[4]

Some university presidents have banks of secretaries to assist them, but for thirty-five years Fr. Ted had only one—Helen Hosinski. Many regarded her as the most important person in his life. She was unmarried and lived alone. Efficient, protective, closed-mouthed, she devoted her working life to watching over her boss. "I would always see that he had everything he needed," she said. So effectively did Hosinski understand Fr. Ted that when he was absent, she judiciously advised other administrators about handling delicate situations. While advising Fr. David Tyson on how to handle a dean, she said, "I think that Fr. Ted would probably not take this kind of strong position at this particular moment." "I listened to her," Tyson said. "She was right 99 percent of the time." Fr. Ted deeply appreciated his outstanding secretary. He was always kind to her and remembered to bring her gifts from his trips.[5]

Most of Fr. Ted's closest advisors were also his closest friends. Fellow priests or successful professional laymen, they were intelligent men with integrity who were exceptionally devoted to the vision of making Notre Dame a great Catholic university.

A close friend and major collaborator was Fr. Charles Sheedy, C.S.C., a brilliant moral theologian, who as dean for sixteen years helped reshape Notre Dame's College of Arts and Letters. Fr. Ted's appointment of Dr. George Shuster as his assistant starting early in 1961 was regarded by many as one of his smartest personnel moves. A Notre Dame graduate, polished writer, and former editor of *Commonweal*, Shuster had just retired as President of Hunter College, New York, when Fr. Ted convinced him to spend his sunset years at Notre Dame. Shuster directed the Center for the Study of Man in Contemporary Society, which sponsored and raised funds for a wide variety of social science research projects. He bolstered Notre Dame where it was academically weak, in the social sciences. Beyond his official role, however, he was Fr. Ted's confidant and senior advisor. "I was attracted by the personality of Fr. Hesburgh and the ideas he had for this place," Shuster said. "He's always about five miles ahead of everybody." For his part, Fr. Ted viewed Shuster as the personification of the urbane, sophisticated, and intelligent Catholic layman, and as a "Father-Confessor," who "listened sympathetically and always gave wise counsel." (Shuster died in 1977.)

Fr. Hesburgh's secretary, Helen Hosinski, sorting through the thousands of telegrams and letters received after his "15 minutes or out" speech in the late 1960s.

Over the years Fr. Ted developed an informal network of people within the university who advised him. One was Fr. John Egan, former president of the Association of Chicago Priests, who served as Fr. Ted's special assistant from 1970 to 1983. Periodically he met with Fr. Egan over spaghetti dinner in South Bend. "He would confide in me and ask for my suggestions," Egan recalled. "He would ask my opinion about particular people that he thought I knew on the campus, as to whether or not they merited advancement, preferment and honors."[6]

After their first meeting in 1946, Fr. Ted gradually pulled Edmund Stephan into active involvement with Notre Dame. An Irish-Catholic Democrat, Stephan became senior partner and chairman of Mayer, Brown, and Platt, a large, century-old, prestigious law firm in Chicago. Stephan was the first chairman of Notre Dame's new Board of Trustees, serving fifteen years until his retirement in 1982. Thoughtful and judicious, Stephan provided Fr. Ted with a sounding board for ideas, particularly about delicate situations involving key administrators and potential donors. They spent many Thanksgivings at Stephan's home in Evanston, Illinois, and vacationed together at Stephan's second home in Florida. "[There's] hardly a week that goes by that we don't talk on the phone several times," Fr. Ted said in 1977. "It really was more than chairman and president," Stephan reflected. "We were very close friends. I've always viewed him as practically a brother."[7]

Fr. Edmund Joyce, C.S.C., was Fr. Ted's executive vice president and right hand man. For three-and-a-half decades the pair labored at desks in offices only a few yards apart. Both were the same age (although Fr. Ted was ordained six years earlier). Like his boss, Fr. Joyce was intelligent, understanding, and exceptionally dedicated to improving Notre Dame. Otherwise, there were major differences, making them an unusual team. Fr. Ted was visionary and idealistic; Fr. Joyce was practical and cautious. "He's a Southerner, I'm a Yankee," noted Fr. Ted. "He's quite conservative, I'm quite liberal. He's good with numbers, I'm better with words. He knows how to raise money, I'm better at spending it. He's also more into athletics than I've ever been." Despite their strange chemistry, they worked effectively together, talked out differences, and never fought.

By his own design, said a writer who profiled Fr. Joyce, he "labored quietly in the shadow of the more charismatic Hesburgh, never courting publicity, seeking credit, or revealing much about himself." A certified public accountant, Fr. Joyce supervised budgets and investments, assisted in fund-raising, presided over the construction or remodeling of more than forty campus buildings, and kept the athletic program above reproach.

Fr. Ted relied on his advice and judgment about every major decision facing the university. If Fr. Ted envisioned an extravagant plan for physical expansion, Fr. Joyce cautioned him to move more slowly. "Let's not overdo it," he advised his boss. "I would try to keep the reigns on," Fr. Joyce reflected. A gentleman, he always acted deferentially toward Fr. Ted. "He never forgets who the president is," said James Murphy. Moreover, he never had any desire to succeed Fr. Ted. "I didn't have any ambition to be the president," he said.[8]

Once a month Fr. Ted met with all the officers of the university to review the previous month and project the following month. The officers met with him once a year for a three-day session to review the year and project the following year. At officers' meetings, agenda items were solicited from all participants. If a vice president wanted something on the agenda, he had the item inserted, and at the meeting he made his presentation. Fr. Ted decentralized authority by delegating responsibilities; he wanted the university to run itself. "When I became president, I had more power than Hitler," he said. "I could do anything because we didn't have all these structures we've created."

"The secret is really to get the very best people you can get, even if they are better than you are, and to get them in the right slot," he said of his delegation. "But once you get them appointed to that slot and get their agreement to do the work, then leave them alone. Don't try to second guess them. . . . I always told them: 'You do your work, and I'll do mine. Whatever you do, you are going to get the credit for it, and whatever you do I'll back you on it. Unless you make an absolute mess of it, I'm with you all the way.'" Asked how often he called back to the university when he traveled, Fr. Ted responded: "I never call back. I've hired good people to do their jobs. And when I'm gone, I expect the university to run without me. . . . They know where to get me if they need me."

Those who worked with him liked his approach. "He delegated better than any senior executive I was ever close to," said Philip Faccenda. "He picks people to do a job and then backs away and lets them do it," John Gilligan agreed.

He abided by a few axioms: never handle the same piece of paper twice; never have two people worrying about the same thing. He resented instances when he gave a task to someone and later would get the same task back; he expected the person delegated with the responsibility to solve the problem.

One other extraordinary axiom guided him. Occasionally his profound faith had to be factored into budget decisions of the university. Thomas Mason became vice president of business affairs at Notre Dame in 1976. At one of his first meetings, discussion focused on a proposal to construct a new building. Mason had prepared carefully for the meeting, drawing up a solid financial plan for the building proposal, including a construction schedule, projected costs, and cash flow estimates. He expressed concern that the proposal had a financial shortfall of several million dollars and questioned if the project should proceed under the daunting financial circumstances.

After Mason's presentation, Fr. Ted remarked, "What you are suggesting, Tom, is that we haven't identified all the sources of financing [and] that we don't have it totally funded." Mason agreed. Fr. Ted responded with a mini-lecture about the role of faith in financial planning at Notre Dame.

"Let me tell you a story about your formula and Notre Dame's method," Fr. Ted advised. He explained that when Cardinal Giovanni Battista Montini (later Pope Paul VI) visited Notre Dame, Fr. Ted showed him the huge hole in the ground where construction had just begun on the new, expensive fourteen-story library.

"How much is it going to cost?" asked Montini. Fr. Ted gave him the multi-million dollar estimate.

"Where did you get the money?" Montini wondered.

"We haven't got it yet, but we'll get it," said Fr. Ted.

When Montini expressed astonishment that the university didn't have the money in hand to pay for the library, Fr. Ted simply responded: "Cardinal, you've got to have *faith.*"

After relating the story, Fr. Ted asked Mason, "Is that library causing you [financial] problems today?"

"No," said Mason. "It's paid for."

"That's right," said Fr. Ted. "But if we had adopted your formula, we never would have dug the hole because we didn't have the financing all lined up. A formula here has to have a good degree of faith in it or it won't work. And your formula doesn't have faith. I'm trying to indoctrinate you in the university. Everything we do around here has an element of faith. And if it doesn't have faith, it probably isn't applicable to us." Reflecting on the financial lesson, Mason said, "Fr. Ted really believed that [Our Lady on the Dome] was getting things done around here."[9]

Fr. Ted had exceptional capacity to motivate. Optimistic, energetic, his attitude inspired the faculty and staff. "He always gave us the impression we were dong something terrific here," said a faculty member. He tried to inspire by projecting his vision, his dream, that Notre Dame could become a great Catholic university. James Frick "wanted to work like hell for him." He made subordinates feel that their work was significant. "It is not [just] the words he uses," said Timothy O'Meara. "It is the whole way in which he communicates or his presence communicates. He gives people the feeling of being important." Even when he exaggerated Notre Dame's potential, he still inspired. "He had a way of projecting a definition of Notre Dame that was factually [not verifiable]," observed Professor Ralph McInerny, "but it became something we were—By God!—going to become." Through his own example he created an expectation of excellence. "You always knew," said Faccenda, "[that] Fr. Ted expected you to be the best in your field."[10]

Although he delegated responsibilities, he made many of the decisions affecting Notre Dame and all of the major ones. "Those decisions made without his signature are infrequent," according to O'Meara. He gave O'Meara an enormous amount of independence. "But," added the provost, "obviously we have to see eye-to-eye . . . from the beginning." Decisions made by others usually bore his imprint. "The fact that I'm in this job indicates a certain compatibility of point of view," said O'Meara.

Fr. David Tyson, an assistant to Fr. Ted and a professor who specialized in management, described Fr. Ted as an "entrepreneurial manager," who exploited an opportunity even if it deviated from a set plan. Fr. Ted wanted consensus, but he could not tolerate lengthy process, and did not think he needed a consensus from every committee before he acted. With so many diverse views within the university community, to operate effectively he felt he had to make major decisions. He trusted his intuition. Subordinates had opportunities to express their own ideas, but he knew where he was going and usually steered a discussion or a meeting toward his ultimate goal. "He would listen," said O'Meara, "but ultimately he would get to where he wanted unless he heard powerful arguments to the contrary."

Whether it was a meeting with trustees, his vice presidents, or a university committee, Fr. Ted always dominated. At meetings of the Academic Council, his presence was very imposing. As the chair he brilliantly used persuasion to win support for his position or to reach a consensus. (He was so successful that a few suspicious faculty thought he was manipulating them.) "In dealing with the Academic Council," observed Fr. Ernest Bartell, "he never had to veto anything—ever—because he always got a vote his way." After he expressed his opinion about a proposal, the outcome was predictable. "It was a moot point to have a vote on it," said Mario Borelli, a faculty member, "because out of his own strength of character, presence, and [his] proprietoriness about Notre Dame, [the proposal] moved the way he wanted."

His dominance irritated some subordinates. "He is not a team member," said a former officer of the university. "The trappings are there, but he's not a team member. . . . Once he speaks in those officers' meetings, it's pretty clear how it is all going to turn out." His administrative style, contended Fr. David Burrell, "while genial, personable, and, indeed, pastoral was nonetheless always autocratic." One-time Notre Dame administrator Isabel Charles agreed. "He was very autocratic," she said. "It was *his* vision that people were to fulfill. He knew what [the vision] was, and he wanted everyone else to join in." For the most part, he persuaded people within the university to join him. "But even when people didn't [join him], he went ahead," said Charles. "He knew he was in charge; he took charge; and he brought everyone else along with him."[11]

Although he didn't micromanage and didn't interfere with his subordinates, he kept himself informed and insisted that his subordinates also keep him informed on major issues. He told the people who worked for him that he didn't like surprises. "I'm responsible," he said. "If I don't know about it, I'm double responsible." During the long nights in his office, he carefully read university reports and releases, and the minutes of department meetings. Frederick Crosson was astonished to learn that Fr. Ted studied in detail the minutes of every department meeting in all sixteen departments in the College of Arts and Letters. Fr. Ted closely questioned Fr. John Walsh about the details of a memo Walsh had sent him. "Having grasped the central significance [of the memo]," observed Walsh, "he would also be very concerned about the specific detail."

In most cases he made quick, efficient decisions. Fr. Chester Soleta, chairman of the English Department during the 1950s, occasionally presented his arguments to Fr. Ted on behalf of additional faculty for his department. "The answer came [quickly]," said Soleta. "It might be positive; it might be negative. Sometimes he said no; sometimes he said yes. But it was *there.*"

Department chairs found him congenial and easy to work with. If he differed on a proposal, rather than acting arbitrarily, he discussed the issue. "Chet, I disagree with you on this," he told Fr. Soleta. Fr. Ted explained his position; then Soleta presented his arguments. "There were two sides to [the issue]," Soleta recalled. "He was the president [and] had the final responsibility. . . . He always respected my proposals. I always found him a very good man to work with."

Some evenings Fr. Ted studied a four-foot-high stack of tenure and promotion recommendations. Other people had already passed on their recommendations, but he felt obligated to scrutinize every page. "It's a miserable task," he said. "I read myself blind until nine o'clock three or four nights. But I have to do it, because I'm dealing with people's lives. If the answer comes out no, the man or woman is finished here in another year. If it comes out yes and he's 35 years old, we'll have him for the next 35 years."[12]

He modestly claimed that he didn't know much about finance, but he actually knew a lot. "I must say," said Fr. Joyce, "that he is an awfully fast learner in finances. . . . I never had to tell him something twice. He grasped it immediately." Seldom did he need to be told something twice. On one occasion when Faccenda repeated important advice, Fr. Ted looked at him and said simply, "You told me that two days ago." Observed Faccenda: "I never did it again." He plowed through his mail and memos "flew out" of his office to other people instructing them to handle the matter, to reply in his name, or some other instruction. He always replied quickly to anything that anyone sent him. When O'Meara met with him, they handled most matters in a few minutes. "We communicated with each other very quickly," said O'Meara. At times there would be disagreements, but O'Meara added, "He would always let me come back and nag him and get him to change his mind."[13]

Maintaining the confidentiality of the university's business was not one of his strengths. "Fr. Ted was the biggest leak on campus," said a colleague who worked closely with him. "When you had something confidential, he would constantly tell everybody it was confidential, but then he would tell eight or ten other people." Fortunately his action didn't cause major problems. Ironically, he assumed others broke confidentiality, but, said the colleague, "We all knew who passed it on."[14]

Usually Fr. Ted didn't damage his health by worrying. He did the best he could and then moved on to something else. "I doubt if I've been kept awake a half dozen nights in forty years worrying about anything, even though there were a few things to worry about." Normally he put the worries aside, said his prayers, and went to bed.

He was open to new ideas, and he encouraged people to disagree with him. "He doesn't like soft people who say 'Yes' to him on everything, [or] who will break apart just because he . . . disagrees," said Fr. Egan. He liked stimulating discussion and people with strong opinions. Still, added Fr. Egan, "he and the rest of us know who's boss."[15]

Fr. Ted tried to practice a humane philosophy of management. People deserved to be treated with sensitivity even when the administrator's instinct leaned toward brusqueness. A community of learners and teachers should be characterized by "rationality, civility, urbanity, friendship, but especially humanity towards one another, even when they are intellectually or morally in disagreement." There was a humane way of saying no, of denying an impassioned request, of telling a person he has failed and will be terminated. "Even if you've got to let a guy go because he's done a terrible job—you help him get on his feet, maybe recover and do something else. But you don't drive people to jumping off bridges." There was also a humane way of upholding a deeply held conviction, even when it was under brutal attack. "One can be forceful and humane at the same time," he said. "But it is not easy."

He took a personal interest in the people who worked at the university. Besides remembering the names of employees and often the names of their spouses and children and the problems within the family, Fr. Ted wrote thank-you notes to all sorts of people within the Notre Dame community. "The place looks great," he wrote a gardener; "keep it up." To a university garage mechanic he wrote, "Thank you for picking up my car and getting it washed. It is much appreciated. Thanks for all you do for Notre Dame." The recipient was delighted. "People just glowed when they got [the note]," said Marty Ogren.[16]

James Gibbons, who arranged banquets and special events at Notre Dame, almost invariably received a prompt thank-you note for his efforts. Sometimes Fr. Ted sent a special note of gratitude to Gibbons's wife, as well, thanking her for being supportive while her husband was working on special events. "Gratitude was a hallmark of his character," said Gibbons.

Some of his pithy notes to subordinates were humorous one-liners. After receiving abrasive complaints from a student organization, he wrote his assistant, Fr. Tyson, "I will leave these tender concerns for you to handle." After another distasteful complaint, he wrote, "Could you handle this person's concern? Yuk!"[17]

He applauded achievement and gave credit to others. "Great job!" he would say. When McInerny received a grant or published a novel, not only did he receive an official letter of congratulation, but Fr. Ted scribbled a personal note as well. "It was a very pleasant thing," said McInerny. "He really knows how to . . . interact with people," said Francis Castellino. "His style has been very warm, very congenial, very open."[18]

When Fr. Ted became the president in 1952, neither lay nor religious faculty had a significant voice in running Notre Dame; they had little influence on appointments, promotions, priorities, or anything else. All Catholic universities were the same way. Fr. Ted supported the move toward more decentralized and democratized control. In 1968 a faculty manual was adopted which in part described the roles of the faculty and administration in governance. The university also established institutions which increased the faculty's influence on the university's affairs. "[Fr. Ted] initiated that whole movement to decentralize the authority of the university," observed Frederick Crosson. Still, Fr. Ted was not disposed to grant too much power to faculty. "I firmly believe that administrators, not professors, should administer."

He won respect from many faculty members because of his inspiration, persuasiveness, forceful personality, and accomplishments. "People have respect for him and can see what he has accomplished," said Timothy O'Meara. They were touched that he remembered their names. Many faculty favored extending Fr. Ted's presidency for five more years in 1982. "With a 30-year president, that kind of [attitude ordinarily] just doesn't happen," said Castellino.[19]

Although many faculty were pleased with the way the university was governed, Fr. Ted's management style annoyed others, who thought he was paternalistic and insensitive to collegial governance. "The whole structure of the university is designed to keep other sources of power from emerging," said Vaughn McKim, professor of philosophy and chairman of the faculty senate in 1982. "There is no direct access to decision making." "He didn't have a strong feel for faculty democracy," contended Fr. Ernan McMullin.

The Faculty Senate was a consultative body virtually without power. The Academic Council acted as an outlet for faculty opinion, but Fr. Ted chaired the meetings and the Council had more administrators than faculty. Some faculty were frustrated because they strongly supported Notre Dame, yet felt impotent about influencing its direction. They wanted more collegiality, broad consultation, and democratic process, plus more input on teaching, financial aid, admission standards, priorities for new buildings, and the appointment of top administrators.[20]

Despite differences of opinion, faculty critics who disliked the limited governance role Fr. Ted granted faculty nonetheless usually praised his overall presidency. "The many pluses in his career far overshadow short-term negatives," said McKim. Disgruntled faculty restrained from public criticism because of his imminent retirement, respect for his great contributions to Notre Dame, and a disinclination to embarrass him. "He engenders so much respect that all the closet problems never came out in his presence," said Castellino. It was unlikely, however, that critical faculty would have remained patient if he wasn't near retirement. "A good number of the faculty, myself included, were beginning to think that the time was arriving for more participation in governance by the faculty," said Mario Borelli. "It would have been hard for Fr. Hesburgh to accept the changes the faculty wanted. . . . I think he retired at the right time." "It was providential that Fr. Ted left when he did," agreed Isabel Charles, "because he might have really faced [an] uprising of the faculty."[21]

For the most part, Fr. Ted found that being a university president was a great vocation: exciting, demanding, surprising, at times satisfying, and occasionally fun. He also found it to be very hard work, tiring to the point of exhaustion, repetitive, and often exasperating. As long as he kept a positive attitude about his job, he didn't find it dull or hopeless.[22]

Like most university presidents, he had to spearhead fundraising activities. "I have to do the most of the thing I really like the least," he often said. "I sometimes think my friends run when they see me coming." Nonetheless, he did everything his fundraising experts asked him to do and seldom showed public displeasure with his role. His alter ego in fundraising was James W. Frick, who perfected the art of fundraising at Notre Dame. Persuasive, organized, hard working, and intense (a "Type A+ personality," said a colleague), Frick had a touch of genius for raising funds. Like Fr. Ted, he met potential benefactors on even terms, unintimidated by wealth, affluence, or prominence.[23]

Frick's methods were methodical, calculating, and exceptionally effective. His system had five stages. First, identify the potential benefactors. The prospect had to have both the financial "resources" and the "disposition" to give to Notre Dame. Of course, many alumni fit the mold, but most of Notre Dame's support did not come from alumni. (Some benefactors were not even Catholic.) How, then, do you identify potential benefactors? Frick used third parties, including "agents of wealth" (brokers, bankers, real estate and insurance agents). "There is hardly any information you can't find out about someone if you go at it," said Frick. Second, educate the potential benefactors about Notre Dame (send them literature, meet them for lunch). Third, involve them in the university. "People give to institutions that they perceive reinforce their own values, so you have to get them involved." Notre Dame involved potential benefactors through councils, advisory boards for each college, special presidential committees, alumni clubs, and board of directors. "So you have them involved," said James Murphy, Frick's associate; "Notre Dame becomes their school." "There is a hierarchy of involvement," Frick continued. "And we move you along to the extent that you respond to the previous stimulus. . . . If you don't respond over a period of time, we simply abandon the idea of trying to get you involved." Fourth, cultivate their commitment to the university, provide them with invitations to special events. "It's a kind of a light being turned on," said Frick. Finally, after they have made their commitment to Notre Dame, Frick solicited their contribution. "Once they make that commitment," Frick observed, "the contribution is just automatic, just follows. It is just a question of how high that contribution will go." Neither Fr. Ted nor Frick regarded themselves simply as crass fundraisers. "Look, we're doing a great thing at Notre Dame," Frick told a faculty colleague, "and I give these people a chance to get in on it."[24]

"He hates to ask people for money," Frick said of Fr. Ted. "He really, truly hates to ask people for money." Fortunately, Fr. Ted didn't have to. His role was to create the environment in which Frick could effectively operate. Fr. Ted was to become friendly with important potential benefactors and articulate an exciting vision of Notre Dame's potential that would inspire listeners. After painting a beautiful picture, he stopped. He never could bring himself to ask for the money. He wasn't the finisher, the closer. Frick and his assistants closed. "Fr. Ted didn't have to close," said an observer. "It just happened around him."[25]

Speaking to a Notre Dame alumni reunion, Fr. Ted lavished praise on the university's alumni throughout the world. They were the "real story" of Notre Dame, he said, a "spectacular group," "fantastic Christians," who have produced excellent marriages and splendid professional careers. Subtly connecting the alumni with a financial investment in Notre Dame, he pointed out that they had a "degree" from Notre Dame in much the same way they had a "share of stock" in a corporation. "When the corporation gets better, your stock is worth more. If the university gets better, your diploma is worth more."

Notre Dame students were "special," unlike some students at secular universities who were merely "brains on stilts." He praised the large number of students who spent a good part of their time helping the less fortunate in the South Bend area, tutoring, caring for the elderly, sitting with the dying, and helping mongoloid children.

He waxed nostalgic, pulling at the heartstrings of the alumni. While showing the Cardinal Archbishop of Paris around campus, Fr. Ted stopped with his guest at the Grotto. A student who had been jogging around the lakes also stopped at the shrine. Fr. Ted approached the sweating young lady, introduced her to the distinguished church leader, and, as Fr. Ted translated, the cardinal asked her to explain why she stopped at the Grotto. "She said," Fr. Ted told his audience, "'What else do you come here for, I come to pray.' So I said to him, look, in the middle of her jogging she stops here to pray. All he could say was, 'My God'! He never saw anything like that in France, at least along the Seine." After touring the campus, Fr. Ted related, the French church leader was overwhelmed. "I am [most] impressed by something I don't see in Europe," Fr. Ted quoted him as saying. "Young people who believe. Young people who pray. Young people who are fervent. Young people who are full of idealism. That impresses me so much I just don't know what to say about it. I just find it unbelievable." [26]

In the mid-1980s Fr. Ted met regularly with small groups of potential benefactors who were flown to Notre Dame on weekends. "Believe it or not," he wrote David Rockefeller, explaining his inability to get away from the university, "I have 25 such weekend encounters in the year ahead [1986] which just wipes out about half of my weekends." The effort was crucial, though, he told Rockefeller. "Since I'll be retiring from the Presidency following graduation in May of 1987, I believe I have to give this last full commitment to the University so that our endowment will reach a half a billion dollars before I leave. This is my least interesting endeavor, but it has to be done."

Fr. Ted was so persuasive and inspiring that people were excited about donating. "Would a million dollars for an endowed chair for my mother be acceptable, Father?" some would say. "He had them eating out of his hand," said Fr. Egan. "Nobody could give a better fundraising talk than Ted." "People *want* to give money to us," said Timothy O'Meara. "People are *eager* to give."

Notre Dame's fundraising efforts produced spectacular results. In the 1960s, when the Ford Foundation failed to make a third pledge, Notre Dame went ahead with its SUMMA campaign (1967–72) which raised $62.5 million for endowed distinguished professorships, graduate education, minority scholarships and student loans, and other special projects. The Campaign for Notre Dame (1975–81) raised $180.5 million for a variety of campus projects plus a dramatically increased endowment. "Twenty-four new structures, four major renovations, and two building additions completed during the 1952–76 period drastically transformed Notre Dame," observed Notre Dame's historian Thomas Schlereth. The last campaign, Notre Dame: A Strategic Moment, started in 1987, planned to raise $300 million, but far exceeded its goal, raising $463 million.[27]

Not only did Fr. Ted need to attract talent and money to Notre Dame, he needed to define what made Notre Dame unique. Early in his presidency he had modeled Notre Dame after Princeton, but that was only as an academic model. "I want this to be a great university," he said, "a great *Catholic* university. . . . I want to be the greatest Catholic university in the world." (Trying to make Notre Dame a top-ranking Catholic university, wrote Christopher Driver in the *Manchester Guardian* in 1969, was, "in view of the competition, not inordinately ambitious." There had not been a great Catholic university anywhere for centuries.)

Fr. Ted assumed the primary role for articulating the goal of creating a great Catholic university. "It is probably true that the President has to dream longer and more intensely than others," he told a faculty assembly of his effort to promote the Catholic character of Notre Dame. He tried to shape a university where Catholic faith, values, and commitment were cultivated as well as academic competence.[28]

A major challenge confronting Catholic universities was to develop a truly integrated educational approach in which philosophy, and particularly theology, played an important role. A great Catholic university had to take a special philosophical and theological look at most subjects, as well as a secular look, he thought. It must act as if the Incarnation has taken place and that God has given the world the Good News.

The Catholic university, Fr. Ted said many times, must be a "beacon, a bridge, and a crossroad" where the world's problems find assistance toward their solution. The Catholic university and its members should act as mediators, should "match secular or state universities in their comprehension of a vast spectrum of natural truths in the arts and sciences, while at the same time . . . must be in full possession of our one true heritage of theological wisdom."

The Catholic university must have a Catholic intellectual community. Not everyone had to belong to it, but it must be predominant. After Vatican II, Fr. Ted thought, the Catholic university must also be ecumenical. "We have Protestants and Jews in our Theology Department," he observed in 1982. Still, a Catholic university could not be nondenominational. It was Catholic and the non-Catholics should share its values, esprit, and mystique. "It's just about impossible to create a great Catholic university without Catholic scholars as to create a great Jewish university without Jewish scholars, or a great black university without black scholars," he said.[29]

Fr. Ted mostly succeeded in maintaining and promoting the Catholic character of Notre Dame. The casual observer was often impressed by the signs of abiding religious faith at the university. The school year began with Mass at Sacred Heart Church. Throughout the year there were liturgies, worship services, and religious exercises; many people stopped to pray at the Grotto. The Holy Cross community was noticeably present, and priests and nuns dotted the faculty. There were religious symbols in all the classrooms and a prayer before many classes. All students took two courses in theology and two in philosophy as prerequisites for graduation. "Notre Dame is one of the most Catholic environments you could possibly imagine," Fr. McBrien said.

Because of the Reformation and the French Revolution, Catholic universities founded in the Middle Ages were secularized and the teaching of theology was mostly relegated to the seminaries outside the universities. Many scholars and intellectuals did not even recognize theology as a valid academic discipline. Giving only lip service to theology, most Catholic universities didn't hire distinguished faculty, demand scholarship, or provide the Theology Department with a decent budget. Fr. Ted thought it was a disgrace that the most obvious weakness in Catholic universities was their faculty of theology, which should be their greatest strength, particularly in the wake of the complicated world of post–Vatican II, "so needful of theological insights from the university."[30]

In the 1950s, Fr. Ted had scoured Europe for excellent recruits for Notre Dame's Theology Department; he lured back to the university young Holy Cross priests who had studied for their doctorates in Europe. "We've got our Jacques Maritains coming up," he told *Time* in 1962. By the 1980s, professors with doctorates dominated in the much-improved Theology Department.

Students had become more religious in a different and better way, he thought. He didn't want to return to the spiritual life that he witnessed on campus in the 1930s, when students were ordered to attend Mass and hardly anyone reached out to the poor and less fortunate in the community. In contrast, in the 1970s when he said Mass in resident hall chapels, large numbers of students voluntarily attended. "They just wanted to be there," he said. "I like that a lot better."

Of the many students who regularly performed community service Fr. Ted spoke with the same pride he showed in discussing high aptitude test scores for new freshmen or the millions of dollars spent on research. Notre Dame's Center for Social Concerns coordinated the students' community service. Students organized collective fasts, donating the proceeds to poor countries. In 1976 more than a thousand students were active in the South Bend community, tutoring underprivileged children, assisting minority industries, helping the elderly, and volunteering at a hospital for crippled children. Students had found a "new sacrament"— serving the poor and the disadvantaged. "If they find and serve Christ in the hungry, the thirsty, the naked, the imprisoned, the essential has been realized," Fr. Ted said. "They find Christ and they serve him, as he himself indicated he might be found and served. . . . They may, if they walk this path, find a deeper and a more realistic spirituality than we found. Perhaps they will avoid the dichotomy of the pious person who was totally lacking in a hunger for justice [or] compassion for the poor of the world."[31]

Fr. Ted also spearheaded the establishment of institutes on campus aimed at exploring moral issues of the day. Among them were institutes on urban studies, peace, international studies, civil rights, government, and ethics and religion. "We like to think of ourselves as the kind of place where any question can be raised—*even* a religious question," Fr. David Burrell said. "In so many academic circles, that's the one you *can't* raise. The population people like to come here because the *value* questions get raised, and they can go beyond simply talking about ways to manipulate interest groups in order to achieve their goals." Some thought Notre Dame was *too* Catholic. Others described it as "a Catholic Disneyland," "a Catholic paradise," "an island of Catholicism at its idealistic best."

The Catholic dimension of the university needed constant attention, needed to remain uppermost on the priority list. "Guard your Catholic character as you would your life," was Fr. Ted's special warning to Catholic universities. For many people, a Catholic university was still alien in the secular world. "Obviously, we are swimming against the current when we profess the eternal and the spiritual to an age completely caught up in temporal and material concerns," he said. "It is not easy to engage in intellectual inquiry in the context of the Christian message in a world that often rejects the Good News . . . to teach students to cherish values, prayers, grace, and eternal life when they are surrounded by a sea of vice, unbelief, cynicism, and anomie, all dressed up to look sophisticated and modern, something they mostly aspire to be."[32]

In the mid and late 1960s there was a noticeable trend among Notre Dame students to reject Catholicism openly. Mass attendance fell off. Possibly as many as 25 percent of the students didn't regard themselves as Catholics. When asked about the trend, Fr. Ted sometimes resorted to wry humor. "If a boy is going to lose his faith, I can't think of a better place than Notre Dame to do it." He argued, though, that students were simply adopting a new attitude toward religion. "These kids no longer see religious truth as a body of doctrine to be memorized and believed. Religion for them is a search, a quest for God through service to their fellow men. Although it is sometimes confused and obscure, I think it is a better kind of religion than the older variety, which Notre Dame taught for so long." Mass attendance improved after the 1960s.[33]

Still, traditionalists in the Church and at Notre Dame worry that the university will eventually go the way of Presbyterian, Methodist, and Baptist colleges in the United States and become secular. Many faculty are uncertain that Notre Dame can retain its Catholic character. Is Notre Dame becoming more or less Catholic? "That's a hard question," answered Professor Frederick Crosson. That's a "tough question," echoed Professor Vaughn McKim. In 1969 Notre Dame sociologist Robert Hassenger thought the victory of secularism was inevitable. "I have a feeling that places like Notre Dame and Fordham are going to wake up one morning and find that they've made it, for all the wrong reasons. They'll get research contracts, they'll get an image as good as general universities—but making it in this context means becoming a Stanford or a Northwestern. Remember that several of Northwestern's trustees have to be elected by the Methodist church—but nobody thinks of Northwestern as a Methodist or church-sponsored school."[34]

The biggest concern focused on the faculty. In the early 1950s, observed historian Philip Gleason, the prevailing view at Notre Dame was that the challenge facing Catholic higher education was to form its distinctive vision more systematically. The curriculum was to be rearranged to exhibit more clearly the religious and philosophical synthesis worked out by Thomistic philosophers and theologians. In 1953 a lengthy report by a special committee recommended numerous curricular changes so that the Thomistic synthesis would "penetrate, animate, and dynamize" all other subjects studied. Notions of "form and matter" were to underlie the sophomore course in literature and criticism.

"This was carrying things a little far even for those willing to grant that there was such a thing as a Catholic world view," Gleason observed. By the time Gleason joined the faculty in 1959, few people regarded curricular integration as a priority. "Everyone was then emphasizing the need for scholarship, for research, for upgrading intellectual standards," said Gleason. "Nobody came right out and said it was time to put the Catholic world view on the shelf, but that was what happened."

Many Catholic professors suffered an identity crisis. In the 1930s the American Catholic Sociological Society was founded on the premise that there was such a thing as "Catholic sociology." Thirty years later Catholic scholars had repudiated that belief. Why have an organization explicitly for Catholic sociologists if Catholic sociologists did not differ from secular sociologists in the way they studied, researched, or taught sociology?[35]

By the mid-sixties, assimilation had brought the Catholic population to the point where it differed only marginally from the rest of American society. "Catholic scholars in various disciplines," noted Gleason, "were discarding the belief that their faith dictated an approach different from that of non-Catholic workers in the same fields. Leading Catholic universities accepted the model of outstanding secular institutions, pledging their readiness to 'pay any price, break any mold' in their pursuit of academic excellence." The general trend was clearly in the secular direction.

There were disturbing trends among the Notre Dame faculty. Over the years of Fr. Ted's presidency, fewer of Notre Dame's faculty were members of the Holy Cross clergy and more were laymen and women, some non-Catholics or nonbelievers. Occasionally it seemed that Catholicism was secondary when it came to hiring. "I told them I was an agnostic," a philosophy professor said in 1974 after he had been lured from a prestigious Midwestern university. "They said it didn't matter." Some younger faculty, drawn to the university by high salaries, were uninterested in Notre Dame's spiritual identity. "When they hear Notre Dame's rhetoric about Catholicism," said one professor, "they regard it as they would football talk; they don't consider themselves part of a Catholic agenda."

Some thought Notre Dame was on an inexorable course toward secularism. Few philosophy professors taught Thomism any more; in

1976 the Philosophy Department's introductory survey text was the same as the one used by Harvard. The desire for academic excellence had resulted in hiring policies no different from elite, secular research universities. Departments had no Catholic criteria in their hiring policies. Science and engineering posed special problems. ("We don't even know what it means to have Catholic departments in those areas," said a professor.)[36]

"We've entered into a period now when the very nature of the place as a Catholic university is confused," contended Professor McInerny, who worried that Notre Dame was losing its Catholic character. "We probably now have, or are approaching, a majority of tenured professors who are neither Catholic or . . . if they still are Catholics, that doesn't mean anything to them in doing the work they do at the university. And they will hire more like themselves. So I think the thing will simply fade away in a fashion that is inevitable." Some alumni also felt that Notre Dame was abandoning its religious absolutes. "Other universities have the courage to be secular," said one graduate. "Why doesn't Notre Dame have the courage to be Catholic?"

Fr. Ted admitted that not every faculty member at Notre Dame shared his vision, making a connection between their academic discipline, their intellectual culture, and their Catholic faith. "We have some faculty who probably believe that the Catholic character of the university is a drag on its trajectory upwards as a great university."[37]

Self-conscious about maintaining the university's Catholic character, some faculty and administrators have vigilantly tried to stop any erosion. When university officials converted to lay control in 1967, they sought to avoid secularization by ensuring that the president would always be a Holy Cross priest. In the late 1970s administrators concluded that, given current hiring trends, in fifteen or twenty years many departments would have few Catholic members and some would have none. Therefore, top officials began to make the appointment of Catholics a priority. Some departments and deans tried to organize packages of candidates to insure a high percentage of Catholics in the pool of applicants. "Affirmative action for us is maximizing the number of Catholics, blacks, hispanics, and [Holy Cross] priests in the pool of applicants," observed Francis Castellino. "But once the pool is there, we look for the best person. If there is a good Catholic scientist out there, we want [the person] in the pool," said Castellino. "Then the pool is judged according to quality."

In the late 1970s, Fr. Ted worried that Notre Dame's Theology Department was losing its Catholic identity. Some recently hired faculty were non-Catholics who seemed noticeably antagonistic toward the Catholic tradition. A disagreement had emerged between those who wanted an essentially ecumenical department and those who desired a Catholic department with ecumenical overtones. Fr. Ted strongly favored the latter course. He was also disturbed that students could fulfill their requirements in theology by taking non-Christian courses or frivolous ones, like religion and magic.

In 1980 Fr. Ted brought in Fr. Richard McBrien to chair the department and gave him substantial funds to hire excellent faculty. McBrien tightened course requirements, making all students take their basic courses in Catholic theology. "The Theology Department was not moving in the direction [Fr. Ted] wanted it to move," said McBrien. "He knew he was coming up on retirement, and he regarded this as one of the things he wanted to fix before he left his job. He felt the Department was not Catholic enough, that it had lost its center."

Fr. Ted and others disagreed with skeptics who doubted the university could maintain its Catholic character. "I think Notre Dame is as Catholic [in 1990], and probably more Catholic, than 20 years ago," said Fr. William Beauchamp. "There is something very alive here in terms of the Catholic spirit," echoed Timothy O'Meara. "We can't be a great Catholic university unless we're a great university," said Fr. McBrien. "The trick is to try to attend to both, but never sacrifice the one for the other." Despite the complex challenges facing Notre Dame, Fr. Andrew Greeley judged that if there is a major Catholic university, "Notre Dame is the place."[38]

Academic freedom was a recurring problem within the Catholic university. Notre Dame and other Catholic universities differ from public institutions in that they have to reconcile freedom of inquiry and unfettered search for truth while upholding Church doctrine. Before Vatican II the emphasis was on upholding Church doctrine and those with unconventional ideas were restricted or suppressed. Increasingly, however, scholars at Catholic universities, embarrassed by the deficiencies of Catholic intellectual life, sought the same professional norms as their colleagues at public institutions. Fr. Ted agreed and became a catalyst for academic freedom.

Like all freedom, Fr. Ted believed, academic freedom was rooted in the nature of man. Man cannot be true to himself unless he is free to follow any argument, any research, or any point of inquiry. Scholars had to be left free to share their convictions and conclusions with their colleagues and students, in their teaching and in their writing, without fear of reprisal.

As a consequence of Vatican II a new atmosphere prevailed at Catholic universities. "Freedom of inquiry is clearly the most significant advance," said Church historian Jay Dolan. "Suppression of theological dissent was a feature of pre–Vatican II Catholicism, but this is no longer true." By the middle 1960s, observed Philip Gleason, "Catholic professors were asking for full academic freedom, and the institutions in which they taught resembled more and more the standard secular model of the American university."

Despite Vatican II, things did not always go smoothly, and intense debate and bitter confrontations took place over academic freedom. In 1963 The Catholic University of America, in Washington, D.C., banned four distinguished priest-scholars from speaking on campus. In 1965 thirty-three professors at St. John's University in New York were dismissed, most of them immediately and without a hearing. The specific issue was the faculty's right to organize, but the larger issue was academic freedom. The American Association of University Professors censured St. John's for its action.[39]

The greatest danger to academic freedom and the autonomy of the Catholic university seemed to come from the church's hierarchy. Ironically, while some were concerned that secularization would ruin Notre Dame's Catholic character, others worried that Vatican intervention would make Notre Dame too rigidly Catholic.

Since the Protestant Reformation, Catholic universities had been strictly controlled by juridical ties to Rome, the local bishop, or to a religious order controlled by Rome. This older, classical point of view insisted that a Catholic university exercised its autonomy and freedom only within the parameters of the dogmatic and moral definitions laid down by the Church. By the early 1960s, however, the interpretation desired by leaders of most Catholic universities in the U.S., modeling themselves after secular universities, was that the university community should be allowed to pursue the truth without restrictions or conditions.

The problem was enormously complex. What essentially constituted a Catholic university? Was it the university's juridical link with the ecclesiastical authorities or was it the animating presence of the Catholic faith? Or both? How does a professor or a university achieve autonomy and academic freedom if the professor or the university is supposed to be obedient to the teaching authority of the Church? The issue would cause misunderstanding and disagreement between the Vatican bureaucracy and U.S. Catholic universities. And starting in 1963 Fr. Ted spearheaded the movement for more autonomy and academic freedom.[40]

In 1963 Fr. Ted was elected president of the International Federation of Catholic Universities (IFCU) at a meeting in Washington D.C. (He had left the meeting early and was elected in absentia.) Established in 1951, the IFCU had been in shambles, having practically no money, no independence, no organization, no decent constitution, and a small membership. Inspired by Vatican II, the members who still cared about the organization sought to revitalize it. Almost overwhelmed with work, Fr. Ted reluctantly accepted the new position. Somehow, he thought, "I'll manage and we'll make this organization amount to something."

The Federation in 1963 was strictly dependent on the Sacred Roman Congregation of Seminaries and Universities (soon to become the Sacred Congregation for Catholic Education). Shortly after his election, Fr. Ted was summoned to Rome for a meeting with leading Vatican officials. ("They did not ask, they just told me," he recalled in his autobiography.) Monsignor Georges LeClercq, president of the Catholic University of Lille in France and newly elected secretary general of the IFCU, was also summoned. Former officers of the IFCU, resentful at being voted out of office, were present as well. ("I was certain they had whispered in the right ears in Rome," Fr. Ted later said.) At the meeting a powerful archbishop declared the election invalid because it hadn't followed canon law. He was setting up a six-member council to run the IFCU, a group which included Fr. Ted but was dominated by members loyal to the archbishop and the Congregation. Fr. Ted boldly rejected the proposal, and LeClercq backed him up.

The archbishop countered by saying he would leave the room while the group worked things out. In his autobiography Fr. Ted described his reaction.

I stopped him in his tracks, saying that I had just come four thousand miles at my own expense and would be traveling another four thousand miles back, also at my own expense, and that I expected him to stay right there and hear everything I had to say and that I wanted to hear everything he had to say. There would be no private deals that he could agree or disagree with later, I insisted.

Then I went even further. I told him that we would not stand for his autocratic plan and neither would the people who had elected us, and if he persisted he would just end up being in charge of nothing. I really let the fur fly. My Irish mother would have been very proud of me. After some more inconsequential discussion, he dismissed us. I shook his hand and asked for his blessing, which just about killed him, I'm sure.

LeClercq corroborated Fr. Ted's version of events at the four-hour meeting, underscoring Fr. Ted's exceptional poise and courage. Fr. Ted's final gesture "impressed me profoundly," said LeClercq. "He knelt before [the archbishop] who had presided over the meeting, and asked for a blessing. I followed his example, admiring his inspiration. Some may see a certain skillfulness in his gesture. If such was the case, though it is not clearly so, it was a skill tempered by faith."[41]

Four days after the tense confrontation with the archbishop in Rome, Fr. Ted appealed to a higher authority to clarify the role of the IFCU. Writing the Vatican's Secretariate of State, he complained of the "juridical roadblocks," preventing the IFCU from functioning effectively.

Unfortunately, even in the Rome meeting, the most important questions, most central to the life of the Federation, were not discussed. These questions are: What is the purpose of the Federation in the world today? How can it best serve the Church in the field of Higher Catholic Education? And how should it be constituted to serve these purposes?

Then he answered his own questions. The purpose of the IFCU was twofold:

1. To give the Church a strong, vital, and consistent presence in the international scene of the university world. This world is served *publicly* by UNESCO's international meetings, symposia, and study projects; and *privately* by such organizations as the International Association of Universities. Both are located in Paris, where the Federation should have a permanent secretariate, and consultant status at UNESCO Headquarters.

2. The second purpose of an International Federation of Catholic Universities is to share the growing strength of Catholic higher learning by confederating the existing national and regional groupings of Catholic universities, e.g. in Latin America, the United States and Canada, and in France, and to promote fruitful relationships between these universities, especially between those of the developed and less-developed regions.

The current constitution of the Federation was an "anachronism" in the field of international higher education, he stated, and a new one was needed. Juridical considerations should aid the cause, not impede it. "Organization is a means, not an end," he wrote. He was willing to step aside if doing so would advance the Federation.

If the writer is personally objectionable to some because of the strong stand he has taken on behalf of the Federation, then he would willingly resign. . . . My sole interest in all of this is to make the Federation capable of service to the Church in the field of Higher Catholic Education, both internally in the perfecting of Catholic universities throughout the world, and externally in providing a fruitful presence for Catholic higher learning in the rapidly expanding organizations of international life.[42]

After the meeting in Rome had ended in a deadlock, the archbishop went ahead with his plan, notifying heads of universities throughout the world that a commission would run the IFCU until the next election. "It was one of the most arrogant letters I had ever read," said Fr. Ted.

But Fr. Ted had an ace in the hole: his friend, the newly elected Pope Paul VI. After Fr. Ted wrote to the Pope, explaining the events, Paul VI called the archbishop on the carpet. In his autobiography Fr. Ted explained his recollection of what happened next.

Paul VI called the archbishop and gave him three clear orders. First, he was to write to all those universities again and apologize for waiting from September to January to approve Father Hesburgh and the others who were elected. Second, he would approve Father Hesburgh and the others immediately and give them full power to conduct the affairs of the Federation. Third, he would instruct them to write a new constitution for the Federation in which the Congregation of Seminaries and Universities would not even be mentioned. Then he instructed the archbishop to send an apology to Father Hesburgh, with a copy to all those to whom he had sent his previous letter. I have to give the archbishop credit for one thing: he wrote a fifteen-page letter in excellent Latin and he ate crow on every page.[43]

As president of the IFCU, Fr. Ted was constantly trying to put out fires. In 1966 he learned of a meeting in Rome in which Cardinal Ottaviani had given a list of moral and doctrinal positions to the leaders of several Catholic universities. Ottaviani told the university leaders that they should reflect the positions—and no other—in all their conferences, classes, and publications. "This would, of course, ruin the university as a place in which ideas are freely discussed with all due liberty and autonomy," Fr. Ted wrote his colleague Georges LeClercq.

It reflects a vision of the university as a propaganda agency, not as a place of inquiry. Of course, there are established Catholic positions which a Catholic

university should reflect, but there is also a wide area of opinion and specula-
tion which should be open to free inquiry.[44]

Under Fr. Ted's direction the IFCU engaged in profound reflection
on the nature and the mission of the Catholic university. Lengthy discussions took place at General Assemblies in Tokyo (1965), Kinshasa,
Congo (1968), and Boston (1970), as well as at intervening regional conferences.

The most significant regional conference took place in July 1967,
when Fr. Ted assembled twenty-six church leaders from the U.S. and
Canada at a special meeting at Land O'Lakes. For four days Fr. Ted acted as the main strategist in developing a statement which he hoped
would be adopted as the policy of six hundred Catholic institutions
throughout the world at the IFCU's meeting in Kinshasa in 1968. "He
did this," wrote a reporter, "knowing it would bring anguished cries
from Vatican officials and run-of-the-mill Notre Dame alumni."

What emerged from the conference in Wisconsin was viewed as the
Magna Carta of Catholic higher education. The crucial passage in the
Land O'Lakes Statement declared independence from the Vatican and
the local bishop. "The Catholic university today must be a university in
the full modern sense of the word, with a strong commitment to and
concern for academic excellence. To perform its teaching and research
functions effectively, the Catholic university must have a true autonomy
and academic freedom in the face of authority of whatever kind, lay or
clerical, external to the academic community itself." The entire world of
knowledge must be open to students. There "must be no outlawed
books or subjects."

A "historic" statement, wrote a reporter in *The New York Times*.
"Now at last," declared another commentator, "Catholic universities
had signaled their willingness to accept the openness characteristic of
many secular institutions." The Land O'Lakes document, Jay Dolan observed, "became a key statement on behalf of academic freedom and the
value of the Catholic university."[45]

Throughout most of his nine years as president of the IFCU, Fr. Ted
dealt with Cardinal Gabriel Garrone, Prefect of the Sacred Congregation for Catholic Education. Unlike his predecessors, Garrone was open
minded and willing to listen, and he and Fr. Ted built a warm, respectful relationship. Still, Fr. Ted had to explain and justify why Catholic
universities needed autonomy and academic freedom.

When the Plenaria of the Sacred Congregation for Catholic Education proposed general "norms and regulations" as guidelines for Rome to govern American Catholic universities, Fr. Ted composed a series of powerful letters to Garrone, arguing that the guidelines dangerously infringed on the independence and freedom of Catholic universities in the United States.

To enforce Rome's norms and rules would be a "disaster," he wrote Garrone in March 1970. Diplomatically but firmly, he instructed the cardinal about the American scene.

It has taken us the better part of a century to qualify for governmental funds, and only one of our universities receives any financial assistance from the Church. Lawyers who are challenging our freedom and autonomy as qualifying us to receive public funds would use the Roman declaration of general norms and regulations to destroy the position we have established and to disqualify all Catholic colleges and universities from receiving state and federal assistance.

If Rome implemented the norms and rules, major U.S. Catholic universities would have to stop being Catholic to survive.

The fact is that we are Catholic today, basically governed by Catholic principles and a Catholic philosophy of life, and inspired by the Gospel in our essential being. Theology within the universities is very free and autonomous because, otherwise, theology would not be accepted as a valid university discipline by the university faculties. Without theology, we do not think it possible to be Catholic.

American Catholic universities would prefer to remain Catholic and at the service of the Church, he told Garrone, but the price for doing so and still being recognized as American universities was to be "free and autonomous." This would not prevent the Magisterium (the teaching authority of the Church) from declaring that a theologian was not orthodox in his teaching and writing. "However, action against individual university theologians should be according to the rules of the institution," Fr. Ted insisted.

The Catholic university needed a vision that would provide leadership and inspiration for the "good things" taking place. Instead of the positive approach, he wrote Garrone in May 1971, the Congregation took a "negative and critical approach," which added discouragement to an already difficult task.

Speaking for just this one university, Notre Dame, I can honestly say that we have had not one cent of support from the Church in over a century, and that almost every letter we have had from the Congregation has been critical, rather than encouraging. If I were less optimistic, I would be tempted to say, "Why keep trying to create a Catholic university under such conditions?" The 95% of good that is being done is not recognized, whereas the 5% of foolishness that occurs is immediately open to criticism and rebuke.

He had personally undergone seven years of "controlled" theology, Fr. Ted explained, referring to his seminary training, and had found it a "deadening and regressive" influence on his intellectual formation.

What I am really saying is that the control exercised in the past did not work for the good of theology or the growth of theology, and that we must find new methods of leadership and inspiration that will make for theological growth that will assure orthodoxy and faith in some manner different than the control of the past.[46]

After working together for so many years on behalf of the IFCU, Fr. Ted paused to graciously thank Georges LeClercq: "You have been a good friend over many years and there never has been anyone in my life with whom I have been able to work more easily and more effectively than with you. This is probably because you did most of the work."

Actually, it was Fr. Ted who had done the crucial work, and his colleagues in Catholic universities throughout the U.S. lavished praise on him for his adroitness and courage. "He did a masterful job on Garrone," said Fr. Paul Reinert. "Ted has the knack and ability to go to . . . the top," added Reinert. "He thought nothing of going right to Rome on a lot of these problems. He was very courageous and smart politically. . . . He did more than any other single individual to make the essence of Catholic higher education in the U.S. intelligible to the Roman mentality."[47]

In 1972, after three terms, Fr. Ted stepped down as president of the IFCU. By establishing an office in Paris, a much larger dues-paying membership, a workable constitution, and a good-sized budget, he had helped revive the moribund organization. As he stepped down he also thought he had achieved a measure of autonomy and freedom for Catholic universities, but his hopes were soon dashed when the Sacred Congregation for Catholic Education subsequently reaffirmed the need for direct control of Catholic universities. "Just when I and others thought we had seemed to have gotten the message through to Rome," said Neil McCluskey, "then all of a sudden another document would come out and somebody else [would say] to go back to square one." "This has been a 50-year struggle," agreed Reinert. "We think we have it all understood in Rome, and then they change the head of one of these commissions . . . and we start all over again."[48]

In the mid-1980s the Vatican's threat started over again. The U.S. had far more Catholic colleges and universities—235 in 1985—than any other country in the world. With the exception of The Catholic University of America in Washington, D.C., which as a pontifical university was subject to special rules from Rome, they were enjoying considerable academic freedom. But in April 1985, the Sacred Congregation for Catholic Education issued a draft ("schema") document which threatened to extend some of the Vatican's rules to every Catholic campus in the world. The schema included forty-nine complex and detailed "norms," or regulations, to which Catholic universities must adhere. No Catholic university could consider itself "a purely private institution." More ominously, the document stipulated that Catholics who teach theological subjects at any "institution of higher studies must have a mandate from the competent ecclesiastical authority." Experts interpreted that to mean that an authority outside the university—a local bishop—would approve Catholic theologians who taught at Catholic universities and could remove those who contradicted church doctrine.

The schema aroused consternation among Catholic educators in the U.S. Critics argued that it was impossible for the Vatican to make one set of rules for universities that operated in multiple cultural and political environments. The schema would create enormous church-state problems in the U.S. and would jeopardize the half-billion dollars Catholic universities and its students received from the government. Beyond the possible financial loss would be the loss of freedom and autonomy.[49]

In the fall of 1986, Fr. Ted helped organize Catholic college and university presidents in opposition to the Vatican schema and then served as the point man for 111 Catholic college presidents in publicly criticizing the document. In a major article in *America* on November 1, 1986, Fr. Ted insightfully critiqued the Vatican's proposals and in the process forcefully restated and clarified his thoughts on Catholic higher education. "Those of a juridical mind-set seem to think that an institution is Catholic only if they charter it or fully control it," he wrote. "If this were true, all of the Catholic universities they charter and control should be very Catholic. Almost the opposite is true. I have visited practically all of them and, in my judgment, most of the Catholic universities and colleges in the United States chartered by the states and under the control of lay boards are far more Catholic than the pontifical universities throughout the world." In the U.S. students at Catholic universities and colleges studied Catholic philosophy and theology. "Not true elsewhere," he observed. "The vast majority of our faculty are committed, practicing Catholics. Not true elsewhere. Most of our Catholic students practice their religion at daily or at least weekly participation in Mass and Holy Communion. In the best pontifical university I know in Europe, three percent of the Catholic students attend Sunday Mass."

The central problem was that the norms established by the schema ran counter to the requirements of *any* university, namely, that it possess academic freedom and autonomy. "Obviously, if church or state or any power outside the university can dictate who can teach and who can learn, the university is not free and, in fact, is not a true university where the truth is sought and taught. It is, rather, a place of political or religious indoctrination."

U.S. Catholic higher education was unique in the world, he argued. There were few Catholic universities in Europe; those in Latin America were poorly financed and weak in philosophy and theology; in much of the rest of the world there were no Catholic universities at all. In Canada the two strongest Catholic universities had recently secularized and were no longer Catholic universities. "Against this background, it might be hoped that the strong Catholic presence in American higher education would be cherished and supported by the church, not threatened." Who would jeopardize the strongest segment of Catholic universities and colleges in a world where so few existed?[50]

For the next four years, Fr. Ted and many Catholic educators and their allies argued against the schema and worried what the Vatican might impose on them. Other drafts followed, written in a more collegial fashion, and in 1990 a new draft removed the most offensive portions of the 1985 schema, satisfying most of the concerns of U.S. Catholic educators. "A sigh of relief is in order," wrote *Commonweal*.[51]

On several specific occasions Fr. Ted steadfastly fought for academic freedom at Notre Dame. In the early 1960s Notre Dame hired history professor Samuel Shapiro, who had been fired from a college in Michigan and blackballed by some other Midwestern universities for defending the legitimacy of Fidel Castro's government in Cuba. Subsequently, Frank Mankiewicz, who was handling public relations for the Peace Corps, phoned Fr. Ted and objected that Shapiro was teaching Peace

Corps trainees in a summer program. "I was not about to give into that kind of pressure," Fr. Ted reflected in his autobiography. "In no uncertain terms, I informed Mankiewicz that the Peace Corps had a contract with Notre Dame and that we would decide who would teach what. If Washington had any difficulty with that, they could take their contract and give it to someone else. Then I hung up." The next day Mankiewicz phoned to apologize and retracted his objection to Shapiro.[52]

In 1968 Pope Paul VI issued his controversial encyclical, *Humanae Vitae,* upholding the church's traditional view of birth control. Almost immediately, theology professor Fr. James Burtchaell denounced the encyclical in a lecture ("The Bitter Pill") to students on the campus. Among other things, he did not agree with the Pope's assertion that procreation was the primary end of marriage. Such logic, he contended, would suggest that the "primary end of the Noble Prize banquet is nutrition, the primary end of the Mexican Olympic Games is exercise and the primary end of baptism is hygiene." The Pope had been overly concerned with "sexual plumbing," and his encyclical expressed a narrow biological view of the marital act. Burtchaell added: "Conjugal love, unless I am gravely mistaken, is a many-splendored thing." The encyclical, he concluded, was "grossly inadequate and largely fallacious."

Burtchaell's harsh criticism received extensive media attention and cries of wrath arose from alumni and Catholic leaders elsewhere. Two days after the talk, in a rare 75-minute news conference, Fr. Ted manfully came to Burtchaell's defense. "I think the faculty are perfectly free . . . to speak according to their competence." He wanted students and faculty to openly discuss the great social issues of the time rather than react apathetically. "That's what we exist for, to look at tough questions and try to find answers. As far as I'm concerned, a university, if it is going to be true to itself, ought to be willing to sit down and confront these things."

It was against the "spirit of a university" for any group to say they disagreed with someone so they would not let him speak. "I'm against half of the stuff that's talked about around here, but that's irrelevant, because anyone with a mind has to take a stand, and you take it as you wish. That's the very reason for the existence of a university, and if you can't do that, then we ought to cancel out higher education."

Asked if the Vatican might censure Notre Dame for Burtchaell's criticism, Fr. Ted responded: "It's possible, always possible. . . . There are a lot of people around who want to get [Notre Dame] into trouble. As soon as something comes out, they put it in an envelope and send it over to Rome. It happens all the time." But he denied being worried about the prospect, noting that the lay board of trustees controlled Notre Dame.

Asked on another occasion if a "risk for error" should be allowed in teaching Catholic theology, Fr. Ted emphatically responded, "Yes. You have to take a risk to think new thoughts and to express yourself. If theologians are constantly beat over the head if they get two meters off the main-trod path, then they will lose heart and they won't let their imaginations run."[53]

Fr. Ted would not allow a Notre Dame benefactor to use financial leverage to stifle opinions on campus. "I don't interfere in your business, do I?" he told them. In 1970 when theology professor Fr. David Burrell inadvertently angered J. Peter Grace, the wealthy shipping and industrial magnate, Grace threatened to withdraw a substantial financial commitment he had made to Notre Dame. "I think maybe I lost you a million dollars yesterday," Fr. Burrell told Fr. Ted. "Yea, I heard about it," said Fr. Ted. "Don't worry about it. We'll get it somewhere."

Fr. Ted prided himself on being the protector of different points of view within the faculty. "He lets right-wingers do their right-wing things [and] left-wingers do their left-wing things," said Fr. McBrien. When Professor McInerny started *Crisis*, a conservative Catholic magazine, he thought many of his liberal colleagues would have liked to muzzle him. But McInerny felt protected by his president. "[Hesburgh] was not about to have [*Crisis*] declared out of bounds," said McInerny. "He was more 'liberal' in that sense than most liberals."[54]

In the 1970s and 1980s Notre Dame provided a forum for a widely diverse array of speakers ranging from presidents, theologians, comedians, ex-fugitives, and poets to right-wingers, left-wingers, singers, saints and sinners. An article on academic freedom at Notre Dame observed, "Abbie Hoffman passed out 'AIDS to the Contras' buttons. Eleanor Smeal urged those who support abortion to be more vocal. Jerry Falwell talked about the role of evangelical Christians in politics. Timothy Leary pushed the religion of drugs."[55]

Sometimes, though, Fr. Ted and other administrators at Notre Dame drew the line on student freedoms, particularly when the freedom involved sex. Notre Dame has hedged on its endorsement of academic freedom on the issue of sex. In 1963 publication of the student magazine *Scholastic* was suspended partly because it criticized the policy of banning women from visiting the men's dorms. Two years later, the vice president of student affairs, Fr. Charles McCarragher, vetoed a campus appearance by *Playboy* publisher Hugh Hefner, viewing him as an evil mercenary of the flesh. In their book, Joel Connelly and Howard Dooley said that McCarragher worried that Hefner would bring along bunnies and pose them in front of the Golden Dome. Hefner wasn't interested in free speech, McCarragher argued; he wanted to use Notre Dame for public relations purposes. In 1968, during the Pornography Conference, Fr. McCarragher impounded an art exhibit that had arrived from New York.

In the mid-1980s, Notre Dame refused to recognize formally the organization known as Gays and Lesbians at Notre Dame/Saint Mary's College. In 1986 the university ordered the campus radio station to stop airing a public service announcement for the group. (Two station managers resigned in protest.) Although the issue of homosexuality was discussed by speakers on campus, the administration would not deal directly with the gay/lesbian organization, assigning that responsibility to the University Counseling Center and the Office of Campus Ministry. The gay/lesbian group was not pleased. "The administration knows it can't stifle these debates," said a spokesman. "So to a certain extent it lets them take place—just so long as they aren't done in a way that could embarrass the University."[56]

Overall, though, Fr. Ted acted as a catalyst for academic freedom in Catholic higher education. His efforts extended beyond the United States. After the military deposed Salvador Allende's government in Chile in 1973, one of the first things the new military government did was to put military officials in charge of each university. Upset, Fr. Ted met with the admiral who ran the Catholic University in Santiago. He asked the admiral, "Since you would be upset if I tried to tell you how to run the navy, what makes you think you know anything about running a university?" The admiral responded, "It was out of control. I am just purifying it." Commenting later on the lesson of his encounter, Fr. Ted said: "Purify us and we die. Long live academic freedom."[57]

In the late 1940s and early 1950s Fr. Ted went through a stage in which he put football at Notre Dame "in its place." His in-house victory over Coach Frank Leahy achieved that goal. After Leahy retired, Fr. Ted seemed more relaxed about football on the campus and more confident that it occupied an important but not all-important role at Notre

Dame. Nonetheless, there were problems to solve and, most important, high standards to meet. He often reminded everyone to keep intercollegiate athletics in proper perspective. Those who favor intercollegiate athletics, he said, "praise them out of all proportion to their merits," while those who deny them worth "are quite blind to the values" they possess.

On December 9, 1975, Fr. Ted reiterated simply and clearly his philosophy on college football in his speech at the Hall of Fame Banquet in New York City. He reminded his audience that a university is "first, foremost, and always dedicated to higher education. That is why it was created, why it exists, why it does everything it does, including football."

Players were students first and were expected to take standard courses (not "jock courses") like other students. Besides a scholarship, a player should expect no additional favors—no job for his father, no scholarship for his brother or girlfriend, no athletic dorm, no cash under the table, no special rules. He should receive "a good education, no more, no less." If the student-athlete performed poorly in his classes or became a discipline problem, he should be treated the same as any other student. "On the other hand, if athletes get hurt the first day of practice, if they decide for good reasons not to play football, no matter, the offer is good for four years, the NCAA notwithstanding." He also praised the value of football because it imbued the athlete with discipline, spirit, and a will to win. "In a quite discouraged and discouraging world, I ask, what's wrong with that?"

Personally, though, Fr. Ted didn't enjoy most competitive sports. He seldom attended Notre Dame's basketball games; baseball was boring and slow; boxing was savage. He took a modest interest in Notre Dame's football team. "He enjoys the games," insisted Fr. Joyce. "He hates to lose. He likes to win at everything we do, including football." He appreciated football at Notre Dame because of its mystique, tradition, financial benefits, and enrichment of campus life. When the Irish scored a touchdown, he reacted with polite enthusiasm, clapping and trading congratulations with those seated around him.

During the game, however, he was just as likely to chat with friends about a foreign policy problem. In the middle of a play he turned to Edmund Stephan and asked, "What do you think about the situation in Yugoslavia?" "We'd get involved in many discussions that were quite irrelevant to the game," said Stephan. "When we would lose an important game, he'd brush it off. . . . In five minutes, he'd forget it and go on to something else." After Notre Dame lost an important game, Fr. Ted told an administrative colleague at dinner the same evening, "I want to tell you two things: When you get up [tomorrow] morning, the clock will be going around, and the sun will be coming up. The world didn't end today."[58]

Only once did he perform out of character after a big football victory. On the afternoon of the Cotton Bowl in January 1979, quarterback Joe Montana led the Irish to an improbable comeback victory over Houston, 35–34. As Notre Dame partisans cheered wildly, Fr. Ted scrambled down to the field, and there he led the band in playing the Notre Dame Victory March. Later, when a university official teased him about the "overemphasis" he placed on football, he replied smiling, "There's a time and place for everything, and that was the time and place for that."

Still, questions directed to him about the football team often irritated him. "How's the football team gonna do?" he was asked. He demurred politely but seemed to churn inside. "How the heck should I know?" he responded rhetorically. However, he willingly discussed academic standards for athletes. "An athlete who can't read? That's immoral. We have high standards here, and our coaches keep 'em."[59]

He delegated to Fr. Joyce the responsibility of overseeing athletics, and Joyce ran the program like a fiefdom. Fr. Ted, though, kept well informed about details of the athletics program and was particularly interested in the academic performance of the student-athletes. "He knew exactly what was going on," said associate athletic director, Roger Valdiserri. "He used to amaze me by talking about a game [or] a player." Fr. Ted and Fr. Joyce constantly reminded people that Notre Dame existed not to win football games but to become a great Catholic university. Both refused to be intimidated by football and tried to keep it healthy but under control. Both had one recurring nightmare. "The worst thing that could ever happen to us would be to have an athletic scandal," said Fr. Joyce. "It would kill me," added Fr. Ted. Consequently, the measures employed by Notre Dame to keep athletics in line were among the most severe in the nation. Moreover, plenty of evidence showed that Notre Dame abided by the spirit and the letter of the rules of college athletics.[60]

"Admissions are gone over with a fine-tooth comb," wrote John Underwood in *Sports Illustrated* in 1983. "Notre Dame requires an incoming freshman athlete to have a combined score of at least 900 on his SATs, rate in the top third of his high school graduating class and be credited with 16 units of English, foreign language, social studies, science and math at a minimum 2.0 average." Notre Dame didn't offer physical education or "life science" majors because Fr. Ted thought they shielded the athlete from the rigors of scholarship. "There's no such thing as a jock curriculum in South Bend," Underwood observed. The athlete had to make it in the humanities, business, science, or engineering, the same as other students.

Notre Dame pushed its athletes to graduate in four years. They had to maintain a 2.0 grade point and couldn't lag in credit hours or they had to attend summer school. Red-shirting, the practice in which an athlete was held out of competition for a year for seasoning to enhance his ability for another year, was banned. (Exceptions were made for injuries.) "In [Hesburgh's] view," commented athletic director Gene Corrigan in 1986, "there are certain evils connected with athletics, and delaying someone's graduation is an evil. When Father Hesburgh thinks something, we all think it."

Normally Notre Dame didn't accept junior college or transfer athletes, who have long provided other major college programs with a steady supply of proven talent. There were no athletic dorms either because Notre Dame didn't believe in segregating athletes. "Nothing we do here sends the message that they're somehow special," said Fr. Ted.[61]

Booster clubs, dedicated to raising athletic funds and often the source of embarrassments (illegal payoffs to athletes; recruiting misdeeds), were forbidden. Alumni clubs raised funds, but all the proceeds had to be funneled into the general fund of the university. "Notre Dame alumni clubs are notorious for complaining about the Irish football coach's won-lost record," observed Underwood, "and consistent in getting nowhere with their complaints."

Fr. Ted was proud that over the years Notre Dame's graduation rates for football and basketball players were among the highest of major schools. One survey of the National Football League in the early 1980s found that of the thirty-one former Notre Dame players in the NFL, thirty had their degrees. Of 490 scholarship football players who entered Notre Dame from 1965 to 1981, all but five graduated. "[Hesburgh's] football goal isn't to win every game," Roger Valdiserri said in 1982. "It's to graduate every player. He isn't satisfied with the 97 percent we graduate now."

"Equally illuminating," wrote Underwood, "is Notre Dame's police record with the NCAA." Two hundred and sixty-one major public penalties were handed down by the NCAA against colleges from 1952 to 1983. "It would seem only natural that with its high profile Notre Dame would have gotten nabbed at one time or another, for one thing or another." And it did. The NCAA twice reprimanded the university for minor violations. "But that's it," noted Underwood. "Two misdemeanors—reprimands are the NCAA equivalent of parking tickets." In 1983 NCAA director of public relations David E. Cawood commented, "The astonishing thing our enforcement people find is that they get so few complaints [about Notre Dame]. For a school that attracts so much envy, and even hate, you would expect it would be defending itself all the time. But nobody points a finger."[62]

Occasionally there were problems caused by overzealous, rowdy students. In the fall of 1964, for example, some students attacked the Michigan State band as it marched across the Notre Dame campus following a game. The band director complained that some students knocked one of his musicians unconscious, damaged instruments, and stole band caps. Notre Dame students also chanted tasteless cheers and toted embarrassing signs during halftime. Fr. Ted deplored such behavior. A year later, before another encounter with Michigan State, he warned in a letter to students that "spirit is more than noise" and that students should refrain from "turning the campus into a jungle [by] embarking on an emotional binge." Spirit "should not be confused with rowdiness, buffoonery or inhospitality to opponents." He even threatened to end intercollegiate competition if such behavior continued.[63]

He enjoyed visiting with each new coach, but in the course of their visit he gave virtually the same cautionary speech to each one: Gerry Faust, Ara Parseghian, Dan Devine, and basketball coach Digger Phelps. "You've got [at least] five years," he told Faust. "We don't say boo to you if you lose. I think you'll have the tools here to win more than you lose; it seems to work out that way. But if you don't [win], you won't hear from me." Then, a blunt warning: "You're familiar with our rules?" Fr. Ted asked.

"Yes, sir," Faust said.

"You know we run a program that's clean as a hound's tooth?"

"Yes, sir."

"All right, then, you keep the rules," Fr. Ted said, "and I'll keep the alumni off your back." As his new head coach got up to leave, Fr. Ted said: "One more thing. If anybody on your staff gets out of line, you'll be gone before midnight. You and all your coaches."

"Yes, sir."[64]

When Notre Dame appointed Gene Corrigan athletic director in 1980, Fr. Ted cautioned him as well. Fixing his eyes on Corrigan, he said: "We will not have a violation of the spirit or the letter of the law at Notre Dame. If we do, those people will be gone by midnight. . . . You are going to be held responsible for your coaches."

As long as the head coach followed the rules, Fr. Ted insisted on upholding the university's commitment to the coach, without concern for the team's record. In the third year of his five-year contract, Gerry Faust was being criticized in the media because of his less than stellar record, and rumors circulated that Faust would be fired. At one point, while being interviewed by the *Chicago Tribune*, Corrigan hesitated in supporting Faust. "I didn't sound very supportive," Corrigan reflected. "Not as much as I should have [been]." Fr. Ted read the *Tribune's* article, phoned Corrigan, and discussed the athletic director's struggle with the Faust predicament. "How long is Gerry's contract?" Fr. Ted asked.

"Five years," Corrigan responded.

"Well, unless he dies," said Fr. Ted, "he will be here five years. We promised him five years, and we're going to give him five years." The phone conversation clarified Corrigan's confusion. "That made it very simple for me," he recalled. "My job, then, was to garner all the resources that we had in the athletic department to try to help Gerry win. [Hesburgh] always simplified things."[65]

Throughout his presidency Fr. Ted rejected suggestions that he build a new football stadium or remodel the old one. He thought the "psychological effect" would be "demoralizing" and revive charges that Notre Dame's primary commitment was to football. "I was concerned that a new or bigger stadium would send out the wrong message," he reflected in his autobiography. "I feared it would reinforce the widely held misconception that Notre Dame was emphasizing athletics at the expense of academics. I was not about to do anything that would send this message. The time will probably come when we will enlarge the stadium, but I never could face that decision." He also valued symbolic victories of academics over athletics. He insisted that the library completed in 1963 cost more than the Athletic Convocation Center completed five years later. (It did: $12.5 million to $8.6 million.)[66]

"Notre Dame's special quality when it comes to athletics," concluded Underwood, "isn't a superior morality, but a superior and deeply involved leadership." Notre Dame wasn't pure or above reproach and never had been. But, Underwood contended, "it strives mightily to attain purity and be above reproach. The heart of the matter is that Notre Dame is proud of being righteous. This creates a perpetuating kind of morality. In a way, this makes obeying the rules easier. When you build for yourself a glass house, you watch what you wear to the breakfast table." [67]

9 ⸺ RETIREMENT

A S FR. TED was about to step down as President of Notre Dame in May 1987, he didn't want to move into retirement overly organized. "I literally have not sat down and planned out a lot of stuff," he said. Still, he knew he wanted to travel and fish, read lots of books, continue his outside public service, perform pastoral work, and do whatever Notre Dame's new administration wanted him to do. He stacked yellow legal pads near his desk. "I intend to write every day as a kind of discipline for retirement," he said.

Both of his sisters worried about him. "I don't think he knows how to take care of himself," said Anne Jackson. "He doesn't know how to cook, as far as I know. The secretaries have been taking care of him and Father Joyce for so long." But Fr. Ted seemed to manage fine.[1]

The first order of business was a year of travel and vacation. Fr. Ted had traveled millions of miles throughout the world but had seen his own country mostly from airports, meeting rooms, and hotels. A little over a month after his valedictory speech, therefore, on the morning of June 11, 1987, he and Fr. Joyce set out from Notre Dame in a Skyline recreational vehicle headed for the Western United States. A hundred friends and well-wishers gathered to send them off. Because the pair had never cooked or done laundry, some had teased them that they wouldn't get beyond Gary, Indiana, eighty miles away. So as they pulled out of Notre Dame, Fr. Ted held a sign in the window saying, "Gary or Bust."

The trip out West brought a monumental change of pace. "The university seems miles and miles away and, of course, it is," he wrote fifteen days into the journey. "The former life of hustle and bustle seems miles away, too. When the mechanic at the garage said today that it would take forty minutes to recharge our battery, we simply said, 'No problem.' Ned went off to mail a letter and I went off to collect the second batch of laundry."

For two-and-a-half months the pair toured seventeen national parks and twenty-nine national forests. Fr. Ted had visited over a hundred countries, had seen most of the natural wonders of the world, but he thought the West surpassed all of them in its "composite beauty and splendor."[2]

In the fall of 1987, on the second phase of their sabbatical, he and Fr. Joyce traveled throughout Central and South America from Mexico to Tierra del Fuego. Next came a one-hundred-day cruise aboard the ocean liner Queen Elizabeth II, where they served as chaplains. From January to May 1988, they traveled 30,000 miles by sea, visiting New Zealand, Australia, China, Korea, Japan and Hawaii.

Fr. Ted engaged in pastoral counseling in Latin America and aboard the Queen Elizabeth II. When a cleaning lady had a "spiritual problem," he spent over an hour talking with her in Spanish. "Human problems seem to be the same worldwide these days," he reflected in his diary. After a counseling session with another troubled person, he wrote. "It's amazing how many stories are packed into a ship like this, how many tragedies, and how many opportunities."

Irritated with some elderly passengers aboard ship who were preoccupied with death, dying, inactivity, and loss of power, he preached a sermon criticizing the "obtuse spirit." The result? The offertory collection declined. "Maybe I was too tough in the sermon," he noted. "People voting with their dollars. No matter, my task is giving them the truth, not getting big collections." The two priests completed the final portion of their travel during the last two weeks of December 1988, visiting Antarctica.[3]

On his return to Notre Dame, Fr. Ted had a new office. His desk, books, and his secretary Helen Hosinski were moved to the thirteenth floor of the newly named Theodore M. Hesburgh Library, and Fr. Joyce was moved to an adjacent office. "My new office fulfilled all my desires," he said. It had bookshelves from floor to ceiling and a window gave him a beautiful panoramic view of the campus with the gold dome and the

Sacred Heart Church spire in the center. He and Fr. Joyce both believed that the "best gift" they could give to the new president, Fr. Edward Malloy, and new executive vice president, Fr. William Beauchamp, was to disappear for a year, and then to slip back quietly and undertake some unobtrusive tasks useful to the university.[4]

When Fr. Ted was about to retire a commentator expressed the hope that his retirement be enjoyable but that it not last too long because "neither the church nor the nation can afford to let him disappear permanently into private life." Actually, Fr. Ted never intended to disappear permanently into private life; he said he wanted to retire—not slow down. Shortly after his sabbatical, still energetic, he spoke about the nuclear arms race to the Notre Dame Club of Delaware in Wilmington on Wednesday evening; the following day he addressed students at a Wilmington high school, talked with six seniors about to enter Notre Dame, was interviewed on television, and visited the Wilmington Free Library where he read stories to a group of preschoolers.[5]

Reading his breviary, celebrating Mass, and praying the rosary remained the constants in his life. Otherwise his days were a mixture of domestic and foreign travel, phone calls and correspondence, writing articles and speeches, guest lectures in Notre Dame classrooms, presiding over liturgies in campus dormitories, and advancing the interests of the five institutes he helped found. He arrived at the library about noon, took the elevator to the eighth floor, then, to get his exercise, walked five flights of stairs to his office on the thirteenth floor. It was exactly 100 steps. He often worked until 2:00 A.M., as he had before his retirement.

Faculty invited him to present guest lectures. He spoke on the history of the civil rights movement, affirmative action, disarmament, venture capital, leadership, and presidents he had known. In lecturing to a class in American history about the civil rights movement, he used his personal experiences. "The students enjoy it very much," said the instructor, Fr. Thomas Blantz. Altogether, Fr. Ted received between ten and fifteen requests to speak per week and had to reject most of them. "People think that because you're retired, you have nothing else to do," he said. "If I never gave another outside talk, I'd have more than enough to do."[6]

He served on fifty boards and committees, but he focused on the development of five institutes affiliated with Notre Dame: the Ecumenical Institute for Theological Studies at Tantur, Jerusalem; the Center for International Human Rights; the Helen Kellogg Institute for International Studies; the Institute for International Peace Studies; and the Hank

Family Environmental Research Center (an environmental, education-al, and research laboratory at Notre Dame's spacious forest and lake re-serve at Land O'Lakes). Each institute had an executive director, reliev-ing Fr. Ted of administrative responsibility. He discussed programs with the staff and board of directors and raised funds for developing the insti-tutes.

He was the ideal facilitator for the five institutes because he sat on the board of so many other advisory councils—some with similar focus-es—and could bring back ideas for Notre Dame's institutes. Fr. Ernest Bartell, the director of the Helen Kellogg Institute for International Studies, appreciated his advice and fundraising, but Fr. Ted didn't play an active role in governing the institute. Although Fr. Ted chaired the Advisory Council, Bartell and his staff did all the preparation for meet-ings. "We . . . set the agenda, and, frankly, we sit right next to him while he chairs it so that he can follow along with it."[7]

In the spring of 1990, Fr. Ted was asked to deliver fifteen college commencement addresses, but he had time for only four. He told grad-uates of Loras College in Iowa to combine their newly acquired compe-tence with compassion and commitment. "You have to work constantly to become more competent. Don't ever settle for less than competency. God isn't served by mediocrity." But competence wasn't enough in a world filled with poverty and hunger. Compassion was needed. "And compassion isn't worth a darn without commitment."

He was given scores of awards and honors. In the spring of 1994, af-ter he received honorary degrees from Marian College (Indianapolis) and Avila College (Kansas City), his total came to 129. He attributed his American record-holding title to being president of Notre Dame for thirty-five years and for working on the issues of civil rights and higher education. What did a person do with all those honors? "I put them in the archives," he stated. He always received a framed degree and a doc-toral hood.

In the fall of 1991, he received his fifteenth presidential appointment when President Bush named him a member of the Board of Directors of the United States Institute of Peace in Washington, D.C. Congress had created the board in 1984 to oversee a variety of programs, grants, fel-lowships, conferences, and publications relating to world peace. Al-though Fr. Ted accepted the post, the institute's meager $5 million budg-et disturbed him. "The government spends 800 times more on one air-plane than they do on total work for peace. It's enough to give me heartburn," he said.[8]

He flew throughout the world on behalf of various projects. In a five-week period he traveled to Brazil, Uruguay, West Germany, Moscow, and Washington, D.C., with stops back home between each trip. "I write these lines at 41,000 feet, enroute to Moscow, having been in six other countries in the last ten days," he said about another trip.

In the summer of 1989, Fr. Ted was among twelve people selected to observe political conditions in Namibia, monitoring the Southwest African nation's progress toward a freely elected government. For more than a decade there had been war in Namibia between the occupying forces of South Africa and guerrillas of SWAPO (the South-West Africa People's Organization). The United Nations and the International Court of Justice had declared illegal South Africa's occupation and administration of the country.

Shortly after being selected to go to Namibia, he encountered Fr. Oliver Williams, a Notre Dame professor and South African expert. When Fr. Ted asked Fr. Williams about the difficulty of traveling in Namibia and the inoculations needed before traveling there, Fr. Williams responded that travel would be very difficult, that many shots were needed because of Namibia's severe water and food problems, and that Fr. Ted would probably have to live in a tent. Fr. Williams strongly urged him not to make the trip. But Fr. Ted was adamant and excited. "I wouldn't miss this for anything!" he told Williams. (He made the trip; his observer group reported some encouraging progress in election preparations in Namibia, but was mostly critical of South Africa for placing "formidable barriers to free and fair elections".)[9]

He also continued to monitor the Cold War and to warn of possible nuclear destruction. In 1988 he became a trustee of a new organization set up in Moscow, the International Foundation for the Survival and Development of Humanity. He described it as the first private, independent, autonomous foundation in the history of the Soviet Union. Of the twenty trustees, five were Americans and five were Russians, including Andrei Sakharov, the Nobel Prize–winning physicist, Soviet dissident, and human rights activist.

The foundation hoped to reduce armaments, increase trust, and improve economic and social development in the Third World. A special Human Rights Commission planned to investigate worldwide problems with religious freedom, penal systems, and the freedom to emigrate. Because he visited the Soviet Union so often, he was given a free visa that allowed him to come and go as he pleased with no baggage check.[10]

In late September 1988, while meeting in Moscow with Sakharov's group, he was asked to celebrate Mass in an Orthodox chapel at the invitation of an archbishop of the Russian Orthodox Church. He casually invited all the officials at the meeting to attend his Sunday Mass on September 25, and not only did the Americans come, but so did the Soviets. "I've never been to Mass in my whole life," a Soviet official told him, "and it really caught me deep in my heart."

To Fr. Ted the incident was another symptom of changes in the Soviet Union. Earlier he had detected increasing receptiveness by Soviet officials for human rights. "Something really *is* happening [in the Soviet Union]," he wrote in his diary on January 5, 1988, after a conference in Amsterdam. "I've never seen the Russians more open and conciliatory than they are here."

In 1989, while speaking on religious freedom in the conference room of the Soviet Central Committee in Moscow, he told a group of top Soviet lawyers: "It's cruel and obscene that you don't let your parents teach their kids what they believe—their faith." He was shocked that many Soviet officials agreed with him. One told the group, "I'm an atheist, but the more [Father Hesburgh] talked, the more he dragged me into his orbit. I have to say this honestly—I believe 100 percent of what he is saying." Fr. Ted returned from Moscow astonished by the changes in the Soviet Union. "The atmosphere is different, the conversation is different, the openness is fantastically different. It told me that we really are in a new world." "We used to say three Hail Marys after Mass for the conversion of Russia," he later said; "I think it is happening." He attributed the changes in the Soviet Union to Mikhail Gorbachev, "one of the great visionaries of our time."

The reduction of East-West tensions was a moment to be seized. The problem, he argued in January 1989, was that people had lived so long in a climate of mistrust and fear—even hatred—that it was difficult suddenly to go down a new road together. "I think we are on a new road together. We have to . . . test them at every move, but that's not a bad thing to do, and they ought to test us." He wanted U.S. defense spending shifted to resolving monumental social problems at home: shelter for the homeless, equal educational opportunities for minorities, turning hopelessness into hopefulness.[11]

When the threat of nuclear disaster dramatically declined, Fr. Ted urged Americans to focus on environmental dangers. In a speech to faculty and students in November 1991, he discussed global warming, destruction of rain forests, and water pollution. Placing much of the blame on his own countrymen, he argued that Americans made up 5 percent of the world's population but consumed 26 percent of the world's oil supply and produced 290 million tons of toxic waste yearly. Americans should "think globally but act locally," he advised. They could not solve the world's problems, but they could improve the environment in their own communities. On another occasion, he expressed frustration that "we're the only planet in the solar system that has air you can breathe, water you can drink, and land where you can grow food. So what are we doing? We're making our air unbreathable, our water undrinkable and our land polluted." The prospect of environmental catastrophe seemed to replace the possibility of nuclear catastrophe as Fr. Ted's primary fear, but he wasn't able to muster the energy to pursue the environmental issue with the same passion that he had approached the nuclear dilemma in the 1980s.

One unusual idea he impulsively put forth seemed imprudent. In September 1991, he told a reporter for the *South Bend Tribune* that he had a "plan" to eliminate and replace "all ghetto schools." Just bulldoze 1,000 acres of a slum and build a K-12 complex, educating 30,000 students. The complex would be totally fenced so if "any drug dealer tried to get in, he would be electrocuted." His plan would provide health, nutrition, and recreational services, "total security" for teachers, and a beautiful environment with a lake in the middle where kids could fish. "I would pay for it with [the cost of] one nuclear submarine."[12]

He also wrote two books of memoirs (with the assistance of Jerry Reedy, a professional writer and Notre Dame graduate) and helped edit another book. In 1982 Richard Conklin had spent a week at Land O'Lakes tape recording Fr. Ted's memories. In 1989 they brought the story up to date. Reedy organized the resulting one thousand pages of transcripts into the manuscript of Fr. Ted's autobiography. The book, *God, Country, Notre Dame* (1990), spent six weeks on *The New York Times'* best seller list.

In the book he recalled his childhood, his rigorous training in the seminary, and his meteoric rise to the presidency of Notre Dame. He described his regular visits to the halls of power, his struggle for civil rights and academic freedom, and his handling of anti-war protesters in the 1960s. Mostly he told engaging stories—about his personal diplomacy with Soviet officials, friendship with Pope Paul VI, firing by

Richard Nixon, flight aboard the SR-71 reconnaissance plane, and Christmas vacations in Mexico.

Although engaging, the book was not all-encompassing. It ignored exceptionally sensitive topics, specifically Fr. Ted's squabble with anti-abortionists and the traumatic dismissal of Fr. James Burtchaell as provost. On the other hand, modesty compelled him to underestimate his outstanding attributes and leadership qualities. In addition, the book overlooks the insights of friends, colleagues, and observers.[13]

Some critics thought the oral history approach produced thin results. "Those who are looking for the inner, private Hesburgh, will not find it here," wrote the reviewer for the *Washington Post.* "A great life," said the review in *America.* "A disappointing book."

Most reviewers, though, liked the book, judging it as amiable as the storyteller himself. The stories "are simply wonderful," praised one reviewer; "enthralling," said another. The book had "spirit," said the review in *Chicago Tribune.* "[Its] warmth and humanity are infectious, and most readers will not have the nerve to fight off the pleasure of going along."[14]

In the fall of 1992, Doubleday published an edited version of the travel diaries Fr. Ted wrote during his retirement. *Travels with Ted and Ned* wasn't just about the fun of travel, Fr. Ted wrote. "Fundamentally it's a book about totally changing one's ordinary, lifelong way of living without coming apart at the seams. It's a book about enjoying, not dreading retirement. And yes, it's about stopping—stopping, at long last, to smell the roses."

The book was not reviewed widely, and the reviews it did receive were mixed. "Reading his diary is akin to viewing the vacation slides of a competent but uninspired photographer," said the critical review in *Library Journal.* The book was too superficial, the reviewer thought; "those looking for an illuminating travel narrative will likely be disappointed." However, the reviewer for *Publisher's Weekly* liked Fr. Ted's "humor and urbanity," and thought the book vividly captured the many ports of call as well as the performance of ministry.[15]

In the summer of 1994, the University of Notre Dame Press published a book Fr. Ted helped edit, *The Challenge and Promise of a Catholic University.* He and twenty-nine prominent members of Notre Dame's faculty and administration wrote essays examining central issues affecting Catholic higher education: could a Catholic university simultaneously avoid secularization and insular sectarianism; should a majority of the faculty be practicing Catholics; should Catholicism be defined in terms of culture, belief, practice, or all of these; and, finally, what level of commitment to intellectual inquiry and the possibility to dissent was appropriate on a Catholic campus? As usual, Fr. Ted wrote and edited hastily. "We have never done a book so fast," he said afterwards.[16]

In 1989, responding to incidents of major scandals in college athletics, the Knight Foundation, an offshoot of the Knight-Ridder news organization, established a twenty-two-member commission on intercollegiate athletics. Creed Black, head of the Knight Foundation, met with Fr. Ted at the Morris Inn during the fall of 1989 and asked him to co-chair the commission. Fr. Ted tried to beg off; his schedule was too full. But Black appealed to his heart.

"I thought you cared about the integrity of higher education," said Black.

"I do," Fr. Ted responded.

"Well, then do something about it," urged Black.

Fr. Ted agreed, later explaining that although he wasn't an avid fan of college sports, he accepted the role because "I don't want to see athletics tarnish the institution I love, the American University." Disgusted with the corruption in college athletics, he added: "It's gotten so bad that everybody has contempt for the integrity of our institutions of higher education in regard to athletics." He co-chaired the commission together with William Friday, retired President of the University of North Carolina at Chapel Hill.

Because of his renown, Fr. Ted brought instant credibility to the commission. He was also the perfect role model for cleaning up college athletics. "If all the schools were like Notre Dame and run by a president like Hesburgh," said a reporter for the *Chicago Tribune*, "[athletic] reform would be a moot point."[17]

When Fr. Ted arrived in Washington, D.C., for the first meeting of the commission, he had several yellow sheets of paper filled with ideas. "Fr. Ted had really gotten fired up," said Creed Black. At the beginning of the commission's work Fr. Ted and Friday issued a joint statement explaining their reasons for accepting leadership of the commission:

First, we both cherish institutions of higher learning and are disgusted at the way their standing in the eyes of the American public is being seriously impugned by a long series of athletic and related academic scandals. Secondly, we both believe in the potential value of intercollegiate athletics when conducted with integrity. We both believe that if we can do something to insure that integrity and to restore the good name of universities, both public and private, it would be worth the effort involved.

The co-chairs also said they didn't want to be just another commission, "the latest in a long series, that spins its wheels, emits pious platitudes, and finally reports and walks away leaving the problem a bit embellished with ambiguous solutions that never take root and, in reality, leave the festering problems still festering to the detriment of university integrity."[18]

The commission didn't want to rewrite the NCAA manual, propose new rules, or suggest sanctions. It was interested, said Fr. Ted, in the "big picture." Early in the commission's study Fr. Ted proposed the "one-plus-three plan," the fundamental feature ultimately adopted by the commission. "One" meant presidential control over all aspects of the university's athletic programs; and "three" meant financial integrity, academic integrity, and continuous independent auditing to certify compliance with the rules.

Some commissioners wanted to add a fourth principle, gender equity, to the three already agreed upon. Although Fr. Ted supported gender equity, he wanted to focus on corruption in college athletics and urged that gender issues be handled in a different context. He listened patiently as commissioners discussed whether to add the item to the other three. Then he expressed his view, concluding, "These are all great ideas and we could spend a lot of time on each. . . . But you will have to excuse me. I am accustomed to Trinitarian principles." His fellow commissioners howled with laughter.

In its much-heralded interim report in 1991, the high-profile panel recommended the "one-plus-three" plan. The commission emphasized a method to control athletics long used by Fr. Ted at Notre Dame: the empowerment of university presidents. The presidents must remain vigilant to prevent future abuses in college athletics. As for those who didn't want to accept the new reforms and continued their unethical conduct, Fr. Ted had a recommendation: "If people could not comply with our one-plus-three model, they could go by themselves and form the Outlaw League for Illiterate Athletes."

In March 1993 the Knight Commission completed more than three years of study with a warning not to allow its push for reform to die with it. Staff director Christopher Morris estimated that the NCAA had implemented 65 percent of the Knight Commission's specific recommendations by early 1994, including raising academic standards for athletic eligibility and reducing the number of scholarships in some sports. "Our role was advisory," Fr. Ted said proudly, "but we changed the face of intercollegiate athletics."[19] Public opinion supported the Knight Commission's reform efforts and most of the commission's recommendations were welcomed.

Two other causes Fr. Ted espoused, however, were intensely controversial. One involved a major espionage case. Jonathan Pollard was a civilian intelligence analyst for the U.S. recruited for espionage by the Israeli Defense Ministry in the mid-1980s. Pollard delivered suitcases full of U.S. military documents to the Israelis, including satellite photographs and information on Arab military systems. (He admitted receiving $50,000 in cash from Israel.) In 1987 he was convicted of espionage and given a harsh punishment—life in prison.

Fr. Ted had known the Pollard family for almost thirty years. Jonathan's father, Morris Pollard, who is Jewish, had joined the Notre Dame faculty in 1961, and during his long career at the university had engaged in cancer research, chaired the Microbiology Department, and directed the LOBUND Laboratory. His young son Jonathan had attended Notre Dame social functions with his parents and met Fr. Ted; later, when Jonathan took summer school classes at Notre Dame, he and Fr. Ted discussed world affairs and Greek history.

Feeling deep compassion for the Pollards, Fr. Ted took the initiative in contacting the family to offer his assistance. "They are part of the [Notre Dame] family," he later explained. "When part of the family has difficulty of any kind, my inclination was always to jump in and try to help them."

After studying the case, Fr. Ted concluded that there were mitigating circumstances in Jonathan's actions and irregularities in his trial. Although Fr. Ted didn't dispute the fact that Jonathan had given military secrets to Israel, he joined other Pollard sympathizers in arguing that a plea bargain had not been kept; that Israel was not an "enemy" nation and therefore Jonathan had not engaged in "treason"; that he had been unjustly placed in solitary confinement; and that his life sentence was disproportionately severe compared to sentences handed down for similar crimes.[20]

Fr. Ted advised and encouraged Morris and Mildred Pollard, sought assistance from an expert Washington attorney, wrote letters to Presidents Bush and Clinton seeking clemency, informally lobbied other White House officials, and wrote letters to the court. An official in the Bush Administration leaked the news of Fr. Ted's quiet lobbying to a prominent newspaper columnist, who phoned Fr. Ted and tried to dissuade him from helping Jonathan. "I thought that was out of order," reflected Fr. Ted. He told the columnist, "What I do is my business!"

Worried, depressed, and embarrassed about her son's arrest, Mildred Pollard was reluctant to be seen in public. Learning of her reticence, Fr. Ted phoned her and said, "There is no reason why you should . . . [hide] from society. I hereby invite you to come to the Morris Inn and have lunch with me in the center table of the dining room." Mrs. Pollard declined, but Fr. Ted's bold invitation boosted her spirits. "I thought [the invitation] was magnificent," said Morris Pollard. "He has really been consistently supportive, to the extent that we feel very emotional about the contact we have [had] with him."

Israel, American Jewish groups, and some members of Congress urged that Pollard be granted clemency. But the Justice and Defense Departments, as well as the Central Intelligence Agency, unanimously recommended against clemency. A review of the case coordinated by the Justice Department recommended to President Clinton that freeing Pollard would send a dangerous message that the U.S. would be lenient with someone whose espionage or spying caused grave damage to the U.S.

On March 23, 1994, President Clinton rejected clemency for Pollard. "The enormity of Mr. Pollard's crime," said the President, "the harm his actions caused to our country and the need to deter every person who might even consider such actions, warrant his continued incarceration."[21]

To avoid alienating alumni and others, Fr. Ted had repeatedly said that he would not become involved in partisan politics. But he bent the rule in June 1994, when he agreed to become co-chair of the legal defense fund for President Bill Clinton and First Lady Hillary Rodham Clinton.

President Clinton and his wife faced mounting legal bills stemming from their partnership in the Whitewater real estate development while he was governor; a federal independent counsel was investigating their activities. In addition, Paula Jones, a former Arkansas state employee, accused Bill Clinton of sexual harassment and filed a law suit. Jones claimed she had to rebuff then Governor Clinton in May 1991, when he asked her to perform oral sex. Clinton categorically denied the accusation; his attorney, Robert Bennett, asked a federal court to seek dismissal of the suit until Clinton left the presidency. Observers estimated that the Clintons' legal bills might run as high as $2 million a year. Their 1993 income was approximately $293,000.

Co-chairing the Presidential Legal Defense Trust was former Democratic Attorney General Nicholas Katzenbach. Overseeing the fund was an executive director and trustees made up of prominent Democrats and Republicans, including former Republican Attorney General Elliot Richardson, former Democratic Congressman from the South Bend area John Brademas, and former Texas Democratic Congresswoman Barbara Jordan. The fund would accept donations of no more than $1,000 per individual. No other president had ever set up such a fund while in office, but supporters of the Clintons claimed that the problem of huge legal expenses was also unprecedented. "No previous president has had to face the enormous personal legal expenses confronting President Clinton, because of current legal proceedings based on events that allegedly occurred well before he took office. These expenses will be many times his total compensation as president," Fr. Ted and Katzenbach said in a statement. "Whatever the merits or motivations of these proceedings, we believe it is in the public interest to assist the president in meeting a financial burden that could otherwise distract him from performing his public responsibilities."

Critics, however, wondered why a prominent Catholic leader wanted to expend energy on a controversial political issue when there were many other worthy causes he could champion. In a letter to the *South Bend Tribune*, a critic wrote that he was "perplexed" and "astonished" that Fr. Ted would use such "poor judgment." Surely, "there are many other humanitarian needs that would seem to warrant the efforts of a man of Hesburgh's stature."[22]

Other new responsibilities were less controversial. On April 10, 1994, Fr. Ted was elected president of the Harvard Board of Overseers. (First elected to the Board in 1990, he was the first Roman Catholic clergyman to be elected as an overseer at Harvard.) Fr. Ted knew something was up when he was asked to leave the room for a few minutes during the election meeting. When he returned, the overseers asked him to accept the post as president. He reminded them that he would be seventy-seven on May 25 and that, because of his failing eyesight, it would be difficult for him to read a lot of documents. But Hanna Gray, the committee chairperson, replied that the Board had considered all those factors, and Harvard's president approved the selection. So Fr. Ted accepted. "Father Hesburgh is among the most extraordinary and accomplished educational leaders of our time, and it is Harvard's privilege to have him serve as the next president of the Board of Overseers," said Harvard's President Neil L. Rudenstine.[23]

Did Fr. Ted miss being president of Notre Dame? He didn't say. "I think he misses his active role in the administration of the university," speculated his niece, Mary Flaherty, three years after he retired. Not the day to day problems. "But I think he misses . . . running the big picture. . . . It is probably difficult for him that things are not done exactly the way he may have done them."[24]

He scrupulously avoided interfering with his successor, seldom venturing inside the Main Building where his old office was. "I've been in the building just five times in more than five years," he said with satisfaction in 1993. "Occasionally if I have what I think is a bright idea, I'll just send a note over and tell them they can do whatever they want with it. I'd say everybody's quite relaxed around here on this whole subject. The new administration is doing well, and if there's any way I can back them, I do, at least indirectly."

When faculty friends stopped by to discuss a problem, he made sure everybody understood there was one subject he refused to discuss. "They all know that there's one piece of ground I don't walk on, and that's discussing the present administration. I think it's important that I adhere to that policy very strictly."

Despite his repeated public endorsement of Fr. Malloy's administration, there persisted rumors of tension between Fr. Ted and the new administration. "I think he's biting his tongue about what the new crowd is doing versus what his priorities were," said an official in the Malloy administration in 1993. Some believed that Fr. Ted had been slighted. "The administration which followed him and whom he personally picked . . . have treated him very snottily," said a former administrator under Fr. Ted's presidency. Although Fr. Ted conscientiously stayed out of the way of the Malloy administration, said the same official, "after a while he didn't need to because he and Fr. Joyce were both stiff-armed in ways that were gratuitous and unnecessary." Perhaps the rumors were baseless; no one has come forward with any examples of Fr. Ted being stiff-armed. And if Fr. Ted had any complaints about his successor, he was not vocal about them.

Fr. Ted was an emeritus trustee, but at meetings he seldom spoke. "He's never spoken . . . except when a question has been directed to him," observed trustee Sr. Alice Gallin in March 1994. At a meeting of the trustees Fr. Ted sat quietly, as he usually did, until Fr. Malloy asked him to explain his long-time battle to keep the Vatican from regulating Catholic universities. Fr. Ted spoke eloquently, but later told a friend, "I did not speak until I was called on." [25]

For relaxation Fr. Ted spent two or three weeks at the Holy Cross property at Land O'Lakes, fishing, reading, writing, and listening to classical music. In 1992 he caught a 25-pound muskie under exceptional circumstances. He was fishing with two friends, Jerry Hank, a Notre Dame trustee and benefactor, and Gerry Schoesser, the manager of the property. Fr. Ted told the fish story to Jerry Reedy, the co-author of his autobiography:

I was casting an orange bucktail with a minnow hooked on behind. I had just reeled it in and had it alongside the boat slightly out of the water, when a muskie lunged at it. He missed, cartwheeled in the water and lunged once more. He missed again, but this time his momentum carried him into the boat—or, more precisely, onto Gerry Schoesser's lap. The fish was thrashing around a lot. Gerry tried to wrestle it to the bottom of the boat so it couldn't jump back into the lake.

During the struggle, Jerry Hank tried several times to bash the muskie with an oar without bashing Gerry. It seemed that every time he tried, Gerry's head was in the way. In the meantime, this round-bottomed boat we were in was rocking back and forth, threatening to dump all of us in the lake. To keep Jerry from falling overboard as he attempted to swing the oar at the fish, I grabbed him from behind by the belt. Finally, he managed to get in one good whack, which stunned the fish long enough for him to get a stringer into its mouth. [26]

He sensed that the aging process was affecting him. His joints were beginning to "creak;" his memory wasn't as good. When he started experiencing weakness in his legs, he began peddling a stationary bicycle every day, while simultaneously trying to learn Chinese. He claimed he put 3,000 miles on the bicycle, and although he strengthened his legs, his Chinese didn't improve. "I learned that when you're past 70 you're not going to learn Chinese." In 1993 he suffered back pain, but doctors at the Mayo Clinic didn't find anything seriously wrong with his back. His vision, though, posed the most serious health problem. The retina in his right eye deteriorated, making it more difficult for him to read. When he put his hand over his left eye, he saw only a blur, but he still could read using his left eye. [27]

Fr. Hesburgh pursuing a favorite retirement pastime.

Overall, though, he still felt energetic. He preferred to stay overcommitted than undercommitted. ("I'd rather wear out than rust out.") Many people took retirement too seriously, he thought. "They shut off the lights, lock the door, and vegetate. Others may drink too many martinis or play too much gin rummy. That isn't retirement; it's quitting while still having much to give, much to enjoy, much to love, much living yet to do."

"I assume the old body is going to start wearing down," he told a group of senior citizens. "So it wears down. But I'll get all I can out of it as long as it lasts. It's like driving an old car. You don't have to put it on the junk heap as long as it starts and runs," and, he joked, "you have a good friend that's a mechanic." He castigated the "mindless" diversion of watching television all day. Senior citizens shouldn't waste time watching the tube. "That's a great anesthesia. But who wants anesthesia when you're alive and there are still things your mind can do."[28]

On May 6, 1993, Fr. Ted celebrated his jubilee Mass, marking fifty years in the priesthood. The ceremony took place in the university's Sacred Heart Church where he had been ordained in June 1943. In his fifteen-minute homily, Fr. Ted spoke reflectively about Jesus being "the great high priest and one true mediator." He expressed gratitude for being able to preach and to practice "the apostolate of just being there . . . as a living symbol of Jesus when he was present in flesh and blood." He told the gathering of 400 people: "If I could use this moment to ask one more benefit, one more grace from the Lord, I would ask to be able to offer the sacrifice of the Mass every day until I die. Then I will die happy."

He said he was "not anywhere near as holy, not anywhere near as humble, not anywhere near as loving, not anywhere near as giving as I would like to be because I have the impossible model of Jesus Christ himself, but I am trying."[29]

One day during his retirement, while reading his breviary, he was struck by the notion that life was often referred to as a journey. In his diary he wrote, "We are constantly getting new insights, surmounting new difficulties, suffering some defeats, and rejoicing in a few victories as the journey continues as we work our way towards God and eternity. One has to develop a capacity for enjoying surprises, facing new challenges, growing in a lot of little ways, and not being discouraged if some things aren't always perfect."[30] His moment of reflection actually applied to his own journey through life. Often insightful, he had surmounted difficulties, suffered some defeats, faced scores of new challenges, grew in many ways, and remained hopeful and optimistic, all the while continuing to work toward God and eternity. And he had many reasons to rejoice.

NOTES

For information on the methods of research and the manner of citation used in this work, the reader is referred to the Sources essay, pp. 343ff. The following abbreviations have been used in the notes.

DPRI   Department of Public Relations and Information Papers,
              University of Notre Dame.

TMHP   Theodore M. Hesburgh Papers, University of Notre Dame Archives.

UNDA   University of Notre Dame Archives.

USCCR   United States Commission on Civil Rights.

NOTES TO INTRODUCTION

1. *Notre Dame Magazine,* Summer 1987; *St. Anthony Messenger,* May 1987; *The Tidings,* October 24, 1986.

2. *America,* May 30, 1987; *Chicago Tribune,* November 9, 1986; *Houston Chronicle,* February 7, 1981; *South Bend Tribune,* May 17, 1987; interviews, John Brademas, Edmund Stephan.

3. *Chicago Tribune,* June 26, 1977, and November 9, 1986; *National Catholic Reporter,* May 22, 1987; *South Bend Tribune,* May 17, 1987.

4. *Chicago Sun-Times,* May 3, 1987.

5. *The Chronicle of Higher Education,* May 13, 1987; *National Catholic Reporter,* May 22, 1987; interview, Richard Conklin.

6. *The Boston Globe,* May 18, 1987; *Time,* May 18, 1987.

7. *The Boston Globe,* May 18, 1987; *The New York Times,* May 22, 1987.

NOTES TO CHAPTER ONE

1. Theodore M. Hesburgh, "Education," in John Marks Templeton (ed.), *Looking Forward: The Next Forty Years* (New York: HarperBusiness, 1993), pp. 148–49; Thomas

Stritch, "A Short Biography of Theodore Hesburgh," in Charlotte A. Ames (ed.), *Theodore M. Hesburgh: A Bio-Bibliography* (New York: Greenwood Press, 1989), p. 4; Theodore Hesburgh, *God, Country, Notre Dame* (New York: Doubleday, 1990), pp. 1–2; John C. Lungren Jr., *Hesburgh of Notre Dame: Priest, Educator, Public Servant* (Kansas City: Sheed and Ward, 1989), pp. 10–11.

2. Stritch, "Theodore Hesburgh," p. 4; Hesburgh, *God, Country, Notre Dame*, p. 5.

3. Hesburgh, *God, Country, Notre Dame*, p. 5; interview, Theodore Hesburgh.

4. *Los Angeles Times,* June 21, 1982; Hesburgh, *God, Country, Notre Dame*, pp. 6, 11, 12; interviews, James Hesburgh, Theodore Hesburgh, John O'Connor, Elizabeth O'Neill, Donald Roth.

5. *Chicago Tribune,* November 12, 1978; *The Courier Journal,* December 7, 1986; *South Bend Tribune,* July 1, 1952; Hesburgh, *God, Country, Notre Dame*, p. 6; interviews, Theodore Hesburgh, Newton Minow, Elizabeth O'Neill, Donald Roth, Mary Waters.

6. *The Courier Journal,* December 7, 1986; *The Observer,* Spring 1987; *Syracuse Herald-American,* December 17, 1978; *Time,* February 9, 1962; Hesburgh, *God, Country, Notre Dame*, pp. 9, 11; Frank Corso to author, July 14, 1989; interviews, John O'Connor, Elizabeth O'Neill.

7. *South Bend Tribune,* May 3, 1964; *Syracuse Herald-American,* December 17, 1978; Hesburgh, *God, Country, Notre Dame*, p. 10; interviews, John O'Connor, Elizabeth O'Neill.

8. "Commencement Program," June 24, 1934, unprocessed Most Holy Rosary School Papers, Syracuse, N.Y.; *Syracuse Post-Standard,* May 8, 1991; *America,* October 4, 1986; David O'Brien, *Faith and Friendship: Catholicism in the Diocese of Syracuse: 1886–1986* (Syracuse: Catholic Diocese of Syracuse, 1987), pp. 244–45; Frank Corso to author, July 14, 1989; John O'Connor to author, October 1989; interviews, Frank Corso, John O'Connor, Theodore Hesburgh.

9. Hesburgh, *God, Country, Notre Dame*, p. 133; Trevor Kennedy (ed.), "Theodore Hesburgh," *Top Guns: Seventeen World Leaders in Politics, Media and Business Tell How They Made It to the Top—and Stayed There* (South Melbourne: Sun Books, Macmillan Company of Australia, 1988), p. 73.

10. Diary of Theodore Hesburgh, "Travels with Ted and Ned, I. North America," DPRI (1987), p. 155; *South Bend Tribune,* May 17, 1987.

11. *The Observer,* Spring 1987; *Syracuse Post-Standard,* May 8, 1991; interviews, Elizabeth O'Neill, Theodore Hesburgh.

12. Clipping, Newspaper Clipping File, Hesburgh Office File, TMHP; *The Indianapolis News,* March 4, 1987; *Syracuse Herald-American,* December 17, 1978; Hesburgh, *God, Country, Notre Dame*, pp. 189–90; interview, Elizabeth O'Neill.

13. Clipping, Newspaper Clipping File, Hesburgh Office File, TMHP; clipping, Theodore Hesburgh News Clippings, DPRI; Robert Sam Anson, typescript of an interview with Theodore Hesburgh, 1981, p. 1, Theodore Hesburgh News Clippings, DPRI; *Boston Sunday Globe,* November 16, 1986; *Our Sunday Visitor,* March 13, 1966; *America,* October 4, 1986; Hesburgh, *God, Country, Notre Dame*, p. 7; interviews, James Hesburgh, Theodore Hesburgh, Anne Jackson, Elizabeth O'Neill.

14. *The Courier Journal,* December 7, 1986; *South Bend Tribune,* July 1, 1952; *Time,* February 9, 1962; Andrew Greeley, *The American Catholic: A Social Portrait* (New York: Basic Books, 1977), p. 11; Hesburgh, *God, Country, Notre Dame*, pp. 7, 8; O'Brien, *Faith and Friendship,* pp. 199–207; Garry Wills, *Bare Ruined Choirs* (Garden City, N.Y.: Doubleday, 1972), pp. 15–16; interviews, Donald Roth, Mary Waters.

15. Lungren, *Hesburgh of Notre Dame,* p. 7; Frank Corso to author, July 14, 1989; interviews, Theodore Hesburgh, John O'Connor, Donald Roth, Mary Waters.

16. Hesburgh diary, "Travels with Ted and Ned, I" (1987), p. 20; *Notre Dame Magazine,* June 1972, p. 13; *Syracuse Herald-American,* December 17, 1978; Hesburgh, "Education," in Templeton (ed.), *Looking Forward,* p. 156; Hesburgh, *God, Country, Notre Dame,* p. 8; interviews, Donald Roth, John O'Connor.

17. *Time,* February 9, 1962; Frank Corso to author, July 14, 1989; interview, John O'Connor.

18. Untitled article by Theodore Hesburgh in *The Rosarian* (1934), unpublished Florence Lynch Papers, Syracuse, N.Y.; "Literary Guild Notes," probably *The Rosarian* (1934), Most Holy Rosary School Papers; John O'Connor to Theodore Hesburgh, September 14, 1985, unprocessed John O'Connor Papers, Winchester, Massachusetts; *The Book Review Digest 1927* (New York: The H. W. Wilson Company, 1928), p. 358; James Walsh, *Father McShane of Maryknoll* (New York: Dial Press, 1932), p. 225; interviews, Theodore Hesburgh, John O'Connor.

19. Untitled article by Theodore Hesburgh, *The Rosarian* (1934), Lynch Papers; *The Book Review Digest 1933* (New York: The H. W. Wilson Company, 1934), p. 458.

20. *Syracuse Herald-American,* December 17, 1978; *Parent's Magazine,* December, 1968; "Rev. Theodore M. Hesburgh," *A Celebration of Teachers* (Urbana: National Council of Teachers of English, 1985), p. 24; Hesburgh, *God, Country, Notre Dame,* p. 8; Wills, *Bare Ruined Choirs,* p. 27; interviews, John O'Connor, Theodore Hesburgh.

21. "Catholic Sun Editorial," April 26, 1934, Most Holy Rosary Papers; *The Observer,* Spring 1987; interview, Mary Waters.

22. *Syracuse Post-Standard,* May 8, 1991; interview, Donald Roth.

23. "Honors Awarded For Excellence" (1934), Most Holy Rosary Papers; "Commencement Program," June 24, 1934, Most Holy Rosary Papers.

24. "Class Prophecy," probably in *The Rosarian* (1934), Most Holy Rosary School Papers; Anson interview, p. 1; *The Observer,* Spring 1987; Hesburgh, *God, Country, Notre Dame;* interview, Elizabeth O'Neill.

25. *The Indianapolis News,* March 4, 1987; *The Observer,* Spring 1987; *The Sign,* March 1961; *Syracuse Herald-American,* December 17, 1978; Edward Fischer to author, July 10, 1989; interview, Elizabeth O'Neill.

26. "Silverlake Property, Rolling Prairie, Indiana," typescript, Miscellaneous Papers, The Province Archives Center, Notre Dame, Indiana; *Notre Dame Alumnus,* August 1971; *Our Sunday Visitor,* March 13, 1966; *Scholastic,* October 11, 1957; Hesburgh, *God, Country, Notre Dame,* pp. 13–14.

27. "Rolling Prairie," Miscellaneous Papers, The Province Archives; Diary of Theodore Hesburgh, "Around the World," DPRI (1978), p. 126; *Notre Dame Alumnus,* August 1971; *Scholastic,* October 11, 1957; Hesburgh, *God, Country, Notre Dame,* pp. 14–15; interview, Theodore Hesburgh.

28. "Order of the Day, Winter Program 1934–1935," Typescript, Miscellaneous Papers, The Province Archives; "Obituary for Bro. Seraphim Herrmann," Miscellaneous Papers, The Province Archives; Hesburgh, *God, Country, Notre Dame,* pp. 15–21; interviews, Richard Conklin, Theodore Hesburgh.

29. *The Courier Journal,* December 7, 1986; Hesburgh, *God, Country, Notre Dame,* pp. 19–24; interview, Theodore Hesburgh.

30. *Notre Dame Report,* November 13, 1981; *Scholastic,* October 11, 1957; Hesburgh, *God, Country, Notre Dame,* pp. 14, 24–25; interview, Theodore Hesburgh.

31. *The Courier Journal,* December 7, 1986; Stritch, "Theodore Hesburgh," p. 6;

Hesburgh, *God, Country, Notre Dame,* pp. 26–33; interviews, Theodore Hesburgh, Emmett O'Neill, Herman Reith, Chester Soleta.

32. Hesburgh, *God, Country, Notre Dame,* pp. 29–33; interviews, Emmett O'Neill, William Schreiner.

33. Stritch, "Theodore Hesburgh," p. 6; Lungren, *Hesburgh of Notre Dame,* p. 13; Hesburgh, *God, Country, Notre Dame,* pp. 30–32; interviews, Theodore Hesburgh, Emmett O'Neill, Louis Putz, Herman Reith, Roy Rihn, William Schreiner.

34. *Ave Maria,* August 10, 1940.

35. Theodore Hesburgh to Thomas Steiner, June 15, 1940, Thomas Steiner Papers, The Province Archives Center, Notre Dame, Indiana; Diary of Theodore Hesburgh, "July 15–August 31, 1982," DPRI (1982), p. 11; Hesburgh, *God, Country, Notre Dame,* pp. 34–36; interviews, Emmett O'Neill, William Schreiner.

36. "Unpublished Memoirs of Dennis Geaney," pp. 53–55, unprocessed Dennis Geaney Papers, Calumet City, Illinois; *U.S. Catholic,* May 1979; Hesburgh, *God, Country, Notre Dame,* pp. 37, 190; interviews, Dennis Geaney, Theodore Hesburgh.

37. Theodore Hesburgh, sermon, "50th Anniversary of Ordination," May 6, 1993, DPRI; unpublished sermon, late 1940s, CPHS, 141/01, TMHP; clipping, Lynch Papers; Hesburgh, *God, Country, Notre Dame,* pp. 37–40.

38. Hesburgh, sermon, "50th Anniversary of Ordination," May 6, 1993, DPRI; Hesburgh, *God, Country, Notre Dame,* pp. 41–42.

39. Hesburgh, *God, Country, Notre Dame,* pp. 39–40; interview, Theodore Hesburgh.

40. Hesburgh, *God, Country, Notre Dame,* p. 40; Theodore Hesburgh, *Letters to Service Women* (Washington D.C.: National Catholic Community Service, 1943), pp. 10–15, 20–29; interview, Theodore Hesburgh.

41. *The Catholic University of America Announcements: The School of Sacred Theology and the School of Canon Law, 1945–1946* (Washington, D.C.: Catholic University of America, 1945), pp. 15, 18; *The Catholic University of America Announcements, General Information, 1945–1946* (Washington, D.C.: Catholic University of America, 1945) pp. 32, 39; Hesburgh, *God, Country, Notre Dame,* pp. 42–44; interview, Theodore Hesburgh.

42. Dennis Geaney, "Catholic Action," *New Catholic Encyclopedia,* Vol. III (New York: McGraw-Hill Book Co., 1967), p. 263; Jay Dolan, *The American Catholic Experience* (Garden City, N.Y.: Doubleday, 1985), pp. 408–9, 415–16; interview, Theodore Hesburgh.

43. *America,* October 4, 1986; Hesburgh, *God, Country, Notre Dame,* pp. 44–45; interviews, Dennis Geaney, Theodore Hesburgh.

44. *Our Sunday Visitor,* January 30, 1977; Theodore Hesburgh, *The Theology of Catholic Action* (Notre Dame: Ave Maria Press, 1946), pp. 1, 3, 15–17, 185–86; Hesburgh, *God, Country, Notre Dame,* p. 45; interview, Dennis Geaney.

45. Theodore Hesburgh to Gabriel Cardinal Garrone, May 17, 1971, CPHS, 98/11, TMHP; John Tracy Ellis (ed.), *The Catholic Priest in the United States: Historical Investigations* (Collegeville, Minnesota: Saint John's University Press, 1971), pp. 39–40, 351–53; Philip Gleason, *Keeping the Faith: American Catholicism Past and Present* (Notre Dame: University of Notre Dame Press, 1987), pp. 166–71; Samuel Stumpf, *Socrates to Sartre: A History of Philosophy,* 4th Edition (New York: McGraw-Hill Book Co., 1988), pp. 175, 184–90; interview, Theodore Hesburgh.

46. Thomas Horton (ed.), "Theodore M. Hesburgh, C.S.C.," *What Works for Me: 16 CEOs Talk About Their Careers and Commitments* (New York: Random House, 1986), p. 168; interview, Theodore Hesburgh.

1. Hesburgh to Steiner, May 6, 1945, Steiner Papers; *Boston Sunday Globe,* November 16, 1986; *Look,* October 24, 1961; Thomas Schlereth, *The University of Notre Dame: A Portrait of Its History and Campus* (Notre Dame: University of Notre Dame Press, 1976), p. 3.

2. *Look,* October 24, 1961; *Time,* February 9, 1962; John C. Lungren Jr., *Hesburgh of Notre Dame: Priest, Educator, Public Servant* (Kansas City: Sheed and Ward, 1989), p. 19; Schlereth, *Notre Dame,* p. 145.

3. *Look,* October 24, 1961; Schlereth, *Notre Dame,* pp. 147, 149.

4. *Notre Dame Magazine,* Winter 1986; Joel Connelly and Howard Dooley, *Hesburgh's Notre Dame: Triumph in Transition* (New York: Hawthorn Books, 1972), pp. 11–12.

5. *Time,* February 9, 1962; Ellis (ed.), *The Catholic Priest,* p. 295; Gleason, *Keeping the Faith,* pp. 72, 186; Andrew Greeley, *The American Catholic: A Social Portrait* (New York: Basic Books, 1977), p. 6; Margaret Reher, *Catholic Intellectual Life in America* (New York: Macmillan Publishing Co., 1989), p. 130; Schlereth, *Notre Dame,* pp. 183–84; Wills, *Bare Ruined Choirs,* pp. 35–46.

6. Clipping, Hesburgh News Clippings, DPRI; *The New York Times,* May 11, 1969 and March 15, 1970; *Notre Dame Magazine,* June 1972; *Time,* May 2, 1977; Connelly and Dooley, *Hesburgh's Notre Dame,* p. 33; Theodore Hesburgh, *God, Country, Notre Dame* (New York: Doubleday, 1990), p. 65; interviews, David Burrell, Frederick Crosson.

7. *Chicago Tribune,* November 9, 1986; *Notre Dame Magazine,* Spring 1987; *Bulletin of the University of Notre Dame,* Vol. XLII (Notre Dame: University Press, 1945), p. 68; Hesburgh, *God, Country, Notre Dame,* pp. 46, 47; interview, John Schneider.

8. *Scholastic,* October 8, 1948; *Time,* February 9, 1962; Hesburgh, *God, Country, Notre Dame,* pp. 48–49; Thomas Stritch, "A Short Biography of Theodore Hesburgh," in Charlotte A. Ames (ed.), *Theodore M. Hesburgh: A Bio-Bibliography* (New York: Greenwood Press, 1989), p. 9; interview, Patty Crowley.

9. *The Indianapolis Star,* March 8, 1970; *The New York Times,* May 11, 1969; *Notre Dame Magazine,* Summer 1989; Stritch, "Theodore Hesburgh," p. 9.

10. *The New York Times,* May 11, 1969; Connelly and Dooley, *Hesburgh's Notre Dame,* p. 18.

11. *Notre Dame,* Fall 1952; *The Observer,* Spring 1987; *Our Sunday Visitor,* January 30, 1977; *South Bend Tribune,* May 3, 1964; *Time,* February 9, 1962; Stritch, "Theodore Hesburgh," p. 9; Hesburgh, *God, Country, Notre Dame,* pp. 51–53; Schlereth, *Notre Dame,* p. 192; interviews, John Schneider, Dorothy Webb.

12. *Scholastic,* October 8, 1948; Hesburgh, *God, Country, Notre Dame,* p. 53; interview, John Schneider.

13. *Scholastic,* October 8, 1948; Hesburgh, *God, Country, Notre Dame,* p. 53; interview, John Powers.

14. Clipping, Newspaper Clipping File, TMHP; clippings, unprocessed University of Notre Dame Press Papers, Notre Dame, Indiana; Theodore Hesburgh, *God and the World of Man,* 2nd Edition (Notre Dame: University of Notre Dame Press, 1960), p. 14; Hesburgh, *God, Country, Notre Dame,* p. 47, 53.

15. *Chicago Tribune,* November 9, 1986; *South Bend Tribune,* May 3, 1964; Hesburgh, *God, Country, Notre Dame,* p. 54.

16. *The New York Times,* January 26, 1958 and December 30, 1979; *Time,* April 28,

1952; Stritch, "Theodore Hesburgh," p. 9; Jay Dolan, *The American Catholic Experience* (Garden City, N.Y.: Doubleday, 1985), p. 400; Schlereth, *Notre Dame,* p. 198; Robert Schmuhl, *The University of Notre Dame: A Contemporary Portrait* (Notre Dame: University of Notre Dame Press, 1986), p. 14.

17. *Chicago Tribune,* November 12, 1978; *Notre Dame Magazine,* May 1982; Lungren, *Hesburgh of Notre Dame,* p. 23; interview, Edmund Stephan.

18. Hesburgh, *God, Country, Notre Dame,* pp. 55–56.

19. Ibid., pp. 56–57.

20. Theodore Hesburgh to John Cavanaugh, July 28, 1949, UPCC, Box 2, John J. Cavanaugh Papers, Archives, University of Notre Dame, Notre Dame, Indiana; Hesburgh, *God, Country, Notre Dame,* pp. 57–59.

21. John Cavanaugh to Theodore Hesburgh, September 20, 1949, UPCC, Box 2, Cavanaugh Papers; Hesburgh, *God, Country, Notre Dame,* p. 58.

22. *Notre Dame,* Fall 1952; Hesburgh, *God, Country, Notre Dame,* pp. 58–59.

23. Theodore Hesburgh to John Cavanaugh [1951] UPCC, Box 2, Cavanaugh Papers.

24. Clipping, Hesburgh News Clippings, DPRI; *The New York Times,* June 22, 1973; *Sports Illustrated,* January 10, 1983; Hesburgh, *God, Country, Notre Dame,* pp. 76–77; Schlereth, *Notre Dame,* p. 180.

25. Theodore Hesburgh to John Cavanaugh, September 16, 1949, UPCC, Box 2, Cavanaugh Papers; *Notre Dame Report,* January 18, 1980; Hesburgh, *God, Country, Notre Dame,* pp. 78–80.

26. Theodore Hesburgh to John Cavanaugh, August 3, 1951, UPCC, Box 2, Cavanaugh Papers.

27. Ibid., July 28, 1949.

28. Unpublished speech by Theodore Hesburgh, June 7, 1986, Hesburgh/University Profiles, 1981–1989, DPRI; *Chicago Sun-Times,* November 9, 1986; *Notre Dame Report,* January 18, 1980; Theodore Hesburgh, *The Hesburgh Papers: Higher Values in Higher Education* (Kansas City: Andrews and McMeel, 1979), pp. 4–8.

29. *The Dome 1951,* p. 22; *The New York Times,* May 11, 1969; *Notre Dame Magazine,* June 1972; Connelly and Dooley, *Hesburgh's Notre Dame,* p. 17.

30. *Chicago Tribune,* November 9, 1986; *The New York Times,* December 30, 1979; Hesburgh, *God, Country, Notre Dame,* pp. 60–61; Schlereth, *Notre Dame,* p. 208.

31. *South Bend Tribune,* July 1, 1952; *Notre Dame,* Fall 1952.

32. *Scholastic,* February 8, 1952; *Chicago Tribune,* November 9, 1986; Connelly and Dooley, *Hesburgh's Notre Dame,* p. 19; Hesburgh, *God, Country, Notre Dame,* pp.66–68; interview, Chester Soleta.

33. *Notre Dame Magazine,* Summer 1989; Hesburgh, *Hesburgh Papers,* p. 7; Hesburgh, *God, Country, Notre Dame,* pp. 64, 72, 73.

34. *The Elkart Truth,* October 27, 1986; Schmuhl, *University of Notre Dame,* p. 18.

35. *The New York Times,* June 22, 1973, and May 14, 1987; *Notre Dame,* Fall 1952; Hesburgh, *God, Country, Notre Dame,* p. 83.

36. *The Chicago American,* May 24, 1958; *South Bend Tribune,* December 18, 1955; *St. Louis Globe-Democrat,* April 12, 1953; *Notre Dame,* Fall 1952.

37. Theodore Hesburgh, "Sermon delivered . . . at the dedication of Saint John Church and Catholic Student Center, Michigan State University, East Lansing, Michigan, January 12, 1958," UNDA: UDIS, Biographical Files, TMHP; Theodore Hesburgh, Review of *The Idea of the University: A Reexamination,* by Jaroslav Pelikan. *Catholic Historical Review* 78 (October 1992): 621–23; *Notre Dame,* Fall 1952; Connelly and Dooley,

Hesburgh's Notre Dame, p. 19; Thomas Horton (ed.), "Theodore M. Hesburgh, C.S.C.," *What Works for Me: 16 CEOs Talk About Their Careers and Commitments* (New York: Random House, 1986), p. 154; Hesburgh, *God, Country, Notre Dame,* p 70; interviews, John Dunne, James Hesburgh, Theodore Hesburgh.

38. *St. Louis Globe-Democrat,* April 12, 1953; Hesburgh, *God, Country, Notre Dame,* 74.

39. Clipping, Department of Information Services Papers, Biographical Files, TMHP; *Time,* May 7, 1956.

40. Hesburgh, *God, Country, Notre Dame,* pp. 223–26.

41. John Cavanaugh to Amedee Dugas, February 1, 1947, UPHS 50/24, TMHP; William Storey to Theodore Hesburgh, January 15, 1954, UPHS 50/25, TMHP; Herman Reith to Theodore Hesburgh, September 27, 1954, UPHS 50/25, TMHP; Theodore Hesburgh to Herman Reith, October 1, 1954; Theodore Hesburgh to Charles Ehinger, October 19, 1954, UPHS 50/25, TMHP; Isidore Hodes to Theodore Hesburgh, March 21, 1959, UPHS 51/02, TMHP; Theodore Hesburgh to Steve Griffin, April 13, 1965, UPHS 50/08, TMHP; *Columbia University Forum,* Summer 1963; Redmond Burke, *What is the Index* (Milwaukee: The Bruce Publishing Company, 1952), pp. 27, 91–93; Anne Haight, *Banned Books,* 3rd Edition (New York, R. R. Bowker Company, 1970), p. 109; interview, Theodore Hesburgh.

42. Theodore Hesburgh, *Patterns for Educational Growth* (Notre Dame: University of Notre Dame Press, 1958), pp. xiii–xiv, 19.

43. *Dartmouth Alumni Magazine,* July 1958.

44. *The Chicago American,* May 24, 1958; *The Sign,* March 1961.

45. *The Indianapolis Star,* May 24, 1987; *Notre Dame,* Fall 1952; interviews, John Schneider, Chester Soleta.

46. *The Chicago American,* May 24, 1958; *Notre Dame,* Summer 1958; Schlereth, *Notre Dame,* p. 205.

47. *The New York Times,* January 26, 1958; *South Bend Tribune,* May 17, 1987; *Time,* May 7, 1956; Connelly and Dooley, *Hesburgh's Notre Dame,* p. 34; Schlereth, *Notre Dame,* p. 205; interview, Ernan McMullin.

48. *The Chicago American,* May 24, 1958; *The Tablet,* November 7, 1987; Hesburgh, *God, Country, Notre Dame,* p. 71.

49. *South Bend Tribune,* May 17, 1987; *Change,* February 1976; *Saturday Review,* March 2, 1963; Ellis (ed.), *The Catholic Priest,* pp. 354–55; Theodore Hesburgh, *Thoughts for Our Times,* no. 1 (Notre Dame: University of Notre Dame, 1962), p. 14; Theodore Hesburgh, "The Priest as Mediator and Ambassador," in Madonna Kolbenschlag (ed.), *Between God and Caesar: Priests, Sisters and Political Office in the United States* (New York: Paulist Press, 1985), p. 282; Trevor Kennedy (ed.), "Theodore Hesburgh," *Top Guns: Seventeen World Leaders in Politics, Media and Business Tell How They Made It to the Top—and Stayed There* (South Melbourne: Sun Books, Macmillan Company of Australia, 1988) p. 65.

50. *Chicago Tribune,* November 9, 1986; *South Bend Tribune,* October 1, 1956; *The Sign,* March 1961; *Time,* May 2, 1977.

51. *Cleveland Plain Dealer,* December 16, 1957; *Minneapolis Tribune,* December 4, 1957.

52. *Chicago Daily News,* June 18, 1965; *Look,* October 24, 1961; *Newsweek,* January 5, 1959; *Sports Illustrated,* January 5, 1959; Hesburgh, *God, Country, Notre Dame,* p. 85.

53. *Sports Illustrated,* January 19, 1959.

54. Ibid.; Hesburgh, *God, Country, Notre Dame,* p. 85.

55. *South Bend Tribune,* May 17, 1987; *The Sign,* March 1961.

56. Walter Langford, "My Adventures with Father Hesburgh," unpublished manuscript, p. 2, unprocessed Walter Langford Papers, Creve Coeur, Missouri; *The Chicago American,* May 24, 1958; *South Bend Tribune,* December 18, 1955 and May 3, 1964; *The Observer,* Spring 1987.

NOTES TO CHAPTER 3

1. *Los Angeles Times,* February 8, 1973; *Notre Dame Magazine,* June 1972; *Time,* November 18, 1957; Robert Dallek, *Lone Star Rising: Lyndon Johnson and His Times 1908–1960* (New York: Oxford University Press, 1991), p. 526; Foster Rhea Dulles, *The Civil Rights Commission: 1957–1965* (Michigan State University Press, 1968), pp. 1, 2, 12, 15.

2. *Catholic Digest,* August 1960; *Time,* November 18, 1957; Dulles, *Civil Rights Commission,* p. 19; Steven Lawson, *Black Ballots* (New York: Columbia University Press, 1976), p. 214; John C. Lungren Jr., *Hesburgh of Notre Dame: Priest, Educator, Public Servant* (Kansas City: Sheed and Ward, 1989), p. 49; Harris Wofford, *Of Kennedys and Kings: Making Sense of the Sixties* (New York: Farrar, Straus, Giroux, 1980), p. 463.

3. *South Bend Tribune,* November 8, 1957.

4. Clipping, CPHS, 24/12, USCCR, TMHP; *Catholic Digest,* August 1960; Dulles, *Civil Rights Commission,* p. 19; Theodore Hesburgh, *God, Country, Notre Dame* (New York: Doubleday, 1990), p. 192; Wofford, *Kennedys and Kings,* pp. 463–64; interviews, Berl Bernhard, William Taylor, Harris Wofford.

5. Hesburgh, *God, Country, Notre Dame,* pp. 192, 194, 195; Dulles, *Civil Rights Commission,* pp. 34, 39; Lawson, *Black Ballots,* pp. 215–16; Wofford, *Kennedys and Kings,* p. 470.

6. *Catholic Digest,* August 1960; *MSU Alumni Magazine,* Winter 1989; Hesburgh, *God, Country, Notre Dame,* p. 199; Wofford, *Kennedys and Kings,* pp. 477–78.

7. *MSU Alumni Magazine,* Winter 1989; Hesburgh, *God, Country, Notre Dame,* p. 199; Wofford, *Kennedys and Kings,* p. 478; interview, Berl Bernhard.

8. Minutes, July 14–15, 1959, CPHS, 20/23, USCCR, TMHP; clipping, CPHS, 24/12, USCCR, TMHP; *MSU Alumni Magazine,* Winter 1989; *South Bend Tribune,* September 8, 1959; Hesburgh, *God, Country, Notre Dame,* p. 201; James Sundquist, *Politics and Policy: The Eisenhower, Kennedy, and Johnson Years* (Washington, D.C.: The Brookings Institution, 1968), p. 244; Wofford, *Kennedys and Kings,* p. 478.

9. Clipping, CPHS, 24/12, USCCR, TMHP; *The Philadelphia Sunday Bulletin,* December 13, 1970; Lawson, *Black Ballots,* pp. 213–14; Wofford, *Kennedys and Kings,* pp. 482–83.

10. *Catholic Digest,* August 1960; *The New York Times,* June 30, 1963; *Notre Dame Magazine,* Spring 1987; *Our Sunday Visitor,* April 9, 1961; *South Bend Tribune,* June 13, 1960; *Voice of St. Jude,* February 1961; Theodore Hesburgh, *Thoughts for Our Time V,* No 5 (Notre Dame: University of Notre Dame, 1969), p. 23.

11. Clipping, Newspaper Clipping File, Hesburgh Office File, TMHP; *Los Angeles Times,* February 8, 1973; *The New York Times,* November 17, 1961; *Scholastic,* December 15, 1961; Lungren, *Hesburgh of Notre Dame,* p. 57.

12. *The New York Times,* November 19, 1961; *Scholastic,* December 15, 1961.

13. *Catholic Digest,* August 1960.

14. *Notre Dame Magazine,* June 1972; Dulles, *Civil Rights Commission,* pp. 105, 106; Hugh Graham, *The Civil Rights Era* (New York: Oxford University Press, 1990), p. 63.

15. Dulles, *Civil Rights Commission,* pp. 80, 258, 259.

16. John McClellan to Theodore Hesburgh, March 8, 1960, CPHS, 17/15, USCCR, TMHP; minutes, November 9, 1969, CPHS, 21/09, USCCR, TMHP; Hesburgh, *God, Country, Notre Dame*, p. 204; interview, Berl Bernhard.

17. *The New York Times*, June 11, 1971; *U.S. Catholic*, May 1979; interview, Berl Bernhard.

18. *Notre Dame Magazine*, June 1972; *The Reporter*, July 4, 1963; Lawson, *Black Ballots*, pp. 258–60, 289; Sundquist, *Politics and Policy*, p. 256; Wofford, *Kennedys and Kings*, p. 161.

19. Minutes, March 29, 1963, CPHS, 21/03, USCCR, TMHP; minutes, January 28, 1965, CPHS, 21/05, USCCR, TMHP; Dulles, *Civil Rights Commission*, p. 181; Wofford, *Kennedys and Kings*, p. 420; interviews, Berl Bernhard, William Taylor.

20. *Civil Rights Digest*, Summer 1973; *St. Louis Post-Dispatch*, July 17, 1974.

21. Minutes, January 28, 1965, CPHS, 21/05, USCCR, TMHP; minutes, April 6, 1966, CPHS, 21/06, USCCR, TMHP; *The New York Times*, April 5, 1966; Dulles, *Civil Rights Commission*, pp. 232–33; Lawson, *Black Ballots*, p. 313; interview, William Taylor.

22. *Civil Rights Digest*, Summer 1973; *Los Angeles Times*, February 8, 1973; *Meridian Magazine*, December, 1984; *MSU Alumni Magazine*, Winter 1989; Dulles, *Civil Rights Commission*, p. 210; Hesburgh, *God, Country, Notre Dame*, p. 203.

23. *New Republic*, December 22, 1973; Dulles, *Civil Rights Commission*, pp. 136, 211, 245.

24. Theodore Hesburgh to Sargent Shriver, March 21, 1961, CPHS, 115/16, TMHP; Walter Langford, "My Adventures with Father Hesburgh," unpublished manuscript, p. 2, unprocessed Walter Langford Papers, Creve Coeur, Missouri; *Detroit News*, March 19, 1961; Hesburgh, *God, Country, Notre Dame*, p. 97.

25. Langford, "Adventures with Hesburgh," pp. 2–4; Hesburgh, *God, Country, Notre Dame*, p. 96; interview, Harris Wofford.

26. Theodore Hesburgh to Sargent Shriver, May 4, 1961; CPHS, 115/16, TMHP; interview, Walter Langford.

27. Theodore Hesburgh to Walter Langford, May 23, 1962, CPHS, 115/29, TMHP; Langford, "Adventures with Hesburgh," pp. 4–5; interviews, Mike Curtin, Walter Langford, Tom Scanlon.

28. Theodore Hesburgh, "My Visit to the Chilean Peace Corps" (1962), pp. 1, 2, 19, 20, CPHS, 116/20, TMHP; Langford, "Adventures with Hesburgh," p. 6; interviews, Walter Langford, Tom Scanlon.

29. Theodore Hesburgh to Walter Langford, April 28, 1962, CPHS, 115/29, TMHP; Hesburgh, "Chilean Peace Corps," pp. 7, 16, 25, 26; Langford, "Adventures with Hesburgh," pp. 6–7; interviews, Walter Langford, Sargent Shriver, Tom Scanlon.

30. Clippings, UPHS, 43/06, TMHP; clippings, Newspaper Clipping Files, Hesburgh Office File, TMHP; *Life*, December 18, 1964; *Los Angeles Times*, December 9, 1964; *The New York Times*, December 8, 1964; Joel Connelly and Howard Dooley, *Hesburgh's Notre Dame: Triumph in Transition* (New York: Hawthorn Books, 1972), pp. 89–90; interviews, Philip Faccenda, Theodore Hesburgh, John Walsh.

31. Theodore Hesburgh to G. Kerry Smith, December 17, 1960, UPHS, 69, TMHP; *The Indianapolis Star*, May 24, 1987; *Notre Dame Magazine*, June 1972; *The Observer*, Spring 1987; Stritch, "Theodore Hesburgh," p. 14; Connelly and Dooley, *Hesburgh's Notre Dame*, pp. 20–21; interview, Edmund Joyce.

32. Clipping, Newspaper Clipping File, Hesburgh Office File, TMHP; *The Louisville Times*, February 10, 1981; *Look*, October 24, 1961; *Scholastic*, April 21, 1961; Connelly and Dooley, *Hesburgh's Notre Dame*, pp. 30–31.

33. *Harper's Magazine,* May 1967; Connelly and Dooley, *Hesburgh's Notre Dame,* pp. 8, 44, 45, 107; interview, Christopher Murphy.

34. Connelly and Dooley, *Hesburgh's Notre Dame,* pp. 42, 105.

35. *South Bend Tribune,* May 3, 1964 and May 17, 1987; *Commonweal,* May 31, 1963; *Scholastic,* February 22, 1963; *Time,* May 3, 1963; Thomas Blantz, *George N. Shuster: On the Side of Truth* (Notre Dame: University of Notre Dame Press, 1993), p. 331.

36. *America,* October 5, 1963; *Commonweal,* May 31, 1963 and June 28, 1963.

37. *Chicago Tribune,* November 9, 1986; Thomas Schlereth, *The University of Notre Dame: A Portrait of Its History and Campus* (Notre Dame: University of Notre Dame Press, 1976), p. 221; interviews, David Burrell, Philip Faccenda, Edmund Stephan, John Walsh.

38. *America,* October 4, 1986; *Harper's Magazine,* May 1967; Hesburgh, *God, Country, Notre Dame,* p. 171; Neil McCluskey (ed.), *The Catholic University: A Modern Appraisal* (Notre Dame: University of Notre Dame Press, 1970), p. 153; Schlereth, *Notre Dame,* p. 221; interview, David Burrell.

39. *Ave Maria,* January 28, 1967; *The Chronicle of Higher Education,* January 27, 1967; *Notre Dame Magazine,* June 1972; Hesburgh, *God, Country, Notre Dame,* pp. 171, 174; interviews, Newton Minow, Paul Reinert.

40. *Detroit News,* April 8, 1969; *South Bend Tribune,* May 6, 1967; *St. Anthony Messenger,* May 1987; Schlereth, *Notre Dame,* p. 221.

41. Interviews, Robert Galvin, Clark Kerr, Ralph McInerny, Ernan McMullin, Edmund Stephan.

42. *The New York Times,* May 11, 1969; Connelly and Dooley, *Hesburgh's Notre Dame,* p. 165; interviews, Frederick Crosson, Ralph McInerny, John Walsh. Confidential interview.

43. *The New York Times,* June 7, 1961 and July 4, 1964; *Time,* February 9, 1962; Connelly and Dooley, *Hesburgh's Notre Dame,* p. 91; interview, Frederick Crosson.

NOTES TO CHAPTER 4

1. *The New York Times,* October 10, 1967; Joel Connelly and Howard Dooley, *Hesburgh's Notre Dame: Triumph in Transition* (New York: Hawthorn Books, 1972), p. 89; William Manchester, *The Glory and the Dream* (Boston: Little Brown and Company, 1973), pp. 131–34; Norman and Emily Rosenberg, *In Our Times: America Since World War II,* 3rd Edition (Englewood Cliffs, New Jersey: Prentice-Hall, 1987), p. 160.

2. Connelly and Dooley, *Hesburgh's Notre Dame,* pp. 174–75; Thomas Schlereth, *The University of Notre Dame: A Portrait of Its History and Campus* (Notre Dame: University of Notre Dame Press, 1976), p. 215.

3. *Chicago's American,* March 27, 1969; Connelly and Dooley, *Hesburgh's Notre Dame,* p. 214; Schlereth, *Notre Dame,* p. 215; interviews, Edmund Joyce, David Krashna, Richard Rossie.

4. Clipping, Hesburgh News Clippings, DPRI; *South Bend Tribune,* May 17, 1987; interview, David Krashna.

5. Connelly and Dooley, *Hesburgh's Notre Dame,* pp. 249–51.

6. Ibid., p. 169; *The New York Times,* May 11, 1969; *Look,* November 18, 1969; *Time,* February 15, 1971; interview, Philip McKenna.

7. *Catholic Transcript,* May 16, 1969; *National Catholic Register,* June 7, 1970; James Armstrong, *Onward to Victory: A Chronicle of the Alumni of the University of Notre Dame du Lac: 1842–1973* (Notre Dame: University of Notre Dame, 1974), p. 426; interviews, J. Peter Grace, James Riehle.

8. Connelly and Dooley, *Hesburgh's Notre Dame,* pp. 42, 290; interview, Richard Rossie.

9. Theodore Hesburgh to Students, October 11, 1971, Hesburgh News Clippings, DPRI; *The New York Times,* May 11, 1969; *The Seattle Times,* March 21, 1971; *South Bend Tribune,* May 17, 1987; Connelly and Dooley, *Hesburgh's Notre Dame,* p. 143.

10. Theodore Hesburgh, "Dear Notre Dame Faculty Members and Students," November 25, 1968, UNDA: UDIS, Biographical Files, TMHP; *Chicago's American,* March 27, 1969; *New York Post,* March 22, 1969.

11. Philip Faccenda to Theodore Hesburgh, February 6, 1969, UPHS, 77, TMHP; Theodore Hesburgh to John Mroz, February 6, 1969, Department of Information Services Papers, Biographical Files, Theodore Hesburgh, Archives, University of Notre Dame; *National Catholic Reporter,* February 26, 1969; Connelly and Dooley, *Hesburgh's Notre Dame,* pp. 229–30; Schlereth, *Notre Dame,* p. 216; interview, Richard Rossie.

12. Anson interview, p. 7; *The New York Times,* May 11, 1969.

13. *Chicago's American,* March 27, 1969; *Scholastic,* May 2, 1977; Connelly and Dooley, *Hesburgh's Notre Dame,* p. 228; Theodore Hesburgh, *The Hesburgh Papers: Higher Values in Higher Education* (Kansas City: Andrews and McMeel, 1979), p. 162.

14. Theodore Hesburgh, "The Hesburgh Letter on Student Unrest," February 17, 1969, Hesburgh News Clippings, DPRI.

15. Clippings, Hesburgh News Clippings, DPRI; *The Indianapolis News,* February 24, 1969; *The New York Times,* February 18, 21, 25 and May 11, 1969; *South Bend Tribune,* February 18, 1969; *Washington Post,* February 24, 1969; *Notre Dame Magazine,* Winter 1989; Thomas Horton (ed.), "Theodore M. Hesburgh, C.S.C.," *What Works for Me: 16 CEOs Talk About Their Careers and Commitments* (New York: Random House, 1986), p. 160; Thomas Stritch, "A Short Biography of Theodore Hesburgh," in Charlotte A. Ames (ed.), *Theodore M. Hesburgh: A Bio-Bibliography* (New York: Greenwood Press, 1989), pp. 11–12.

16. *Look,* November 18, 1969; *Manchester Guardian,* April 13, 1969; *The Observer,* February 21, 1969; Connelly and Dooley, *Hesburgh's Notre Dame,* pp. 242–45.

17. *Chicago's American,* March 27, 1969; *National Catholic Reporter,* February 26, 1969; *The New York Times,* May 11, 1969.

18. *Commonweal,* March 14, 1969.

19. *Chicago's American,* March 27, 1969; *New York Post,* March 22, 1969; *Scholastic,* May 2, 1977; Hesburgh, *Hesburgh Papers,* p. 164; interview, Edmund Joyce.

20. Richard Nixon to Theodore Hesburgh, February 22, 1969, UPHS, Richard Nixon Letters, TMHP.

21. Theodore Hesburgh to Spiro Agnew, February 27, 1970, Biographical Files, Theodore Hesburgh, Department of Information Services Papers; *The New York Times,* February 28, 1969; Hesburgh, *God, Country, Notre Dame,* pp. 119, 123.

22. *The New York Times,* May 11, 1969; *Notre Dame Magazine,* June 1972; Connelly and Dooley, *Hesburgh's Notre Dame,* pp. 5, 259–60; Hesburgh, *Hesburgh Papers,* viii; interview, John Houck.

23. *The Indianapolis Star,* March 8, 1970; *The New York Times,* May 11, 1969; *Time,* February 15, 1971.

24. Richard Conklin to Theodore Hesburgh, September 10, 1969, UPHS, 81, TMHP; *The Indianapolis Star,* March 8, 1970; *The New York Times,* March 15, 1970; *Notre Dame Magazine,* June 1972; Thomas Blantz, *George N. Shuster: On the Side of Truth* (Notre Dame: University of Notre Dame Press, 1993), pp. 321–22.

25. *The Observer,* October 17, 1969; *The Progressive,* February 1973; *U.S. Catholic,*

March 1976; Connelly and Dooley, *Hesburgh's Notre Dame,* p. 261; interviews, David Burrell, John Dunne. Confidential interview.

26. *The New York Times,* May 11, 1969; *The Observer,* November 19 and 20, 1969; Schlereth, *Notre Dame,* p. 219; Theodore Hesburgh, *God, Country, Notre Dame* (New York: Doubleday, 1990), p. 128; interview, James Riehle.

27. *The Observer,* October 2, 1969 and Spring 1987; *Look,* November 18, 1969; Stritch, "Theodore Hesburgh," pp. 10, 12; interview, David Krashna.

28. Interviews, Richard Conklin, Ernan McMullin.

29. *Notre Dame Magazine,* June 1972; Connelly and Dooley, *Hesburgh's Notre Dame,* pp. 251, 286; Hesburgh, *God, Country, Notre Dame,* pp. 123–25.

30. *The Observer,* February 10, 1970; *Phi Delta Kappan,* September 1969; Connelly and Dooley, *Hesburgh's Notre Dame,* pp. 254, 255, 262, 263; Theodore Hesburgh, *Thoughts for Our Time V,* No 5 (Notre Dame: University of Notre Dame, 1969) p. 14; Hesburgh, *Hesburgh Papers,* p. 86; Theodore Hesburgh, "The Priest as Mediator and Ambassador," in Madonna Kolbenschlag (ed.), *Between God and Caesar: Priests, Sisters and Political Office in the United States* (New York: Paulist Press, 1985), pp. 284–86; interviews, Ernest Bartell, Frankie Freeman, John Walsh.

31. *Chicago's American,* March 28, 1969; *Detroit News,* April 8, 1969; *The New York Times,* May 11, 1969.

32. George Herring, *America's Longest War: The United States and Vietnam, 1950–1975,* 2nd Edition (New York: Alfred A. Knopf, 1986), p. 236; Manchester, *Glory and Dream,* p. 1211; James Patterson, *America in the Twentieth Century: A History,* 3d Edition (San Diego: Harcourt, Brace, Jovanovich, Publishers, 1989), p. 446.

33. *Notre Dame Magazine,* Winter 1989; Schlereth, *Notre Dame,* p. 220; Hesburgh, *God, Country, Notre Dame,* pp. 108–9.

34. "Remarks of the Rev. Theodore M. Hesburgh, May 4, 1970," Hesburgh Files, Department of Information Services Papers; *Notre Dame Alumnus,* May/June 1970; *Notre Dame Magazine,* June 1972 and Winter 1989.

35. *South Bend Tribune,* May 5, 1970; *Notre Dame Magazine,* Winter 1989; *The Observer,* May 5, 1970; Schlereth, *Notre Dame,* p. 220.

36. Interview, David Krashna.

37. *Notre Dame Alumnus,* May/June 1970; *Notre Dame Magazine,* Winter 1989.

38. *Notre Dame Alumnus,* May/June 1970; *Notre Dame Magazine,* Winter 1989; interviews, David Burrell, James Riehle.

39. *Notre Dame Alumnus,* May/June 1970; *South Bend Tribune,* May 6 and 7, 1970.

40. Theodore Hesburgh to J. M. Haggar, June 30, 1970, Box 28, Department of Information Services Papers; *National Catholic Register,* June 7, 1970; *Notre Dame Alumnus,* May/June 1970.

41. Theodore Hesburgh to Richard Nixon, May 18, 1970, UPHS, Nixon Letters, TMHP; Hesburgh to Haggar, June 30, 1970, Box 28, Department of Information Services Papers; *Notre Dame Alumnus,* May/June 1970.

42. Theodore Hesburgh to George Leclerc, June 4, 1970, CPHS, 97/02, TMHP; *Daedalus,* Fall 1974; Blantz, *George Shuster,* p. 333.

43. Theodore Hesburgh to Richard Nixon, February 17, 1969, UPHS, Nixon Letters, TMHP; Anson interview, p. 16; *Scholastic,* May 2, 1977; Hesburgh, *God, Country, Notre Dame,* pp. 206–7.

44. Theodore Hesburgh to Richard Nixon, November 26, 1952, UPHS, Nixon Letters, TMHP; Hesburgh to Nixon, March 6, 1969, UPHS, Nixon Letters, TMHP; Anson interview, p. 15; *Scholastic,* May 2, 1977.

45. Clipping, Newspaper Clipping Files, Hesburgh Office File, TMHP minutes,

August 27–29, 1971, CPHS, 20/03, USCCR, TMHP; *The Philadelphia Sunday Bulletin*, December 13, 1970; *St. Louis Post-Dispatch*, July 12, 1970; Hugh Graham, *The Civil Rights Era* (New York: Oxford University Press, 1990), pp. 319–20; Hesburgh, *Hesburgh Papers*, viii; Steven Lawson, *Running For Freedom* (New York: McGraw-Hill, 1991), pp. 134–38, 140; Tom Wicker, *One of Us: Richard Nixon and the American Dream* (New York: Random House, 1991), pp. 522–23.

46. *The Progressive*, February 1973; *Look*, November 18, 1969.

47. Minutes, March 8, 1970, CPHS, 2/10, USCCR, TMHP; Anson interview, p. 20; *Christian Science Monitor*, March 13, 1970; *The Indianapolis Star*, December 30, 1979.

48. *The New York Times*, October 13, 1970; *The Philadelphia Sunday Bulletin*, December 13, 1970; *Notre Dame Magazine*, June 1972; Hesburgh, *God, Country, Notre Dame*, p. 209.

49. Minutes, November 9, 1970, CPHS, 21/10, USCCR, TMHP; Howard Glickstein to Commissioners, October 30, 1970, CPHS, 19/25, USCCR, TMHP; *The Indianapolis Star*, November 10, 1970; *Washington Star*, November 9, 1970; *The Progressive*, February 1973; interview, Stephen Horn.

50. *The New York Times*, May 11 and 14 and November 17, 1971; *Washington Post*, May 24, 1970; *Washington Star*, November 17, 1970; *Commonweal*, March 24, 1972; interview, Leonard Garment.

51. *Washington Post*, March 2, 1972; *Washington Star*, May 16, 1971; *Origins*, March 16, 1972; *The Progressive*, February 1973.

52. *Chicago Tribune*, July 29, 1972; *Washington Post*, March 2, 1972; *Notre Dame Magazine*, June 1972; John C. Lungren Jr., *Hesburgh of Notre Dame: Priest, Educator, Public Servant* (Kansas City: Sheed and Ward, 1989), pp. 57–58.

53. *Los Angeles Times*, February 8, 1973; *Notre Dame Magazine*, June 1972; Theodore Hesburgh, *The Humane Imperative: A Challenge for the Year 2000* (New Haven: Yale University Press, 1974), p. 35.

54. Anonymous letter to Theodore Hesburgh, April 13, 1971, UPHS, 22/16, TMHP; *Look*, November 18, 1969; *Notre Dame Magazine*, June 1972; Lungren, *Hesburgh of Notre Dame*, p. 56.

55. *Philadelphia Daily News*, November 4, 1972.

56. *The New York Times*, October 29, 1972; *South Bend Tribune*, October 29, 1972; Lungren, *Hesburgh of Notre Dame*, p. 63.

57. Clipping, CPHS, 24/15, USCCR, TMHP; handwritten note on cover of minutes, November 13, 1972, CPHS, 21/12, USCCR, TMHP; Hesburgh, *God, Country, Notre Dame*, pp. 210–11; Lungren, *Hesburgh of Notre Dame*, pp. 65, 67.

58. Clipping, CPHS, 24/15, USCCR, TMHP; Lungren, *Hesburgh of Notre Dame*, pp. 71–72.

59. *South Bend Tribune*, November 22, 1972 and May 17, 1987; *The Crisis*, January 1973; *Christian Century*, December 6, 1972; *Commonweal*, December 8, 1972; *Washington Post*, December 7, 1972.

60. Richard Nixon to Theodore Hesburgh, December 20, 1972, UPHS, Nixon Letters, TMHP; clipping, Newspaper Clipping Files, Hesburgh Office File, TMHP; *The Progressive*, February 1973; Lungren, *Hesburgh of Notre Dame*, pp. 74–75.

61. *Washington Post*, February 12, 1973.

62. Clipping, Hesburgh News Clippings, DPRI; *The Indianapolis Star*, December 30, 1979; *South Bend Tribune*, May 17, 1987; *St. Louis Post-Dispatch*, July 17, 1974; *The Catholic Transcript*, May 16, 1969; *The Progressive*, February 1973; Lungren, *Hesburgh of Notre Dame*, p. 75–76.

63. Interviews, John Brademas, John Houck, Ralph McInerny.

64. Interview, Richard Conklin.

65. Theodore Hesburgh to Richard Nixon, April 23, 1985, UPHS, Nixon Letters, TMHP; *Chicago Tribune,* June 26, 1977; Hesburgh, *God, Country, Notre Dame,* p. 212.

NOTES TO CHAPTER 5

1. *Chicago's American,* March 28, 1969; *Chicago Tribune,* November 12, 1978; *The Observer,* January 27, 1987; Theodore Hesburgh, *God, Country, Notre Dame* (New York: Doubleday, 1990), p. 179; Thomas Schlereth, *The University of Notre Dame: A Portrait of Its History and Campus* (Notre Dame: University of Notre Dame Press, 1976), pp. 221–22.

2. Clipping, Newspaper Clipping Files, Hesburgh Office File, TMHP; *The Chronicle of Higher Education,* October 13, 1982; *National Catholic Reporter,* August 10, 1979; *The Observer,* January 27, 1987; Hesburgh, *God, Country, Notre Dame,* p. 183; Schlereth, *Notre Dame,* pp. 221–22; interviews, Josephine Ford, Oliver Williams.

3. *The Observer,* January 27, 1987; Hesburgh, *God, Country, Notre Dame,* pp. 182–83; Schlereth, *Notre Dame,* p. 222.

4. Schlereth, *Notre Dame,* p. 224. Confidential interview.

5. *National Catholic Reporter,* October 27, 1978; *The Observer,* August 27, and September 7, 1977. Confidential interview.

6. *The New York Times,* December 5, 1979 and January 28, 1980.

7. Diary of Theodore Hesburgh, "Cambodia," etc., DPRI; (1980), p. 94; clipping, Hesburgh News Clippings, DPRI; *The New York Times,* January 28, 1980; *U.S. Catholic,* May 1979; John C. Lungren Jr., *Hesburgh of Notre Dame: Priest, Educator, Public Servant* (Kansas City: Sheed and Ward, 1989), pp. 97–99.

8. Theodore Hesburgh to Michael Carlson, May 1, 1972, UPHS 22/33, Chase Manhattan Bank, TMHP; Thomas Horton (ed.), "Theodore M. Hesburgh, C.S.C.," *What Works for Me: 16 CEOs Talk About Their Careers and Commitments* (New York: Random House, 1986), p. 170; interview, David Rockefeller.

9. *Common Sense,* April/May 1987; *Notre Dame Magazine,* Spring 1987.

10. *U.S. Catholic,* May 1979; interviews, John Connor, David Rockefeller.

11. *South Bend Tribune,* May 17, 1987; *U.S. Catholic,* May 1979; Horton, *What Works for Me,* p. 171; interview, David Rockefeller.

12. Theodore Hesburgh to David Rockefeller, September 22, 1978, UPHS 22/39, TMHP; Owen Frisby to Theodore Hesburgh, August 20, 1975, UPHS 22/36, TMHP; Hesburgh to Frisby, September 6, 1975, UPHS 22/36, TMHP; Frisby to Hesburgh, September 16, 1975, UPHS 22/36, TMHP; Hesburgh to Frisby, September 19, 1975, UPHS 22/36, TMHP; Trevor Kennedy (ed.), "Theodore Hesburgh," *Top Guns: Seventeen World Leaders in Politics, Media and Business Tell How They Made It to the Top—and Stayed There* (South Melbourne: Sun Books, Macmillan Company of Australia, 1988), pp. 81–82; *Change,* February 1976; interview, John Connor.

13. James Grant to Theodore Hesburgh, March 10, 1978, UPHS, 74, TMHP; Theodore Hesburgh to Jimmy Carter, January 2, 1979, UPHS, 73, TMHP; Theodore Hesburgh to George Bush, July 23, 1981, UPHS, 73, TMHP; typescript of "Today Show," April 10, 1974, unprocessed Overseas Development Council Papers, Washington D.C.; *Overseas Development Council Report, 1973–1975* (Washington D.C.: Overseas Development Council, 1975); interviews, John Gilligan, James Grant.

14. *Denver Post,* April 11, 1974; *St. Louis Post-Dispatch,* April 10, 1974; interviews, James Grant, John Sewell, Davidson Sommers.

15. Theodore Hesburgh to James Grant, June 21, 1976, CPHS, 94/28, TMHP; *Chicago Tribune,* November 12, 1978; *The Denver Catholic Register,* April 20, 1972; *Kalamazoo Gazette,* April 5, 1976; *Change,* February 1976; *Chief Executive,* July/August/September 1977; Lungren, *Hesburgh of Notre Dame,* p. 94.

16. Theodore Hesburgh, *The Hesburgh Papers: Higher Values in Higher Education* (Kansas City: Andrews and McMeel, 1979), p. 200.

17. *Chicago Tribune,* June 26, 1977 and November 12, 1978; *Time,* May 2, 1977; interview, Stephen Horn.

18. *South Bend Tribune,* June 19, 1977; *Meridian Magazine,* December, 1984; *Notre Dame Magazine,* October 1977; Theodore Hesburgh and Louis Halle, *Foreign Policy and Morality: Framework for a Moral Audit* (New York: Council on Religion and International Affairs, 1979), pp. 8, 47, 55.

19. "Memorandum of conversation with Chinese officials," June 25, 1979, CPHS, 108/14, TMHP; "memorandum of conversation with Cyrus Vance," August 14, 1979, CPHS, 108/14, TMHP; *BioScience,* February 1978; *C&EN,* September 3, 1979; *The Chronicle of Higher Education,* September 10, 1979; Kennedy (ed.), *Top Guns,* p. 66; Theodore Hesburgh, "The Priest as Mediator and Ambassador," in Madonna Kolbenschlag (ed.), *Between God and Caesar: Priests, Sisters and Political Office in the United States* (New York: Paulist Press, 1985), pp. 286–87; interview, Jean Wilkowski.

20. *Chicago Tribune,* February 28, 1980; Gil Loescher and John Scanlan, *Calculated Kindness* (New York: The Free Press, 1986), pp. 156–57, 163.

21. *Chicago Tribune,* February 28, 1980; Loescher and Scanlan, *Calculated Kindness,* pp. 156–57, 163; Theodore Hesburgh to Jimmy Carter, October 24, 1979, CPHS, 95/23, TMHP; James Grant to Theodore Hesburgh, October 26, 1979, UPHS, 73, TMHP; Theodore Hesburgh to Edward King, August 11, 1980, CPHS, 88/30, TMHP; *Los Angeles Times,* November 14, 1979; *Washington Post,* October 25, 1979; *Washington Star,* October 25, 1979.

22. Theodore Hesburgh to Lennie Hershey, February 27, 1980, CPHS, 87/15, TMHP; Theodore Hesburgh to Thomas Drohan, May 5, 1980, CPHS, 87/18, TMHP; Theodore Hesburgh to Edward King, August 11, 1980, CPHS, 80/30, TMHP; Theodore Hesburgh to Lane Kirkland, August 14, 1980, CPHS, 88/30, TMHP; clipping, Hesburgh News Clippings, DPRI; Hesburgh diary, "Cambodia" (1980), pp. 110–12, 126, 136–37, 174; *Los Angeles Times,* August 28, 1980.

23. Hesburgh diary, "Cambodia" (1980), pp. 128–29, 174.

24. Theodore Hesburgh to Lane Kirkland, August 14, 1980, CPHS, 88/30, TMHP; Theodore Hesburgh to Richard Lyman, October 27, 1980, UPHS 85, TMHP; clipping, Hesburgh News Clippings, DPRI; *Los Angeles Times,* August 28, 1980.

25. *The New York Times,* September 17, 1974; Hesburgh, *God, Country, Notre Dame,* p. 265; Lungren, *Hesburgh of Notre Dame,* pp. 82, 91; Robert Schmuhl, *The University of Notre Dame: A Contemporary Portrait* (Notre Dame: University of Notre Dame Press, 1986), p. 22.

26. *The New York Times,* September 17, 1974; Hesburgh, *God Country, Notre Dame,* pp. 266–68; Lungren, *Hesburgh of Notre Dame,* p. 90.

27. Lungren, *Hesburgh of Notre Dame,* p. 112; interview, Larry Fuchs.

28. Clipping, Hesburgh News Clippings, DPRI; Hesburgh, *God, Country, Notre Dame,* pp. 277–79; Lungren, *Hesburgh of Notre Dame,* pp. 113–15.

29. *Los Angeles Times,* June 21, 1982; *The Sooner Catholic,* April 13, 1980; Hesburgh, *God, Country, Notre Dame,* pp. 132, 134, 143–52.

30. Clipping, Hesburgh News Clippings, DPRI; Hesburgh diary, "Cambodia"

(1980); Walter Langford, "My Adventures with Father Hesburgh," unpublished manuscript, unprocessed Walter Langford Papers, Creve Coeur, Missouri, p. 7; Hesburgh, *God, Country, Notre Dame,* p. 143.

31. Lungren, *Hesburgh of Notre Dame,* p. 132.

32. Diary of Theodore Hesburgh, "Mainland China," DPRI (1979), pp. 7–8; Diary of Theodore Hesburgh, "China, Nepal, India, the Seychelles, and Kenya," DPRI (1984), pp. 38, 39, 43; interview, Francis Castellino.

33. *Los Angeles Times,* November 14, 1979; *The Observer,* Spring 1987; Schmuhl, *University of Notre Dame,* p. 22.

34. "Vocations Interview for Our Sunday Visitor," 1963, UNDA: UDIS-Biographical Files, TMHP; *Chicago Sun-Times,* November 9, 1986; *Los Angeles Times,* November 14, 1979; *U.S. Catholic,* March 1976; Kennedy (ed.), *Top Guns,* pp. 64–67; Kolbenschlag (ed.), *Between God and Caesar,* pp. 282–90; Schmuhl, *University of Notre Dame,* p. 24; interview, John Brademas. Confidential interview.

35. *National Catholic Reporter,* October 27, 1978 and May 2, 1986; *South Bend Tribune,* January 16, 1979; *The Wanderer,* July 30, 1987; *Washington Post,* May 10, 1987.

36. Clipping, Hesburgh News Clippings, DPRI; *The Chronicle of Higher Education,* October 13, 1982; *The Indianapolis News,* March 4, 1987; *National Catholic Reporter,* May 22, 1987; interview, John Powers.

37. Diary of Theodore Hesburgh, "Trip to South Africa," DPRI (1978), pp. 53–54; *Chicago Tribune,* November 9, 1986; *The Dartmouth Review,* April 16, 1986; Walter LaFeber, *America, Russia, and the Cold War, 1945–1990,* 6th Edition (New York: McGraw-Hill, 1991), p. 311.

38. Richard Zang to Theodore Hesburgh, February 18, 1981, UPHS 91, TMHP; *Chicago Tribune,* October 26, 1985; *The Dartmouth Review,* April 16, 1986; *National Catholic Register,* November 10, 1985; *National Catholic Reporter,* May 2, 1986; Lungren, *Hesburgh of Notre Dame,* p. 105; interview, Oliver Williams.

39. *Chicago Tribune,* November 9, 1986; *The Nation,* July 2/9, 1988; *National Catholic Reporter,* May 2, 1986; Lungren, *Hesburgh of Notre Dame,* p. 106.

40. *Chicago Tribune,* November 9, 1986; *The Dartmouth Review,* April 16, 1986; Lungren, *Hesburgh of Notre Dame,* p. 105.

41. *The Indianapolis Star,* May 24, 1987; *South Bend Tribune,* May 26, 1985; Horton, *What Works for Me,* p. 162; interviews, Vaughn McKim, Ernan McMullin, Franklin Murphy.

42. *Chicago Sun-Times,* November 9, 1986; *Houston Chronicle,* February 7, 1981; *The Indianapolis News,* March 4, 1987; *The Indianapolis Star,* May 24, 1987; *Los Angeles Times,* November 14, 1979; *National Catholic Reporter,* October 27, 1978; *South Bend Tribune,* May 26, 1985; *South Bend Tribune Magazine,* May 3, 1964; Horton, *What Works for Me,* p. 158; interview, John Houck.

43. Clippings, Newspaper Clipping Files, Hesburgh Office File, TMHP.

44. *National Catholic Reporter,* May 22, 1987; interview, John Gilligan.

45. Clipping, Newspaper Clipping Files, Hesburgh Office File, TMHP; *South Bend Tribune,* May 17, 1987; *Time,* May 2, 1977; *U.S. News and World Report,* April 18, 1977.

46. *National Catholic Reporter,* January 28, 1983; Theodore Hesburgh, review of *The Challenge of Peace: God's Promise and Our Response* by the National Conference of Catholic Bishops, *Journal of Law and Religion* 2 (1984): 435; Theodore Hesburgh, forward to Philip Murnion (ed.), *Catholics and Nuclear War* (New York: Crossroad, 1983), xi; interview, Theodore Hesburgh.

47. Memorandum, "Project: Science and Religion Against Nuclear War" [1982],

CPHS, 139/01, TMHP; clipping, Hesburgh News Clippings, DPRI; *Moment,* July/August 1983; *National Catholic Reporter,* January 28, 1983; interviews, John Gilligan, Theodore Hesburgh.

48. *Moment,* July/August 1983; *South Bend Tribune,* May 17, 1987; Hesburgh in Murnion (ed.), *Catholics and Nuclear War,* xii.

49. *Moment,* July/August 1983; *South Bend Tribune,* May 17, 1987; Hesburgh in Murnion (ed.), *Catholics and Nuclear War,* xii; memorandum, "Project: Science and Religion Against Nuclear War" [1982], CPHS, 139/01, TMHP; Theodore Hesburgh to Franz Cardinal Konig, October 1, 1982, CPHS, 139/06, TMHP; *National Catholic Reporter,* January 28, 1983.

50. *Moment,* July/August 1983; *National Catholic Reporter,* January 28, 1983; interview, Thomas Malone.

51. *Bulletin of the Atomic Scientists,* April 1985; Hesburgh review, *Journal of Law and Religion* 2 (1984): 436–37; interviews, Theodore Hesburgh, Thomas Malone.

52. Theodore Hesburgh to Gerald Smith, January 7, 1982, CPHS, 138/15, TMHP; Norman Cousins and Theodore Hesburgh to George Bush, April 20, 1982, CPHS, 109/05, TMHP; Theodore Hesburgh to Paul Laxalt, June 21, 1982, CPHS 109/05, TMHP; memorandum, "Project: Science and Religion Against Nuclear War" [1982], CPHS, 139/01, TMHP; Hesburgh review, *Journal of Law and Religion* 2 (1984): 435–41; *National Catholic Reporter,* January 28, and April 22, 1983; *Notre Dame Magazine,* February and May 1983; *The Observer,* October 13, 1983; *South Bend Tribune,* May 17, 1987; Roald Sagdeev, *The Making of a Soviet Scientist* (New York: John Wiley and Sons, 1994), p. x.

53. Clipping, Hesburgh News Clippings, DPRI; *Los Angeles Times,* December 15, 1985; Lungren, *Hesburgh of Notre Dame,* p. 135; interview, John Gilligan.

54. Diary of Theodore Hesburgh, "Trip to Moscow and Beijing," DPRI (1986), pp. 3–7; interview, William Beauchamp.

55. Clipping, Hesburgh News Clippings, DPRI; *The Indianapolis Star,* May 24, 1987; *The Chronicle of Higher Education,* October 13, 1987.

56. *Chicago Tribune,* November 9, 1986; *The Elkhart Truth,* September 22, 1986; *Notre Dame Magazine,* Spring 1987; *South Bend Tribune,* June 19, 1977 and September 21, 1986.

57. Clipping, Hesburgh News Clippings, DPRI; *Chicago Tribune,* November 9, 1986; Dolan, *American Catholic Experience,* p. 443.

58. "The Hesburgh Era: Comparative Statistics," press release, August 1986, DPRI; *The Indianapolis Star,* May 24, 1987; *Time,* May 18, 1987; Dolan, *American Catholic Experience,* p. 69.

59. *The Indianapolis Star,* May 24, 1987; *Washington Post,* May 9, 1987; Thomas Stritch, "A Short Biography of Theodore Hesburgh," in Charlotte A. Ames (ed.), *Theodore M. Hesburgh: A Bio-Bibliography* (New York: Greenwood Press, 1989), p. 2.

NOTES TO CHAPTER 6

1. *Scholastic,* April 1987; *Syracuse Herald-American,* December 17, 1978; interviews, Frederick Crosson, Newton Minow.

2. Diary of Theodore Hesburgh, "Travels with Ted and Ned, IV. Around the World on the QE2," DPRI (1988), p. 222; interviews, James Frick, Robert Gordon, Timothy O'Meara, David Tyson.

3. *The Chronicle of Higher Education,* October 13, 1982 and May 13, 1987; *Time,* May

2, 1977; Thomas Stritch, "A Short Biography of Theodore Hesburgh," in Charlotte A. Ames (ed.), *Theodore M. Hesburgh: A Bio-Bibliography* (New York: Greenwood Press, 1989), p. 23; interview, Timothy O'Meara.

4. *The Indianapolis News,* March 4, 1987; *Notre Dame Magazine,* June 1977; *South Bend Tribune,* May 17, 1987; interviews, Thomas Blantz, James Grant, Marty Ogren, Morris Pollard, John Schneider. Confidential interview.

5. *Chicago Tribune,* November 12, 1978; *The Indianapolis News,* March 4, 1987; interviews, James Frick, Neil McCluskey, Roger Valdiserri.

6. *The Indianapolis Star,* March 8, 1970; *Los Angeles Times,* June 21, 1982; interviews, Francis Castellino, Robert Griffin.

7. John C. Lungren Jr., *Hesburgh of Notre Dame: Priest, Educator, Public Servant* (Kansas City: Sheed and Ward, 1989), p. 28; interview, James Frick.

8. Theodore Hesburgh to Pope John Paul II, August 2, 1979, UPHS 77, TMHP; Theodore Hesburgh to John Sewell, January 5, 1981, UPHS, 73, TMHP; *Chicago Tribune,* November 9, 1986; *Look,* November 18, 1969; *The Observer,* Spring 1987; Lungren, *Hesburgh of Notre Dame,* p. 29; interviews, Landrum Bolling, John Brademas, John Egan, Donald Keough, James Murphy, David Rockefeller, Roger Valdiserri, Jean Wilkowski.

9. Clipping, Newspaper Clipping File, Hesburgh Office File, TMHP; diary of Theodore Hesburgh, "Travels with Ted and Ned, II. Central and South America," DPRI (1988), p. 16; Hesburgh diary, "China" (1984), p. 60; *The New York Times,* February 15, 1960; interviews, Larry Fuchs, Edmund Joyce.

10. Interviews, Richard Conklin, John Egan, Clark Kerr.

11. *National Review,* July 20, 1979; *50 Plus,* December, 1983; Theodore Hesburgh, *God, Country, Notre Dame* (New York: Doubleday, 1990), p. 313; interviews, Richard Conklin, Walter Langford.

12. Hesburgh diary, "Cambodia" (1980), p. 2; *Chicago Tribune,* November 12, 1978; *The Indianapolis News,* January 4, 1962 and March 4, 1987; *The New York Times,* May 11, 1969; *Notre Dame Magazine,* June 1977; *Syracuse Herald-American,* December 12, 1978; *50 Plus,* December, 1983; interview, James Frick.

13. *Notre Dame Magazine,* June 1977; *The Sooner Catholic,* April 13, 1980; interview, Philip Faccenda.

14. *Chicago Tribune,* November 9, 1986; *Dynamic Years,* March/April 1984; *Notre Dame Magazine,* Spring 1987.

15. Hesburgh diary, "China" (1984), p. 124; *Chicago Tribune,* November 9, 1986; *Notre Dame Magazine,* June 1977; interviews, Frederick Crosson, Philip Faccenda, Edmund Joyce, Marty Ogren, Elizabeth O'Neill, John Walsh.

16. Theodore Hesburgh to Robert Schmidt, February 8, 1979, UPHS, 32/14, TMHP; clipping, unprocessed Theodore M. Hesburgh Papers, Onondaga County Public Library, Syracuse, New York; *The Courier Journal,* December 7, 1986; *The Long Island Catholic,* March 29, 1984; *Notre Dame Magazine,* June 1977; *Syracuse Herald-American,* December 17, 1978; interviews, John Brademas, Theodore Hesburgh, Sargent Shriver.

17. Lungren, *Hesburgh of Notre Dame,* p. 28; interviews, Derek Bok, Larry Fuchs, John Gilligan, Andrew Greeley, John Powers.

18. *National Catholic Reporter,* May 22, 1987.

19. *The Indianapolis Star,* May 24, 1987; *Time,* May 2, 1977; interviews, John Egan, James Frick, James Grant, Clark Kerr, John Ryan.

20. Interviews, Thomas Carney, Larry Fuchs.

21. "Father Theodore M. Hesburgh. Interviewed by Lois Ferm. March 25, 1987."

Billy Graham Oral History Program: O.H. 795. 1987. Photocopy of typescript. UNDA; Theodore Hesburgh, "Living Philosophy," typescript (October 1988), Current News File, DPRI, p. 1; see also the jacket cover of Hesburgh, *God, Country, Notre Dame;* interview, Timothy O'Meara. Confidential interview.

22. Interviews, Richard Conklin, Mike Curtin, James Frick. Confidential interview.

23. *The Indianapolis News,* March 4, 1987; interviews, John Dunne, J. Peter Grace, Robert Griffin, Chester Soleta, John Walsh.

24. Interview, John Walsh. Confidential interview.

25. Clipping, Hesburgh News Clippings, DPRI; *The Catholic Messenger,* November 13, 1986; interviews, Frederick Crosson, Richard McBrien, Timothy O'Meara. Confidential interview.

26. *Time,* May 18, 1987. Two confidential interviews.

27. Interviews, Paul Beichner, Landrum Bolling, Thomas Carney, Francis Castellino, Andrew Greeley, John Powers, Jerry Reedy, David Tyson.

28. *Chicago Sun Times,* November 9, 1986; *The Indianapolis Star,* May 24, 1987; *National Catholic Reporter,* May 22, 1987; Joel Connelly and Howard Dooley, *Hesburgh's Notre Dame: Triumph in Transition* (New York: Hawthorn Books, 1972), p. 277.

29. *The Catholic Messenger,* November 13, 1986; *Time,* May 2, 1977; interview, Robert Griffin.

30. *The Observer,* Spring 1987; *Time,* May 2, 1977; interviews, Isabel Charles, John Gilligan, Philip Gleason, Edmund Joyce, Clark Kerr, Walter Langford, Newton Minow. Confidential interview.

31. *Scholastic,* May 2, 1977; Kennedy (ed.), *Top Guns,* p. 71; interviews, William Beauchamp, David Burrell, Donald Keough, Timothy O'Meara.

32. *Syracuse Herald-American,* December 17, 1978; Kennedy (ed.), *Top Guns,* pp. 65–66; interviews, Alice Gallin, Theodore Hesburgh, Walter Langford, Thomas Mason, Joseph Sandman.

33. Walter Langford, "My Adventures with Father Hesburgh," unpublished manuscript, unprocessed Walter Langford Papers, Creve Coeur, Missouri, p. 10; *Chicago Tribune,* November 12, 1978; *The Courier Journal,* December 7, 1986; *Los Angeles Times,* June 21, 1982; Lungren, *Hesburgh of Notre Dame,* p. 14; interviews, Theodore Hesburgh, Walter Langford.

34. Hesburgh diary, "July 15–August 31, 1982" (1982), pp. 20, 39; Hesburgh diary, "Moscow and Beijing" (1986), p. 83; *The Indianapolis News,* January 4, 1962; *South Bend Tribune,* May 3, 1964; interviews, James Grant, Theodore Hesburgh.

35. Hesburgh diary, "China" (1984), p. 60; *The Indianapolis Star,* March 8, 1970; *Today's Health,* November 1972; Thomas Horton (ed.), "Theodore M. Hesburgh, C.S.C.," *What Works for Me: 16 CEOs Talk About Their Careers and Commitments* (New York: Random House, 1986), p. 168; Trevor Kennedy (ed.), "Theodore Hesburgh," *Top Guns: Seventeen World Leaders in Politics, Media and Business Tell How They Made It to the Top—and Stayed There* (South Melbourne: Sun Books, Macmillan Company of Australia, 1988), pp. 72–73; interview, David Burrell.

36. Clipping, Newspaper Clipping Files, Hesburgh Office File, TMHP; Hesburgh diary, "July 15–August 31, 1982" (1982), pp. 7, 38.

37. Interviews, Richard Conklin, James Frick.

38. Thomas Karam, "A Rhetorical Analysis of Selected Speeches on Higher Education by Reverend Theodore M. Hesburgh" (Master's thesis, Louisiana State University and Agricultural and Mechanical College, 1979), p. 19; Theodore Hesburgh, *Still More Thoughts for Our Times,* No 3 (Notre Dame: Public Relations and Development, 1966),

p. 20; Theodore Hesburgh, *Three Bicentennial Addresses* (Notre Dame: University of Notre Dame, 1976), p. 32; interviews, Derek Bok, Theodore Hesburgh, Emil Hofman, Christopher Murphy, Edmund Stephan.

39. Karam, "Rhetorical Analysis," pp. 18, 48, 69–71; *America,* May 28, 1960; interviews, James Frick, Clark Kerr, Ernan McMullin.

40. Interviews, Thomas Carney, Robert Galvin, Robert Gordon, J. Peter Grace, Richard McBrien, Chester Soleta.

41. *South Bend Tribune,* May 17, 1987; interviews, Ernest Bartell, Isabel Charles, Frederick Crosson, Josephine Ford, John Houck, Ernan McMullin.

42. Theodore Hesburgh, *Thoughts for Our Time V,* No 5 (Notre Dame: University of Notre Dame, 1969), p. 1; Hesburgh diary, "July 15–August 31, 1982" (1982), p. 54; Charlotte A. Ames (ed.), *Theodore M. Hesburgh: A Bio-Bibliography* (New York: Greenwood Press, 1989), p. 32; "Rev. Theodore M. Hesburgh," *A Celebration of Teachers* (Urbana: National Council of Teachers of English, 1985), p. 24; Charles Moritz (ed.), "Theodore M. Hesburgh," *Current Biography Yearbook: 1982* (New York: The H. W. Wilson Company, 1982), p. 158; interview, John Gilligan.

43. Clippings, Yale University Press, file of reviews of Theodore Hesburgh, *The Humane Imperative,* unprocessed Yale University Press Papers, New Haven, Connecticut.

44. *Los Angeles Times,* May 27, 1979; *Library Journal,* June 15, p.979.

45. *Choice,* July/August 1974.

46. Hesburgh diary, "Cambodia" (1980); Ames, *Hesburgh: Bio-Bibliography,* pp. 169–72.

47. Hesburgh diary, "July 15–August 31, 1982" (1982), p. 58; Diary of Theodore Hesburgh, "Travels With Ted and Ned, III. The Caribbean at Christmas Time," DPRI (1988), pp. 22–23; *Dynamic Years,* March/April 1984; Hesburgh, *Humane Imperative,* p. 2; interviews, Richard Conklin, Michael Crowe, Andrew Greeley. Confidential interview.

48. Clipping, Hesburgh News Clippings, DPRI; *Notre Dame Magazine,* Spring 1987; *The Observer,* Spring 1987.

49. *The New York Times,* October 1, 1970; Lungren, *Hesburgh of Notre Dame,* p. 100.

50. Hesburgh, "Living Philosophy" (1988), pp. 6–8; *Notre Dame Report,* June 13, 1973.

51. *The Indianapolis Star,* December 30, 1979; *The Times-Herald,* February 9, 1980; *Today's Education,* November/December, 1974; Theodore Hesburgh, *The Hesburgh Papers: Higher Values in Higher Education* (Kansas City: Andrews and McMeel, 1979), p. 116; Theodore Hesburgh, *Thoughts for Our Times,* no. 1 (Notre Dame: University of Notre Dame, 1962), no. 1, p. 17; Theodore Hesburgh, *More Thoughts for Our Times,* no. 2 (Notre Dame: University of Notre Dame, 1964), p. 45; Lungren, *Hesburgh of Notre Dame,* p. 36. Confidential interview.

52. *Notre Dame Magazine,* June 1972; Hesburgh, *Hesburgh Papers,* pp. 26–27; interview, Ernest Bartell.

53. *Chicago Sun-Times,* November 9, 1986; *Dynamic Years,* March/April 1984; *Today's Education,* November/December, 1974; Hesburgh, *Hesburgh Papers,* pp. 114, 117.

54. *The Boston Globe,* June 2, 1987; *Current,* April 1976; *Notre Dame Alumnus,* August 1971; *Notre Dame Report,* June 13, 1973.

55. *The New York Times,* November 18, 1962; *Saturday Review,* March 2, 1963; *Scientific Research,* August 19, 1968.

56. *Notre Dame Magazine,* June 1977; Horton, "Theodore Hesburgh," *What Works for Me,* p. 169; interviews, Richard Conklin, James Hesburgh, James Frick, John Walsh.

57. Theodore Hesburgh to Nina Solarz, September 6, 1982, UPHS, 50/21, TMHP; *South Bend Tribune,* September 22, 1985; *Dynamic Years,* March/April 1984; *The Observer,* Spring 1987; Hesburgh, *Hesburgh Papers,* p. ix; interview, Thomas Mason.

58. Hesburgh, *God, Country, Notre Dame,* pp. 214–21.

59. *The Chicago American,* May 24, 1958; *Chicago Tribune,* November 12, 1978; *The Indianapolis News,* March 4, 1987; Stritch, "Theodore Hesburgh," p. 22; interview, Philip Gleason.

60. Diary of Theodore Hesburgh, "The San Salvador Elections," DPRI (1982), p. 5; Hesburgh diary. "Travels With Ted and Ned, IV" (1988), p. 3; clipping, Newspaper Clipping Files, TMHP; *Notre Dame Magazine,* June 1977; *50 Plus,* December, 1983; Kennedy, *Top Guns,* pp. 73–74; interviews, Neil McCluskey, Elizabeth O'Neill.

61. *Ms,* January 1976; *Our Sunday Visitor,* June 7, 1987; *University of Waterloo Courier,* June 1985; Kennedy (ed.), *Top Guns,* p. 74; interviews, David Burrell, Isabel Charles, Richard Conklin, Mary (Hesburgh) Flaherty, David Tyson. Confidential interview.

62. Interviews, Stephen Horn, Neil McCluskey, Franklin Murphy, John Schneider, Jean Wilkowski.

63. Theodore Hesburgh to Anne O'Grady, January 28, 1963, CPHS, 115/28, TMHP; interviews, Anne (O'Grady) Curtin, Mary (O'Grady) Den Dooven.

64. Hesburgh, *God, Country, Notre Dame,* pp. 186; interviews, Anne Curtin, Mary Den Dooven, Hely (Merle) Shork.

65. Hesburgh, *God, Country, Notre Dame,* p. 188.

66. Interview, Edmund Stephan.

67. Hesburgh diary, "Travels With Ted and Ned, IV" (1988), pp. 179, 275–76; Anson interview, p. 35; interviews, Anne Jackson, Elizabeth O'Neill, Joseph Sandman.

68. Interview, Mary Flaherty.

NOTES TO CHAPTER 7

1. *The Chronicle of Higher Education,* October 13, 1982; *The Observer,* Spring 1987; *Scholastic,* December, 1980; interview, John Egan.

2. *Notre Dame Magazine,* June 1977; *Our Sunday Visitor,* March 10, 1963.

3. Terrance A. Sweeney, *God And* (Minneapolis: Winston Press, 1985), pp. 169–70; interview, John Walsh.

4. *Syracuse Herald-American,* December 17, 1978; *The Observer,* Spring 1987; Theodore Hesburgh, *God, Country, Notre Dame* (New York: Doubleday, 1990), pp. 154, 169; interview, John Walsh.

5. Clipping, Newspaper Clipping Files, Hesburgh Office File, TMHP; *Notre Dame Magazine,* June 1977; Hesburgh, *God, Country, Notre Dame,* p. 160; interviews, Thomas Carney, Edmund Stephan.

6. *The Indianapolis Star,* June 21, 1993; *The Observer,* Spring 1987; *Syracuse Herald-American,* December 17, 1978; Hesburgh, *God, Country, Notre Dame,* p. 155.

7. Clipping, Newspaper Clipping Files, Hesburgh Office File, TMHP; *Chicago Tribune,* November 9, 1986; Robert Schmuhl, *The University of Notre Dame: A Contemporary Portrait* (Notre Dame: University of Notre Dame Press, 1986), p. 25; interviews, David Burrell, John Egan, Alice Gallin, Edmund Stephan. Confidential interview.

8. *Our Sunday Visitor,* September 27, 1953; Sweeney, *God And,* pp. 170–72.

9. *Chicago American,* March 1, 1959; *Our Sunday Visitor,* June 14, 1987; *The Sooner Catholic,* April 13, 1980; *U.S. Catholic,* March 1976; Hesburgh, *Thoughts,* no. 4, pp. 37–39; Hesburgh, *God, Country, Notre Dame,* p. 154; Sweeney, *God And,* pp. 170–71; in-

terviews, Alice Gallin, Robert Griffin, Neil McCluskey, Ernan McMullin, Martin Ogren, Chester Soleta.

10. *Scholastic,* December 1980; *U.S. Catholic,* May 1979.

11. *Saturday Review World,* August 24, 1974; *The Serran,* March 1985.

12. Hesburgh speech at the Annual Convention of the National Federation of Priests' Councils, March 15, 1971, CPHS, 142/04, TMHP; *Saturday Review World,* August 24, 1974; Hesburgh, *God, Country, Notre Dame,* p. x.

13. Hesburgh speech, National Federation of Priests' Councils, March 15, 1971; CPHS, 142/04, TMHP; Theodore Hesburgh, *God and the World of Man,* 2d Edition (Notre Dame: University of Notre Dame Press, 1960), p. 7; Theodore Hesburgh, *The Theology of Catholic Action* (Notre Dame: Ave Maria Press, 1946), pp. 52–55; interviews, Anne Curtin, Theodore Hesburgh.

14. *CGA World,* Fall 1987; *The Chronicle of Higher Education,* October 13, 1982; *Our Sunday Visitor,* April 9, 1961; *The Progressive,* February 1973; *University of Waterloo Courier,* June 1985; Joel Connelly and Howard Dooley, *Hesburgh's Notre Dame: Triumph in Transition* (New York: Hawthorn Books, 1972), p. 23; interviews, William Beauchamp, Theodore Hesburgh.

15. *Notre Dame Magazine,* June 1977; interviews, Ernest Bartell, Ernan McMullin.

16. *Notre Dame Magazine,* June 1972; Edward Fischer to author, July 10, 1989.

17. *The Long Island Catholic,* March 29, 1984; *Our Sunday Visitor,* March 10, 1963; *Time,* February 15, 1971; interview, Erwin Griswold.

18. *The Observer,* Spring 1987.

19. Theodore Hesburgh to Lucy Sullivan, February 2, 1987, Hesburgh News Clippings, DPRI; *Dynamic Years,* March/April 1984; *Notre Dame Magazine,* June 1972; *Time,* May 2, 1977; *Woman's Day,* August 4, 1987; interview, John Gilligan.

20. Hesburgh speech, National Federation of Priests' Councils, March 15, 1971, 142/04 TMHP; Hesburgh diary, "July 15–August 31, 1982" (1982), p. 11; Hesburgh diary, "Travels With Ted and Ned, IV" (1988), pp. 87–88; *The Observer,* Spring 1987; *The Serran,* March 1985; interviews, John Egan, John Gilligan, Edmund Joyce.

21. *The Indianapolis News,* March 4, 1987; interviews, Richard Conklin, Frederick Crosson, John Egan, Philip Faccenda, Edmund Joyce, Clark Kerr, Ann Landers, Walter Langford, John Walsh.

22. Draft document, Fr. Hesburgh and Fr. Waldschmidt, August 1, 1968, CPHS 124/25, TMHP; Theodore Hesburgh, "Living Philosophy," typescript (October 1988), Current News File, DPRI, pp. 2–3; *Critic,* Winter 1986; Hesburgh, *God, Country, Notre Dame,* pp. x–xi.

23. Hesburgh speech, National Federation of Priests' Councils, March 15, 1971, CPHS, 142/04, TMHP; Hesburgh, "Living Philosophy" (1988), p. 3; *The Indianapolis Star,* April 3, 1983 and June 21, 1993; *Notre Dame Alumnus,* April/May 1971; *Notre Dame Magazine,* June 1972; *The Serran,* March 1985; John C. Lungren Jr., *Hesburgh of Notre Dame: Priest, Educator, Public Servant* (Kansas City: Sheed and Ward, 1989), p. 122; William Maestri, *A Priest to turn to: Biblical Reflections on the Priesthood* (New York: Alba House, 1989), p. 213; Douglas Morin, *Instrument of Peace: Personal and Spiritual Goal of the Priest* (New York: Alba House, 1989), pp. 63–65; Joseph Wade, *Chastity, Sexuality and Personal Hangups* (New York: Alba House, 1971), p. 2; interview, Theodore Hesburgh.

24. *The Indianapolis Star,* April 3, 1983; *Time,* May 2, 1977; Edgar C. Cummings (ed.), *Social Hygiene Papers: A Symposium on Sex Education* (New York: American Social Hygiene Association, 1957), pp. 18, 22; Theodore Hesburgh, *The Hesburgh Papers: High-*

er Values in Higher Education (Kansas City: Andrews and McMeel, 1979) p. 87; Lungren, Hesburgh of Notre Dame, pp. 121–22.

25. Hesburgh, "Living Philosophy" (1988), p. 4; Critic, Winter 1986; Theodore Hesburgh, Travels with Ted and Ned (New York: Doubleday, 1992), p. xv; Hesburgh, God, Country, Notre Dame, pp. xi–xii; interviews, Robert Griffin, Louis Putz.

26. Hesburgh diary, "Travels With Ted and Ned, II" (1988), p. 148; Notre Dame Magazine, June 1972; The Observer, Spring 1987; interviews, William Beauchamp, Thomas Blantz, David Burrell, Robert Griffin, Louis Putz.

27. The Critic, Fall 1975; Thomas Bokenkotter, A Concise History of the Catholic Church (Garden City, N.Y.: Doubleday, 1977), pp. 387–88; Jay Dolan, The American Catholic Experience (Garden City, N.Y.: Doubleday, 1985), pp. 424–26; Ellis (ed.), The Catholic Priest, pp. xii–xiii; Philip Gleason, Keeping the Faith: American Catholicism Past and Present (Notre Dame: University of Notre Dame Press, 1987), p. 85.

28. Dolan, American Catholic Experience, pp. 426, 429; Gleason, Keeping the Faith, p. 174.

29. Hesburgh, God and the World of Man, pp. 14, 170, 189, 210, 211, 222.

30. Clipping, Newspaper Clipping Files, Hesburgh Office File, TMHP.

31. Notre Dame Alumnus, August 1971; Hesburgh, Hesburgh Papers, pp. 179–85; Hesburgh, God, Country, Notre Dame, p. 249; Lungren, Hesburgh of Notre Dame, p. 120.

32. Hesburgh interview, Billy Graham Oral History Program; Chicago Sun-Times, November 2, 1967; 50 Plus, December 1983; Hesburgh, Thoughts, no. 4, pp. 47–59.

33. Hesburgh interview, Billy Graham Oral History Program; Notre Dame Magazine, June 1972; South Bend Tribune, June 19, 1977; "Reverend Theodore M. Hesburgh, CSC." In Christian Jewish Relations: A Documentary Survey 18 (September 1985): 23–27; "In Spite of Everything." In Against Silence: The Voice and Vision of Elie Wiesel, selected and edited by Irving Abrahamson, vol. 3, p. 259; Lungren, Hesburgh of Notre Dame, pp. 129–31; interview, Landrum Bolling.

34. Theodore Hesburgh to Pope Paul VI, May 14, 1964, CPHS, 96/14, TMHP; Chicago Sun-Times, October 14, 1972; Moment, July/August 1983; Hesburgh, Humane Imperative, p. 15; Lungren, Hesburgh of Notre Dame, pp. 129–30; interview, Landrum Bolling.

35. Clipping, Hesburgh News Clippings, DPRI; Moment, July/August 1983.

36. Hesburgh diary, "Trip to South Africa" (1978), p. 34; U.S. Catholic, May 1979; interview, Neil McCluskey.

37. Anson interview, pp. 22–23; Hesburgh, God, Country, Notre Dame, p. 264; interviews, Neil McCluskey, Edmund Stephan.

38. Clipping, Hesburgh News Clippings, DPRI; clipping, News Clipping Files, Hesburgh Office File, TMHP; Notre Dame Magazine, June 1972; Syracuse Herald-American, December 17, 1978; Connelly and Dooley, Hesburgh's Notre Dame, p. 294; interview, John Egan.

39. The Elkhart Truth, October 27, 1986; Time, May 2, 1977; Lungren, Hesburgh of Notre Dame, p. 120; interviews, Robert Griffin, Theodore Hesburgh, Neil McCluskey.

40. Theodore Hesburgh to Andrew Greeley, May 21, 1971, UPHS, 58, TMHP; Hesburgh speech, National Federation of Priests' Councils, March 15, 1971, CPHS, 142/04; Chicago Tribune, November 9, 1986; Notre Dame Alumnus, April/May 1971; Hesburgh, God, Country, Notre Dame, p. 173; interviews, David Burrell, Theodore Hesburgh.

41. See the handwritten memo by Theodore Hesburgh on the clipping dated September 22, 1975 in the News Clipping Files, Hesburgh Office File, TMHP.

42. Chicago Tribune, November 9, 1986; The New York Times, May 11, 1969; Hes-

burgh, *God, Country, Notre Dame,* pp. 260–61; interviews, John Brademas, Gene Corrigan, Tom Scanlon, Jean Wilkowski.

43. *Our Sunday Visitor,* April 9, 1961; *The Times-Herald,* February 9, 1980; *Notre Dame Magazine,* June 1977; *Time,* May 2, 1977; Lungren, *Hesburgh of Notre Dame,* p. 121; interviews, Richard Conklin, Philip Faccenda, Edmund Stephan, John Walsh.

44. *The Times-Herald,* February 9, 1980; *Notre Dame Magazine,* June 1977; *Time,* May 2, 1977; *U.S. Catholic,* March 1976; Hesburgh, *Travels with Ted and Ned,* p. xiv; Lungren, *Hesburgh of Notre Dame,* p. 121; interview, Philip Faccenda.

45. Theodore Hesburgh Speech, "The Christian Family," Feast of the Holy Family, Notre Dame, 1947. Typescript, UNDA; *National Catholic Reporter,* May 22, 1987; *The New York Times,* January 15, 1960; *The Times-Herald,* February 9, 1980; *Foreign Policy Bulletin* 39 (May 15, 1960): 132; Bokenkotter, *History of Catholic Church,* p. 394; Lungren, *Hesburgh of Notre Dame,* p. 121; Richard McBrien, *Report on the Church: Catholicism After Vatican II* (San Francisco: HarperSanFranciso, 1992), p. 36; interviews, Ernest Bartell, Theodore Hesburgh, Richard McBrien, Neil McCluskey.

46. Interview, Theodore Hesburgh. Two confidential interviews.

47. *Chicago Sun-Times,* October 10, 1976; Theodore Hesburgh, *The Humane Imperative: A Challenge for the Year 2000* (New Haven: Yale University Press, 1974), p. 33; interview, Ralph McInerny.

48. Clippings, Hesburgh News Clippings, DPRI; clippings, News Clipping Files, Hesburgh Office File, TMHP; *Change,* February 1976; *The Wanderer,* May 30, 1974.

49. Clipping, News Clipping Files, Hesburgh Office File, TMHP; *Notre Dame Magazine,* October 1974; *The Observer,* April 20, 1977; *Our Sunday Visitor,* January 30, 1977.

50. Clipping, News Clipping Files, Hesburgh Office File, TMHP; *National Catholic Register,* May 1, 1977; *The Observer,* April 20, 1977; *Our Sunday Visitor,* February 3, 1970.

51. Clippings, News Clipping Files, Hesburgh Office File, TMHP; *The Wanderer,* February 24, 1977.

52. Clipping, News Clipping Files, Hesburgh Office File, TMHP; *Our Sunday Visitor,* February 3, 1980.

53. John Knowles to Theodore Hesburgh, December 21, 1978, UPHS, 85, TMHP; Theodore Hesburgh to John Knowles, January 8, 1979, UPHS, 85, TMHP; Theodore Hesburgh to Charles Rice, March 12, 1973, UPHS, 163, TMHP; clippings, News Clipping Files, Hesburgh Office File, TMHP. Conklin's remark is written on one of the clippings.

54. *Our Sunday Visitor,* December 2, 1979 and January 13, 1980.

55. *The Harmonizer,* August 17, 1986; Lungren, *Hesburgh of Notre Dame,* p. 125; *Notre Dame Journal of Law, Ethics and Public Policy* 1 (1984): 54–55.

56. *Notre Dame Journal of Law, Ethics and Public Policy* 1 (1984): 54–55; *Notre Dame Magazine,* Summer 1988; Lungren, *Hesburgh of Notre Dame,* p. 126.

57. *The Times-Herald,* February 9, 1980.

NOTES TO CHAPTER 8

1. *National Catholic Reporter,* May 22, 1987; *Notre Dame Report,* October 18, 1983; interviews, Isabel Charles, Ernan McMullin, Edmund Stephan.

2. *The Nation,* March 6, 1972; interviews, Richard Conklin, Robert Gordon.

3. *South Bend Tribune,* May 17, 1987; interview, Timothy O'Meara.

4. Thomas Horton (ed.), "Theodore M. Hesburgh, C.S.C.," *What Works for Me: 16*

CEOs Talk About Their Careers and Commitments (New York: Random House, 1986), pp. 153–56; John C. Lungren Jr., *Hesburgh of Notre Dame: Priest, Educator, Public Servant* (Kansas City: Sheed and Ward, 1989), p. 33; interviews, Mario Borelli, Richard Conklin, Richard McBrien.

5. *Chicago Tribune,* November 12, 1978; interviews, John Egan, Mary Flaherty, Helen Hosinski, Edmund Joyce, Martin Ogren, Thomas Mason, David Tyson.

6. *Chicago Tribune,* November 12, 1978; *Los Angeles Times,* February 21, 1966; *Notre Dame Magazine,* Summer 1989; *Notre Dame Report* 6 (1977);Thomas Blantz, *George N. Shuster: On the Side of Truth* (Notre Dame: University of Notre Dame Press, 1993), pp. 302, 325, 326, 361; interviews, Thomas Blantz, David Burrell, John Egan, James Frick, John Gilligan.

7. *Notre Dame Magazine,* June 1977 and May 1982; interviews, Edmund Joyce, Edmund Stephan.

8. *Notre Dame Magazine,* Winter 1986; *The Observer,* Spring 1987; interviews, Theodore Hesburgh, Edmund Joyce, James Murphy, John Walsh.

9. *Chicago Tribune,* November 9, 1986; Schmuhl, *The University of Notre Dame: A Contemporary Portrait,* p. 22; interviews, Richard Conklin, Gene Corrigan, Philip Faccenda, James Frick, James Gibbons, John Gilligan, Thomas Mason.

10. *The Indianapolis Star,* May 24, 1987; interviews, John Dunne, Philip Faccenda, James Frick, Clark Kerr, Ralph McInerny, Timothy O'Meara, Roger Schmitz.

11. *The Indianapolis Star,* May 24, 1987; *The Chronicle of Higher Education,* October 13, 1982; interviews, Ernest Bartell, William Beauchamp, Thomas Blantz, Mario Borelli, David Burrell, Thomas Carney, Isabel Charles, Timothy O'Meara, David Tyson. Confidential interview.

12. *Notre Dame Magazine,* June 1977; Horton, *What Works for Me,* p. 165; interviews, Francis Castellino, Frederick Crosson, Emil Hofman, Chester Soleta, John Walsh.

13. Interviews, Richard Conklin, Philip Faccenda, Edmund Joyce, Timothy O'Meara.

14. Confidential interview.

15. *The Indianapolis Star,* May 24, 1987; *The Chronicle of Higher Education,* October 13, 1982; Horton, *What Works for Me,* p. 153.

16. Trevor Kennedy (ed.), "Theodore Hesburgh," *Top Guns: Seventeen World Leaders in Politics, Media and Business Tell How They Made It to the Top—and Stayed There* (South Melbourne: Sun Books, Macmillan Company of Australia, 1988), p. 84; interview, Martin Ogren.

17. Interviews, James Gibbons, David Tyson.

18. *The Catholic Messenger,* November 13, 1986; Theodore Hesburgh, *The Hesburgh Papers: Higher Values in Higher Education* (Kansas City: Andrews and McMeel, 1979), p. 9; Lungren, *Hesburgh of Notre Dame,* p. 35; interviews, Francis Castellino, John Dunne, John Gilligan, Ralph McInerny, Morris Pollard.

19. *Los Angeles Times,* February 22, 1966; *The Chronicle of Higher Education,* October 13, 1982; *Notre Dame Magazine,* June 1972; interviews, Francis Castellino, Frederick Crosson, Emil Hofman, John Walsh.

20. *Los Angeles Times,* February 22, 1966; *The Chronicle of Higher Education,* October 13, 1982; *Common Sense,* April/May 1987; *Notre Dame Magazine,* June 1972; interviews, Mario Borelli, Isabel Charles, Philip Gleason, Vaughn McKim, Ernan McMullin.

21. Interviews, Mario Borelli, Francis Castellino, Isabel Charles, Vaughn McKim, Ernan McMullin.

22. Hesburgh, *Hesburgh Papers,* p. 3.

23. Clipping, News Clipping Files, Hesburgh Office File, TMHP; *Look,* October 24, 1961; Stritch, "Theodore Hesburgh," p. 16; interviews, Richard Conklin, James Gibbons, J. Peter Grace, James Murphy.

24. *The Observer,* Spring 1987; interviews, David Burrell, James Frick, James Murphy, Joseph Sandman.

25. Interviews, James Frick, J. Peter Grace, Christopher Murphy, James Murphy, Joseph Sandman.

26. Unpublished speech by Theodore Hesburgh, June 7, 1986, Hesburgh/University Profiles, 1981–1989, DPRI.

27. Theodore Hesburgh to David Rockefeller, November 13, 1985, UPHS, 95, TMHP; *The Observer,* Spring 1987; Lungren, *Hesburgh of Notre Dame,* p. 37; Thomas Schlereth, *The University of Notre Dame: A Portrait of Its History and Campus* (Notre Dame: University of Notre Dame Press, 1976), pp. 208–9; interviews, John Egan, Timothy O'Meara.

28. *Chicago Tribune,* November 12, 1978, and November 9, 1986; *Manchester Guardian,* April 13, 1969; *Commonweal,* June 5, 1987; *Harper's Magazine,* May 1967; *Notre Dame Report,* November 13, 1981; Hesburgh, *Hesburgh Papers,* pp. 38–39.

29. Clipping, News Clipping Files, Hesburgh Office File, TMHP; *National Catholic Register,* July 18, 1982; *Commonweal,* October 6, 1961; Joel Connelly and Howard Dooley, *Hesburgh's Notre Dame: Triumph in Transition* (New York: Hawthorn Books, 1972), p. 24; James Armstrong, *Onward to Victory: A Chronicle of the Alumni of the University of Notre Dame du Lac: 1842–1973* (Notre Dame: University of Notre Dame, 1974), p. 371.

30. Neil McCluskey (ed.), *The Catholic University: A Modern Appraisal* (Notre Dame: University of Notre Dame Press, 1970), pp. viii–xi; interviews, John Dunne, Richard McBrien, Neil McCluskey.

31. *Chicago Tribune,* November 12, 1978; *The New York Times,* May 11, 1969; *Change,* February 1976; *Notre Dame Magazine,* Spring 1987; *Time,* February 9, 1962; Hesburgh, *Hesburgh Papers,* p. 79; interview, Emil Hofman.

32. Clippings, News Clipping Files, Hesburgh Office File, TMHP; *Chicago Tribune,* November 12, 1978; *The New York Times,* May 11, 1969; *St. Anthony Messenger,* May 1987; *America,* October 4, 1986.

33. *The New York Times,* May 11, 1969; Connelly and Dooley, *Hesburgh's Notre Dame,* p. 115.

34. *Chicago's American,* March 29, 1969; *Chicago Tribune,* November 12, 1978; interviews, Frederick Crosson, Vaughn McKim.

35. *Notre Dame Magazine,* Winter 1986; Philip Gleason, *Keeping the Faith: American Catholicism Past and Present* (Notre Dame: University of Notre Dame Press, 1987), p. 87.

36. *Change,* February 1976; *Chicago's American,* March 29, 1969; *National Catholic Register,* May 17, 1987; Gleason, *Keeping the Faith,* p. 77; interview, Ernest Bartell. Confidential interview.

37. Clipping, News Clipping Files, Hesburgh Office File, TMHP; clipping, Hesburgh News Clippings, DPRI; *Chicago's American,* March 29, 1969; *National Catholic Register,* May 17, 1987; interview, Ralph McInerny.

38. *Chicago Tribune,* November 9, 1986; *The Chronicle of Higher Education,* October 13, 1982; Andrew Greeley, *From Backwater to Mainstream* (New York: McGraw-Hill Book Company, 1969), p. 22; interviews, William Beauchamp, Francis Castellino, John Dunne, Thomas Mason, Richard McBrien, Vaughn McKim, Timothy O'Meara.

39. *Chicago Sun-Times,* November 9, 1986; *Our Sunday Visitor,* December 2, 1979;

Jay Dolan, *The American Catholic Experience* (Garden City, N.Y.: Doubleday, 1985), pp. 443–45, Gleason, *Keeping the Faith*, p. 87; Hesburgh, *Hesburgh Papers*, p. 64; McCluskey (ed.), *The Catholic University*, pp. 256–57.

40. *Change*, February 1976; McCluskey (ed.), *The Catholic University*, pp. 9–19.

41. *News in brief*, November 1987; Theodore Hesburgh, *God, Country, Notre Dame* (New York: Doubleday, 1990), pp. 227–29; McCluskey (ed.), *The Catholic University*, p. 14.

42. Theodore Hesburgh to Paul Marcinkus, November 20, 1963, CPHS, 96/13, TMHP.

43. Theodore Hesburgh to Pope Paul VI [1963], CPHS, 96/12, TMHP; Hesburgh, *God, Country, Notre Dame,* p. 230.

44. Theodore Hesburgh to Georges LeClercq, November 29, 1966, CPHS, 96/26, TMHP.

45. *Change*, February 1976; *News in brief*, November 1987; *The New York Times,* May 11, 1969; Connelly and Dooley, *Hesburgh's Notre Dame*, p. 177; Dolan, *American Catholic Experience*, p. 444; Hesburgh, *Hesburgh Papers*, pp. 64–65; James Hennesey, *American Catholics* (New York: Oxford University Press, 1981), p. 322; McCluskey (ed.), *The Catholic University*, pp. 4–6; interview, Neil McCluskey.

46. Theodore Hesburgh to Gabriel Cardinal Garrone, March 30, 1970, CPHS, 98/09, TMHP; Hesburgh to Garrone, May 17, 1971, CPHS, 98/11, TMHP; McCluskey (ed.), *The Catholic University*, pp. 13–14.

47. Theodore Hesburgh to Georges LeClercq, June 4, 1970, CPHS, 97/02, TMHP; interview, Paul Reinert.

48. *Change*, February 1976; Hesburgh, *God, Country, Notre Dame,* p. 262; interviews, Neil McCluskey, Paul Reinert.

49. *America*, October 20, 1990; *The New York Times*, November 16, 1986; *Newsweek,* November 11, 1985; *Notre Dame Magazine,* Winter 1986; Lungren, *Hesburgh of Notre Dame*, pp. 127–28.

50. *America*, November 1, 1986; *Time*, May 18, 1987.

51. *America*, October 20, 1990; *Commonweal*, November 9, 1990.

52. *Harper's Magazine*, May 1967; Hesburgh, *God, Country, Notre Dame,* p. 102.

53. Clipping, News Clipping Files, Hesburgh Office File, TMHP; *Chicago Sun-Times,* October 16 and 17, 1968; *The New York Times,* May 11, 1969; *Our Sunday Visitor,* December 2, 1979.

54. *Common Sense,* April/May 1987; interviews, David Burrell, Richard McBrien, Ralph McInerny.

55. *Notre Dame Magazine*, Summer 1988.

56. Ibid.; *National Catholic Reporter,* February 26, 1969; *South Bend Tribune,* May 17, 1987; Connelly and Dooley, *Hesburgh's Notre Dame*, pp. 160, 230; interview, Richard Rossie.

57. Hesburgh, *Hesburgh Papers*, pp. 62–63; interview, Ernan McMullin.

58. Hesburgh speech, Hall of Fame Banquet, New York City, December 9, 1975, DPRI; *Chicago Tribune,* November 9, 1986; *People,* September 26, 1977; *Sports Illustrated,* January 10, 1983; *Today's Health,* November 1972; interviews, Richard Conklin, Edmund Joyce, Thomas Mason, Edmund Stephan.

59. Clipping, Hesburgh News Clippings, DPRI; *Chicago Tribune,* November 9, 1986; *Los Angeles Times,* June 21, 1982.

60. Clipping, Hesburgh News Clippings, DPRI; *Sports Illustrated,* January 10, 1983; interview, Roger Valdiserri.

61. Clipping, Hesburgh News Clippings, DPRI; *Sports Illustrated,* January 10, 1983; interview, Roger Valdiserri; *The Pittsburgh Press,* September 14, 1986.

62. Clipping, Hesburgh News Clippings, DPRI; *Los Angeles Times,* June 21, 1982; *Sports Illustrated,* January 10, 1983.

63. *Scholastic,* December 1964; *South Bend Tribune,* November 14, 1965.

64. Clipping, Hesburgh News Clippings, DPRI; *Los Angeles Times,* June 21, 1982; *The Observer,* Spring 1987; *Sports Illustrated,* January 10, 1983.

65. Interview, Gene Corrigan.

66. Clipping, Hesburgh News Clippings, DPRI; *The Observer,* February 5, 1970; Hesburgh, *God, Country, Notre Dame,* p. 90.

67. *Sports Illustrated,* January 10, 1983.

NOTES TO CHAPTER 9

1. *Notre Dame Magazine,* Summer 1987; *The Observer,* Spring 1987; interview, Elizabeth O'Neill.

2. Hesburgh diary, "Travels with Ted and Ned, I" (1987), pp. 1, 2, 43; Theodore Hesburgh, *God, Country, Notre Dame* (New York: Doubleday, 1990), p. 303.

3. Hesburgh diary, "Travels with Ted and Ned, II" (1988), p. 75; Hesburgh diary, "Travels with Ted and Ned, IV" (1988), pp. 162–63.

4. Hesburgh, *God, Country, Notre Dame,* p. 304.

5. Clippings, Hesburgh News Clippings, DPRI; *The Dialog,* May 5, 1989; *South Bend Tribune,* December 7, 1988 and February 25, 1990.

6. Clipping, Hesburgh News Clippings, DPRI; *The Criterion,* May 11, 1990 and March 20, 1994; *Notre Dame Magazine,* May 20, 1944; Hesburgh, *God, Country, Notre Dame,* p. 306; interview, Thomas Blantz.

7. *Notre Dame Magazine,* Summer 1993; interview, Ernest Bartell.

8. Clipping, Hesburgh News Clippings, DPRI; *Des Moines Register,* May 14, 1990; *Notre Dame Magazine,* Summer 1993; *South Bend Tribune,* September 15 and November 21, 1991.

9. "Notre Dame News," news release, September 6, 1989, DPRI; interview, Oliver Williams.

10. Clippings, Hesburgh News Clippings, DPRI; *The Criterion,* May 11, 1990; *South Bend Tribune,* October 10 and December 7, 1988.

11. Clippings, Hesburgh News Clippings, DPRI; Hesburgh diary, "Travels with Ted and Ned, III" (1988), pp. 32–33; *The Dialog,* May 5, 1989; *South Bend Tribune,* February 25, 1990; interview, Theodore Hesburgh.

12. "Notre Dame News," news release, November 19, 1991, DPRI; *South Bend Tribune,* September 15, 1991.

13. *New York Daily News,* December 30, 1990; Hesburgh, *God, Country, Notre Dame,* pp. 315–16; interview, Richard Conklin.

14. *America,* December 1, 1990; *Chicago Tribune,* December 23, 1990; *The Economist,* November 24, 1990; *Religious News Service,* January 7, 1991; *Washington Post,* January 28, 1991.

15. *The Indianapolis Star,* January 2, 1993; *Library Journal,* November 1, 1992, p. 107; *Publishers Weekly,* October 5, 1992, p. 63; *South Bend Tribune,* November 8, 1992; Theodore Hesburgh, *Travels with Ted and Ned* (New York: Doubleday, 1992), xvi.

16. Clipping, Hesburgh News Clippings, DPRI; "Notre Dame News," news release, May 24, 1994, DPRI.

17. Clippings, Hesburgh News Clippings, DPRI; *Chicago Tribune,* March 29, 1992; interview, Creed Black.

18. William Friday and Theodore Hesburgh, "Joint Statement of the Co-chairmen" [no date], unprocessed Knight Commission Papers, Miami, Florida; interview, Creed Black.

19. *NCAA News,* March 17, 1993; *Notre Dame Magazine,* Summer 1993; interviews, Christopher Morris, Roger Valdiserri.

20. *The New York Times,* March 23 and 24, 1994; interviews, Theodore Hesburgh, Morris Pollard.

21. *The New York Times,* March 23 and 24, 1994; interviews, Theodore Hesburgh, Morris Pollard.

22. Clipping, Hesburgh News Clippings, DPRI; *Catholic News Service,* June 30, 1994; *South Bend Tribune,* July 8, 1994.

23. *The Criterion,* May 20, 1994; *Harvard University Gazette,* April 15, 1994.

24. Interview, Mary Flaherty.

25. *Notre Dame Magazine,* Summer 1993; interview, Alice Gallin. Two confidential interviews.

26. *Notre Dame Magazine,* Summer 1993.

27. *The Criterion,* May 20, 1994; *Notre Dame Magazine,* Summer 1993.

28. *South Bend Tribune,* September 29, 1991; Hesburgh, *Travels,* xvi; interview, Theodore Hesburgh.

29. *Catholic News Service,* May 10, 1993; Theodore Hesburgh sermon, "50th Anniversary of Ordination," May 6, 1993, DPRI.

30. Hesburgh diary, "Travels with Ted and Ned, I" (1987), p. 9; Hesburgh, *God, Country, Notre Dame,* p. 310; Hesburgh, *Travels,* xvi.

SOURCES

This essay does not include a complete list of all the sources used for this study. Readers should consult endnote citations for specific sources.

MANUSCRIPTS

The most important single source for the study of Theodore Hesburgh is Charlotte A. Ames (compiler), *Theodore M. Hesburgh: A Bio-Bibliography* (New York: Greenwood Press, 1989). This extraordinary volume describes the archival and manuscript material held in the Archives of the University of Notre Dame and provides a bibliography of Hesburgh's major published and unpublished works, as well as selected works about him. In the bio-bibliography Notre Dame archivist Kevin Cawley provides a nine-page summary of the manuscripts relating to Hesburgh's career. Ordinarily, university records remain closed for fifty years after the date of their creation, but the university has lifted its absolute restriction on Hesburgh's files. Still, the files are partially restricted by the University Archivist, who reviews pertinent files requested by the researcher and decides if they contain confidential material or if permission to use may be granted. I received permission to inspect about 80 percent of the manuscript materials I requested.

The most helpful collection was the United States Commission on Civil Rights records (1958–73). This huge collection consists of reports, press releases, statements, resolutions, court material, correspondence, memoranda, proposals, minutes, agenda, pamphlets, clippings, transcripts of testimony given in hearings, and transcripts of speeches, press conferences, and broadcasts.

The other Hesburgh Papers that I found most valuable were the Rockefeller Foundation records (1962–82), National Cambodia Crisis Committee and Cambodia Crisis Center records (1979–80), Overseas Development Council records (1971–78), Chase Manhattan Bank records (1972–81), United Nations Conference on Science and Technology for Development records (1977–79), Peace Corps records (1961–65), and the Select Commission on Immigration and Refugee Policy records (1980–81).

Significant letters and memoranda about Hesburgh's tenure as Vice President of Notre Dame are located in the John J. Cavanaugh Papers (University of Notre Dame Archives, University of Notre Dame). The Department of Public Relations and Information Papers (University of Notre Dame) contains a large collection of clippings and press releases about Hesburgh. Another notable collection is the Overseas Development Council Papers (Washington, D.C.).

Other small manuscript collections that contain useful material on Hesburgh are the Walter Langford Papers (Creve Coeur, Missouri), Florence Lynch Papers (Syracuse, New York), Most Holy Rosary School Papers (Syracuse, New York), John O'Connor Papers (Winchester, Massachusetts), Onondaga County Public Library Papers (Syracuse, New York), Thomas Steiner Papers (Province Archives Center, Notre Dame, Indiana), and the Yale University Press Papers (New Haven, Connecticut).

BOOKS AND ARTICLES

No major scholarly biography of Hesburgh exists. John Lungren's *Hesburgh of Notre Dame: Priest, Educator, Public Servant* (Kansas City: Sheed and Ward, 1987) is a brief and superficially researched biography. Joel Connelly and Howard Dooley, *Hesburgh's Notre Dame: Triumph in Transition* (New York: Hawthorn Books, Inc., 1972), presents an occasionally insightful but sometimes unreliable account of Hesburgh and Notre Dame during the 1960s by two former Notre Dame students. Thomas Schlereth, *The University of Notre Dame: A Portrait of Its History and Campus* (Notre Dame: University of Notre Dame Press, 1976), is a judicious account of the history of the university. Harris Wofford, *Of Kennedys and Kings: Making Sense of the Sixties* (New York: Farrar, Straus, Giroux, 1980), has an important appendix on Hesburgh's work for the U.S. Civil Rights Commission.

Fr. Hesburgh's five major books were: *The Theology of Catholic Action* (Notre Dame: Ave Maria Press, 1946), originally his doctoral dissertation; *God and the World of Man* (Notre Dame: University of Notre Dame, 1950), a theology textbook; *The Humane Imperative: A Challenge for the Year 2000* (New Haven: Yale University Press, 1974); his autobiography, assisted by Jerry Reedy, *God, Country, Notre Dame* (New York: Doubleday, 1990); and his retirement travel diary, edited by Jerry Reedy, *Travels with Ted and Ned* (New York: Doubleday, 1992).

Of the published collections of his speeches and essays the most important is *The Hesburgh Papers: Higher Values in Higher Education* (Kansas City: Andrews and McMeel, Inc., 1979). Other noteworthy collections of speeches and essays include *Thoughts for Our Times*, no. 1 (Notre Dame: University of Notre Dame, 1962); *More Thoughts for Our Times*, no. 2 (Notre Dame: University of Notre Dame, 1964); *Still More Thoughts for Our Times*, no. 3 (Notre Dame: Public Relations and Development, University of Notre Dame, 1966); *Thoughts IV: Five Addresses Delivered During 1967*, no. 4 (Notre Dame: Public Relations and Development, University of Notre Dame, 1967); *Thoughts for Our Time V*, no. 5 (Notre Dame: President's Office, University of Notre Dame, 1969); and *Three Bicentennial Addresses*, (Notre Dame: Office of the President, University of Notre Dame, 1976).

Hesburgh's views on the connection between foreign policy and morality are found in Theodore Hesburgh and Louis J. Halle (eds.), *Foreign Policy and Morality: Framework for a Moral Audit* (New York: Council on Religion and International Affairs, 1979). Prominent members of Notre Dame's faculty and administration express their thoughts on the Catholic character of the university in Theodore Hesburgh (ed.), *The Challenge* and *Promise of a Catholic University* (Notre Dame: University of Notre Dame Press, 1994).

Several books provide important context for Hesburgh's activities, including Thomas Blantz, *George N. Shuster: On the Side of Truth* (Notre Dame: University of Notre Dame, 1993); Jay Dolan, *The American Catholic Experience* (Garden City: Doubleday and Company, 1985); Foster Rhea Dulles, *The Civil Rights Commission: 1957–1965* (Lansing: Michigan State University Press, 1968); John Tracy Ellis (ed.), *The Catholic Priest in the United States: Historical Investigations* (Collegeville: Saint John's University Press, 1971); Philip Gleason, *Keeping the Faith: American Catholicism Past and Present* (Notre Dame: University of Notre Dame Press, 1987); Neil McCluskey (ed.), *The Catholic University: A Modern Appraisal* (Notre Dame: University of Notre Dame Press, 1970); David O'Brien, *Faith and Friendship: Catholicism in the Diocese of Syracuse: 1886–1986* (Syracuse: Catholic Diocese of Syracuse, 1987); Margaret Reher, *Catholic Intellectual Life in America* (New York: Macmillan Publishing Company, 1989).

An illustration of the comprehensiveness of Ames's *Bio Bibliography* is the 42 pages devoted to listing 205 published articles, addresses, and essays written by Hesburgh from 1940 to 1988. I studied almost all of them.

Among the most noteworthy articles written about Hesburgh are Robert Ajemian, "Prince of Priests, Without a Nickel," *Time*, May 2, 1977; Ezra Bowen, "His Trumpet Was Never Uncertain," *Time*, May 18, 1987; Robert Cross, "Priest, college president, citizen of the world," *Chicago Tribune Magazine*, November 12, 1978; Thomas Fleming, "Hesburgh of Notre Dame," *The New York Times Magazine*, May 11, 1969; "God and Man at Notre Dame, *Time* (cover story), February 9, 1962; Joe Ingalls, "For God, for Country, and for Notre Dame," *The Chronicle of Higher Education*, October 13, 1982; Gary MacEoin, "Notre Dame's Father Hesburgh," *Change*, February 1976; Jerry Reedy, "A Priest Forever," *Notre Dame Magazine*, Summer 1993; Carol Schaal, "Twilight of a Presidency," *Notre Dame Magazine*, Summer 1987; Robert Schmuhl, "Seven Days In May," *Notre Dame Magazine*, Winter 1989–90; Peter Schrag, "Notre Dame: Our First Great Catholic University?" *Harper's Magazine*, May 1967; Charles E. Sheedy, "The Priest as President," *Notre Dame Magazine*, June 1977; Jim Spencer and Bruce Buursma, "Reaching for Greatness," *Chicago Tribune Magazine*, November 9, 1986; Thomas Stritch, "A Short Biography of Theodore Hesburgh" in Charlotte Ames (compiler), *Theodore M. Hesburgh: A Bio-Bibliography* (New York: Greenwood Press, 1989); John Underwood, "Casting a Special Light," *Sports Illustrated*, January 10, 1983; Linda Witt, "Bio: Father Theodore Hesburgh," *People*, September 26, 1977; and Gereon Zimmermann, "Notre Dame's Father Hesburgh," *Look*, October 24, 1961. Also see "The Hesburgh Years . . . an Observer Special Issue," *The Observer*, Spring 1987, and the special issue devoted to Hesburgh in *Notre Dame Magazine*, June 1972.

A sample of the most notable articles written by Theodore Hesburgh includes "Election of Pius XII," *Ave Maria*, August 10, 1940; "The Facts of the Matter," *Sports Illustrated*, January 19, 1959; "Every Man has a Right to Vote," *Catholic Digest*, August 1960; "The Work of Mediation," *Commonweal*, October 6, 1961; "Looking Back at Newman," *America*, March 3, 1962; "Science is Amoral; Need Scientists be Amoral, Too?" *Saturday Review*, March 2, 1963; "Father Hesburgh's Program for Racial Justice," *The New York Times Magazine*, October 29, 1972; "Catholic Education in America," *America*, October 4, 1986; "The Vatican and American Catholic Higher Education," *America*, November 1, 1986; "Reflections on Cuomo: The Secret Consensus," *Notre Dame Journal of Law, Ethics and Public Policy*, Volume 1 (1984); "Reflections on Priesthood," *The Serran*, March 1985; "The 'Events': A Retrospective View," *Daedalus*, Fall

1974; "The Examined Life," *Dartmouth Alumni Magazine*, July 1958; "Are Religious Orders Obsolete? Theodore Hesburgh Responds," *Critic*, Winter 1986.

Many interviews with Hesburgh have been published. Two of the best are in Thomas Horton (ed.), *What Works for Me: 16 CEOs Talk About Their Careers and Commitments* (New York: Random House, 1986); and Trevor Kennedy (ed.), *Top Guns: Seventeen World Leaders in Politics, Media and Business Tell How They Made It to the Top—and Stayed There* (South Melbourne, Australia: Sun Books, 1988).

In seventeen unpublished diaries, totalling over twenty-two-hundred pages, written between 1973 and 1989, Fr. Ted described his thoughts and activities during his foreign trips. I used copies of the diaries located in the Department of Public Relations and Information Papers (University of Notre Dame).

NEWSPAPERS AND PERIODICALS

Research into newspapers and periodicals proved exceptionally time consuming, but the results were indispensable. One hundred and twelve different newspapers and periodicals provided voluminous coverage of Fr. Hesburgh's long career. (Some of them came from clipping files.) Those nineteen studied most comprehensively were *America* (1960–90), *Chicago's American* (1958, 1964, 1969), *Chicago Sun-Times* (1966–87), *Chicago Tribune* (1969–90), *Commonweal* (1987–90), *The Indianapolis News* (1953, 1962, 1969, 1987), *The Indianapolis Star* (1979–87), *Los Angeles Times* (1964–90), *National Catholic Register* (1970–87), *National Catholic Reporter* (1969–87), *The New York Times* (1952–87), *Notre Dame Alumnus* (1959–71), *Notre Dame Magazine* (1972–87), *Notre Dame Report* (1973–83), *The Observer* (University of Notre Dame, student newspaper, 1969–87), *Our Sunday Visitor* (1952–80), *The Scholastic*, (1948, 1952, 1957–87), *South Bend Tribune* (1952–90), and the *Washington Post* (1969–87).

INTERVIEWS

Valuable intimate material was gathered in interviews with 117 persons. One fifth of the interviews were conducted in person; four fifths were telephone interviews. The "live" interview is most desired, of course, but the telephone approach had one compelling, practical benefit: since the persons I needed to interview were scattered over forty states, the travel costs would have been prohibitive. I found the telephone interview to be almost as effective as the live one. A few interviews were brief; some persons were interviewed at length or more than once. Almost all the interviews were tape-recorded. All the taped interviews are in my possession, and, at some future date, I intend to donate them to an historical depository.

Bartell, Ernest	Burrell, David	Crowe, Michael
Beauchamp, E. William	Carney, Tom	Crowley, Patty
Beichner, Paul	Castellino, Francis	Curtin, Anne (O'Grady)
Bernhard, Berl	Chapleau, Melanie	Curtin, Michael
Black, Creed	Charles, Isabel	DenDooven, Mary
Blantz, Thomas	Conklin, Richard	(O'Grady)
Bolling, Landrum	Connor, John	Dunne, John
Bok, Derek	Corrigan, Gene	Egan, John
Borelli, Mario	Corso, Frank	Faccenda, Philip
Brademas, John	Crosson, Frederick	Fischer, Edward

Flaherty, Mary
  (Hesburgh)
Ford, Josephine
  Massyngberde
Freeman, Frankie
Frick, James
Fuchs, Larry
Gallin, Alice
Galvin, Robert
Gannon, James
Garmet, Leonard
Geaney, Dennis
Gibbons, James
Gilligan, John
Gleason, Philip
Glickstein, Howard
Gordon, Robert
Grace, J.Peter
Grant, James
Greeley, Andrew
Griffin, Robert
Griswold, Erwin
Hesburgh, James
Hesburgh, Theodore
Hofman, Emil
Horn, Stephen
Hosinski, Helen
Houck, John
Jackson, Anne
  (Hesburgh)
Jones, John Miriam

Joyce, Edmund
Keough, Donald
Kerr, Clark
Krashna, David
Landers, Ann
Langford, Walter
Malone, Thomas
Mason, Thomas
McBrien, Richard
McCluskey, Neil
McInerny, Ralph
McKenna, Philip
McKim, Vaughn
McMullin, Ernan
Merle, Hely
Minow, Newton
Morris, Christopher
Murphy, Christopher
Murphy, Franklin
Murphy, James
Murphy, John
Murphy, Michael
O'Connor, John
Ogren, Marty
O'Meara, Timothy
O'Neill, Elizabeth
  (Hesburgh)
O'Neill, Emmett
Pollard, Morris
Powers, John
Putz, Louis

Reedy, Jerry
Reinert, Paul
Reith, Herman
Riehle, James
Rihn, Roy
Rockefeller, David
Rossie, Richard
Roth, Donald
Ryan, John
Sandman, Joseph
Scanlon, Tom
Schmitz, Roger
Schneider, John
Schreiner, William
Sewell, John
Shriver, Sargent
Soleta, Chester
Sommers, Davidson
Stephen, Edmund
Taylor, William
Tyson, David
Valdiserri, Roger
Walsh, John
Waters, Mary
Webb, Dorothy
Wharton, Clifton
Wilkowski, Jean
Williams, Oliver
Wofford, Harris
Two confidential
  interviews

LETTERS TO AUTHOR

Corso, Frank
Fischer, Edward
Walsh, John

INDEX

198–200, 211; money interests, 143–44, 261–62, 265; personal qualities, 163, 181–82, 183, 186, 188, 190, 194–95, 197–98, 201, 213, 244–45, 266; politics, 184, 189; publications, 203–6; student discontent and, 94–95, 105, 107–8; salesman, 183–84, 192–93, 201–3; schedule, 160, 163, 167–68, 187–89; visionary, 256; women, regard for, 213–14

Hesburgh, Theodore Bernard, 5–7
Hesburgh Declaration, 120–22
Hesburgh Papers, 187, 204
HEW, 127
hierarchy, 244
Holy Cross, Order of, 97–98
Holy Cross College, 28
homosexuality, 249
Horn, Stephen, 136
Hosinski, Helen, 55, 258, 297
Houck, John, 137
Howard University, 29
Hubbard, Fr. Bernard Rosecrans, 16
human rights, 148–49, 168
Humanae Vitae, 248, 287
Humane Imperative, 204
humanism, 223
humanities, 93
hunger, 147–48, 152

ICBM, 92
Idea of a University, The, 57
illegitimacy, 15
immigration, 157–58
in loco parentis, 93
Incarnation, 220
Index Librorum Prohibitorum, 59–61, 238
Inquisition, modern, 238
Institute of Rural Education, 87
integration, 83
intellectualism, 41–42
International Federation of Catholic Universities, 64, 279–82
International Foundation for the Survival and Development of Humanity, 300
International Rice Research Institute, 142
Islam, 240–41

Jesuits, 241, 242
Jesus, savior, 239
Jews, 9–10, 240–41
jobs, 14
John XXIII, Pope, 234–35, 239, 242, 358
Johnson, Pres. Lyndon, 85, 99
Johnston, Sen. Olin, 77
Jones, Charles, 212
Joyce, Fr. Edmund, 55, 92, 101, 258, 260, 291, 296
jubilee Mass, 312
Justina, Sister, 17

Kant, Immanuel, 60
Katzenbach, Nicholas, 308
Keating, Sen. Kenneth, 85
Kelley, Mary Eleanor, 14
Kennedy, Pres. John, 83, 84, 87, 210
Kennedy, Robert, 83, 84
Kent State University, 118, 121
Keough, Donald, 184, 196
Kim, Stephen Cardinal, 148
King, Martin Luther, 83
Kirk, Pres. Grayson, 99–100
Knight Foundation, 304, 305
Knights of Columbus, 10
Konig, Franz Cardinal, 170
Krashna, David, 102, 115, 118–20
Kroc, Joan B., 176

laity, role of, 34–35
Lalande, Fr. Germain M., 97
Lamont, Bishop Donal, 148
Landers, Ann, 230
Langford, Walter, 87–88
Loras College, 299
Latin, 223
Laxalt, Sen. Paul, 174–75
leader, definition of, 191
Leahy, Frank, 49–51, 56
LeClercq, Msgr. Georges, 279
Legion of Decency, 12
Lent, 180–81
Leo XIII, Pope, 36
Library, Hesburgh, 297
Lincoln, Pres. Abraham, 16
Lindbergh, Charles, 9
liturgy, 222, 228, 234
LOBUND, 42, 49, 54
Luther, Martin, 237, 239

Mahon, Fr. George, 8
Malloy, Fr. Edward, 298, 309
management, philosophy of, 265
Manion, Clarence, 54
March, Fredric, 14
Marian College, 299
marriage, theology of, 287
Marshall, Edison, 15
Mary, Blessed Virgin, 31, 224
Mass, 219, 221–23, 235
Mason, Thomas, 261–62
McBrien, Fr. Richard, 257, 277
McCarragher, Fr. Charles, 93
McCarthy, Sen. Eugene, 19
McClellan, Sen. John, 82
McCluskey, Fr. Neil, 241
McDowell, Fr. Howard, 13
McGlynn, Fr. Edward, 5
McGovern, Sen. George, 134
McInerny, Ralph, 137, 276
McKenna, Philip, 103

Rockne, Knute, 39, 49–50
Rolling Prairie, life at, 22–23
Roman collar, 229
Rome, American universities and, 282–84
Rossie, Richard, 101, 106
ROTC, 163, 204–6

sacraments, 219–23, 229–30, 246, 273
Sacred Congregation for Catholic Education, 245
Sagdeev, Roald, 174
sainthood, 228
Sandburg, Carl, 99
Save the Children, 206
Scanlon, Tom, 89
Schlereth, Thomas, 96, 106
Schmidt, Benno, 177
Schmul, Robert, 121
Schneider, John, 63
Schoesser, Gerry, 310
scholarship, 228
science, 92, 93, 142, 160–61, 211, 226
Science and Religion Against Nuclear War, 171
secularism, 34
segregation, 10
Select Commission on Immigration and Refugee Policy, 157–58
self-sufficiency, 142
seminarians, life of, 20–22
service, 225
sex, 10, 13, 23, 233
sex discrimination, 126, 139–40
sexual harrassment, 139
Shapiro, Samuel, 286
Shaw, George Bernard, 42
Sheedy, Fr. Charles, 31, 46, 55, 69, 258
Shriver, R. Sargent, 86–88
Shuster, Dr. George, 52, 113, 234, 258
sit-ins, 105
Smith, C. R., 212
social functions, 14
social outreach, 142
social responsibility, 144–46, 165, 171, 208, 246
sociology, 275
Soleta, Fr. Chester, 24, 63
Sorin, Fr. Edward, 39
South Africa, 164–66
South America, 66
Spirit, Holy, 241
St. John's University, 278
St. Louis University, 97
St. Mary's College, 139
St. Patrick's Cathedral, 9
St. Paul, 224
Stanford University, 274
Steiner, Fr. Thomas, 38, 98
Stephan, Edmund, 184, 259–60

Storey, Robert, 72
Strathmore, N.H., 9
student activism, 102–10, 114–18, 120–22, 109–10
Students for a Democratic Society, 100
Stumpf, Samuel, 36
Sullivan Principles, 165
South West Africa People's Organization, 300
Soviet Union, 300–301
Syracuse, Diocese of, 8
Syracuse University, 13

Taylor, William, 85
technology, 210
Thailand, 152
theater, 17
theology, 223, 235–37, 272
Theology of Catholic Action, 35
Thomism, 35, 274–75
Thurmond, Sen. Strom, 72, 77
Travels with Ted and Ned, 303
Tyson, Fr. David, 258

U.S. Institute of Peace, 299
U.S. wealth, 147–48
UNICEF, 153
unionization, 141
United Nations, 149–50
university: as Catholic, 271, 278–79, 282; church affiliation, 274; reason for 287, 290
urban renewal, 85
USO, 31

Valparaiso University, 95
Vatican, 59, 278, 285, 287
Vatican II, 36, 96, 234–39, 246, 271, 277–79
Velikhov, Yevgeny, 172–73, 177
Veronica, Sister, 17
veterans, WWII, 43–45
Vietnam War, 113–14, 118–19, 123, 130
Vietnamese government, 154
virtue, 242
VISTA, 206
vocation, 10, 11, 18
voting, 74–76, 83
vows, 23, 231

Wallace, Gov. George, 73, 127, 131
Walsh, Fr. John, 96 120, 220
Walshe, Peter, 166
Walt, Gen. Lewis W., 157
WASPS, 163
Watergate, 137, 209
Waters, Mary, 13
Wilkins, Ernest, 72
Wilkowski, Jean, 149, 151
Williams, Fr. Oliver, 300

Hesburgh: A Biography was designed and composed in Adobe Garamond by Kachergis Book Design, Pittsboro, North Carolina; printed on 60-pound Glatfelter Supple Opaque and bound by Thomson-Shore, Inc., Dexter, Michigan.